Individual Differences in Arithmetic

Standards in numeracy are a constant concern to educational policy makers. However, why are differences in arithmetical performance so marked? In *Individual Differences in Arithmetic*, Ann Dowker seeks to provide a better understanding of why these differences in ability exist, encouraging a more informed approach to tackling numeracy difficulties.

This book reviews existing research by the author and by others on the subject of arithmetical ability and presents strong evidence to support a componential view of arithmetic. Focusing primarily on children, but including discussion of arithmetical cognition in healthy adult and neuro-psychological patients, each of the central components of arithmetic is covered. Within this volume, findings from developmental, educational, cognitive and neuropsychological studies are integrated in a unique approach. This book covers subjects such as:

- Counting and the importance of individual differences.
- Arithmetic facts, procedures and different forms of memory.
- Causes of, and interventions with, mathematical difficulties.
- The effects of culture, language and experience.

The educational implications of these findings are discussed in detail, revealing original insights that will be of great interest to those studying or researching in the areas of education, neuroscience and developmental and cognitive psychology.

Ann Dowker is a University Research Lecturer in the Department of Experimental Psychology, University of Oxford.

Individual Differences in Arithmetic

Implications for psychology, neuroscience and education

Ann Dowker

 **Psychology Press**
Taylor & Francis Group

HOVE AND NEW YORK

First published 2005
by Psychology Press
27 Church Road, Hove, East Sussex BN3 2FA

Simultaneously published in the USA and Canada
by Psychology Press
270 Madison Avenue, New York, NY 10016

Psychology Press is part of the Taylor & Francis Group

Typeset in Times by Garfield Morgan, Rhayader, Powys
Printed and bound in Great Britain by MPG Books Ltd, Bodmin,
Cornwall
Cover design by Anú Design
Cover image: Stockbyte Platinum/Getty Images

This publication has been produced with paper manufactured to strict
environmental standards and with pulp derived from sustainable
forests.

British Library Cataloguing in Publication Data
A catalogue record for this book is available from the British Library

Library of Congress Cataloging-in-Publication Data
Dowker, Ann.
  Individual differences in arithmetic : implications for psychology,
neuroscience, and education / Ann Dowker.
       p. cm.
  Includes bibliographical references and index.
  ISBN 1-84169-235-2
  1. Mathematical ability. 2. Number concept. I. Title.
  BF456.N7D69 2005
  513'.01'9–dc22
                                                    2005009940

ISBN 1-84169-235-2 (hbk)

Dedication

To the memories of Bob Hiorns and Neil O'Connor

Contents

Acknowledgements

I am very grateful to all the staff and children in the schools and nursery schools involved in the various studies reported here, for all their help and co-operation over the years. I also thank the following Oxfordshire primary schools: Barton Village Primary School, Charlbury Primary School, Cutteslowe Primary School, Edward Field Primary School, New Hinksey Primary School, New Marston Primary School, St Aloysius' Primary School, St Barnabas' Primary School, St Ebbes' First School, St Francis' Primary School, St Mary and St John Primary School, St Michael's Primary School, St Nicholas' Primary School, St John Fisher Primary School, St Philip and St James' Primary School, Windmill Primary School and Wood Farm Primary School.

I also thank the following Oxford nursery schools and day nurseries: Bartlemas Nursery School, Elms Road Nursery School, Julia Durbin Day Nursery, Kiddies Korner Day Nursery, Sandfield Day Nursery, St Anne's College Nursery, St Thomas' Day Nursery, Slade Nursery School and Summertown Nursery School.

In addition, my students and collaborators have been helped by numerous other schools in the United Kingdom and overseas; although I cannot list all these schools by name, I am extremely grateful to all of them.

I would also like to thank all the adults who have taken part in my studies.

The book, and the research that led up to it, have benefited from valuable discussions, at various stages, with many people, including Daniel Ansari, Sir Christopher Ball, Brian Butterworth, Yi-Ping Chen, Tim Coulson, Richard Cowan, Stanislas Dehaene, Margarete Delazer, Chris Donlan, Karen Fuson, Herbert Ginsburg, Silke Goebel, Ati Hermelin, Nancy Jordan, Liane Kaufmann, Deborah King, Tim Miles, Alison Price, Sonia Sciama, Kathy Sylva, Ian Thompson, Anne Watson, Bob Wright and all members of the Numeracy Intervention email discussion group. The opinions – and the errors – in this book are, of course, my own.

Elizabeth Warrington kindly provided me with her Dot Counting test and permitted me to use it.

I am grateful to all members of the SRU for their valuable assistance with the research.

I am grateful to the British Academy, the ESRC, and the Esmee Fairbairn Charitable Trust for financial assistance at various stages.

Arithmetic by Carl Sandburg

Arithmetic is where numbers fly like pigeons in and out of your head.

Arithmetic tells you how many you lose or win if you know how many you had before you lost or won.

Arithmetic is seven eleven all good children go to heaven – or five six bundle of sticks.

Arithmetic is numbers you squeeze from your head to your hand to your pencil to your paper till you get the answer.

Arithmetic is where the answer is right and everything is nice and you can look out of the window and see the blue sky – or the answer is wrong and you have to start all over and try again and see how it comes out this time.

If you take a number and double it and double it again and then double it a few more times, the number gets bigger and bigger and goes higher and higher and only arithmetic can tell you what the number is when you decide to quit doubling.

Arithmetic is where you have to multiply – and you carry the multiplication table in your head and hope you won't lose it.

If you have two animal crackers, one good and one bad, and you eat one and a striped zebra with streaks all over him eats the other, how many animal crackers will you have if somebody offers you five six seven and you say No no no and you say Nay nay nay and you say Nix nix nix?

If you ask your mother for one fried egg for breakfast and she gives you two fried eggs and you eat both of them, who is better in arithmetic, you or your mother? ('Arithmetic' from *The complete poems of Carl Sandberg*. Copyright © 1970, 1969 by Lilian Steichen Sandberg, Trustee, reprinted by permission of Harcourt, Inc.)

Introduction

What this book is

This book is a review of the extent and nature of individual differences in arithmetic in childhood and after. This book will discuss several important components of arithmetical cognition and performance and will discuss *individual differences* in these components: focusing in particular on children, but also drawing on studies of arithmetical cognition in healthy adults and in neuropsychological patients.

Standards in numeracy have recently become of increasing concern to educational policymakers. However, it may be difficult to ameliorate or prevent numeracy difficulties without a greater understanding of their nature.

The main argument of this book is that there is no such thing as arithmetical ability: only arithmetical abili*ties*. Converging evidence from studies of normally developing children, of adults from the general population, of neuropsychological patients, of others with arithmetical disabilities, of people with exceptional arithmetical talent and from recent brain-imaging studies indicates that arithmetical cognition is made up of many components. Marked individual differences in these components, and discrepancies between these components within an individual child or adult, can be readily observed.

The book will discuss several important components of arithmetic and evidence for individual differences in these components. The components to be discussed include counting principles and procedures; knowledge of arithmetical facts procedures; the understanding of arithmetical principles and ability to use them to devise new, non-standard strategies; arithmetical estimation; and the ability to deal with sums presented in terms of concrete objects, numbers and word problems and to translate between the different versions. The book will discuss the contributions that internal (the brain) and external (environmental, cultural and linguistic) factors make to such individual differences. It will also be emphasized that arithmetical performance has emotional as well as cognitive components; and the book will discuss studies of *emotions* and *attitudes* concerning mathematics. The book will close with a discussion of the educational implications of these findings; of some remedial arithmetic programmes for those with arithmetical difficulties; and in particular of a 'numeracy recovery' intervention project devised by the author on the basis of the theoretical approach and empirical research described in this book.

One major aim: bringing together findings from different times, places and subjects

Arithmetical development and arithmetical thinking have been important topics of study for many years, in many parts of the world and from the point of view of many disciplines. These topics are of concern to teachers, educational policymakers, psychologists, neuroscientists, mathematicians and to all who need to learn arithmetic and to deal with numbers.

Much less work has been carried out on arithmetical development than, for example, the development of reading. At the same time, much more work has been done on the subject than is often realized. This is in part because of lack of transmission of information across *time*, across *place* and across *discipline*.

With regard to transmission across *time* there is a significant body of early work that is sometimes ignored nowadays. In the past, theories and findings were not always transmitted as efficiently as might be the case today; and it is easy for people of the 21st century, when examining something as seemingly topical as mathematics education, to assume that they are coming new to the topic. It can be startling to discover, for example, that the need for individualized intervention programmes for children with arithmetical difficulties was already being pointed out in the 1920s; that 19th-century educational policymakers were already debating the relative importance of rote learning and conceptual understanding (Brown, 2001; McIntosh 1977); and that Maria and Richard Edgeworth were emphasizing the importance of language to children's understanding of arithmetic as early as 1798.

With regard to transmission across *place*, researchers are not always aware of what is going on in other countries. This is particularly true when language barriers are involved; but even communication between Britain and North America is sometimes imperfect. The bibliographies in British and American books on mathematical development often show remarkably little overlap.

With regard to transmission of information across *disciplines*, there is still a tendency for research in different disciplines to proceed independently, so that neuroscientists, developmental psychologists and educationists may not even be aware of mutually relevant work: a situation that limits the scope of such research. Communication between researchers, teachers and other practitioners and policymakers is still more inadequate.

Thus, a key aim of the present book is to bring together work that is relevant to individual differences in arithmetic from *different times*, *different places* and *across the disciplines* of psychology, education and neuroscience

What this book is not

There are several potentially interesting issues that are beyond the scope of this book.

It is *not* about the whole of mathematics. It deals specifically with arithmetic, which is only one of the many aspects of mathematics: for example, it does not deal with geometry.

It does *not* attempt to provide a comprehensive definition of arithmetic and its components from a mathematical, philosophical or educational point of view.

It does *not* investigate individual differences in arithmetic from the point of view of quantitative behavioural genetics, heritability estimates or the 'nature–nurture debate' as such. It does, however, include extensive discussion of contributions that may be made by both nature (the brain) and nurture (the environment) and how these interact and influence one another from the beginning; but it does not attempt to quantify the relative contributions of nature and nurture to arithmetic. There will be only brief reference to the few existing studies of this issue.

It is *not* concerned with the issue of how arithmetic might have evolved.

Note regarding terminology

Such terms as 'skills' and 'abilities' will at times be used to refer to proficiency in arithmetic, its components and other domains. The use of such terms does not imply assumptions about the genetic or environmental causation of such 'abilities', or whether they are innate or learned. Unfortunately, there are no common terms in this area, which have not become associated to some degree with nature/nurture studies. If there were such neutral terms, these would be used.

Main themes of the book

The main themes of the book are as follows:

1   Arithmetical ability is not unitary, but is made up of many different types of process. These can be grouped into several categories (e.g. procedural, factual and conceptual); but each of the categories has numerous subcomponents. For example, procedural knowledge may include written, oral and concrete calculation procedures and includes the procedures applicable to different arithmetical operations. Factual knowledge will include facts corresponding to different operations, e.g.

addition facts and multiplication facts and also the names given to different numbers and operations. Conceptual knowledge is an even broader category, including the understanding of the meaning of word problems; approximate arithmetic; arithmetical principles such as commutativity, associativity and distributivity, etc.

2   Some subcomponents will be easier for children than others; but there can be strong discrepancies, in either direction, between almost any two subcomponents. For example, though counting is generally easier than word problem solving, there are some children who have more difficulty with counting procedures than with word problem solving (see Chapter 4).

3   There are many parallels between the discrepancies that can be observed in 'normal' children and adults and those that can be observed in individuals with arithmetical deficits resulting from brain damage. This should not be seen as implying either that the deficits in brain-damaged people are not real or that discrepancies in the general population must be due to subtle brain damage or abnormal brain functioning. Rather, performance in each of the different subcomponents of arithmetic can best be seen as lying on a continuum, with extreme talent at one end and extreme deficit (sometimes, but not always, due to brain damage) at the other.

4   Levels of performance in different subcomponents are influenced by a multitude of interacting factors: brain based (both innate and acquired), social, cultural and educational. Any statement that arithmetical ability is purely the product of a single factor is oversimplified.

5   Emotional factors make a very important contribution to arithmetical performance. Some people like arithmetic very much, while a worryingly large number of people experience 'math anxiety' or even 'math phobia'. There are many contributory factors to such negative attitudes to arithmetic; but I would suggest that one of these is the tendency of children themselves and of their parents and teachers to regard arithmetic as unitary and to assume that difficulty with any one aspect of arithmetic means that one is 'no good at math'.

6   Arithmetical difficulties can be ameliorated considerably by intervention, especially interventions that are based on the fact that arithmetic is made up of numerous subcomponents and that take account of the specific strengths and weaknesses of individuals.

1 Children, adults; males, females: Weaknesses and talents

'Most people can do maths when they're 4, if they start school when they're 4. And when they're grown up, some people can do maths and some can't.' (Tom, aged 6)

It is well known that individual differences in arithmetical performance are very marked in both children and adults. For example, Cockcroft (1982) reported that an average British class of 11-year-olds is likely to contain the equivalent of a 7-year range in arithmetical ability. Despite many changes in UK education since then, including the introduction of a standard National Curriculum and a National Numeracy Strategy, almost identical results were obtained by Brown, Askew, Rhodes, Denvir, Wiliam, Ranson, and Millett (2002). They found that the gap between the 5th and 95th percentiles on standardized mathematics tests by children in Year 6 (10- to 11-year-olds) corresponded to a gap of about 7 years in 'mathematics ages'. Individual differences in arithmetic among children of the same age are also very great in most other countries, although some studies suggest that they are less pronounced in Pacific Rim countries (TIMSS, 1996).

Individual differences in arithmetic are easier to detect in *children*, who are attending school and taking mathematics tests; but it is clear that they persist throughout life. Some adults have severe difficulties with basic numeracy; and most such adults were already struggling with arithmetic by the age of 7 (Basic Skills Agency, 1997). By contrast, others have a fascination with numbers, are exceptionally skilled calculators and/or reason exceptionally well about numbers. A few are 'lightning calculators' who can perform multi-digit calculations in their heads as fast or faster than the average calculating machine.

Environment, heredity and arithmetical ability

There are numerous environmental influences on arithmetical development. Culture, education, even the language that we speak all play an important part in the way arithmetic is acquired. These influences will be discussed in

Chapter 9 of this book. More rarely, illness or injury can cause brain damage, which has a significant effect on arithmetic. Perinatal factors, such as severe prematurity, can have gross or subtle effects on brain development that influence arithmetic: even when very premature babies go on to develop typically in other respects, they often demonstrate arithmetical difficulties (Isaacs et al., 2001; Tasaka & Shimada, 2000). The effects of brain damage and unusual patterns of brain development will be discussed in Chapter 10.

As regards genes, there are a few genetic disorders, such as Turner's syndrome and Williams' syndrome, that are particularly associated with arithmetical difficulties. Such disorders are rare, but there is a tendency for arithmetical difficulties to run in families, even when not associated with a known genetic disorder. For example, Knopnik, Alarcon, and DeFries (1997) found that monozygotic twins were significantly more likely than dizygotic twins to be concordant for mathematical disabilities. There was also a significant genetic correlation between mathematical disabilities and reading disabilities.

The possible genetic contribution to arithmetical disabilities will be discussed further in Chapter 10. There has been surprisingly little research into the possible genetic contribution to variation in arithmetical performance in the population as a whole.

Heritability is defined as the proportion of variance in a particular characteristic for a given population that can be explained by heredity. It is usually investigated by comparing levels of similarity in identical versus non-identical twins and/or in biological versus adopted relatives. There is considerable controversy both about the accuracy and appropriateness of the methods used to estimate heritability and about the validity of even attempting to separate genetic from environmental contributions to individual differences, since there are undoubtedly strong interactions between genetic and environmental factors.

Bearing these limitations in mind, the few existing (and mostly quite old) relevant studies suggest that there is a significant genetic contribution to individual differences in mathematics. Notably, Vandenberg (1966) carried out a twin study and obtained a heritability estimate for mathematical ability of approximately 50%.

The major debates about genetic and environmental influences on mathematical ability have tended to focus not so much on population variance as on *gender differences*. Although gender differences are not in fact great in most aspects of mathematics, they have been an intense focus for research in the field of individual differences in mathematics. This topic must therefore be considered at some length.

Gender differences in arithmetic

'Girls [or boys] go to Mars
To get more stars.

Boys [or girls] go to Jupiter
To get more stupider.' (British playground rhyme, reversible according to the gender of the speaker)

'I do wish I could do clock sums and those sums about taps running in and out. I wonder whoever invented such nonsense. I wish I could give the man who thought of them my honest opinion of his wits.'
'"How do you know it was a man?"' inquired my brother .'It is girls who think of ridiculous things.'
'Not sums, especially pipe sums. What *girl* would let water in by two taps and out by one if she wanted to fill a bath? It takes a boy to think of *that* way of doing things.' (Maude Forsey: *Mollie Hazeldene's Schooldays*, London: Nelson, 1924, p. 16. Every effort has been made to trace copyright holder and obtain permission to reproduce this extract. Any omissions brought to our attention will be remedied in future editions)

Are males better at mathematics than females?

The folk wisdom is that males are better at mathematics than females. In fact, this statement needs considerable qualification. Males are more likely to be *extremely* good at mathematics. Certainly, the large majority of professional research mathematicians are men. At the other end of the scale, serious mathematical difficulties seem to be *equally* common in males and females (Gross-Tsur, Manor, & Shalev, 1995; Lewis, Hitch, & Walker, 1994).

Findings tend to show that any male advantage in arithmetic does not usually appear until the age of 10 or later (Benbow, 1988; Hyde, Fennema, & Lamon, 1990a; Lummis & Stevenson, 1990).

Studies of preschool and early primary school children generally show no gender differences in arithmetic. For example, Lummis and Stevenson (1990) found no gender differences in arithmetical calculations in kindergarten, first grade and even fifth-grade (10- to 11-year-old) children in the United States of America, Taiwan and Japan. Fifth-grade boys in the Asian countries did, however, show an advantage in word problems.

Gender differences in mathematics have decreased overall (TIMSS, 1996, 1999) over the years. For example, Delgado and Prieto (2004) found no significant gender differences in arithmetic, word problem solving or geometry even in a group of (non-mathematician) university students.

Spatial ability and gender

Spatial ability has frequently been suggested (e.g. by Casey, Nuttall, & Benbow, 1995) to be an important factor in mathematical performance in general, and in gender differences in mathematics in particular.

There is no doubt that gender differences in spatial ability are frequently observed, although they tend to be quite small, and are mainly found for tasks involving three-dimensional than two-dimensional space (Voyer,

Voyer, & Bryden, 1995). There has been much debate as to whether such gender differences are due to biological factors (Geary, 1996) or to environmental factors such as boys being given more constructional toys and more freedom to explore their environment independently. Can this explain gender differences in mathematics?

Spatial abilities are presumably related to geometrical abilities. However, as will be discussed later in this chapter and Chapter 10, it is unclear whether there are strong links between spatial abilities, especially three-dimensional spatial abilities, and non-geometrical mathematical abilities. The spatial abilities involved in arranging numbers on a page for multi-digit calculations are two-dimensional; and it is not clear that most arithmetical and algebraic abilities have a strong spatial component.

Some researchers (e.g. Casey et al., 1995) have found spatial ability to be a strong predictor of mathematical performance, and to account for much of the gender effect on performance. However, a meta-analysis by Friedman (1995) suggests that mathematical ability is not very highly correlated with spatial ability and that correlations between spatial and verbal abilities are higher. In this connection, it may be noted that the factor analytic studies used to construct psychometric tests of 'IQ', such as the WISC and WAIS, have usually placed arithmetical tests in the verbal, rather than the more spatially dominated performance scales (cf. Kaufmann, 1990). The arithmetic subtests of the WISC and WAIS predominantly emphasize word problem solving: one of the skills for which spatial ability differences are sometimes called upon to explain gender differences.

It is sometimes suggested that there may actually be gender differences with regard to the extent to which spatial ability predicts mathematical performance, but findings are contradictory with regard to the nature of such gender differences. Some studies (Casey, Pezaris, & Nuttall, 1992; Connor & Serbin, 1985) have found that spatial ability predicts mathematical performance more in males than in females, while the opposite was found by Friedman (1995).

Thus, the evidence that differences in spatial ability are a major cause of gender differences in mathematics is quite weak. This weakness can be seen on two grounds:

1   differences in spatial abilities are small, and confined to only some forms of spatial skill
2   the relationship between spatial and mathematical skills, other than geometry, is tenuous.

Attention, mathematics and gender

As suggested by Dowker (1996), future consideration of gender differences in mathematics should address the issue of single-minded concentration. Personal communications from several male and female mathematicians suggest that one important factor in mathematical research, to a greater extent than for other academic subjects, is the ability to concentrate single-mindedly on a given problem. There is some evidence that women may be more able than men to pay attention to several topics at once and less willing or able to focus attention in the exclusive way demanded, for example, by advanced mathematics. There are obvious social reasons why this may be the case: women in their traditional role as caregiver to children may need to be able to divide their attention between their own tasks and several children's different needs and requests. There may also be biological factors involved. Males are more likely than females to be diagnosed as having 'attention deficit disorder'. Although this condition is probably over-diagnosed in some places, and there are uncertainties as to the criteria for diagnosis, this difference does suggest that males may be more likely than females to be found at either extreme of the ability to focus attention narrowly.

Mathematics self-concept, mathematics anxiety and gender

As discussed in Chapter 11, mathematics arouses anxiety and other negative emotions in many people: often linked to low estimates of their own ability and expectations of failure. There is also evidence that females tend to experience more anxiety than males with respect to mathematics and to rate themselves lower in mathematics than do males. Studies tend to show that boys *like* mathematics more than girls do and that girls' attitude to mathematics declines more over time than that of boys. However, the gender difference in attitude may be less now than it was some years ago.

Our own recent research with a sample of primary school children in 10 countries found no overall gender differences in younger children's liking for mathematics (Gregory, Snell, & Dowker, 2000; Chapter 11 in this volume). However, girls did tend to give themselves lower ratings in mathematics than boys did, while there were no gender differences in self-ratings for reading. The study found no evidence that children of this age consider that boys are better than girls in mathematics. The children showed no overall tendency to give boys higher ratings than girls on either ability at mathematics or liking for mathematics. They did, however, show some tendency to give higher ratings to their own gender.

It is often suggested that females' greater anxiety and lower self-concept in mathematics may lead to poorer performance and less inclination to choose to study mathematics.

The question is which comes first. Do females find mathematics more difficult for other reasons, and therefore experience more anxiety about it; or is the difficulty due to the anxiety? If the anxiety comes first, then why are females more anxious? They may be more liable to performance anxiety in general; but then why is their literacy development not equally affected by anxiety? One possible explanation is that they experience more negative reactions to their mathematical performance from adults and peers as a result of social stereotypes. If a boy performs badly at a mathematics test, this may be attributed to a temporary cause: he was not feeling well on the day, he did not understand particular questions or he had not revised sufficiently for the test. If a girl performs badly at the same test, she may be more quickly labelled as 'no good at maths'.

Fact retrieval and gender

Some researchers have suggested that the crucial difference between males and females is that males are faster at retrieving facts from memory. One study of Hong Kong Chinese, Anglo-American and Chinese-American children and adults indicated that the males were faster than the females at retrieving arithmetical facts, but not other kinds of information (Royer, Tronsky, Chan, Jackson, & Marchant, 1999). The authors concluded that fact retrieval may be the cognitive mechanism underlying gender differences in mathematical test performance. Of course, questions arise as to which comes first. It could be that females show less good fact retrieval because they do not understand certain concepts, which would make the facts more meaningful, or because they dislike maths and so get less practice at it. In any case, not all studies do show that females have more difficulty at the level of remembering facts or doing basic calculations: some suggest that their difficulties are more with word problems (Geary, 1996).

Changes in attitudes to gender and mathematics

> Of course, boys usually can't understand algebra! (Remark made by female teacher to parents of a 14-year-old boy, Britain, 2002)

In Britain some of the gender-related expectations about mathematical performance may have diminished or even reversed in recent years. As boys' general academic performance has declined in comparison with girls, teachers and policymakers have become increasingly concerned with male underachievement. Until the 1980s, books and papers on gender issues in education tended to be concerned mainly with the disadvantages experienced by girls. Since the 1990s, there have been far more writings on the educational difficulties and disadvantages experienced by boys. It would be of interest to investigate whether this has changed adults' perception of gender differences in mathematics. Anecdotal evidence – e.g. the teacher remark just quoted – suggests that this is a possibility.

People with difficulties in arithmetic

There will be many references in this book to children and adults with 'difficulties' in arithmetic, mathematics or numeracy. The term simply refers to children or adults who struggle or fail to cope with some of the aspects of arithmetic that are necessary or desirable for educational or practical purposes. Since the term 'learning difficulties' is used in some educational and clinical contexts to imply severe and unusual problems that may require special education, it should be emphasized that the use of the term 'difficulties' does not have such an implication here. The term simply refers to children or adults who struggle or fail to cope with some of the aspects of arithmetic that are necessary or desirable for educational or practical purposes. It does not mean that these difficulties are pathological; that they are always classifiable as 'specific learning difficulties' in the technical sense or that they must be either innate or the result of brain damage. Some difficulties with arithmetic do indeed involve a pathological process, as in the case of adults who lose previously established arithmetical concepts or skills as the result of brain damage. However, most difficulties in arithmetic, like most difficulties in learned subjects, lie on a 'normal' continuum between extreme talent and extreme weakness; and are due not to brain damage but to a mismatch between an individual's pattern of cognitive strengths and weaknesses and the way that (s)he is taught.

In recent years, there has been increased emphasis on the possibility that, just as some children have dyslexia, some may have *dyscalculia*: a specific difficulty in doing arithmetic.

Several studies have investigated the prevalence of learning difficulties in mathematics. For example, Lewis, Hitch, and Walker (1994) studied 1056 unselected 9- to 10-year-old-English children (the entire age group within a particular, socially highly heterogeneous, local education authority; excluding only those assessed as having severe general learning difficulties). They were given the Raven's Matrices IQ test; Young's Group Mathematics Test; and Young's Spelling and Reading Test. Of the sample, 1.3% had specific arithmetical difficulties, defined as an arithmetic scaled score of 85 or below despite a Raven's IQ score of 90 or above. A further 2.3% had difficulties in both reading and arithmetic (scaled scores of 85 or below in both the reading and arithmetic tests) despite a Raven's IQ score of 90 or above. Thus, the prevalence of arithmetic difficulties in children of at least average cognitive ability was 3.6%. The children with arithmetical difficulties were equally divided as to gender, which contrasts with the general finding that boys are far more likely than girls to have language and literacy difficulties.

Gross-Tsur et al. (1996) assessed the incidence of dyscalculia in a cohort of 3029 Israeli 11- to 12-year-olds. The 600 children who scored in the lowest 20% on a standardized city wide arithmetic test were selected for further testing. Five hundred and fifty five were located and given an individualized arithmetic test battery previously constructed and standardized by the authors. This included reading, writing and comparing numbers; comparing quantities; simple calculations; and more complex (multidigit) calculations. Of the total, 188 children (6.2%) were classified as having dyscalculia, using the criterion of a score equal or below the mean for children two years younger. Of these children 143 were located and received parental consent for further testing. This included the WISC-R IQ test, and reading and spelling tests standardized on 70 age-matched typically developing children. Three children were excluded from the 'dyscalculic' group because they obtained IQ tests below 80. Of the 140 dyscalculic children, 75 were girls and 65 were boys, once again indicating an approximately equal gender distribution. Their IQs ranged from 80 to 129, with a mean of 98.2. They were assessed for symptoms of other learning problems. The researchers diagnosed 17% as dyslexic and 26% as having symptoms of attention deficit hyperactivity disorder. They came from significantly lower socioeconomic backgrounds than the children without dyscalculia and 42% had first-degree relatives with specific learning disabilities.

Bzufka, Hein, and Neumarker (2000) studied 181 urban and 182 rural German third-grade pupils. They were given standardized school achievement tests of arithmetic and spelling. Twelve children in each sample (about 6.6% of the whole population) performed above the 50th percentile in spelling, but below the 25th percentile in mathematics. When the urban and rural children were compared, they showed little difference in incidence of specific spelling or mathematics difficulties, but the urban children (who were on the whole of lower socioeconomic background) were far more likely than the rural children to have difficulty with both (48.6% as against 3.3%).

Thus, the incidence of mathematical learning difficulties depends widely between studies, depending on the methods and criteria used. For example, they have used different IQ tests; different mathematics tests that may be emphasizing quite different components; and different cut-off points for establishing deficit in both IQ and mathematics. Moreover, it has been pointed out (Desoete, Roeyers, & De Clercq, 2004; Mazzocco & Myers, 2003) that findings about the incidence, nature and outcomes of mathematical difficulties may vary considerably, depending on whether one uses criteria of *discrepancy* between mathematical performance and IQ, *severity* of mathematical weaknesses or *persistence* of mathematical weaknesses. Given the marked differences in criteria between studies, it is perhaps inappropriate to focus too much on the exact numbers obtained. The main conclusion one can gain from most studies is that many children have difficulties with mathematics and a significant number have relatively *specific* difficulties with mathematics.

It is in any case, questionable whether one can or should even attempt to establish a precise figure for the incidence of mathematical difficulties. Arithmetical thinking involves a very wide variety of components (see Chapter 2). Thus, there are many forms and causes of arithmetical difficulty, which may assume different degrees of importance in different tasks and situations. If dyscalculia implies an impairment in all aspects of arithmetic, and *only* in arithmetic, then it would appear to be very rare (Dowker, 1998) probably occurring in far fewer than 6% of the population. If it implies difficulties with certain aspects of arithmetic, which are sufficient to cause significant practical and educational problems for the individual, then they are probably considerably more frequent than the 6% figure would imply, perhaps occurring in 15 to 20% of the population if not more. The exact figure is much less important than the fact that there are a large number of people who find arithmetic extremely difficult; fall increasingly behind in it during their school years; often come to fear it; and as adults are restricted by the need to avoid jobs and other activities that involve arithmetic.

Numeracy difficulties in adults

There are considerable individual differences in arithmetical performance in adults. Some adults have a considerable facility with number and enjoy it; others find arithmetic very difficult. Because of the practical problems that may be caused by numeracy difficulties, the lower end of the adult performance range in arithmetic has received rather more attention than the higher end.

Bynner and Parsons (2000) gave some Basic Skills Agency literacy and numeracy tests to a sample of 37-year-olds from the National Child Development Study cohort (which had included all individuals born in Britain in a single week in 1958). The numeracy tests included such tasks as working out change, calculating area, using charts and bus and train timetables and working out percentages in practical contexts. According to the standards laid down by the Basic Skills Agency, nearly one-quarter of the cohort had 'very low' numeracy skills that would make everyday tasks difficult to complete successfully. This proportion was about four times as great as that classed as having very low literacy skills. Women were more likely than men to be in this category: 27% of women, as compared with 19% of men were classed as having very low numeracy skills.

Poor numeracy did indeed seem to have an impact on these people's lives. People who had *both* poor numeracy *and* poor literacy skills had the greatest problems in employment. However, even if literacy were adequate, people with poor numeracy skills had their problems. Among men, 17% of those with only numeracy difficulties were not in full-time employment, as compared with 10% of those with only literacy difficulties, 8% of those with problems in neither area and 31% of those with problems in both areas. Among women, 74% of those with only numeracy difficulties were not in full-time employment, as compared with 58% of those with literacy problems only, 56% of those with problems in neither area and 73% of those with problems in both areas. Among those who were in full-time or part-time employment, the *type* of job was associated with numeracy skills. Among men, 74% of those with only numeracy difficulties were working in a manual occupation, as compared with 69% with only literacy difficulties, 39% of those with problems in neither area and 75% of those with problems in both areas. Among women, 41% of those with only numeracy difficulties were working in a manual occupation, as compared with 18% with only literacy difficulties, 25% of those with problems in neither area and 55% of those with problems in both areas. Although the direction of causation may not be completely one-way – certain forms of occupational training and experience may serve to increase numeracy skills – it does appear that poor numeracy skills do affect people's ability to gain full-time employment and often restrict employment options to manual (usually lower paid) jobs.

The effect of numeracy skills on income was indeed quite significant. Even if only people who left school at 16 are considered (to control for the effects of extended education on earnings), 40% of men and 58% of women with only numeracy difficulties were classed as receiving low wages, as compared with 35% of men and 30% of women with only literacy diffi-culties, 43% of men and 55% of women with problems in both areas and 20% of men and 22% of women with problems in neither area. Moreover, it seems that poor numeracy skills have if anything a *greater* impact than poor literacy skills on employment prospects; although this may be in part because literacy skills did not need to be as severely deficient as numeracy skills to enable people to be rated as having a difficulty in the area.

Does early numeracy performance predict later numeracy performance? There is certainly evidence that adults with numeracy difficulties tend to have already demonstrated numeracy difficulties in childhood. The majority of the adults with numeracy difficulties in Bynner and Parsons' (2000) study had already been rated by their teachers as poor at arithmetic at the ages of 7 and 11. However, the relationship was not perfect: 15% of the adults with numeracy difficulties had been rated as outstanding at arithmetic by their teachers at the age of 7. It seems that, while numeracy difficulties are often consistent throughout life, some people start out with no numeracy problems but then 'something goes wrong' during their development and education.

Severe, and slightly less severe, specific difficulties with arithmetic

There are some individuals who have very severe difficulties with most aspects of arithmetic, while having no apparent difficulties in other areas. Butterworth (1999) described 'Charles', a university graduate, who had no problems with literacy or general reasoning, but who could only solve even single-digit sums by counting slowly on his fingers. He could not subtract or divide at all or carry out any sort of multi-digit arithmetic. He was extremely slow even at comparing numbers: for example, saying which was bigger, 9 or 3. He could only give the answer to such comparison problems after counting on his fingers from the smaller number to the larger number. He took about ten times as long as most people even to state whether two numerals were the same or different. He seemed to lack even the most basic numerical abilities that usually seem to be present in babies. He could not recognize even two dots as two without counting them.

Chapter 10 will discuss some of the possible brain-based reasons for the difficulties of people such as Charles. For now, such cases will be treated as evidence that it is possible to have very severe arithmetical difficulties without having difficulties in other aspects of language, memory or reading.

Such extreme cases are rare, even among those with diagnosed dyscalculia. Nicola, for example, is an adult whom I am currently studying. She is a 19-year-old woman who has been diagnosed as having dyscalculia. She has always had severe difficulties with school arithmetic. Her WAIS arithmetic subtest score is 2. On the British Abilities Scales Basic Number Skills subtest, designed for children, she obtained an age equivalent score of 8 years 9 months. This test places considerable emphasis on the ability to read two- and three-digit numbers, which Nicola can do. It is possible that a test that places less emphasis on number reading would have resulted in an even lower age equivalent. She deals with most arithmetical problems by counting on her fingers: counting on from the larger number for addition; counting down from the larger number for subtraction. What are her more basic numerical difficulties like? Her ability to estimate numerosities is indeed relatively weak; but she *can* recognize quantities up to 3 without difficulty. There is a sharp division for her between 3 and more than 3: for larger quantities she counts on from 3, so that six dots are counted: '3, 4, 5, 6'.

Thus, Charles and Nicola seem to represent quite different forms of dyscalculia. Charles lacks even some of the numerical abilities that appear to be possessed by most babies. Nicola has these numerical abilities, but has difficulty with most forms of arithmetic and relies excessively on somewhat cumbersome counting strategies.

It is important that people like Charles, and even like Nicola, be identified as having difficulties early on, so as to reduce the risks of intellectual confusion and emotional frustration and possibly humiliation if they are expected to cope with the typical school arithmetic curriculum without special help.

Arithmetical difficulties: A difference in kind or a difference in degree?

One question that may be asked about people who have difficulties in any area of functioning is whether they are fundamentally different from individuals without such difficulties, or whether they represent the lower end of a continuum. Do people with arithmetical difficulties lack some function which everyone else has or are they doing the same things as others, but less well or less efficiently?

It is difficult to make generalizations about *all* people with arithmetical difficulties, because, as we have seen, such difficulties take very hetero-geneous forms. However, the evidence is that the majority of such difficulties can be seen as representing the lower end of a continuum. Studies of unselected groups of individuals have indicated that individual variations are considerable even for adults in even such apparently basic numerical skills as counting accuracy and speed (Deloche et al., 1994) and single-digit addition and multiplication (Lefevre, Smith-Chant, Hiscock, Daley, & Morris, 2003). (See also Chapter 3 in this volume.) One study by Szanto (1998) found that adults with arithmetical difficulties performed in a similar fashion on both computational skills and arithmetical reasoning to normally achieving adolescents and children who were at a similar overall arithmetical level.

This does not mean that people with arithmetical difficulties do not have a genuine problem. Many characteristics vary continuously in the population and yet may pose serious problems at the extremes. Body weight varies continuously, but being very overweight or underweight may both indicate and cause serious health problems. IQ varies continuously, but those at the low end of this continuum are likely to experience major difficulties, even when no specific pathological cause can be identified. However, it does mean that people with arithmetical difficulties are not sharply distinct from other individuals, and that most of the difficulties that they show can also be seen to varying degrees in the general population.

Exceptionally high mathematical ability

> 'Do not worry about your difficulties in mathematics; I assure you that mine are greater.' (attributed to Albert Einstein)

> 'To be a scholar of mathematics, you must be born with talent, insight, concentration, taste, drive and the ability to visualize and guess.' (Paul Halmos (1985, p. 400): *I want to be a mathematician*, New York: Springer Verlag)

Much work on individual differences in arithmetic has focused either on the 'normal' range of ability or on the nature of and reasons for arithmetical difficulties. However, there are, of course, some people who have exceptional talent in arithmetic. These may be approximately divided into two groups: those who are unusually fast and accurate calculators; and those who have exceptional ability to reason about numbers and arithmetic. It is possible for one individual to combine both types of ability to an exceptional degree: e.g. the mathematician and talented calculator Professor Aitken, described by Hunter (1962). Such a combination seems, however, to be rare.

Extremely superior calculation skills

Arithmetical skill is usually associated with high levels of ability in other directions; but it does not depend on such levels of ability.

Extremely superior calculation abilities sometimes, albeit rarely, occur in people with very low IQs (Cowan, O'Connor, & Samella, 2003; Hermelin & O'Connor, 1991; O'Connor & Hermelin, 1984; O'Connor, Cowan, & Samella, 2000; Smith, 1988). Some such individuals are globally outstanding at most or all aspects of calculation. More often they are remarkably rapid and accurate at some particular aspect of calculation: surprisingly often, the ability to work out on which day of the week a particular date will fall. Usually, such special calculation skills are associated with a generally relatively good level of arithmetical performance. Most, but not all, of these 'savant' calculators are autistic.

Some people who are not intellectually impaired or autistic are capable of outstandingly rapid and accurate calculations. There have, for example, been a number of professional and semi-professional performers who earned fame and sometimes money by giving public displays of their arithmetical abilities (Flansburg, 1993; Smith, 1988; Weinland, 1948). Such talents have also been recorded in some people working in solitary occupations, such as the shepherds Jacques Inaudi and Henri Mondieux (Smith, 1988).

It is hard to say how frequently such talents occur in the general population. Since the advent of calculators and computers, which perform rapid calculations, there are few practical advantages in being a calculating prodigy. Even people who are capable of such calculations may thus prefer to devote their major efforts to other areas, if not restricted in doing so by their own limitations (as in autism) or their circumstances (as in the isolated shepherds). Richard Cowan (personal communication) has studied two non-autistic primary school boys who demonstrated savant-type abilities in calendrical calculation. One was of average IQ, while the other had an IQ of over 140. Both were very good at other aspects of arithmetic. They had a wide variety of other interests. By the age of 10 or 11, they seemed to have lost interest in calendrical calculation, although they were still able to demonstrate it if required.

Such talents as calendrical calculation may even be seen as suspect by some people. George, an arts graduate, informed me that at the age of five he had been very interested in and good at calendrical calculation; although the extent of his ability in this direction was never recorded. His parents, aware that this is sometimes a 'savant' talent in people with low IQs, had actively discouraged him from pursuing this interest and he felt that this had not only led to the loss of his calendrical calculation ability, but reduced his interest in mathematics as a whole.

The relative lack of value placed on rapid calculation in contemporary western society almost certainly means that some calculating prodigies go unnoticed and are never recorded. Does it also prevent people from becoming calculating prodigies in the first place? Would many more people be rapid calculators if they were encouraged to practice this activity? It does seem that most or all calculating prodigies, whether 'savants', shepherds, public performers or the rare professional mathematicians in this category, do devote a lot of time to practising their skill.

There is evidence that some people who might not otherwise have been outstanding calculators can develop an impressive skill in this direction with sufficient training and practice. Such skills do seem to be commoner in cultures where they have a practical or social value.

Binet (1894) reported the lightning calculation abilities of some French cashiers before the days of calculators: the fastest cashier whom he studied could multiply two three-digit numbers in four seconds. In contemporary Japanese culture, although calculators have removed the practical necessity for rapid calculation, the ability to use an abacus for rapid calculation is still highly valued. Some teenagers join abacus classes and clubs and devote themselves seriously to this pursuit (Hatano, Miyake, & Binks, 1977). Many of these people become very rapid calculators, able to create a mental image of an abacus that they can use almost as efficiently as a real abacus (see Chapter 9 for more details).

Staszewski (1988) taught a group of American students some fast calculation strategies, and gave them about 300 hours of training over a period of two or three years. After this extensive training, they were able to calculate such problems as $59{,}451 \times 86$ in only 30 seconds.

Such findings have led some people such as Howe (1990) to conclude that talent in arithmetic and other domains is just a matter of practice. According to this view, anyone could be a calculating prodigy if they had the time and the will to devote large amounts of time to practising this skill. Savant calculation abilities, according to such theories, are a product of the practice induced by having very little else to do with one's time, combined with the obsessional characteristics of many autistic people.

Yet, although practice is important, it does not seem to be the whole story. It does not seem that *anyone* could be a lightning calculator. What of the people who have real difficulty in remembering and applying calculation facts and procedures? People who receive extensive training and practice in calculation are usually not selected at random. Not everyone in Binet's France chose to become a cashier and presumably not everyone who did apply for a cashier's post was successful in obtaining the job.

In Japan, only about one-sixth of secondary school pupils choose to devote themselves seriously to learning the abacus. Staszewski's students were not *compelled* to devote hundreds of hours to calculations, although they did receive some payment for it. A person with poor initial calculation ability might not have chosen to engage in such activities or might have given up at an early stage.

High levels of arithmetical reasoning ability

Expertise at calculation procedures is not the same thing as the ability to understand and reason about numbers. The two may go together, but often do not. There have been several studies of the characteristics of children and adults with high levels of mathematical reasoning ability. Most such studies have not distinguished between high levels of reasoning about numbers and high levels of reasoning about other aspects of mathematics.

Arithmetical reasoning ability often shows itself quite early in life. Not every child with a strong interest or talent in arithmetic will continue equally interested or equally highly achieving, later on. For one thing, as children grow older, they have more other intellectual activities to choose from. Young children in many cultures are exposed to numbers, but it is only later that they are typically exposed to history or geography or the sciences or music. Thus, children with high IQs and/or intellectual interests are often interested in arithmetic at an early stage and transfer their interests to other spheres later on. For another thing, many children become less interested in intellectual activities in general as adolescence approaches: the peer group, the opposite sex, their appearance, the pursuit of physical, social and economic independence all take priority. Also, secondary school mathematics may not have as broad appeal as primary school mathematics: the young child who is fascinated with numbers is not necessarily destined to be equally fascinated with algebra, calculus or proofs. While the reverse can also be the case – a child who dislikes numbers and arithmetic may later find far more interest in more abstract mathematics – it is probably less common. Children of all levels of mathematical ability tend to show a reduction in liking for mathematics as they get older (see Chapter 11).

There have been several studies of people with high levels of mathematical reasoning, although arithmetical reasoning is typically not treated separately from reasoning about other aspects of mathematics. For the most part, studies of 'mathematically able' individuals, whether children, adolescents of adults, have grouped all such individuals together. Those with high numerical and arithmetical ability have usually not been studied separately from those with talents in geometry and other domains of mathematics.

The best-known study in the area is probably that carried out by Krutetskii (1968) in what was then the Soviet Union. The most important characteristics of the mathematically gifted children were:

- They *liked* mathematics and were enthusiastic about it.
- They could reason quickly, sometimes to a degree that interfered with their ability to 'show their working' in written form or describe it clearly to others.
- They were good at *generalizing*: they could not only find appropriate rules and strategies for solving specific problems, but could often work out general rules that could be applied to a broad category of related problems.
- They could recognize the *mathematical structure* of problems.

- They were able to deal with *abstract concepts*.
- They were inclined to remember not the *details* of a problem, but its *general principles*. If they were shown another problem based on the same general principles as a previous one (e.g. successive problems that involved the inverse relationship between multiplication and division), they often thought that they had seen the same problem before.
- They were *flexible* in their thinking and were able to devise a variety of strategies and to move easily from one type of strategy to another.

Sheffield (1994, 1999) studied mathematically able children in the United States of America and devised a somewhat similar list of characteristics. These included *interest* and *curiosity* about quantitative information; the ability to perceive and generalize *patterns and relationships*; *flexibility* of thought; the ability to reason *analytically, inductively and deductively*; the ability to *vary* and switch between strategies; the ability to *transfer* learning to new situations; a tendency to *formulate* new mathematical questions; and *persistence* with difficult problems. These characteristics are very similar to those discussed by Krutetskii (1976). In addition, Sheffield (1994, 1999) stated that mathematically gifted children were good at organizing and working with *data* and at distinguishing relevant from irrelevant data.

These characteristics were not specific to arithmetic and not all of the mathematical pupils in the studies by Krutetskii and by Sheffield were necessarily very accurate calculators; indeed Sheffield pointed out that some were not. Hope and Sherrill (1987) looked more specifically at children who were skilled at mental calculation. Such children were once again characterized by interest in the subject; flexibility of approach; and ability to perceive and make use of mathematical principles and relationships (in this case, arithmetical principles and relationships between numbers and operations). Memory for number facts was of secondary importance.

There have been several studies of the characteristics of mathematically gifted adolescents and young adults (Benbow, 1988, 1992; Lubinski & Humphreys, 1991; O'Boyle, 2000; O'Boyle, Gill, Benbow, & Alexander, 1994). Once again, most such studies have not separated those who are specifically gifted at dealing with or reasoning about numbers from those who are gifted at other aspects of mathematics such as geometry. Moreover, the mathematically gifted pupils have typically been selected according to test scores or academic performance, which may have excluded some pupils, especially those who were underachieving at school (Sowell, Bergwall, Zeigler, & Cartwright, 1990). Their main findings have been that mathematically gifted individuals tend:

1   to be male. Some suggested reasons for this finding are discussed in the subsection on 'Gender differences'
2   to show a high rate of allergies and autoimmune disorders
3   to be short-sighted

4   to show unusual patterns of brain organization with a high rate of left-handedness.

Benbow (1988, 1992) and her colleagues have suggested that high levels of testosterone may lead both to unusual patterns of brain organization conducive to mathematical talent and to a proneness to immune disorders. This theory, however, is still very much in the realm of speculation.

Importance of flexibility and variability of strategy use: Central to mathematical talent; central to mathematical development

'There are nine and sixty ways of constructing tribal lays
And every single one of them is right.' (Rudyard Kipling: *In the Neolithic Age* (from *Collected Poems*), Ware: Wordsworth Editions, 1994, p. 354. Reproduced with permission of A P Watt Ltd on behalf of the National Trust for Places of Historic Interest or Natural Beauty)

A central theme of this book is that people use a very wide variety of strategies in arithmetic. In this book, this issue will come up repeatedly. For example, it will be discussed with regard to estimation strategy use (Chapter 7); to the use of 'derived fact strategies' based on arithmetical principles such as commutativity and associativity (Chapter 6); and to the ability to represent the same problem in multiple formats – concrete, numerical and verbal – and to translate between them (Chapter 5). It is indeed an issue that permeates all aspects of arithmetic. There appears to be no form of arithmetic – from counting to complex arithmetical reasoning – for which people fail to use a remarkable variety of strategies.

This is an issue that can be obscured for at least two reasons. One reason is that oversimplified interpretations of stage theories of development can lead to an assumption that children at a given stage use only one strategy and then move on to using another single strategy at the next stage. In fact, most stage theorists including Piaget do not actually state this. However, the emphasis on changes with strategy according to stage of development can sometimes obscure the fact that multiple strategies are often used by the same child within the same 'stage'.

The other reason is that educators and psychologists often note the obvious fact that some strategies are more accurate and efficient than others and leap from that fact to the conclusion that there must be one strategy that is 'best' for any given problem, which children should learn to use. This view may have received some impetus from attempts to create 'expert systems' in artificial intelligence. Often such research on 'expert systems' has been based on, and has reinforced, a view that expertise results in effective decision making as to which is the best strategy to use for a given problem and efficient use of that strategy.

In fact, even young children use many different strategies for similar arithmetic problems at the same time. As early as 1928, Alpert studied preschool children's responses to a number of problem-solving tasks and found that the same child would attack one problem in one way and another problem in a different way and no one problem was solved in the same way by all children. More recently, studies by researchers such as Baroody (1988, 1989) and Siegler and his colleagues (Kerkman & Siegler, 1997; Siegler & Jenkins, 1989; Siegler & Robinson, 1982) have shown that 5-year-old children in the early stages of arithmetic use a multiplicity of strategies for simple addition problems and may solve exactly the same problem in different ways at slightly different times. Development consists not of the replacement of a single immature strategy by a single more mature strategy but of the discovery of increasingly more mature strategies, which co-exist for a long time with immature strategies, before gradually supplanting them. Similar results are found for older children with very low IQs (Baroody, 1988; Fletcher, Huffman, Bray, & Grupe, 1998).

This multiplicity of strategy use is not solely due to the fact that young children have not yet worked out how to use a 'best' strategy. Children and novices may be variable in their strategy use; mathematically able adults seem to be even more so – even when dealing with quite simple arithmetic. Some years ago, I gave mathematicians a dull-seeming task that involved estimating the answers to 20 multi-digit multiplication and division problems (Dowker, 1992). The details of the study are described in Chapter 7; but the findings and conclusions are so central to the global theme of this book that they must be mentioned here. The mathematicians were very accurate (although not error-free) estimators; but what was remarkable was the number and variety of the estimation strategies that the different mathematicians used for the same problem. This was not just due to individual differences in strategy preference (between-individual variability) but reflected the fact that the mathematicians were variable and versatile in their strategy use, as shown most strikingly by the fact that when 18 of the mathematicians were retested after a few months, they used different strategies on the two occasions for most of the same problems.

A few years later, the study was extended to other groups of adults: accountants, psychology students and English students (Dowker, Flood, Griffiths, Harriss, & Hook, 1996b; also see Chapter 7 in this volume). The most striking result of the study was that all the groups in the study showed both between-individual and within-individual variability to a very marked degree. All groups used a remarkably large number and variety of strategies for every problem. Within-individual variability was also considerable, as shown both by the number of broad types of strategy used in each protocol and by the fact that those who were retested showed considerable variations in specific strategy use on the two test occasions.

Although great variability in this task was a characteristic of all groups, there were some highly significant individual and group differences. These were mostly in the direction of greater variability being associated with greater arithmetical knowledge and experience. The mathematicians showed more variable strategy use than the accountants or psychology students, who, in turn, showed more variable strategy use than the English students. Within each group, those who used more strategies tended also to be the more accurate estimators.

Such results indicate that the view of an 'expert' as one who is able to work out quickly how to use the 'one best strategy' is inaccurate. Either expertise is consistently associated with variable strategy use, or there may be a U-shaped relationship between expertise and strategy variability as suggested by Dowker et al. (1996b). Novices may use many strategies, often inappropriate or inefficient, because they have not yet fixed on any particular strategy or set of strategies. Experts may use many strategies, mostly appropriate, partly because they have access to more strategies, but mainly because they have a sufficiently good 'cognitive map' of the territory that they do not fear becoming irretrievably lost if they stray from a known path. People at intermediate levels of expertise are more likely to confine themselves to a small set of strategies that they have learned and with which they feel safe.

The findings concerning the remarkable variability of strategy use by mathematicians in apparently simple arithmetic problems also received support from the subsequent findings by Lefevre and her colleagues (Lefevre, Bisanz, Daley, Buffone, Greenham, & Sadesky, 1996a; Lefevre, Sadesky, & Bisanz, 1996b; Lefevre et al., 2003) that educated adults use a wide variety of strategies in solving single-digit addition and subtraction problems. Smith (1995) found great variability in adults' strategy use in problems involving fractions and decimals.

Such findings concerning strategy versatility have important educational implications. If strategy variability even for simple problems is the norm, and becomes startlingly high in 'expert' groups, then it becomes obvious that there is *not* only one way or even one optimum way of solving a problem. This supports the view of Ginsburg (1977) that 'it is nonsense to suppose that there is one dominant mode of learning academic material' and that it is desirable 'to explore different kinds of learning for different kinds of children, or for the same child under different circumstances'. There is now abundant evidence that elementary school children will, if permitted, devise and use a wide variety of appropriate strategies for addition, subtraction, multiplication and division (Ambrose, Baek, & Carpenter, 2003; Beishuizen, Van Putten, & Van Mulken, 1997; Carpenter, Franke, Jacobs, Fennema, & Empson, 1998; Fuson & Burghardt, 2003; Fuson & Smith, 1997; Kamii, 1985; Thompson, 1994, 1997b). Both as cause and effect of such findings, some countries have in recent years placed an increased emphasis on multiple strategy use in the primary school years.

Indeed, some attempts to model human mathematical cognition through artificial intelligence programs have emphasized flexibility and inventiveness in strategy use rather than honing in on one optimal strategy. Defays' (1995) 'Numbo' program is a notable example.

Do numerically gifted people make mistakes in arithmetic?

Professional academic mathematicians are one group who have been selected and self-selected for talent in at least some aspects of mathematics, although not necessarily arithmetic.

There are two common stereotypes about the arithmetical calculation ability of professional mathematicians and others with considerable capacity for abstract mathematical reasoning. One is that such people are 'human calculators' who can solve arithmetical problems with remarkable speed and accuracy. The other is that they are particularly bad at arithmetic and 'cannot even add their laundry lists'. Both stereotypes are inaccurate, except with regard to rare cases. Most mathematicians are more accurate in arithmetic than people with limited mathematical ability, but are far from immune to errors. For example, in the estimation study alluded to earlier and in Chapter 7, only 11 of the 62 protocols by the mathematicians resulted in perfect scores. This is not just an artifact of the scoring technique and the set criterion for an accurate estimate, because when mathematicians' strategies were inaccurate they tended to be *completely* inaccurate. Mistakes were generally due to calculation errors, most frequently involving a failure to adjust the decimal point.

Every one of the five mathematicians studied by Lewis (1981) made at least one error in solving 22 algebra problems and most of these were 'careless' errors in carrying out routine operations. Lewis suggests that: 'No one bothers to become a flawless equation solver'.

Mathematicians who have written about the nature of their own mathematical thinking do indeed emphasize that the avoidance of such errors is not their primary concern. Mary Cartwright (1955), for example, stated that: 'There is no doubt that even the greatest mathematicians make plenty (of mistakes). In fact it was stated of one eminent professor that he says a, he means b, he writes c, but it *should* be d. If the proof is easily rectified and the result holds, we do not worry.'

Generally, even when the mathematicians were making use of learned facts about numbers, such as squares and square roots, their knowledge and their use of strategies based on this knowledge seemed to involve an enjoyment of thinking about and playing with numbers, rather than rote memorization.

Such interest in playing with numbers also characterizes many other people with high level of arithmetical reasoning ability. A similar attitude was described by some of Hope and Sherrill's (1987) talented mental calculators and perhaps best expressed by the outstandingly able 13-year-old mental calculator studied by Hope (1987), who frequently used strategies based on factoring and on a remarkable knowledge of squares. She remarked: 'I'm not very good at memorizing.' (Hope) commented that some people might regard her knowledge of squares as merely 'memorizing'. She exclaimed: 'But that's not memorizing. That's knowing and thinking.'

This remark is just one demonstration of the fact that arithmetic is not a single ability but is made up of many components. This will be the theme of the next chapter and, indeed, of the rest of the book.

2 There is no such thing as arithmetical ability – only arithmetical abilities

Thus far, we have been discussing arithmetical ability as though such a thing existed as a single entity. However, there is extensive and increasing evidence that there is no such thing as arithmetical ability: only arithmetical abilities. Although some people tend to do well on most numerical tasks and some people to do badly on most numerical tasks, it is quite possible for the same person to find some numerical activities easy and some difficult.

This is true whether arithmetic is treated in terms of the *mental processes* involved (e.g. exact calculation versus estimation; facts versus procedures versus concepts) or in terms of *content* (e.g. addition versus subtraction; whole numbers versus fractions).

There have been a few attempts to classify the mental processes involved in learning and doing arithmetic. The classifications differ in detail and in the number of processes that they involve, but they concur that arithmetic cannot be treated as a single system or process.

Ginsburg (1972, p. 10) proposed at least four 'relatively autonomous cognitive systems': a system for calculation procedures, a system for estimation, a system of formal knowledge (involving explicit knowledge of arithmetical facts and concepts such as place value) and a system of informal knowledge (involving arithmetical concepts such as 'more' and 'less', which are acquired by all children without a need for formal teaching).

While there may be disagreement as to what are the most important components of arithmetical understanding and where the boundaries between them should be drawn, it is clear that, as Ginsburg (1972, p. 11) pointed out: 'Children's mathematical knowledge is an enormously rich . . . cognitive system . . . It is not simply a collection of rote responses, or memorized facts, or concepts or the conservation of numbers, or quantitative aptitudes.' Neither, we might nowadays add, is it simply a representational system, a set of social and cultural practices or the operation of a specific piece of the brain.

Levine, Lindsay, and Reed (1992) propose 16 major mathematical subcomponents: facts, details, procedures, manipulations (co-ordinating multiple facts, procedures and details in working memory), patterns, words (mathematical vocabulary), sentences (verbal explanations and word problems), images, logical processes, estimations, concepts, approaches (forming problem-solving strategies), accumulations (being able to remember and build on prior knowledge and skill), applications (ability to see and use the relevance of mathematics in real-life contexts), apprehensions (mathematics anxiety) and affinities (perceiving the cohesion of mathematics and the ways in which different aspects 'go together'). One could argue about the extent to which these are all components of mathematics: some of these (notably 'accumulations') seem to refer more to the way in which mathematical learning was achieved than to mathematical thought processes. Also, some of these subcomponents could be seen as closely related to one another, while others could be subdivided further.

As regards most of the subcomponents, there is room for debate and research as to the extent to which they are likely to be specific to mathematics. To give just one example, there are debates as to whether difficulties in manipulating mathematical information in working memory are typically restricted to mathematical information or involve some sort of central memory mechanisms which affect many forms of information (see Chapter 8).

Evidence that arithmetic consists of multiple components

(a) *Studies of typical adults* show that marked discrepancies can occur between different components of arithmetic. Moreover, it seems that, when investigated, almost no component is so simple as to fail to evoke individual differences in normal adults. Deloche, Seron, Larroque, Magnien, Metz-Lutz, Riva, and Schils, et al. (1994) gave 180 typical adult subjects the EC301, a standardized testing battery for the evaluation of brain-damaged adults in the area of calculation and number processing. Although most of the participants performed well, there were significant individual differences even in such components as written and oral counting and transcoding between digits and written and spoken number words. Moreover, people who did well in one component did not always do well in another.

(b) There have been several *factor analytic studies* of arithmetic in both children and adults, involving identification of tests that cluster together. The assumption is that if several different clusters are obtained, these may represent different components of arithmetic. This method has been used as a technique of investigating the components of mathematical ability for almost as long as factor analysis has existed as a technique (Canisia, 1962; Collar, 1920; Thurstone, 1938; Thurstone & Thurstone, 1941; Very, 1967; Werdelin, 1961). Such studies, supported by later work by Geary and Widaman (1987, 1992), led to the distinction between two mathematical domains: numerical facility and mathematical reasoning.

It should be remembered that the results of factor analysis can depend on the number and nature of tests that are introduced into the study in the first place. A few studies that have incorporated additional tests have appeared to uncover additional factors, e.g. the Dot Counting factor proposed by Thurstone and Thurstone (1941). Werdelin (1961) obtained a factor for dealing with number series and number analogies, which was separable from numerical facility and general mathematical reasoning factors. Very (1967) found a separate Arithmetical Estimation factor.

Whatever the limitations of, and discrepancies between, factor analytic studies, they do concur with one another and with other studies in providing support for componential theories of individual differences in arithmetic (Geary & Widaman, 1992).

(c) Some of the most striking evidence for the componential nature of arithmetic, and the possibility of individual differences in the relative levels of functioning of the different components, comes from *studies of patients* who have become dyscalculic as the result of brain damage. These will be discussed in more detail in Chapter 10. For example patients can show selective impairments in knowledge of arithmetical facts; in carrying out procedures accurately; in understanding arithmetical principles; in reading or writing numbers; or in understanding and comparing the relative sizes of numbers. People may show impairments in any one of these components while showing little or no impairment in any of the other components.

Most such studies have involved patients who have experienced selective injury to particular areas of the brain, e.g. as a result of strokes or head injuries. Similar results are also found for people who develop Alzheimer's disease and similar conditions. Kaufmann, Montanes, Jacquier, Matallana, Eibl, and Delazer (2002) found that people in the early stages of Alzheimer's disease showed a variety of dissociations between arithmetic facts, arithmetic procedures and basic number knowledge (understanding and comparing numbers). No component appeared to be a necessary prerequisite for other components.

(d) Studies of *children with arithmetical disabilities* (Geary, 1993; Jordan, Hanich, & Uberti, 2003; Jordan & Montani, 1995; Rourke, 1993; Russell & Ginsburg, 1984; Shalev, Weirtman, & Amir, 1988; Temple, 1991) also suggest that arithmetic is componential. For example, double dissociations have been reported between factual and procedural knowledge of arithmetic in children (Temple, 1991). Such studies also indicate the possibility of discrepancies between different aspects of arithmetical reasoning: for example, children with arithmetical disabilities are often impaired at arithmetical word problem solving, but not at other aspects of arithmetical reasoning such as derived fact strategy use and estimation (Russell & Ginsburg, 1984).

(e) *Cross-cultural studies* show that different aspects of arithmetic are affected to varying degrees by age and educational experience. Dellatolas, Von Aster, Willadino-Braga, Meier, & Deloche (2000) studied 460 children between the ages of 7 and 10 from three countries: Brazil, France and Switzerland. They found that age (which was strongly associated with educational level, so that it was hard to separate the two) strongly predicted performance in some tasks: e.g. reading and writing numerals; number comparisons; mental calculation; and word problem solving. By the same token, it had only a slight effect on certain other tasks: counting dots; counting backwards; and estimation.

Chapter 9 reviews several studies that show that people who have little or no schooling, or who are performing poorly at school, may perform extremely well at practical mental arithmetic in the workplace, while performing poorly at formal written arithmetic.

Do the components of arithmetic form a hierarchy?

If arithmetic is made up of numerous subcomponents, the question arises: can these be ordered in a hierarchy? Are there some skills that are always prerequisites for other skills, in the sense that one must learn to perform skill A before one can perform skill B? There have been several attempts to establish such hierarchies of skill, with a view both to developing a better understanding of the nature of arithmetical learning and to discovering the optimum order in which to teach arithmetical skills (Gagne, Major, Garstens, & Paradise, 1962; Underhill, 1983; Uprichard & Phillips, 1977).

The best way of investigating whether certain skills are prerequisites for other skills is to carry out longitudinal studies, especially studies that look at the effects of training children in particular skills (Butterworth & Bryant, 1990). Unfortunately, there have been relatively few longitudinal studies in the field of mathematical development. However, all the evidence suggests that arithmetical cognition is much less hierarchical than might at first appear.

Arithmetic tends to be *taught* in a hierarchical way: children are taught 'simpler' skills first and then progress toward more difficult skills. This means that if children have missed or failed to understand teaching early on, they may have difficulty with later instruction that is based on attempts to build on the earlier material. Nevertheless, studies have failed to demonstrate consistent hierarchies between subskills.

Some subskills do facilitate the development of other skills; but there are few subskills that must invariably precede other skills. Discrepancies in both directions can occur between almost any two subskills, however closely related they may be in general. Many examples of such discrepancies will be described in this book. For example, children usually can count accurately before they can perform more advanced arithmetic; and difficulties in counting often lead to difficulties in arithmetic. However, Chapter 4 gives several examples of children who showed serious difficulties with counting procedures and yet were able to perform apparently much more difficult arithmetical tasks.

Underhill (1983, pp. 243–244) rejected earlier views, such as those of Gagne and colleagues, that 'there is one optimal instructional sequence for acquiring specific content and that the sequence is based on a validated learning hierarchy' and considered that 'there is [not] *one* optimal instructional sequence for acquiring specific content for all learners, but many'.

Broad distinction between rote learning and conceptual learning

'A child's seeming stupidity in learning arithmetic may, perhaps, be a proof of intelligence and good sense. It is easy to make a boy, who does not reason, repeat by rote any technical rules that a common writing-master, with magisterial solemnity, may lay down for him; but a child who reasons will not be thus easily managed; he stops, frowns, hesitates, questions his master, is wretched and refractory, until he can discover why he is to proceed in such a manner; he is not content with seeing his preceptor make figures and lines upon a slate, and perform wondrous operations with the self-complacent dexterity of a conjuror. A sensible boy is not satisfied with merely seeing the total of a given sum, or the answer to a given sum, or the answer to a given question come out right, he insists upon knowing why it is right.' (Maria and Richard Edgeworth: *Practical Education*, London, J. Johnson, 1798, pp. 246–247)

'She teaches him arithmetic in some wonderful scientific way that . . . will make him a capital mathematical scholar, though he cannot add up pounds, shillings and pence.' (Charlotte Yonge: *The Daisy Chain*, London: Collins, 1843, p. 513)

'There is a prevailing opinion that the London elementary school children of today are slower and less accurate in computation than they were ten years ago. I have searched for evidence in support of this contention, but have failed to find it . . . But even if there has been a slight loss of accuracy, there has been a great gain in intelligence; and intelligence is an equipment incomparably more valuable than facility in calculation.' (school inspector quoted in: Board of Education: *Special Reports on Educational Subjects*, 1912, 26, 16)

'The idea in New Math is to understand what you are doing, rather than to get the right answer.' (Tom Lehrer: *New Math, That was the Year that was*, Reprise Records, 1964)

For many years, researchers and educators have drawn a distinction between two kinds of arithmetical knowledge. One is gained through repetition, rote learning and habit formation, and involves the mastery of facts and skills without much reference to their deeper meanings. The other is gained through discovery and reflection and involves a deeper conceptual understanding of the meanings of numbers and operations, whether or not such an understanding is associated with rapid and efficient computation.

Different terms are used for these two different forms of mathematical learning. Brownell (1938) styled the former 'learning by repetition' and the latter 'learning by insight'. Skemp (1976) distinguished between 'instrumental learning' and 'relational learning' and Hatano (1988) distinguished between 'routine expertise' and 'adaptive expertise'. Some researchers with young children (Greeno, Riley, & Gelman, 1984) and with patients with brain damage (Delazer & Benke, 1997) have concluded that there is a fundamental cognitive distinction between 'procedural knowledge' (knowing how to use specific strategies in counting or arithmetic) and 'conceptual knowledge' (understanding the mathematical principles underlying these strategies).

As will be discussed later, these two broad categories of arithmetical knowledge are further divisible. Routine expertise involves *both* knowledge of procedures *and* knowledge of facts and these do not always go together (Sokol & McCloskey, 1991; Temple, 1991). So we have at least *three* recognized categories of arithmetical knowledge: *conceptual, procedural* and *factual knowledge* (e.g. Delazer, 2003). These categories can be divided into further subcomponents.

Educational attitudes to rote learning and conceptual learning

At certain times and in certain places, great emphasis has been placed on rote learning, on the assumption either that this form of learning was more important in mathematics than any other or that once the rote learning was in place the concepts would follow. Gupta (1932) argues that Indian education was adversely affected for centuries by the remnants of the ancient Indian system of requiring pupils first to learn a book by heart and only afterwards to receive an explanation. In early 20th-century India, a saying that he translates (p. 76) as 'Getting by heart a thing is to be preferred to the understanding of it' was still current.

At the other extreme, there have been times and places that discouraged rote learning to the extent that some people felt that *any* training in memory for facts and procedures was discouraged or even forbidden. Newson and Newson (1977, pp. 127–128) quote a Nottingham mother of the 1960s:

> We help him with his arithmetic, and now, though the school doesn't approve, we're teaching him his tables. They say at school they're not allowed to teach them their tables . . . I happened to be talking to his teacher about how we taught Steven and Jennifer their tables – because Jennifer found that more help than anything when she got to Mundella [grammar school]. And I says, "Why don't you teach them here?" And

she said, "We're not allowed to teach them tables. If the school inspector came and found us teaching them tables, we'd be in trouble".

Factual knowledge and difficulties in remembering facts

There are extensive individual differences in knowledge of arithmetical facts. Chapter 8 will discuss these from the point of view of their relationships to *memory*. They will be discussed here as evidence that factual knowledge forms a separate category to procedural and conceptual knowledge.

Difficulties in retrieving arithmetic facts are very common, and tend to be persistent (Garnett & Fleischner, 1983). On the whole, children who are performing poorly at arithmetic rarely use retrieval of facts and tend to rely on counting procedures (Gray & Tall, 1994; Ostad, 1998; Siegler, 1988). It is important to distinguish between children who have trouble with factual memory, but use a wide range of back-up strategies including derived fact strategies (see Chapter 6) and those who appear *only* able to use counting-based strategies (Gray & Tall, 1994; Pitta Pantazi, & Gagatsis, 2001). The former group would indeed appear to have a specific weakness in remembering facts. The latter group may also have relatively weak *conceptual* understanding of arithmetic and may be limited to the rather inflexible use of a learned procedure.

It should also be noted that, while difficulty in remembering number facts is a very common component of arithmetical difficulties, not all children with arithmetical difficulties have this problem. Most of the children in my intervention study certainly did experience problems with number facts; but not all did. Some children could remember many number facts, but seemed to lack strategies (including suitable counting strategies) for working out sums when they did not know the answer. Some other children could deal with single-digit arithmetic but had serious difficulty in achieving even limited understanding of tens, units and place value.

Factual memory: Imperfect and variable even in adults

It is often assumed that adults have an efficient store of simple arithmetic facts in memory and that, unlike young children, they do not have to calculate the answers to single-digit addition and multiplication sums: they can retrieve them automatically. However, this does not appear to be completely true. Thevenot, Barouillet, and Fayol (2001) found that adding numbers interfered with adults' recognizing them in a subsequent task, while comparing them did not. This suggests that addition was not a completely automatic process for them.

To what extent *do* adults use strategies other than retrieval in simple multiplication? Quite frequently, it appears. Gilles, Masse, and Lemaire (2001) found that adults were considerably faster at saying that answers to problems involving multiplying by 5 were incorrect if the result did not end in 5 or 0 than if it did but was incorrect. Thus, they were clearly making use not only of their knowledge of multiplication facts, but of the 'five rule' that multiples of 5 must end in either 5 or 0. However, reaction time studies suggested that this was only true for relatively large numbers: for products up to 5 × 5, the strategy seemed not to be used, suggesting that the small number facts were sufficiently well known for additional strategies to be unnecessary.

To what extent do people – even *adults* – show *individual differences* in their use of retrieval versus other strategies? Once again, there do seem to be significant individual differences. For example, Gilles et al. (2001) found that adults with high and low scores on arithmetic tests differed in the speed and accuracy with which they used the 'five rule', although it was used by people in both groups.

Procedural knowledge and procedural difficulties

Many studies have examined children's difficulties with arithmetical procedures and, in particular, their incorrect strategies. A lot of 'mistakes' are not random, but result from the misapplication of rules that children have been taught. Such misapplied rules have been labelled as 'bugs' by Brown and Burton (1978) and VanLehn (1990). For example, in subtraction of numbers with two or more digits, a child may always subtract the smaller number from the larger one; e.g.

$$
\begin{array}{r}
52 \\
-28 \\
\hline
36 \\
\hline
\end{array}
$$

Another faulty technique of subtraction involves *always* 'borrowing' ('exchanging') one, even when this is unnecessary: 'Three from six you can't, so you borrow one.'

The consistent use of such faulty strategies cannot be seen as pure forgetfulness, carelessness or random behaviour; but it is also questionable whether it can be seen as a 'pure' problem with procedures. In most cases, it would seem to be associated with a failure to understand the conceptual basis of the procedures or sometimes even to recognize that there *is* a conceptual basis (Holt, 1966; Tilton, 1947; VanLehn, 1990). Borrowing is seen as a rule set by the teacher or textbook and the reasons for it are not perceived. Sometimes the rule is followed correctly and sometimes incorrectly. In the latter case, children, and indeed often adults, may fail to perceive that the procedure being adopted does not make mathematical sense: if they do change it to a correct one, it is simply because 'Miss Jones says you should only borrow when the bottom number is bigger than the top one.'

Resnick (1982) distinguished between the syntax and semantics of arithmetical procedures. The syntax refers to the series of rules to be followed; the semantics to the principles behind them, e.g. that a borrowed or carried 1 represents a ten.

In many, but not all, children, procedural difficulties represent delay rather than absolute deficit and they seem eventually to 'catch up' in their procedural skills (Geary & Brown, 1991a, 1991b). In some cases, this catching up may be more apparent than real: they learn how to use certain school-taught strategies, but may remain, even as adults, less flexible and sophisticated in their strategy use than people of greater mathematical ability.

In the case of young children, referring to 'procedural difficulties' as a broad category may be misleading. There are several different types of procedure that a child needs to learn to use and these may involve quite different processes: counting-based procedures; mental and written algorithms for multi-digit arithmetic; derived fact strategies, etc. These in their turn may relate to other aspects of arithmetical knowledge. Counting-based procedures are related to counting principles. Multi-digit arithmetic is related both to place value and to working memory. Derived fact strategies are predominantly a manifestation of *conceptual* knowledge, but are mentioned here as well, because many algorithms, if carried out with understanding, are really derived fact strategies in their essence (see Chapter 6 for further discussion).

It is notable that intervention programmes for children with arithmetical difficulties rarely include a broad 'procedural' category. Those programmes, which place considerable emphasis on procedural learning, tend to include many different types of procedure and to break these down into small components. Those that emphasize a combination of conceptual and procedural skills also tend to have more than one category relevant to procedures. For example, my own Numeracy Intervention programme, described in Chapter 10, includes strategies based on counting principles; derived fact strategies; problem solving with tens and units; and word problem solving, as well as some less procedurally based categories.

With older children and adults, it may be more appropriate to describe certain arithmetical difficulties as predominantly procedural. Even here, however, there are several different categories of procedural difficulty:

1   Inability to select a procedure at all, once the individual has to deal with arithmetic problems that are not based on learned facts. This is a relatively uncommon, but not unknown difficulty in young school children. In such young children, the difficulty may be due to lack of teaching, missed schooling, lack of confidence and/or developmental immaturity; and may be ameliorated by appropriate teaching and exposure to appropriate strategies. In older children and adults, this appears to be a much rarer problem, since individuals with severe

arithmetical difficulties usually come to rely on counting procedures. If it does occur, it is likely to represent either very severe arithmetical difficulties indeed or a paralysing level of mathematics anxiety.

2   Inflexible reliance on counting procedures. This has been discussed already.

3   Fixation on incorrect strategies, sometimes known as 'bugs' (Brown & VanLehn, 1980), usually as a result of remembering standard algorithms wrongly or remembering them only partially and then filling the gaps incorrectly.

4   Difficulty in planning and keeping track of the steps needed to solve a problem and in attending to and storing the steps and their results in correct sequence. The individual may start correctly, but becomes confused.

The third and fourth types of difficulty are usually those emphasized in discussions of procedural difficulties in older children and adults. They need to be distinguished as they are likely to have rather different causes, correlates, treatments and outcomes:

Fixation on inappropriate strategies (bugs) has the following characteristics:

- The same incorrect strategy is used consistently for similar problems.
- Errors can occur at any point within a strategy.
- Such 'bugs' may be due to the acquisition of 'bad habits', which then persist or resurface when the individual is distracted. However, they are often associated with much more fundamental conceptual difficulties or even with an assumption that arithmetic cannot be expected to 'make sense'. VanLehn (1990, p. 39) considered that children who use such 'buggy' procedures 'must lack knowledge of the underlying design of the procedure because such knowledge would allow them to not only see why their buggy procedure is wrong but also to understand how to rectify it'. They have learned a 'symbol pushing procedure' without understanding it.
- If due either to a 'bad habit' or to a specific conceptual lacuna 'bugs' may be readily susceptible to remediation. If due to a general lack of conceptual knowledge, especially if combined with an expectation that arithmetic will not make sense, then the outlook is less good: the particular bug may well be overcome, but the conceptual difficulties are likely to persist unless seriously addressed.

Losing track of procedural steps has the following characteristics:

- Incorrect strategies are not consistent, but vary from problem to problem.

- Errors are unlikely to occur right at the beginning of a procedure. The likelihood of error increases with the length of time spent on a problem.
- It is likely to be associated with more general difficulties in working memory and/or attention (see Chapter 8).
- It may improve with maturation and increased working memory capacity. It may also improve with practice and increased 'automatization' of procedures, resulting in reduced load on working memory. Some studies suggest that procedural difficulties tend to improve significantly with age (Geary & Brown, 1991a, 1991b); although this may depend very much on the type of procedural difficulty involved.

Conceptual knowledge: Its different forms

Many studies and tests draw a distinction between arithmetical computation and arithmetical reasoning, but do not always draw a clear distinction between different forms of arithmetical reasoning. On the whole, tests of arithmetical reasoning place much more emphasis on word problem solving than, for example, estimation, derived fact strategy use or the ability to express a concrete sum in numerical terms. Arithmetical reasoning, in all its forms, is generally seen as an aspect of, or result of, *conceptual knowledge* of arithmetic.

Conceptual knowledge has several overlapping definitions and meanings. Sometimes it is used to refer to the underlying concepts about the world that may form the basis for understanding aspects of arithmetic, e.g. the relationships between parts and wholes. Sometimes it is used to refer to concepts about numbers themselves. At other times it is used to refer to the ability to reason about numbers and arithmetic (rather than following rules blindly), which may depend on conceptual knowledge in both of the above senses.

At the core of most definitions of conceptual knowledge of arithmetic is the awareness of relationships between numbers and between arithmetical operations and the ability to use these relationships in solving problems. For example, conceptual knowledge is defined by Hiebert and Lefevre (1986, pp. 3–4) as:

> [K]nowledge that is rich in relationships. It can be thought of as a connected web of knowledge, a network in which the linking relationships are as prominent as the discrete pieces of information . . . In fact, a unit of conceptual knowledge cannot be an isolated piece of information; by definition it is part of conceptual knowledge only if the holder recognizes its relationship to other pieces of information.

Semenza (2002, p. 285) states that: 'Conceptual knowledge of mathematics . . . implies understanding of arithmetical operations, and laws pertaining to these operations. It allows one to make inferences and, unlike [purely] procedural knowledge, can be flexibly adapted to new tasks.'

Thus, conceptual knowledge of arithmetic may be expressed in many ways. It is perhaps most obviously associated with the understanding and use of derived fact strategies (Chapter 6); but is also central to estimation (Chapter 7) and the ability to translate flexibly between different representations and to solve word problems (Chapter 5). Conceptual knowledge is as relevant to *counting* with understanding as to the more advanced arithmetical operations (Chapter 4). Indeed, prediction of the results of counting under different conditions, which do and do not involve changes in quantity, could be seen as the earliest form of derived fact strategy use.

Applying arithmetic: Understanding when and how to use it

'When the pupil learns by means of abstract examples, it very seldom happens that he understands a practical example the better for it; because he does not understand the connexion until he has performed several practical examples, and begins to generalize them.' (Intellectual Arithmetic, by A Teacher of Youth, McIntosh, 1977, in A. Floyd (Ed.) (1981), *Developing mathematical thinking*, Wokingham: Open University Press, pp. 6–11)

'In the first place, some advocates of what they call meaningful arithmetic disregard or minimize arithmetical meanings in favour of social applications, holding that experience in using arithmetical skills will make them meaningful. The fallacy in this thinking has been pointed out several times: experience in using skills may produce some awareness of the usefulness of number (that is, of its significance), but it cannot produce meanings. Meaning is to be sought in the structure, the organization, the inner relationships of the subject itself.' (William Brownell: When is arithmetic meaningful? *Journal of Educational Research*, 1945, 7, 481–498)

'I think using and applying [number and arithmetic] is very hard work because in my view it is demanding the children to make connections themselves. They are actively engaging with the current problem with their current knowledge and trying to make the two meet, and I think that is hard work.' (British Year 5 teacher quoted by Hughes, Desforges, & Mitchell, 2000, p. 1)

Researchers and educationalists have pointed out that there can be a distinction between being able to understand and deal with numbers in the context of an arithmetic problem, and being able to apply them to practical problems. People can understand the relationships between numbers and the procedures for using them appropriately in 'sums', and yet fail to apply them appropriately to real-world problems. Conversely, they may be able to work what sort of mathematical operation is needed to solve a real-world problem, without having the arithmetical skills to carry out the operation successfully. Greeno et al. (1984) proposed *utilizational competence* (being able to apply principles appropriately to practical situations) as a separate form of competence to conceptual and procedural competence.

In contemporary school education, the ability to apply arithmetic and other forms of mathematics appropriately is treated as an important aspect of the mathematics curriculum (Hughes, 2000). The National Curriculum in England and Wales in the 1990s included attainment targets in 'Using and applying mathematics'. The most recent National Numeracy Strategy does not include this as a separate component, but expects it to be integrated with all parts of the numeracy curriculum (DfEE, 1999).

Performance on this aspect of mathematics can differ significantly from performance on other aspects. For example, international comparisons reveal that British pupils perform better than those in most other countries at *applying* mathematics to practical situations, while merely performing close to the international average in most aspects of mathematics.

It is, however, most unlikely that the ability to apply mathematics to real-life situations is a unitary ability. The next question is: '*Which* real-life situations?' The mathematical content of some situations will be more transparent than others. Still more importantly, there will be both individual and cultural differences in terms of which situations are indeed seen to be relevant to 'real life' and what their importance and purpose is seen to be. In Chapter 9, many examples are given of children and adults who are able to apply mathematical skills to a culturally relevant situation (e.g. street trading in areas of Brazil; tailoring in parts of Liberia), but not to formal school situations. It is also not at all clear that they would be able to apply their knowledge to a 'real-life' context that has not been relevant to their own lives: for example, street traders will not necessarily apply their mathematical skills to tailoring, unless that has also been part of their cultural experience.

The same is undoubtedly true of us all; and reflects individual as well as cultural preoccupations. We are all likely to be better at applying mathematics to a subject that is interesting and relevant to us than to one that is not. For example, one person may readily perform calculations connected with football scores but not those associated with political election results; another may show the reverse discrepancy. Ainley (2000, pp. 148–149) proposes that we:

[D]etach the notion of reality from contexts and attach it instead to the perceptions of individuals. So, a problem involving the lengths of curtains in relation to particular windows is a *real* context for [herself] as an adult with an interest in interior decorating, but is not real for most primary school children, or for a colleague who finds the subject of curtains unexciting.

Ainley (2000, p. 149) also points out what is sometimes neglected: that 'real' or relevant does not necessarily equate with 'real world' or 'practical':

> The quality of an individual's engagement with a problem which makes it 'real' for them does not lie solely in its utility of application, nor in its physical existence . . . Abstract problems can be very real in terms of the interest and engagement they arouse. The development of mathematics has been driven by the need to solve problems, both practical and abstract, and by the pure joy of exploration. I do not believe that we have the right to deny children access to huge areas of mathematical understanding, history, culture and pleasure by making the enormously arrogant assumption that only what belongs to the 'real world' can be interesting.

It is worth remembering at this point that children are far more energetic both physically and mentally than most adults and are far more likely to set themselves tasks just for the pleasure of doing them, without needing a practical 'purpose'. They run, jump and practise physical skills that have no immediate application. They engage in endless pretend play, practising both roles that they may one day put to use, such as being parents and those that they will certainly not put into practice, such as being lions or sharks. Like Rudyard Kipling's child with her 'seven million whys', they ask endless questions, with and without practical applications. They play with language, often emphasizing the phonological and grammatical patterns of language over its meaning in such play (Dowker, 1989a, 1991). And they count and do sums for their own sake or to deal with fantasy problems invented in the course of their pretend play.

Here we do indeed need to recognize the importance of individual differences even in an area that might at first sight seem socially and educationally determined. If the perceptions and interests of individuals are crucial in determining the reality and relevance of problems, then individual differences in interests will have a strong influence on the ability to apply mathematical knowledge to a particular problem. Some interests are universal or nearly so; some will depend crucially on an individual's personal characteristics and experiences.

Thus the ability to apply mathematics to situations is at least as componential as other aspects of mathematics: the ability to apply mathematics to one situation need not imply the ability to apply it to another. Nonetheless, it is important that applications as well as content of arithmetic be considered at all ages and levels. In the early years, counting is not just a mechanical skill but must involve an understanding of the purposes of counting (Chapter 3). Students and researchers who learn statistics need not only to learn the techniques, but also when and to what situations they can and should be applied. In between, arithmetic problems need to be seen not just as mechanical activities to be performed in class or in homework, but as applicable to a wide variety of contexts. If they can only be applied, however successfully, in a school context, this constitutes a very serious limitation.

Discrepancies between mental and written calculation

Individuals can also show marked discrepancies between mental and written calculation (Thompson, 1997a). This may reflect certain other characteristics: mental calculation may be dependent on working memory and written calculation on the accurate recognition and processing of written symbols. It may also reflect teaching methods and other aspects of experience. Schools at different times and places give varying degrees of emphasis to mental and written calculation. For example, British educational policies have, in the last few years, placed a greatly increased emphasis on mental calculation in the primary school, whereas written calculation received much more emphasis in the past. On the whole, people tend to use mental rather than written calculation in informal, non-school contexts, even if they have also been taught to carry out written calculations. Individuals who have relatively limited schooling but use arithmetic extensively in the marketplace or workplace tend to be much better at mental than written arithmetic.

It appears that children are often more aware of concepts, and more inclined to reason, when carrying out *mental* arithmetic; and more inclined to carry out procedures as recipes when carrying out *written* arithmetic. This is one reason why some countries have chosen to begin by teaching mental arithmetic before proceeding to written arithmetic. This is the case in Germany and Switzerland (Bierhoff, 1996) and in the Netherlands (Beishuizen & Anghileri, 1998). International comparisons show that children in all these countries perform well in arithmetic. Recently, the British government has placed increasing emphasis on mental arithmetic preceding written arithmetic in the early stages of the curriculum.

As often turns out to be the case, there are old precedents for such an approach. A far more extreme version than anything in current mainstream practice was that of Benezet (1935). Benezet was Superintendent of Schools in Manchester, New Hampshire, in the 1930s and instituted a system of teaching where children were not exposed to formal written arithmetic until the age of 12. In the earlier grades, they received practice in estimating distance, area, weight, time and other measures; in telling the time and using the calendar; using money; reading numbers ('Automobile numbers are a help in this respect'); and, from the age of 9 or 10, mental addition and multiplication. Even after written arithmetic began, mental arithmetic was emphasized. An independent evaluation showed that by the time they had been exposed to written arithmetic for a year, the pupils who had been in the programme performed better, even in written arithmetic, than those who had been in the traditional programme.

Cognitive styles in arithmetic

Some researchers have attempted to distinguish between different 'cognitive styles' in arithmetic. Bath, Chinn, and Knox (1986) distinguished between 'inchworms' and 'grasshoppers'. Inchworms tend to focus on details rather than the problem as a whole; attempt to follow known recipes and formulae; prefer to use pencil and paper to compute; use a single method and carry out the steps in a serial order; and either do not check their result at all or do so by repeating the same procedure. Grasshoppers tend to focus on the problem in a more holistic fashion; form concepts; prefer to compute mentally; use a variety of methods, sometimes combining several at the same time for the same problem; and tend to check their results by using an alternative procedure. Bath et al. considered that teachers should find out their pupils' cognitive styles and teach the different groups by the methods that suited them best. Backhouse, Haggarty, Pirie, and Stratton (1992) felt that where possible children should be encouraged to use 'grasshopper' approaches, as these are likely to lead to greater success in mathematics.

Some individuals will indeed have a global preference for an 'inchworm' or 'grasshopper' cognitive style. But many will vary their cognitive style according to the particular type of arithmetic task; the social context; or their level of knowledge and understanding with respect to the problems being presented. It is a central theme of the book that arithmetical thinking has many components and people may use different cognitive styles for different components. People may rely more on 'inchworm' styles in school than out-of-school contexts (Carraher, Carraher, & Schliemann, 1985; Lave, 1988); and in contexts where 'routine' expertise in a particular activity is emphasized, e.g. the abacus competitions described by Hatano (1988). Also, individuals are likely to adopt 'inchworm' styles when they have acquired a limited number of suitable strategies for solving a particular type of problem, but do not have a sufficiently broad understanding of the domain to be able to stray from known paths without risking getting 'lost' in confusion. I have elsewhere proposed a U-shaped relationship between level of expertise in a domain and flexibility of strategy use in that domain (Dowker, Flood, Griffiths, Harriss, & Hook, 1996b; Chapter 1 in this volume). The 'inchworm' has much in common with the person at an intermediate point on this U-shaped curve; the 'grasshopper' with the person at a higher point. Since the same person may be at different points on curves for different types and levels of arithmetic problem, it will not always be possible to assign a single cognitive style to a person. For example, the same individual might be a 'grasshopper' for whole number arithmetic and an 'inchworm' for fractions and decimals.

Different components of arithmetical content

This chapter has mainly focused on individual differences in the cognitive *processes* involved in arithmetic. But an individual can, of course, perform at very different levels in different aspects of arithmetical *content*. It is possible to show dissociations in either direction between almost any two aspects of arithmetical content (Dowker, 1998; Ginsburg, 1977). However, some aspects of arithmetic do seem to present difficulties more frequently than others. For example, multiplication and division tend to present more difficulty than addition or subtraction; and many people find particular difficulty with concepts of zero and infinity, and perhaps most of all with fractions and decimals.

Differences between different operations

'I'll only come and work with you if I don't have to do any taking-away sums.' (Kerry, aged 6, to a researcher)

'I'm very good at adding but I'm not very good at taking away.' (Andrew, aged 7)

'Addition is the easiest. Subtraction is more difficult, and times is even more difficult.' (Nicola, aged 19, with a diagnosis of developmental dyscalculia; see p. 15)

Most people find some arithmetical operations easier than others. Multiplication and division typically create more difficulty than addition and subtraction. Subtraction is usually found more difficult than addition, although this distinction is not found in the case of preschoolers dealing with small quantities (see Chapter 4).

People often become confused between different arithmetical operations and use one operation where another would be more appropriate. Sometimes this is due to a misunderstanding of a word problem. Children will often respond to problems such as 'Joe has six sweets; Joe has two more sweets than Pat; how many does Pat have?' by adding the quantities, because the word 'more' cues addition: 'Eight, because he has two more.' In many cases, it involves extending a familiar or recently practised operation to problems that require another operation. Although any operation can be overextended in this way, the relative familiarity of addition often leads to a 'when in doubt, add' approach to arithmetic.

Even when individuals do not make actual mistakes, they are often slowed down by the need to overcome confusions between different operations. When people of all ages are asked to say whether an answer to an arithmetic problem is correct or not, they are slower to reject answers that are incorrect for the operation in question, but would be correct for a different operation on the same numbers. For example, they will be slower to reject the answer '2 + 3 = 6' than the answer '2 + 3 = 4', because of interference from the correct multiplication item, '2 × 3 = 6'.

Multiplication and division tend to be more difficult than addition and subtraction

Multiplication and division are often a source of relative difficulty for adults; and both individual and cultural differences are quite marked with regard to these operations. Part of the difficulty is that division often results in fractions; but even when only whole numbers are involved, difficulties still occur. Individual differences seem to arise, in particular, from the following.

Differences in memory for facts: Multiplication, more than other operations, tends to be taught in part in terms of memory for number facts: the 'multiplication tables'. As discussed in Chapter 8, individual differences in memorization and retrieval may be relevant here.

Differences in working memory efficiency. Multi-digit multiplication and division are multi-step operations, and as such rely heavily on working memory.

Differences in conceptual understanding of different forms of multiplication. Multiplication can usually be represented as repeated addition. This is the way it is usually taught and the predominant conception that most people have of it. For example, I asked 38 educated adults (described later in the section on '*The Adult Group: discrepancies between components of arithmetic in adults*') to define the four arithmetical operations. Apart from a very few adults with arithmetical difficulties who could only define multiplication tautologously as 'To multiply' or 'To times', all participants with *or without* arithmetical difficulties defined it in terms of repeated addition.

There are some situations – e.g. those that involve ratio and proportion – where multiplication cannot be reduced to repeated addition. Different researchers and educators differ as to how serious they regard this problem to be. Some consider that the view of multiplication as repeated addition is adequate for most situations, and that difficulties in representing multiplication in other ways are only a serious problem in a limited range of contexts. Others such as Nunes and Bryant (1996) follow Piaget (1970) in considering that multiplicative reasoning is fundamentally different from additive reasoning and that those who can only understand multiplication in terms of addition do not have a true concept of multiplication.

Individual differences in 'number sense'. As pointed out in Chapter 6, some individuals perform better than others at perceiving relationships between numbers and at estimating the likely order of magnitude of the result of a computation. Individual differences in 'number sense' affect all arithmetical operations. However, they may have a greater effect on multiplication and division, where a misplaced decimal point or omitted zero will lead to the result being out by a factor of 10 or more.

Fractions and decimals

> 'With fractions, my teacher says, the more bigger it is, the more smaller it is!' (Megan, aged 9)

> 'I get confused with points and fractions. When numbers aren't whole and when they get messed about like that. When they get bitty. I don't like fractions; they're horrid!' (Claire, aged 28)

Fractions and decimals pose difficulty for many children and adolescents (Hart, 1981) and are often confusing even to adults who have received extended education in mathematics.

As indicated earlier, Hitch (1978) found that industrial apprentices had a lot of difficulty with mathematics. Moreover, unlike most other arithmetical tasks, fraction and decimal arithmetic, and conceptual tasks involving 'ratio, proportion and percentage' showed only a weak correlation with grades obtained on the CSE mathematics examination (an examination given at that time to British school leavers of average or somewhat above average ability). Hitch concluded that: 'Even a high CSE grade [indicating above average achievement in school mathematics] is no guarantee of mastery in fractions.'

Tasks that create difficulty include:

- *Ordering of fractions.*
- *Ordering of decimals.* Sackur-Grisvard and Leonard (1985) studied French school children from the fourth to seventh grades (aged 9 to 13) and found that they tended to respond according to one or more of three implicit and incorrect rules:
  - **Rule 1**: Select as larger the number whose decimal portion is the larger whole number; e.g. 2.16 is larger than 2.4 because 16 is more than 4.
  - **Rule 2**: Select as larger the number that has fewer digits in its decimal portion; e.g. 0.6 is larger than either 0.23 or 0.83, because it has only one digit in its decimal part and the others have two.
  - **Rule 3**: Select as smaller a decimal point that has a zero immediately after the decimal point (e.g. 3.4 is larger than 3.04); otherwise apply Rule 1.

Rules 1 and 3 were the commonest. Rule 1 tended to be used by the younger children and Rule 3 by the older children.

It is not surprising that children would adopt and use incorrect rules while still learning how to deal with decimals and before mastery has been achieved. Unfortunately, mastery is often never achieved and many adults still use such incorrect rules. For instance, Putt (1995) gave Australian and American student teachers tasks involving the ordering of decimals. Over half of 'freshmen' made errors. Even in the third year of teacher training courses, which included some mathematical content, over 40% of the Australian student teachers and 22% of the American student teachers made errors. The majority of the errors were based on some variant of Rule 2.

Grossman (1983) found that fewer than 30% of undergraduates starting at the City University of New York were able correctly to select the smallest of a set of 5 decimals. Since one would expect 20% correct responding by chance alone, this is a startlingly low proportion.

Many studies have indicated that pre-service elementary school teachers often have a poor understanding of fractions and decimals (Lester, 1984; Post, Harel, Behr, & Lesh, 1991; Putt, 1995; Thipkong & Davis, 1991). This is a matter for concern, both because it indicates that many adults do not master these skills and concepts and because teachers may pass on their misunderstandings to their pupils.

There seem to be several important reasons why fractions and decimals present difficulties. These reasons seem to come into two major categories: (1) difficulties in understanding the actual nature and purpose of fractions and decimals; and (2) the fact that some of the central assumptions of whole-number arithmetic do not apply to fraction and decimal arithmetic.

In the study of adults' estimation strategies described in Chapter 7 (Dowker et al., 1996b), many undergraduates studying English at university had difficulty in using fractional relationships and would, for example, describe 943/0.48 as 'about 943 divided by ½, so about 450': i.e. they equated dividing by ½ with multiplying by ½. Even professional mathematicians made such errors occasionally. For mathematicians, such errors were presumably the result of short-term lapses of attention rather than deep conceptual difficulties; but the fact that they could occur at all undoubtedly reflects one of the problems posed by fractions and decimal arithmetic: it contradicts two important assumptions of whole-number arithmetic: that multiplication makes things bigger and that division makes things smaller.

Hecht (1998) investigated the relative importance of several factors in explaining individual differences in adolescents' skills with fractions. He tested the fraction computation skills of 7th- and 8th-graders (12- to 14-year-olds). He also tested their knowledge of basic arithmetic facts (factual knowledge); of the steps involved in fraction computation problems (procedural knowledge) and of part–whole relationships (conceptual knowledge). Basic fact knowledge had relatively little relationship to fraction arithmetic. Both procedural and conceptual knowledge made strong and independent contributions to fraction calculations and to word problems including fractions. Only conceptual knowledge made an independent contribution to performance on *estimation* tasks involving fractions. Thus, once again we see that factual, procedural and conceptual knowledge should be seen as separable components of arithmetic, and make different contributions to different aspects of performance, even within a broad general domain: in this case, fractions.

Very large numbers and the concept of infinity

> *Researcher*: About how many people are there in Oxford?
> *Luke (aged 7)*: Infinity. Because there are always new people being born!

As discussed in Chapter 6, and as pointed out by Hofstadter (1982), most adults find extremely large numbers hard to comprehend. Although, or perhaps because, such numbers are hard to comprehend, many children have a fascination with large numbers and perhaps most of all with 'infinity'. This is commonest in older children of high mathematical ability, but is not unknown in younger children, as we just saw with Luke. Extremely large numbers are sometimes offered when children are asked to make estimates to larger sums than they can calculate or estimate accurately. In my studies of children's estimation (Dowker, 1997, 2003b; Chapter 6 in this volume), children occasionally estimated 'infinity' to large sums. Finite but very large numbers such as 'a googolplex' were occasionally suggested. Eleanor (aged 6) alternated between 'a British billion" and 'a quadrillion' when asked to estimate sums of three-digit numbers.

It is unusual for such preoccupations with large numbers and infinity to occur in young children who have difficulties with arithmetic, but it does happen. Matthew, who is 6, had a lot of difficulties with addition and subtraction. He could add on or take away 1 from a given number, but was usually inaccurate when he had to add or subtract any number larger than 1. He certainly could not perform any multi-digit arithmetic. He could not accurately read two-digit numbers or compare their value. Yet he had a preoccupation with large numbers and with the concept of infinity. He made up the word problem: 'Ben had 5 sweets and Bill 65. They bought infinity more' and wrote the following number:

1000000000000000000

and labelled it as 'infinity'.

Do the children who discuss 'infinity' have any idea of what it means beyond the fact that it is a very large number? This is likely to vary; Luke's comment suggested that he did have some concept of its meaning. Matthew seemed to regard it as a large number; it is less clear that he understood its endlessness.

There has been relatively little work on the subject. Gelman (1980) suggests that children in the early primary school grades achieve an understanding that there is no largest number and that numbers never end. Wistedt and Martinsson (1996) reported that 11-year-olds could use group discussion to reach considerable depth in their understanding of some problems involving infinity. However, even adolescents and adults can demonstrate significant misconceptions on the subject. The extent to which children and adults may vary in their understanding of the concept of infinity and the possible relationships between individual differences in this understanding and in other aspects of arithmetical knowledge and understanding still remains to be studied.

Dealing with zero

'Nought.
0 is not a number. The obvious proof of this is
John had two sweets
Mary had none
John told Mary to eat some sweets
But she had none –
So she could not eat any number of sweets:
You cannot eat a number of sweets, if you have none.
When you are nought, you are not born.
Nothing and nothing make nothing. The obvious proof of this is
John and Mary wanted to collect sweets.
John brought none, Mary brought none, so they had none.
I think:
Nought has no permanent place in the number line. As it belongs with digit 1 in 10, 2 in 20, etc.
You can multiply nought by any number, and it will remain the same old "NOUGHT. Multiply by 9068510819247386015
And you still have 0"
Because in things nought has no form, in a way.' (Rosemary, aged 10, in Rosen, H. & Rosen, C. (1973). *The language of primary school children.* Harmondsworth: Penguin Books. Copyright © Schools Council Publications, 1973. Reproduced by permission of Penguin Books Ltd.)

While few children – or indeed adults – would be able to express the conceptual difficulty of zero as articulately as Rosemary, it is a difficult and puzzling concept for many children. How can something be both nothing and a number?

Many 4-year-olds and most 5-year-olds do have some limited understanding of 0. They realize that if there are no items present, then there are 0 (or 'none'). They realize that if items are repeatedly subtracted from a set, they will eventually end up with '0' or 'none' (or occasionally 'blastoff').

However, understanding the written representation of 0, and especially its role as a placeholder, is much more of a problem. So is the appropriate use of 0 in arithmetic: addition, subtraction and multiplication by 0 and the impossibility of dividing by 0. Nicola, a 19-year-old with a diagnosis of dyscalculia, found it very difficult to understand that one *could* add 0 to, or subtract 0 from, a number.

Understanding and applying rules concerning 0 (e.g. $n \times 0 = 0$; $n + 0 = n$) are a source of difficulty for many in learning arithmetic. They are also a specific problem for some patients (Cacciatori, Grana, Girelli, & Semenza, 2000; Pesenti, Deporter, & Seron, 2000).

Studying the components of arithmetic: Need to combine group studies with individual case studies

Despite all the converging evidence for the componential nature of arithmetical ability, there are still issues that need to be explored further (see also Dowker, 1998). In particular, studies of people from the general population have tended to involve groups rather than individuals, which means that where separable components are identified, it may not be clear whether these components may be further divisible. If two abilities (for example, mental calculation for addition and mental calculation for subtraction) are closely related, and thus describable as a single component, does this mean that they must *always* be associated or are there some individuals in whom they are discrepant?

By contrast, studies of people with acquired dyscalculia usually involve individuals rather than groups; and, moreover, involve individuals whose functioning is highly atypical. These studies have the advantages of making it possible to study dissociations in a very marked form and to facilitate our understanding of the neurological bases of cognition.

However, individual case studies of individuals from the *general population* are also important if we are to gain some idea of the level of encapsulation of different components of arithmetical ability and the nature of individual differences in specific components (see also Ginsburg, 1977). The *combination* of such studies with larger scale, statistically analysable group studies is desirable if we are to explore *both* associations *and* discrepancies adequately.

Some research that integrates group studies with case studies

Several recent and ongoing studies by the present author have involved this combination of techniques. These include a study of 213 unselected children between 5 and 9 (Dowker, 1995, 1998); a study of 178 children undergoing intervention for difficulties in arithmetic (Dowker, 2001; Dowker, in press); and an ongoing study of adults with and without self-reported specific difficulties in arithmetic.

The study of the unselected children had a primary focus on the relationship between calculation skill and the use of derived fact strategies (non-standard calculation strategies based on perceiving and using arithmetical principles such as commutativity and inversion to work out new facts on the basis of known facts) and is discussed in greater detail in Chapter 6. It included measures of calculation performance in addition and subtraction; derived fact strategy use; and, for most of the children, verbal and performance IQ subtests. Sixty children in the study also carried out a task involving estimates for addition (see Chapter 7). Effects of gender and social class were also investigated. As well as investigating overall patterns of performance and relationships between the different measures, the study also included some individual case studies of children within the group.

The results showed strong associations between calculation and estimation; between calculation and derived fact strategy use; and, most of all, between estimation and derived fact strategy use. The strongest associations were between addition and subtraction, with regard to both calculation and derived fact strategy use.

Older children performed better on all tasks than younger children. Gender had no effect on performance on any of the tasks. IQ scores, especially verbal IQ, had significant effects. Moreover, regardless of actual IQ scores, *discrepancies*, in *either* direction between verbal and performance IQ, were associated with a tendency to perform better on derived fact strategy use than on calculation. Social class influenced IQ scores, but had few independent effects on arithmetic performance when IQ was controlled for.

Despite the strong associations that were found, the case studies of individual children revealed that there could be strong discrepancies between almost any pair of components tested. Although some children were weak at arithmetic, most such children were not globally weak at *all* aspects of arithmetic: they appeared to have deficits in *some* but not all components of arithmetic. The weak components varied from child to child. Children who were good at arithmetic also tended to be better at some components than others, although their discrepancies between components were, on the whole, less striking.

For example, some individual children showed strong discrepancies between calculation and derived fact strategy use; between derived fact strategy use and arithmetical estimation; or between addition and subtraction. Examples of children showing such discrepancies – from this study and from others – will be given throughout this book.

These findings were a major inspiration for the Numeracy Recovery programme to be described in Chapter 10, which involves assessing 6- to 7-year-old children with arithmetical difficulties on several different components of arithmetic and providing them with intervention in the particular components with which they are experiencing difficulty. One hundred and seventy eight children were assessed so far, representing approximately the lowest performing 15 to 20% of pupils in their schools in arithmetic. Assessing the children for the programme has provided an opportunity to investigate the characteristics of children with arithmetical difficulties; and findings with regard to the *group's* performance on particular components will be reported in several places in this book (e.g. with regard to counting, derived fact strategies, estimation and translation between problems presented in different formats). The studies of *individual* children in the group indicate, once again, that individuals can show very strong discrepancies between different components of arithmetic. It must be remembered here that, although the children in this intervention group were experiencing arithmetical difficulties, they were, in this respect, representative of a large segment of the general population. They were attending mainstream schools and only a minority of them had 'statements' of special needs or any specific diagnosis. In other words, they were not patients and the discrepancies that they demonstrated cannot be regarded as extraordinary.

For example, let us consider two children in the Numeracy Intervention group: 6-year-old Lewis and 7-year-old Hayley. Both children were attending mainstream schools and were not classified as having any special educational needs; but were considered by their teachers to be weak at arithmetic.

Lewis performed poorly at standardized arithmetic tests: for example, his WISC arithmetic subtest scaled score was 3 (average is 10). Like most children of his age, he had a good understanding of the basic principles of counting. He understood that counting a set of objects in different orders will give the same answer and had no difficulty in answering questions about the results of repeatedly adding 1 to a set of objects. However, he sometimes became confused when asked questions about the results of repeatedly *subtracting* 1 from a set of objects.

He was very weak at formal arithmetic: his responses even to single-digit addition and subtraction problems seemed to be guesses. He is better (although considerably below age level) when the sums are presented as word problems. For example, he estimated $5 + 2$ as 4 and $4 + 3$ as 3; but got the right answers when asked how many are 5 dogs and 2 more dogs and 4 sweets and 3 more sweets. He relied totally on finger counting and does not seem to know any number facts by heart. He sometimes became confused if the result was over 10, forgetting the first 'hand' and thus giving a number that is too low by 5, so that, for instance, he added 5 to 6 and got 6.

By contrast, Lewis had several relative strengths. For example, he could invent word problems (mathematical stories) to represent some simple sums; e.g. for the sum '$4 - 1 = 3$', he told the story: 'Lucy had 4 flowers and 1 died.'

Strikingly, despite his difficulty with single-digit arithmetic, he could read two-digit numbers correctly. He compared the magnitudes of two-digit numbers correctly, so long as there was no conflict between the relative magnitudes of the first and second digits (34 is greater than 32; 45 is greater than 35; 52 is greater than 41). Where there was such a conflict, he tended to rely on the size of the last digit (43 is greater than 51; 24 is greater than 33). In contrast with his difficulties in subtracting 1 from relatively small sets of objects, he was usually able to give the 'number before' a given two-digit number, whether this was presented in oral or written form: thus 53 is before 54; 36 before 37, etc.

Thus Lewis had serious calculation difficulties, but seemed to have a relatively good mental number line; relatively good number reading abilities; and a good basic concept of the meaning of word problems.

Hayley was better at arithmetic than Lewis, even when age was taken into account; for example, her WISC arithmetic scaled subtest score was 8. She could cope well with single-digit arithmetic, but often experienced difficulty when she had to add tens and units. What is striking here is that whereas Lewis had a relative strength with word problems, this was Hayley's area of relative weakness. She found it considerably more difficult to solve problems presented in terms of word problems than in numerical form; and was quite unable to create word problems of her own.

Both Lewis and Hayley ended up improving to reach above average levels of performance in arithmetic, following individualized intervention through the Numeracy Recovery programme described in Chapter 10.

Adult Group: Discrepancies between components of arithmetic in adults

Another study involves *adults*, termed 'the Adult Group' in this book. I have been carrying out detailed case studies of adult volunteers who claim to find arithmetic difficult, but most of who have otherwise done quite well in the educational system. So far, 38 adults (16 men and 22 women), who claim to have such relatively specific problems with arithmetic, have been studied and compared with 12 adults (8 men and 4 women) who did not report specific calculation difficulties. Most of the adults, with a few exceptions, were university students and few had extremely severe difficulties.

They have been given Hitch's (1978) Numerical Abilities Test, which makes it possible to isolate various components of whole-number arithmetic, fraction and decimal arithmetic and arithmetical reasoning. They have also been given general cognitive tests (the Wechsler Adult Intelligence Scales and the AH5 tests of verbal and spatial reasoning); tests of computational, length, 'common sense' and numerosity estimation; mathematical reasoning tasks taken from the Stanford-Binet; and tasks, previously used by Warrington (1982), involving knowledge of number facts and definition of arithmetical terms. (See Chapter 5 for a more detailed report on the study, with a focus on estimation.)

So far, the participants with arithmetical difficulties have varied widely in their patterns of arithmetical and general cognitive abilities. In general, but not invariably, they find working with fractions and decimals much more difficult than working with whole numbers. Most are better at arithmetical reasoning than calculation, but some are highly erratic at both types of task. Estimation skills vary widely. Most show a wide scatter of scores on different subtests of the WAIS. There is no consistent pattern to this scatter. Frequently, but not always, verbal IQ is higher than performance IQ, with the arithmetic subtest score being lower than other verbal subtest scores, but not very low. So far, the controls also show a significant amount of within-subtest scatter, but less so than the subjects with calculation difficulties.

Within the group with arithmetical difficulties, different individuals could show very different patterns of strengths and weaknesses in both arithmetic and other aspects of cognition. For example, let us consider Graham and Maureen.

Graham, the youngest person in the sample, is a 17-year-old young man now studying for A-levels. He passed GCSE mathematics at the second attempt. He obtained very low scores indeed on Hitch's whole-number arithmetic subtests, this being more the result of extreme slowness than of inaccuracy. His performance on arithmetical reasoning tasks and most estimation tasks was very good. His performance on decimal and fraction arithmetic was relatively much better than his whole-number arithmetic: imperfect, but at least as good as that of Hitch's (1978) control subjects. He obtained a WAIS verbal IQ score of 106 and a performance IQ score of 111, with individual subtest scaled scores ranging widely from 14 (block design and coding) to 7 (digit span). His WAIS arithmetic scaled score was 11. He showed a more marked spatial/verbal discrepancy on the AH5 tests, performing well on the spatial reasoning test, but poorly on the verbal reasoning test.

Maureen, an arts graduate in her early 30s, had obtained the lowest passing grade in mathematics O-level on her third attempt. She performed extremely well on tests of both arithmetical reasoning and whole-number arithmetic. Her performance on decimal and fraction arithmetic was much weaker, though not significantly worse than that of Hitch's (1978) controls. Her estimation was very good for whole-number arithmetic; somewhat less good for fraction and decimal arithmetic; and very poor for length and quantity. She obtained a WAIS verbal IQ score of 125, with subtest scaled scores ranging from 17 for vocabulary to 11 for comprehension and digit span (13 for arithmetic). Her WAIS performance IQ score was only 80, with subtest scaled scores ranging from 10 for coding to 3 for object assembly. She reports some spatial difficulties in daily life (e.g. she claims that her young children do jigsaw puzzles better than she does); but her academic and professional achievements have been commensurate with her verbal scores.

While both Graham and Maureen could be described as exhibiting better arithmetical reasoning than calculation, there are considerable differences in their detailed patterns of arithmetical strengths and weaknesses and still more between their patterns of *cognitive* strengths and weaknesses.

The markedly uneven patterns of arithmetical and cognitive functioning shown by a significant number of 'normal' adults has important implications. If such patterns were only found in children, then they could simply reflect uneven patterns of development of different abilities. If they were only found in the adults, then they could be purely the result of educational and environmental influences. Since they were found in both children groups investigated in this study, we may at least suspect that such unevenness is relatively common in the general population and is not purely the result of teaching, although teaching may influence it.

From the point of view of cognitive psychology and neuroscience, it appears that a significant degree of functional independence of abilities is not confined to patients with neurological damage. This supports theories of the componential nature of arithmetic and perhaps of other cognitive functions.

We have already seen that arithmetic is not just one part of general intelligence. Moreover, even the view of multiple intelligence theorists such as Gardner (1983) that there is a single 'mathematical intelligence' is too limited. Arithmetic is many abilities, not one. It comprises many content areas; and, even more importantly, comprises many cognitive processes and forms of understanding. As we shall see in Chapter 10, it also involves multiple areas of the brain.

3 Relationships between arithmetic and other abilities

This book deals with arithmetic predominantly as a specific ability; or rather, as a constellation of potentially separable abilities. There are many examples in this book of people with specifically impaired, or specifically preserved, arithmetic. However, arithmetic does *on average* correlate with other abilities. When discussing individual differences in arithmetic, it is necessary to consider how it relates to these other abilities.

Arithmetic and IQ

Although arithmetic can, and often does, dissociate from other abilities, it is significantly related to overall IQ. People with high IQs are usually better at arithmetic than people with lower IQs (Geary, Liu, Chen, Peng, Saults, & Hoard, 1999; Kolshy, 2001; Krutetskii, 1968). Among unselected people, those who have mathematical difficulties tend to have somewhat lower overall IQs (although still in the normal range) than those who do not have mathematical difficulties (Greiffenstein & Baker, 2002).

There are several reasons why arithmetic may be related to overall IQ. For one thing, almost everything is correlated with overall IQ (Mackintosh, 1998), despite the frequency of discrepancies between IQ and specific abilities in individuals. For another, many IQ tests, such as the Wechsler scales for both children and adults, include arithmetic subtests. In addition, there are two particularly important reasons: arithmetic is related to abstract logical reasoning, which is what IQ tests are often regarded as measuring; and also IQ involves certain other more specific abilities – namely verbal and spatial ability – that may directly affect aspects of arithmetic.

Arithmetic in people with general intellectual impairments

There are certain forms of brain damage and of genetic disorder that not only lead to general intellectual impairment, but to disproportionate difficulties in arithmetic (see Chapter 10). Williams syndrome is a notable example. There are also some individuals who show savant talents in arithmetic despite generally below average IQs (see Chapter 1).

In general, however, even people with severe intellectual impairments tend to show similar arithmetical performance and strategy use to typically developing individuals of the same mental age (Baroody, 1988; Fletcher, Huffman, Bray, & Grupe, 1998). They show the same strategy variability that is usual in typically developing young children.

There have been similar findings for the much larger group of people with *mild* intellectual impairments. For example, Hoard, Geary, and Hamson (1999) compared 19 American first-grade children with low IQs (mean IQ 78) with 43 children of the same age with average or above average IQ (mean 108). The children with low IQs were less good at number naming and number writing and magnitude comparisons. They performed worse than their peers at detecting counting errors, especially when set sizes increased beyond 5.

They made more errors in simple addition, but used a similar range of strategies: an important point when one remembers that they were being compared with children of similar *chronological* age. It would have been desirable to compare them directly with preschoolers of the same mental age. However, it appears that their arithmetic and number skills were delayed but not markedly deviant and that the nature and variability of their strategies were not even delayed, at least at this early age.

There are, however, a few aspects of arithmetic that do seem to present particular difficulty for people with intellectual impairments. Judd and Bilsky (1989) compared adolescents with mild intellectual impairments and younger children matched for mental age and computational ability. The adolescents with low IQs experienced more difficulty in distinguishing between relevant and irrelevant details in word problems and were more influenced by the amount of context that was given for the story.

How important is it whether arithmetical difficulties are specific?

We have established that arithmetical difficulties often but not always occur in people who have generally impaired cognitive abilities. We have also established that many people have arithmetical difficulties that are not associated with low IQ. Does the nature or severity of the arithmetical difficulties actually differ according to their level of specificity?

A few studies have suggested that the level of specificity may not, in fact, be important in predicting the nature of the arithmetical difficulties. Gonzalez and Espinel (1999) found that children whose arithmetical achievement was much worse than would be predicted from their IQ did not differ much in their arithmetic performance from those whose poor arithmetic performance was consistent with below average IQs. The two performed similarly on addition and subtraction word problem-solving tasks and on some working memory tasks. Similar results were obtained by Jimenez and Garcia (2002). If there *are* differences between specific and non-specific mathematical difficulties, they are probably in the direction of specific difficulties being milder and less pervasive than non-specific ones (Jordan & Montani, 1997).

Thus, the evidence so far is that specific arithmetical difficulties are not fundamentally different in their nature from arithmetical difficulties that are associated with other cognitive difficulties. This supports the view that arithmetical difficulties are usually part of a continuum of arithmetical ability, rather than representing a qualitative difference from the rest of the population. More speculatively, they may imply that general intellectual impairments (associated with low IQ) involve a combination of weaknesses that frequently come together, but may occur separately: i.e. general intelligence is a statistical correlation between potentially separable abilities (Thurstone, 1941).

From an educational point of view, it appears that distinguishing specific arithmetical difficulties from difficulties associated with low IQ is important from the point of view of understanding a child's *general* educational needs, but may not be crucial to planning arithmetical intervention as such. (Of course, good general reasoning abilities may be used in helping children to develop compensatory arithmetical strategies; but many children develop such strategies even when their IQs are relatively low.)

Arithmetic and verbal and spatial abilities

There has also been a lot of work on arithmetic in relation to the abilities that are often treated as partly separable in IQ: verbal and spatial ability.

Reasoning, including arithmetical reasoning, can be carried out in many ways. Two broad categories that are often discussed with regard to individual differences are verbal and spatial reasoning. Information can be represented, manipulated and analyzed in words; it can also be represented, manipulated and analyzed in terms of visual–spatial imagery.

As with most classifications, classifying reasoning into 'verbal' and 'visual spatial' is an oversimplification. Other forms of representation can be used; e.g. tactile; motor; or highly abstract forms that cannot be properly classified as either verbal or spatial. Moreover, 'verbal' and 'spatial' reasoning are not themselves unitary categories. Verbal reasoning can, for example, emphasize vocabulary or grammar and can deal with spoken or written words. Spatial reasoning can, for example, be two-dimensional or three-dimensional; and in any case visual imagery need not always be related to space, while motor imagery, for example, could be spatial. However, the broad categories of verbal and spatial reasoning seem to have some validity. The factor analyses used to construct IQ tests (e.g. the Wechsler Intelligence Scale for Children and the Wechsler Adult Intelligence Scale), have typically resulted in 'verbal' and 'spatial' (sometimes termed 'performance') factors. The former includes vocabulary, comprehension, digit span, etc.; and the latter includes picture arrangement, block design, etc. While verbal and spatial IQ scores do tend to correlate with one another, marked discrepancies between the two are not uncommon: for example, Kaufmann (1994) found that 40% of an unselected group of American school children showed discrepancies of 11 points or more, in either direction, between verbal and spatial IQ scores on the Wechsler Intelligence Scale for Children.

A number of researchers have investigated the issue of whether arithmetical skills are particularly associated with verbal or spatial reasoning and/or with discrepancies between the two. The factor analytic studies used to construct the IQ scales have consistently placed the arithmetic subtest (one which emphasizes word problem solving) within the verbal scale. However, it has sometimes been suggested that spatial difficulties are particularly associated with difficulties in arithmetical reasoning (e.g. Rourke, 1993) and that gender differences in advanced mathematics may be explainable by the generally superior spatial ability of males (e.g. Geary, 1996).

On the whole, the relationship between verbal ability and arithmetic has been predominantly studied with regard to the effect of verbal *deficits* on arithmetic, while spatial ability has been studied with regard to the effects of both weaknesses and strengths.

Verbal ability and arithmetic

There is no doubt that mathematical difficulties often co-occur with dyslexia and other forms of language difficulty. People with dyslexia usually experience at least some difficulty in learning number facts such as multiplication tables. Miles (1993) found that 96% of a sample of 80 9- to 12-year-old dyslexics were unable to recite the 6×, 7× and 8× tables without stumbling.

Miles, Haslum, and Wheeler (2001) used data from the British Births Cohort Study of 12,131 children born in England, Wales and Scotland between 5 and 11 April 1970. The children were given a word recognition test, the Edinburgh Reading Test of reading comprehension, the British Abilities Scales spelling test and the Similarities and Matrices 'intelligence' subtests of the British Abilities Scales. The children were categorized as normal achievers (49% of the sample; IQ scores of at least 90, and no significant mismatch between IQ, reading and spelling); low ability children (25% of the sample; IQ scores below 90); moderate underachievers (13% of the sample; reading and/or spelling score 1 to 1.5 standard deviations below the prediction); and severe underachievers (7% of the sample; reading and/or spelling score more than 1.5 standard deviations below the predictions). Due to insufficient data, 6% were excluded. Of the 907 severe underachievers 269 were considered as probable dyslexics, on the grounds of poor performance on a digit span test and on the left–right, months forwards and months reversed subtests of the Bangor Dyslexia Test. These dyslexic children performed less well on average on a calculation task, the Friendly Maths Test, than the normal achievers, and even than underachievers who did not meet full criteria for dyslexia. Items that were particularly difficult for the dyslexics were those that involved several steps (e.g. borrowing from two columns and thus placed a heavy load on working memory; and those which involved fractions and decimals).

Yeo (2001) is a teacher at Emerson House, a school for dyslexic and dyspraxic primary school children, and has written extensively about the mathematical difficulties of some dyslexic children. She reports that while many dyslexic children have difficulties only with those aspects of arithmetic that involve verbal memory, some dyslexic children have more fundamental difficulties with 'number sense'. They comprehend numbers solely in terms of quantities to be counted and do not understand them in more abstract ways or perceive the relationships between different numbers. Yeo suggests that the counting sequence presents so much difficulty for this group that it absorbs their attention and prevents their considering other aspects of number. This sort of difficulty occurs in some children who are not dyslexic (Gray & Tall, 1994); and at present the extent to which it characterizes dyslexics more than others is not clear.

Children with spoken language and communication difficulties usually have some weaknesses in arithmetic, but once again some components tend to be affected much more than others. Fazio (1994) compared 20 5-year-olds with diagnosed specific language impairments with 20 age-matched controls and 20 language-matched younger children.

The children with language difficulties resembled the younger children in the range and accuracy of their counting, but the age-matched controls in their understanding of counting-related concepts, such as the fact that the last item in a count sequence indicates the number of items in the set. Two years later, Fazio (1996) followed up 16 of the children with language difficulties, 15 of the age-matched controls and 16 of the language-matched controls. The children with language difficulties were still poor at verbal counting, but resembled their age-matched controls in counting objects and in reading numerals. They were worse at calculation than the age-matched controls, but no worse than the language-matched controls.

Grauberg (1998) has written a book based on her experiences of teaching mathematics to pupils with language difficulties. She notes that pupils with language difficulties tend to have difficulties in particular with:

1 *Symbolic understanding.* This includes difficulty in understanding how one item can 'stand for' another item or items, and effects can range from difficulties in understanding how a numeral can represent a quantity to difficulties in understanding how a coin of one denomination may be equivalent to a set of coins of a smaller denomination. Typically, developing children under the age of 4 may have problems in distinguishing the cardinal use of numbers to represent quantities from their use as labels ('I am four'; 'I live at number 63'). For children with language difficulties, such problems can persist for far longer. Place value – the use of the position of a digit to represent its value – can

present problems for any child, but such problems are likely to be far greater for those with language difficulties.

2   *Organization.* Children with language difficulties often have difficulties with organizing items in space or time, which may, for example, affect their ability to arrange quantities in order; to organize digits spatially on a page; and to 'talk through' a problem, especially a word problem.

3   *Memory.* Poor short-term and long-term verbal memory are frequent characteristics of individuals with language difficulties (see studies quoted earlier) and will affect learning to count, remembering number facts and keeping track of one step in an arithmetic problem while carrying out subsequent steps.

In addition, language difficulties will directly affect the child's ability to benefit from oral or written instruction and to understand the language of mathematics.

Studies of adults with acquired language impairment (aphasia) following damage to the left hemisphere of the brain have suggested that arithmetic is often but not always impaired and that some aspects of arithmetic are more likely to be impaired than others. For example, Delazer, Girelli, Semenza, and Denes (1999) found that aphasic patients were particularly impaired in the retrieval of multiplication facts. They suggested that verbal processing is particularly important in the memory for multiplication tables.

Excellent mathematical performance can, however, be preserved in the face of quite severe developmental or acquired language impairments (Gopnik, 1992; Hermelin & O'Connor, 1991) and more specific impairments of verbal memory (Butterworth, Cipolotti, & Warrington, 1996).

The emphasis here has been on the effect of verbal *deficits* in arithmetic, because there has been far more discussion of this issue than of the relationship between verbal and arithmetical abilities in the population as a whole (despite the inclusion of arithmetic in verbal IQ scales, mentioned earlier), or in talented individuals. A recent study by Delgado and Prieto (2004) suggests that verbal ability is indeed important in arithmetic in general. They examined the role of lexical access (a verbal task) and mental rotation (a spatial task) as predictors of performance on mathematical tasks. Lexical access and mental rotation were both independent predictors of word problem solving and geometry. Lexical access, but *not* mental rotation, predicted performance in arithmetic. Thus, verbal ability seems to be important in *all* aspects of mathematics, and may be much *more* important than spatial ability to arithmetic.

Spatial ability and arithmetic

There are frequent suggestions that spatial abilities are important in arithmetic; although the exact nature of their contribution to arithmetic – as opposed to certain other components of arithmetic such as geometry – is not always made clear (Delgado & Prieto, 2004; Chapter 1 in this volume).

Some genetic disorders such as Williams syndrome, Turner syndrome and the chromosome 22q11.2 deletion syndrome are associated with both arithmetical and spatial difficulties. These disorders are, of course, relatively rare. However, some studies have indicated that both children and adults with mathematical difficulties tend to be worse at nonverbal (usually meaning spatial) than verbal reasoning. Many such studies do not distinguish between performance in arithmetic and in other aspects of arithmetic. However, some researchers (e.g. Greiffenstein and Baker, 2002) have found an association between arithmetical difficulties and specific weaknesses in nonverbal reasoning.

Such findings may indicate an association between arithmetical difficulties and relative nonverbal weaknesses, which would imply that certain nonverbal skills are particularly important for the understanding of arithmetic. There is, however, another possible explanation. There is some evidence (Dowker, 1995, 1998) that some forms of arithmetical difficulty are associated with discrepancies, in *either* direction, between verbal and nonverbal reasoning. Thus, a group of people with arithmetical difficulties is likely to include a significant proportion of individuals with either a much higher verbal than nonverbal IQ or a much higher nonverbal than verbal IQ. Many (although, of course, not all) people with much higher nonverbal than verbal IQs will have reading difficulties. Some studies of samples of people with arithmetical difficulties exclude those with additional reading difficulties. Therefore, such samples are likely to end up including a high proportion of people with higher verbal than nonverbal IQ, while excluding many of those with higher nonverbal than verbal IQ.

Spatial skills are often invoked to explain not only arithmetical deficits, but the broad spectrum of variation in arithmetical ability. In particular, it is sometimes suggested, for example by Casey, Nuttall, and Benbow (1995) that the reason why males often do better at advanced mathematics than females is that males are better at spatial skills: especially three-dimensional spatial skills.

Many studies (e.g. Hermelin & O'Connor, 1986) do suggest that exceptional mathematical talent in older children is often associated with superior spatial ability. However, this need not mean that *arithmetic* and spatial ability are closely linked; mathematical talent could include superior abilities at geometry, which one might well expect to be related to spatial ability. In fact, the evidence for a relationship between spatial and arithmetical abilities is far from clear cut. Some researchers (e.g. Casey et al., 1995) have found spatial ability to be a strong predictor of mathematical performance. However, a meta-analysis by Friedman (1995), suggests that mathematical ability is not very highly correlated with spatial ability and that correlations between mathematical and verbal abilities are higher (see also earlier section on 'Verbal ability and arithmetic').

Some degree of spatial ability is necessary for the correct placement and alignment of digits and, as such, must play a part in multi-digit arithmetic, especially written arithmetic. Inversions, misplacements and misalignments of digits occur in what is sometimes referred to as 'spatial dyscalculia' (Hartje, 1987).

Moreover, there are suggestions that mental arithmetic, and the ordering of numbers, can be represented by spatial positions on an imaginary number line. Trabasso (1977) suggested that ordinal relationships are represented in memory in a spatial fashion: the items may be ordered from left to right, or from top to bottom of a ladder, to represent the range from biggest to smallest. This could obviously influence arithmetical performance. It is also possible that spatial representations of the mathematical relationships in a word problem can facilitate its solution (Geary, 1996). Some researchers (Geary, 1996; Lehmann & Juling, 2002) consider that spatial skills are important in both arithmetic and algebra, by increasing the possible range of strategies for representing numerical relationships.

Such theories about the role of spatial ability in mental arithmetic are still, however, controversial. First of all, there is much evidence for individual differences in the ways in which number and arithmetic are represented. Some individuals make very strong use of internal number lines and other spatial representations (Seron, Pesenti, Noel, Deloche, & Cornet, 1992b); some people make much less use of such representations. It would be interesting to investigate the extent to which individual differences in mode of representation are associated with individual differences in arithmetical performance. The evidence so far suggests that there may be little or no such association: people of similar arithmetical ability may represent numbers and arithmetical operations in quite different ways. Studies of mathematicians have suggested that some of them represent numerical problems in a mainly spatial way; some in a mainly verbal way; and some in an abstract way that cannot be properly defined as either.

There do seem to be some important associations between number and space. Dehaene and his colleagues (Dehaene, Bossini, & Giraux, 1993) have discovered the SNARC effect (spatial-numerical association of response codes). Adults were given tasks where they had to press either a left-hand or right-hand key to indicate a characteristic of a digit that they were shown. In some tasks, this involved the numerical size of the digit (e.g. whether it was larger or smaller than 65); in some it involved other numerical characteristics of the digit (e.g. whether it was odd or even); in some it involved non-numerical characteristics of the digit (e.g. whether its name started with a consonant or a vowel). Whatever the task, people were faster in pressing the right-hand key to numbers that were large in relation to other numbers used in the experiment. This suggests that most people use a sort of internal number line, with large numbers on the right and small numbers on the left.

However, further studies have suggested that this internal number line is culturally determined and not based on universal characteristics of the brain. In particular, it seems to be associated with reading from left to right. Iranians, who read from right to left, do not show this SNARC effect (Dehaene & Akhavein, 1995).

Are verbal and spatial weaknesses associated with different types of arithmetical difficulty?

As we saw in Chapter 2, arithmetic is not one ability but many; and it is possible that spatial and verbal abilities may be associated with different *forms* of arithmetical ability.

Rourke and his colleagues (Deluka, Deldotto, & Rourke, 1987; Rourke, 1993; Rourke & Finlayson, 1978) have indeed proposed that there are two main subtypes of arithmetic disabilities, the first associated with right hemisphere dysfunction and the second with left hemisphere dysfunction. In the first, reading is unimpaired; verbal IQ is superior to nonverbal IQ, and there may even be 'nonverbal learning disabilities' involving spatial and social learning deficits and indications of right hemisphere dysfunction; and the arithmetical disabilities involve predominantly conceptual deficits. In the second, reading is also impaired; nonverbal IQ is superior to verbal IQ; and the arithmetical disabilities are mostly memory related.

A few studies (e.g. Robinson, Menchetti, & Torgesen, 2002) have supported the view that children with both reading and mathematical deficits tend to have more memory difficulties but fewer conceptual difficulties than those with just mathematical deficits.

However, there has been no consistent support for the view that 'left hemisphere'-type verbal deficits are associated with procedural and factual memory difficulties in arithmetic, while 'right-hemisphere'-type nonverbal deficits are associated with conceptual difficulties in arithmetic. Shalev, Manor, and Gross-Tsur (1997) found no differences in the type of mathematical difficulty demonstrated by dyscalculic children with higher verbal versus higher nonverbal IQ.

Jordan and Hanich (2000) studied 76 American second-grade children. They were divided into four achievement groups: 20 children with normal achievement in reading and mathematics (NA); 10 children with difficulties in both reading and mathematics (MD-RD), 36 children with difficulties in reading only (RD); and 10 children with difficulties in mathematics only (MD). They were given tests of four areas of mathematical thinking: number facts, story problems, place value and written calculation. Children with MD/RD performed worse than NA children on all aspects of mathematics; those with MD performed worse than NA children only on story problems.

Hanich, Jordan, Kaplan, and Dick (2001) similarly divided 210 2nd-graders into four achievement groups: children with normal achievement in reading and mathematics; children with difficulties in both reading and mathematics (MD–RD), children with difficulties in reading only (RD) and those with difficulties in mathematics only (MD). Both MD groups performed worse than the other groups in most areas of arithmetic. The MD-only group outperformed the MD–RD group in both exact mental calculation and problem solving. The two MD groups performed similarly on written calculation, place value understanding and approximate arithmetic.

Geary, Hoard, and Hamson (1999a) studied 90 first-grade children in the average IQ range. They included 35 children with normal achievement in reading and mathematics (N); 15 children with mathematical difficulties (MD; as shown by scores below the 30th percentile on the mathematical reasoning subtest of the Wechsler Individual Achievement Test); 15 children with reading difficulties (RD; as shown by scores below the 30th percentile on the word attack subtest of the Woodcock Johnson Psycho-Educational Battery; and 25 children with both mathematical and reading difficulties (MD–RD). Both MD groups showed problems in fact retrieval and in using counting strategies correctly in arithmetic. Children who had difficulties with both mathematics and reading tended to show problems in understanding counting principles and detecting counting errors; those with only MD or RD did not. However, about half of the MD children made double-counting errors. The MD–RD children, and those MD children who made double-counting errors, had lower backward digit spans than the other children.

The studies by Jordan and her colleagues and by Geary et al. (1999a) would suggest, therefore, that children with combined mathematical and reading disabilities tend to perform badly on more aspects of mathematics than children who only have mathematical difficulties; but do not support the type of dichotomy suggested by Rourke.

Thus, while signs of verbal or spatial weaknesses should serve as a warning signal that a child *may* experience mathematical difficulties, they cannot be used as definite predictors of either the existence or type of mathematical difficulty that a child may have.

There is still less evidence that, within the general population, verbal and nonverbal ability are associated with consistently different forms of strengths and weaknesses within arithmetic. (This is not to say that there might not be such patterns within the broader domain of mathematics; e.g. geometry is likely to be more specifically associated with spatial ability than is arithmetic.) My own research (Dowker, 1995, 1998; Chapter 2 in this volume) has indicated that both verbal and performance IQ predict performance on tasks of both arithmetical calculation and derived fact strategy use. Verbal IQ is a stronger predictor than performance IQ of both types of arithmetical task. Children who are much better at derived fact strategy use (see Chapter 6) than calculation often show marked discrepancies between WISC performance and verbal IQ scores. These discrepancies are equally likely to be in either direction: it is the existence of such a discrepancy, not its direction, that seems to be associated with a superiority of derived fact strategy use over calculation.

Research does indicate that people with dyslexia and other language difficulties are not equally impaired at *all* aspects of arithmetic, but tend to be particularly impaired at those that involve verbal memory.

Many, if not most, dyslexic individuals show poor short-term and long-term memory for number facts, while being unimpaired at dealing with arithmetical concepts and principles (Miles & Miles, 1992; Pritchard, Miles, Chinn, & Taggart, 1989; Steeves, 1983). Children who have difficulty in remembering arithmetical facts may, like some of the dyscalculic adults described earlier, compensate by using alternative strategies. These include counting strategies; derived fact strategies that involve arithmetical principles such as commutativity, and combinations of the two. For example, Miles (1993) describes dyslexic pupils who were able to work out suitable strategies for solving mathematical reasoning problems from the Superior Adult level of the Terman-Merrill IQ test, but had difficulty with the relatively simple calculations involved. For example, one 16-year-old boy was given the 'tree' item, which involves telling the individual the heights of a tree at planting and at yearly intervals over the next three years. (S)he is then required to work out its height at the end of the fourth year, which involves finding a pattern in its growth over the successive years. The 16-year-old worked out the pattern correctly, but miscalculated $27 - 18$ as 11.

However, despite the general association between dyslexia and specific problems with memory for facts, individuals with dyslexia can have specific strengths and weaknesses in *any* aspect of arithmetic. Macaruso and Sokol (1998) studied 20 adolescents with both dyslexia and arithmetical difficulties and found that the arithmetical difficulties were very heterogeneous and that factual, procedural and conceptual difficulties were all represented.

It should be noted that there are also many individuals without language difficulties, who show strong discrepancies between the factual and conceptual aspects of arithmetic (see Chapter 2). For example, Claire (described in Chapter 10) (also see Dowker, 2003b) showed no signs of dyslexia and had a very high verbal IQ and a gift for learning foreign languages. She had difficulty in memorizing arithmetical facts and at the age of 10 made a very similar type of response to the Terman-Merrill 'tree' problem, working out the pattern correctly and devising a correct strategy, but adding $27 + 13$ as 39.

Other abilities and arithmetic

Besides verbal and spatial ability, there are also other abilities that are sometimes considered to be possibly associated with arithmetic. These include general motor co-ordination, finger awareness and musical skills.

Motor co-ordination

As well as the cognitive functions that might be associated with arithmetic, we should consider the potential effects of individual differences in motor co-ordination, specifically as it relates to the motor skills involved in using the fingers for counting. There is some evidence that difficulties with the motor skills involved in counting may impair the acquisition of counting and arithmetic (Camos, Fayol, Lacert, Bardi, & Lacquiere, 1998).

However, they certainly do not always do so. As discussed in Chapter 4, children with severe procedural counting difficulties can still be very able at arithmetical calculation and reasoning. One of the children to be discussed in Chapter 4 is Daniel, who had cerebral palsy, which prevents his controlling his hands sufficiently well to co-ordinate pointing to objects with verbal counting. At the age of 7, he could not count 10 objects reliably. Yet he obtained a scaled score of 14 (well above average) on the WISC arithmetic subtest and performed better than most of his classmates on calculation and derived fact strategy tasks.

More studies of children with motor difficulties affecting counting would be desirable. Different aspects of counting difficulty need to be separated: for example, differences between counting fingers and counting other objects; and between motor difficulties in performing the act of counting and perceptual difficulties in seeing and interpreting the result.

Finger awareness

Some people, who need not have motor difficulties, combine arithmetical difficulties with a lack of awareness of the position of their fingers. These may be combined with difficulties in writing and with problems in right/left discrimination, a combination of problems that is sometimes described as the 'Gerstmann syndrome'. It can occur in adults as a result of brain damage and can also occur in children without known brain damage (the 'developmental Gerstmann syndrome'). It is possible that the lack of awareness of where the fingers are leads to impairments in finger counting, which, in turn, lead to difficulties in arithmetic. It is also possible that finger awareness and arithmetic do not influence each other directly, but are dependent on adjacent or interconnected areas of the brain, so that impairments in these processes often go together.

The Gerstmann syndrome as such is rare. But are individual differences in finger awareness associated with individual differences in arithmetic in the general population? One study by Fayol, Barouillet, and Marinthe (1998) suggests that this is indeed the case, at least as regards young children. They gave 177 5- and 6-year-old children tests of finger awareness and also of arithmetic and found a significant correlation between them. It may be that this is the case for children in this age group, because of the prevalence of finger-counting strategies in arithmetic and that the relationship would cease to be strong at a later age. Alternatively, it may be that finger counting provides a basis in number understanding that carries over to later arithmetical skills. Longitudinal studies would be necessary to determine whether the effect of finger awareness on arithmetic is short term or long term.

Arithmetic and music: Are they related?

When considering possible relationships between arithmetic and other abilities, researchers tend to focus on possible links with language and spatial ability. Outside the research community, a more common assumption seems to be that ability in mathematics, including arithmetic, is related to musical ability. (When I tell people that I carry out research on the psychology of arithmetic, one of the commonest responses is 'So is it true that mathematics and music go together?')

Despite this popular perception of a relationship between mathematics and music, there has been comparatively little research on possible relationships between the two domains. There has been considerable research on the possible effects of listening to classical music on spatial and other cognitive abilities: the so-called 'Mozart effect'. The major effects studied have not, however, involved arithmetic.

Why might people expect there to be a relationship between arithmetic and music? It is certainly plausible that severe deficits in numerical ability might affect musical performance, given that music does involve some understanding of quantitative relationships (a crotchet takes the same time as two quavers, etc.) and 'counting out' rhythms. However, the popular perceptions are not so much that deficits in the two subjects go together as that high levels of talent in the two subjects go together. It is also plausible that music may 'go with' geometry and other spatial aspects of mathematics, as the right hemisphere of the brain is significantly involved both in some musical skills and some spatial skills. Thus, music may be related to mathematics but not specifically to arithmetic. Finally, it may be that arithmetic and music are related simply because both are influenced by similar social conditions: education-oriented middle-class families may emphasize both.

Music and arithmetic certainly do not *invariably* go together. There are some individuals who perform competently or even exceptionally well at music, despite very poor arithmetical ability. For example, people with the genetic disorder Williams syndrome have generally low IQs and are often particularly weak at tasks which involve number and arithmetic. Their musical abilities are, however, often said to be relatively good. This view that people with Williams syndrome are unimpaired at music received some support from a study by Levitin and Bellugi (1998). They gave a group of children with Williams syndrome an echo-clapping task, in which they had to clap back a rhythm which was presented to them. The children with Williams syndrome performed just as well as controls. Furthermore, the errors that Williams syndrome children made were much more likely to bear a musical relationship to the stimulus (forming an answering phrase or a close rhythmic variation, for example).

There are a number of reports of musical 'savants' who are outstandingly good musical performers despite very low overall IQ (Hermelin, 2001;

Miller, 1989; Sloboda, Hermelin, & O'Connor, 1991). Although in most cases, these savants' arithmetical abilities were not studied in detail, they appeared in general to correspond only to their general intellectual level, in marked contrast with their musical abilities.

Are music and arithmetic correlated in the general population? There have been relatively few studies of this issue. Lynn and Gault (1986) gave schoolchildren the Wing (1968) tests of musical ability and correlated performance on this scale with performance on measures of spatial ability, verbal ability, verbal reasoning, memory and number ability. They found significant correlations between almost all of these measures. Thus, in this study musical ability and number ability *did* correlate significantly with one another, but not more so than with other measures.

In 2001 James Roebuck and I carried out an investigation of relationships between music, vocabulary, reasoning and arithmetic. The participants were 30 primary school children between the ages of 8 and 10. The Wing tests were again used to assess musical ability. Vocabulary was assessed by the Mill Hill vocabulary test; abstract reasoning by Raven's Matrices; and arithmetic by the British Abilities Scale Basic Number Skills Test.

When age was controlled for, musical performance correlated significantly with both the Raven's Matrices measure of abstract reasoning and with arithmetic, but not with vocabulary. This gives a degree of support for the view that music may correlate more with arithmetic than with some other skills. However, different components of music seemed to correlate differentially with the other measures. Only the chord analysis subtest of the Wing scale correlated significantly with the Raven's score and only the pitch change subtest with the arithmetic score. The pitch memory subtest did not correlate significantly with either.

The relationship between chord analysis performance and ability at Raven's Matrices may be indicative of some more general ability to extract component parts from a whole, whether they be notes in a chord or features in a pattern. The link between pitch change and maths ability might be explained by some affinity for ordinal relationships, between numbers or notes.

Conclusions

These findings suggest that arithmetic is related to some degree to many other abilities. Arithmetic is related to IQ; to both verbal and spatial ability; and to some other less 'cognitive'-seeming abilities such as motor co-ordination and finger awareness. There is also modest support for the popular assumption of a relationship between arithmetic and music.

However, there can be, and frequently are, marked discrepancies between arithmetic and any or all of these other abilities. The relationship between arithmetic and other abilities is not clear cut. Neither is there even a clear-cut relationship between particular *aspects* of arithmetic and other specific abilities. The clearest relationship is between dyslexia and other language problems and specific difficulties with memory for arithmetical facts. However, language difficulties can co-exist with other patterns of arithmetical strengths and weaknesses and people with no language difficulties at all can exhibit specific difficulties with fact memory. With regard to these issues, as to many others in the field of arithmetical abilities, nothing is as simple as it might at first sight be predicted to be.

4 Counting and after: The importance of individual differences

'I've been thinking. Next term, why don't you do counting
with us? Not adding; not subtracting; just counting!' (Nadia, aged 5,
to a mathematical development researcher working in her school)

'One, two, three
Dinosaurs for me
On a dinosaur tree.' (song composed by a 4-year-old girl)

It is generally considered that counting is universal; and that except for people with severe learning difficulties, everyone over the age of 6 or 7 will count equally well. Yet there is some evidence for individual differences in counting efficiency even in adults (Deloche et al., 1994; Deloche, Souza, Willadino-Braga, & Dellatolas, 1999; Judd, 1927). It is certainly the case that primary school children can show considerable differences in the speed and accuracy of counting, considerably beyond the age at which counting is generally regarded as automatic (Gray, 1997; Houssart, 2001; Wright, 1994).

It is also possible that early individual differences in the age and order of acquisition of counting principles and procedures could affect the later development of arithmetical concepts and procedures. Little is known about this issue: a point that will be discussed later on in the chapter.

There are many aspects of counting and its applications that develop at different times and in which individual differences could arise. Individual differences have been studied extensively with regard to some of these aspects – notably, at one time, number conservation. However, there are many aspects that have not attracted much study from this point of view, either because they are perceived as universally easy or because controversies about their developmental sequence (e.g. whether certain concepts precede or follow on from counting procedures) have overshadowed consideration of individual differences.

Subitization and perception of quantity

'There's three! I didn't need to count them!' (Lisa, aged 4 years 2 months, on being shown a picture of three rabbits)

Subitization implies the ability to recognize quantities without counting them. There is controversy as to how this occurs: whether it involves some abstract representation of the exact quantities or of their approximate magnitudes; or a nonverbal form of counting; or is related more to a representation of area than of numerical quantity or is closely linked to our representations of objects, so that representing 'two' involves the simultaneous representation of two objects, rather than a representation of a quantity as such. The origins and early development of subitization and nonverbal counting have been extensively discussed and debated elsewhere (e.g. Feigenson, Carey, & Spelke, 2002; Mix, Huttenlocher, & Levine, 2002). They will not be discussed in detail in this book, as they have not been studied with respect to individual differences.

Many studies suggest that babies can distinguish quantities up to three (Starkey & Cooper, 1980; Starkey, Spelke, & Gelman, 1990; Strauss & Curtis, 1981). This is shown by habituation studies, which are based on the principle that if one is exposed repeatedly to a stimulus, it becomes less interesting and one will pay less attention to it. New stimuli elicit more attention, which in babies is assessed through the length of time spent looking at the stimulus. For example, at 6 months, if babies are repeatedly presented with two items – e.g. two circles, two squares, two triangles, etc. – they will appear to become less interested and will look less at the later presentations; and this is so, even if there are considerable variations in the nature of the objects and in their spatial arrangement. If they are then shown three objects, they will look significantly longer, implying that they have registered the change. Similarly, if they are repeatedly presented with three items, they will look less at the later presentations and will look longer again if they are presented with two items. This does not work reliably for quantities over three. One study (Antell & Keating, 1986) gave similar results in babies as young as 2 weeks. Such an ability to distinguish between quantities up to three has also been found in many non-human animals including rats, squirrels and monkeys.

A more controversial issue is that of how abstract such early representations of number may be. So long as the numbers are within their 'subitizing range', they do not seem to be dependent on the pattern in which the objects are arranged. If a baby is habituated to three items arranged in a triangular pattern, (s)he will still treat them as the 'same old boring three', if they are presented in a straight line. (This contrasts with their reactions to numbers over 3. Tan and Bryant (2000) found that these can be recognized if, and only if, the pattern remains the same.)

They also do not appear to depend on the type of objects. Babies, indeed, show more surprise if the *number* of objects is changed than if one of the objects in the set is replaced by a different *type* of object. However, there is currently a lot of debate as to whether babies really represent discrete quantities, or rely on the total area that is occupied (Clearfield & Mix, 1999).

There is even more controversy whether the representations are independent of modality: e.g. whether a baby will perceive three sounds as the same quantity as three objects. Starkey, Spelke, and Gelman (1990) obtained evidence that strongly suggested that they do: that if babies hear three drumbeats, they will look more at three dots than at two, while if they hear two drumbeats they will look more at two dots than at three. Since then, some studies have replicated this finding, while others have not (Newcombe, 2002).

Do babies show individual differences in the perception of quantities? Could some of the contradictory findings of different studies of the same phenomenon, for example the cross-modal perception of quantities, be due to individual differences between the babies taking part in the experiments? It is difficult to draw a firm conclusion, since individual differences found in such experiments may reflect differences in mood or in current levels of attention and alertness, rather than in the ability being studied. There have been a few studies comparing specific groups of infants on subitization tasks. Infants with Williams syndrome do not differ from typical infants on such tests, although they show severe deficits in counting and arithmetic in later childhood (Ansari & Karmiloff-Smith, 2002). It is not known whether there is any correlation, within the normal range, between infants' perception of quantities and their later counting, arithmetic or even subitization. It is known, however, that there are a few adults who cannot subitize even small quantities without counting them, and that this is associated with difficulties in arithmetic (Butterworth, 1999).

Procedural aspects of counting

The most important procedural aspects of counting appear to be *memory for the sequence of counting words*; *nonverbal (e.g. gestural) counting*, whether or not this is combined with verbal counting; and the motor skills involved in counting the objects. The motor skills involved in counting fingers or objects are discussed in Chapter 3.

Memory for the counting sequence

Learning the counting sequence can present difficulty for some children. This is particularly true of children with oral language impairments (Fazio, 1994) or dyslexia (Miles, 1990).

The counting sequence depends in part on rote memory (especially up to 10) and in part on the observance of linguistic rules, as seen in such errors as 'two-teen', 'five-teen' and 'tenty' (Ginsburg, 1977). The effects of different languages and counting systems on counting proficiency will be discussed in Chapter 9. It will simply be noted here that both rote verbal memory and linguistic rule learning are likely to create difficulty for children with language difficulties.

Nonverbal counting

> Jade (6 years 0 months) was being given the WISC arithmetic subtest. She understood the meanings of the word problems very well, but had relatively little experience with formal arithmetic. She used the 'counting on from larger' strategy for sums that added up to 10 or less, and counted on her fingers. When she was given the problem, 'Bob had 8 crayons; he bought 6 more; how many does he have now?' she said, 'I don't have enough fingers – Oh, I know!' and proceeded spontaneously to use other body parts: her elbow for 11, her shoulder for 12, the back of her neck for 13. Armed with this self-invented system, she achieved an extremely high scaled score of 17.

Not all counting is verbal. For example, Jordan, Huttenlocher, and Levine (1992) showed children sets of objects being put into a box, where they could not be seen and then asked the children to take the objects out one by one. The researchers investigated whether the children reached the correct number of times, in accordance with the number that they had seen put into the box. The children were able to do so correctly at a younger age than the age when they could count correctly in words.

Gestures – e.g. pointing in turn to each of the objects to be counted or putting fingers up or down to represent the counting sequence – are a common adjunct to verbal counting at any age and especially in young children. Gestural counting can supplement or substitute for imperfect verbal counting.

At one end of the scale gestural involves complex culturally invented systems such as that of the Oksapmin (Saxe, 1979) or in parts of India, where particular points of the body (each shoulder; the back of the neck; the shoulder; the back of the neck, etc.) – represent particular numbers. At the other end of the scale, we find seemingly implicit counting, where the child looks or turns toward each item. The less sophisticated forms of counting are sometimes accurate when verbal counting is incorrect and reflect implicit knowledge that is sometimes in advance of children's explicit knowledge (Alibali & DiRusso, 1999; Goldin-Meadow, Alibali, & Church, 1993).

In particular, nonverbal counting and arithmetic can be considerably better than verbal counting in children who have vocabulary limitations, whether associated with lack of exposure to mathematical vocabulary (Jordan et al., 1992, 1994a) or with specific language impairment (Fazio, 1994).

Conceptual aspects of counting and integration between conceptual and procedural aspects

A child may be able to count to 10 by rote (i.e. use a counting procedure) without understanding that counting provides information about quantity (i.e. understand counting principles).

Piaget (1952) considered that children do not really understand number until they are 6 or 7 years old and that, until that age, counting is just a rote procedure. By contrast, Gelman and Gallistel (1978) have suggested that children *do* understand counting principles from a very early age and that these inform the development of counting procedures, and later of arithmetic. Children may make a lot of mistakes in their early counting, but this is because of difficulties in learning, remembering and co-ordinating the procedures, not because of a failure to understand the principles of counting. Gelman and Gallistel proposed the following principles as existing prior to counting, and as central to the development of counting:

1 *The one-to-one principle*: there is one number word for each item being counted.
2 *The stable order principle*: the number words always come in the same order, even if for very young children this may be an unconventional order, e.g. '1, 2, 3, 4, 5, 6, 7, H, I, J'.
3 *The abstraction principle*: it is possible to count anything: all kinds of object, sound, movement, idea.
4 *The cardinal word principle*: if you count a set of objects, then the last number word in the count sequence will represent the number of objects in the set.
5 *The order irrelevance principle*: if you count the same set of objects in different orders or directions, you will get the same number.

One important method of testing the understanding of counting principles is the use of error detection tasks: tasks in which a person, toy or puppet makes several counts, some correct and some incorrect, and the child has to state whether each count is correct and, if not, what mistake has been made. This is a method frequently used by Gelman and has indicated that children can often distinguish between correct and incorrect counts and point out mistakes, even when they themselves cannot use counting procedures accurately. For example, they may be able to tell that a puppet is correct when it counts according to the one-to-one principle and wrong when it violates this principle by giving two items the same tag or the same item more than one tag, even though they themselves may fail to apply this principle correctly as the result of motor or memory problems. The use of toys and puppets gets around the problem of children not wishing to correct another person, especially an adult; although it should be noted that a few children are reluctant even to correct puppets. One child in Gelman's study accepted all of the 'Cookie Monster' puppet's incorrect counts and, on one occasion when the puppet made a particularly outrageous mistake, the child patted it and said: 'Never mind, Cookie Monster.'

Another method is to give children tasks that may be solved by appropriate counting, provided that the children realize that counting can indeed serve the purpose, i.e. understand the relevant purpose of counting.

Another method is the use of counting prediction tasks: tasks in which the child has to predict the result of counting or, most often, recounting a set of objects. The predicted recount could, for example, be in a different order from the first count or follow some re-arrangement of the objects, or follow some actual change in quantity. Such tasks have the potential advantage of making it possible to assess not only whether children expect the result of recounting to be the same or different, but to elicit their alternative predictions in cases where they expect a different result to be obtained.

The principles that will be discussed here are the cardinal word principle and the order irrelevance principle, since most research on individual differences in counting principles has focused on one or both of these. In discussing the cardinal word principle, some reference will be made to the *non-cardinal* uses of number.

Cardinal word principle of counting

> 'But counting's just saying the words, isn't it?' (4-year-old girl quoted by Munn, 1997, p. 13)

Of Gelman and Gallistel's (1978) counting principles, the cardinal word principle and the order irrelevance principle seem to be particularly important, as they involve the understanding of what counting is all about.

Piaget considered that children do not really understand how counting establishes the cardinality of a set, as shown by the fact that they fail to use counting to compare the values of different sets or to establish that two sets contain the same number of items. Gelman and Gallistel argued, by way of contrast, that children as young as 2 or 3 do have the 'cardinal word principle' that counting establishes the cardinality of a set, because they tend to emphasize or repeat the last word of a count sequence; and because they can count very small sets of two or three items to establish quantity in a game where they need to establish which of two plates contains the 'winning' number of items.

However, some people have considered Gelman and Gallistel's criteria for understanding the cardinal word principle to be too lenient. Children might emphasize or repeat the last word of a counting sequence as a socially learned habit, without realizing its mathematical significance. It is not clear what children are intending to do when they count sets of two or three items, since they can establish such small quantities without counting: as stated earlier, numbers up to 3 can be subitized.

Wynn (1992) gave children two tasks involving the cardinal word principle. One was to count a set of objects and then answer the question, 'How many are there?' Children over the age of 3½ tended to respond to the 'How many' with the last item of the count sequence, while younger children tended to recount. The other was to give the experimenter a requested number of objects, e.g. 'Give me eight toy dinosaurs.' Children over the age of 3½ tended to count out the objects; those under that age tended to grab some objects and give them to the experimenter, without counting or otherwise checking if the number were correct. It turned out that performances on the two tasks were closely related, suggesting that they were indeed tapping the same thing.

Thus, it appears likely that the cardinal word principle develops at about the age of 3½. However, there seem to be some individual differences. Environmental factors seem to have some influence on when it develops. The children in Wynn's study were American children from middle-class families. When Fluck and Henderson (1996) repeated the study with a group of English working-class children, they found a somewhat later average age for acquisition of the principle: 4 years 2 months.

Fluck and Henderson also found a significant association between acquisition of the cardinal word principle and proficiency in counting. This finding was later replicated by Freeman, Antonucci, and Lewis (2000). Children who are good at counting are more likely to demonstrate understanding of the cardinal word principle than those who are bad at counting. However, both studies demonstrated the existence of exceptions in both directions. There are children who are not proficient at counting, but do demonstrate understanding of the cardinal word principle; and there are proficient counters who do not demonstrate such an understanding. Moreover, Fazio (1994) found that children with specific language impairment were very delayed at learning how to count proficiently, but they were not delayed at acquiring the cardinal word principle.

In summary, it appears that understanding the cardinal word principle does not usually precede experience with counting, but it can occur in the face of very limited counting proficiency. In many children, under favourable conditions, it develops in the fourth year; in some it does not develop until the fifth. It appears, however, to be very unusual for children much over 5 to have difficulty in understanding and using the cardinal word principle.

I would suggest that the cardinal word principle might differ from most of the other subcomponents of arithmetic discussed in this book, in that it may indeed be a true prerequisite for many other arithmetical abilities. One of the central themes of this book is the existence of dissociations and discrepancies between different arithmetical abilities: it is possible to have difficulty with, for example, using counting procedures, remembering number facts or solving word problems, and yet to cope well with other aspects of arithmetic. It is less clear that it could be possible to cope with many aspects of arithmetic without the basic understanding of the central purpose of counting implied by the cardinal word principle. This, at least, is a plausible hypothesis. It may yet, however, turn out that some children who do not demonstrate the cardinal word principle do acquire sufficient understanding of quantity by some other means – e.g. nonverbal gestural counting or some abstract representation of quantity – to develop other arithmetical concepts. Wright (1994, p. 39) indeed points out that it is:

> [T]heoretically possible and conceivable that a child's numerical concepts could be developed through activity that does not involve sequential counting. Thus in cultures where number word sequences were not used or at least were not prominent, abstract concepts of number are likely to have a different developmental path.

The cardinal word principle should not, however, be regarded as something that one either has completely or not at all. As with most mathematical concepts and skills, the cardinal word principle may be used in some situations before it is used in others and with smaller set sizes before it is used for larger set sizes.

Even when children do understand the cardinal word principle for relatively small numbers, they may not extend it to larger numbers even when these are well within their counting range. Munn (1997) found that 4- and 5-year-old children could often count far larger sets of items in a counting task than they were able to give to order in a cardinal word task. For example, one child at 5½ could count 35 blocks accurately, but could only give six blocks to order.

Munn (1997) asked children directly about the purposes of counting, most 4- and 5-year-olds do not say that it is to find out how many, but emphasize other purposes of counting. Of 56 children questioned at the time of school entry, only 5 said that they counted 'to know how many there are'. The rest said that they counted in order to learn about numbers ('So I can learn all my numbers'); to please their parents or other people ('Because my mummy and daddy want me to'); to please themselves ('Because I want to'); or gave no coherent reason. This may in part reflect verbal difficulties in describing and explaining some of the purposes of counting. However, it does at least appear that for young children finding out how many objects there are is not the only, and perhaps not even most salient, purpose of counting.

Non-cardinal uses of number words

'A five-year-old, rugby-mad, was being asked if he knew his numbers. The interrogator pointed to a 9 and asked "What's that?" (presumably hoping for an answer like, 'That's a nine'). The answer immediately came: "Gareth Edwards".' (from Pimm, 1987, p. 17)

One reason why children may have some difficulty in understanding the use of counting and number words to express cardinality is that number words are *not* only used for this purpose. Although a major purpose of counting is to establish quantity and although number words are most commonly used to express cardinal quantities, number words do have other purposes. Children must not only learn how number words express cardinality, but also learn to distinguish situations where number words are used for this purpose from situations where they are used in other ways.

Ordinal numbers

Numbers sometimes represent not cardinal quantities, but positions in an ordered sequence. A person may be Number 3 in a race, because he came third. Understanding ordinal relations is an important part of understanding numbers, as we need to be able to understand, for example, that 6 is more than 5. Piaget (1952) thought that the understanding of ordinality is not fully developed until the age of 7 or 8; and supported this by showing that younger children find it difficult to place objects in an ordered series, for example by height. More recent research (e.g. Cooper, 1984) suggests some understanding of ordinal relations between quantities in the second year of life. However, it is likely that very young babies do not understand ordinality. They may be able to distinguish between two items and three items, but not to realize that three items are more than two items.

Some studies have examined young children's ability to understand the ordinal aspects of number – '3 is more than 2' – and its relationship to their understanding the cardinal aspects of number – '1, 2, 3; there's 3!' Bullock and Gelman (1977) showed children sets of one and two objects and taught them that one of these sets was the 'winner'. They then gave children sets of three and four objects and asked them which of these was the winner. Children over 3 years old made relational judgements: choosing the smaller number if they had previously been taught that one was the 'winner' over two and the larger number if they had previously been taught that two was the 'winner' over one. Children under 3 were less reliable in their judgements.

Huntley-Fenner and Cannon (2000) later found that 3- to 5-year-old children were able to say which of two sets of squares had more and that this was *not* correlated with use of the cardinal word principle in a counting task. However, since most of the children in the study were able both to use the cardinal word principle and to make ordinality judgements, the results may have been distorted by ceiling effects.

Brannon and Van de Walle (2001) asked children to say 'how many' items there were in sets ranging from two to six and also tested them on their ability to choose the larger of two numerical sets ranging in size from one to five. They found that many children as young as 2 could make such ordinal judgements. In this study, ordinality was related to cardinality to a limited extent: children who could not provide a correct numerical label for at least one quantity in the 'how many' task were not able to make ordinal judgements. However, among the children who labelled *any* numerical quantity correctly, cardinal ability did not correlate any further with the ability to make ordinal judgements. The smallest numerical quantity in the 'how many' task was two, which could be recognized without counting; thus the relationship between counting as such and the ability to make ordinal judgements is not strong.

We may conclude that ordinal judgements may be related to the very basic understanding that a quantity can be given a numerical label; but beyond this, cardinal and ordinal abilities may be functionally independent.

Numbers as labels

Number words and numerals are often used in ways that either do not express a cardinal quantity at all or do so in a way that is not transparent to a young child. Such number words are used more as personal names than as quantities. For example, a child may be 4, and may live at number 68, and may watch a programme on Channel 2, and ride on the No. 77 bus. Ginsburg (1977) reports a child who was out walking with her parents and started to count everyone in the group: 'One, two, three [pointing to herself]. But I'm 4 [years old]. I'll try it again. One, two, three. But I'm still 4. You try it, Daddy.'

Order irrelevance principle of counting

Different studies have given different results as to the age at which children realize that the order in which one counts a set of items does not change the number. The evidence seems to be that the exact task conditions have a strong effect.

Baroody (1984) asked children to count a row of objects; asked them how many there were; and then asked them how many they would get if they counted in the opposite direction. Children did not pass this task reliably until the age of 5. Gelman, Meck, and Merkin (1986) argued that asking children two 'how many' questions in succession might lead them to think that their first answer was incorrect and should be changed. They found that if children were asked to count an array three times and then were asked for the cardinal value of the array only once, they were more likely to pass an order irrelevance task than if they counted the array once and were asked the question twice. Gelman et al. argued that children's confidence in the correctness of their count, and therefore the likelihood that they would maintain it when the order was changed, was increased if they counted the array three times and if they were not asked repeated questions that they might interpret as challenging their accuracy. Not all studies have, however, replicated the finding that children perform better on order irrelevance tasks if the question is not repeated (Baroody, 1992b; Cowan, Dowker, Christakis, & Bailey, 1996). Richard Cowan and I have also found that children also do not seem to perform any better if an adult makes the count than if they themselves make the count even though one might assume that they have greater confidence in an adult's counting.

Richard Cowan and I have carried out some studies of 4-year-old children's understanding of the order irrelevance principle. One study (described by Cowan et al., 1996) examined the performance of children on tasks where they first counted a set of nine objects and then had to predict the results of recounts (a) when they had to count the objects in the opposite direction from the first count and (b) when one of the items was in fact taken away. Half of the children were asked, 'If you count them this way again, what number will you get?' and the other half were asked, 'If you count them this way/again, will you get the same number or a different number?' Most children responded incorrectly to questions about the specific number that they would get, but over half responded correctly to questions about whether they would get the same or a different number, in that they said that counting in a different order would give the same number, while counting after the subtraction of an item would give a different number.

This difference between conditions could have been due either to differences between forced choice and open-ended questions or to differences in dealing with questions concerning absolute and relative number. In a subsequent study, children were asked both forced-choice and open-ended questions about specific numbers: 'If you count them this way/again, what number will you get?' versus the other half asked 'If you count them this way/ again, will you still get [9] or will you get a different number?' They did much better on the forced-choice version.

Comparing quantities

The ability to compare quantities was considered by Piaget (1952) to be one of the most central measures of the understanding of quantity. Such comparisons may be made through counting or, quite often, through matching.

Matching involves using or creating one-to-one correspondences between items in sets.

One can construct a set of the same numerosity as an existing set ('Give me the same number of blue blocks as red blocks'), by putting items into one-to-one correspondence with those in the existing set. One can also compare quantities by matching items in two sets in one-to-one correspondence. If they match exactly, the two sets have the same number. If items are left over in one of the sets, then that set has more.

Research suggests that matching for comparison purposes is quite difficult for children (Cowan, 1987; Piaget, 1952). This is partly because of perceptual and motor difficulties in matching sets which are not originally in one-to-one correspondence, especially if the items cannot be moved: such difficulties are significant even for children as old as 10 (Brainerd, 1973).

But even if such difficulties are removed – for example by the experimenter drawing guidelines between the items in the set:

```
0    0
0
0    0
     0
     0
0
0
     0
     0
0
     0
0    0
```

children under 7 still find the task difficult (Cowan, 1987). Young children tend not to use one-to-one correspondence spontaneously for comparison purposes, although they can learn to do so through feedback as to its effectiveness (Bryant, 1974).

Matching to establish a set of the same numerosity as another set or to simultaneously create two sets of the same numerosity is easier for children than matching to compare two different sets (Fuson, 1988). Children from their fourth year often do use a sort of matching – 'One for me, one for you' – to share out quantities equally between people (Desforges & Desforges, 1980; Frydman & Bryant, 1988; Miller, 1984) although – as with so many numerical tasks – the younger children perform much better for small than large numbers (Cowan & Biddle, 1989).

Matching, sharing and the understanding of one-to-one correspondence are very important topics in early mathematics; but there has been little work on individual differences in these areas as such. Contrariwise, the closely related issue of number conservation has been studied very extensively indeed and some studies have involved the investigation of individual differences.

Number conservation

Piaget (1952) regarded number conservation as the key concept that distinguishes between procedural counting without understanding and conceptually based counting.

In Piaget's view, although very young children may be able to count, they do not have a true understanding of number until the concrete operational stage, when they become able to think logically and, in particular, to *conserve number*. Conservation of number, as of any other form of quantity, means understanding that the quantity remains the same in spite of perceptual changes.

In a number conservation task, children are presented with two rows, in one-to-one correspondence.

Children will say that there is the same number in each row. However, if one of the rows is then spread out, then the child will say that the longer row has more. Piaget considered that this meant that the child thinks that this row has actually increased in number by becoming longer. This means that they do not understand the invariance of number. They do not realize that purely perceptual changes do not change the actual quantity.

It is still controversial when children do come to realize that perceptual changes do not necessarily result in changes in quantity; but it is almost certainly significantly earlier than Piaget thought. One problem with Piaget's task is that children may have been confused by the fact that an adult was asking them the same question twice, before the transformation and after it. Usually if adults ask the same question twice in close succession, this means either that something has changed or that the child got the wrong answer the first time and should change it ('What's two and three, Johnny?' 'Four.' '*What's* two and three?') Rose and Blank (1974) tried asking 6-year-old children the question only once: after the transformation had occurred. They found that children did much better when the question was asked only once than when it was asked twice: before and after the transformation. Samuel and Bryant (1984) found that the same was true of 4- and 5-year-olds. McGarrigle and Donaldson (1974) found that children were more likely to conserve their number judgement when the transformation was caused by a 'naughty teddy bear' messing things up than when it was carried out by the adult experimenter.

Moreover, the standard conservation task requires not only that children should understand the invariance of a single quantity (i.e. conserve identity), but also that they should apply this knowledge to the relationship between two quantities (i.e. conserve equivalence). In other words, they must realize that:

1   A is the same as B.
2   B is the same as B spread out.
3   Therefore, A is the same as B spread out.

Tasks that require them only to deal with (2) – the fact that B does not change its number when it is spread out – are usually easier for children than the standard conservation test (Cowan, 1979; Elkind, 1966, 1967; Hooper, 1968). Elkind (1967) suggested that young children's problem with the conservation task is not so much with invariance of number as with transitive inferences. Piaget considered that young children cannot make transitive inferences (e.g. inferences of the form A = B; B = C; therefore A = C) until they have reached the stage of concrete operations. If this were so, then this on its own could explain their failures with conservation.

There is by now a lot of evidence that children as young as 4 can, under certain circumstances, make transitive inferences (Bryant & Trabasso, 1971; Pears & Bryant, 1990). However, there is also evidence that children often do not realize when it is necessary or appropriate to make such inferences (Bryant & Kopytinska, 1976). Thus, the inferential component of the conservation task may indeed create problems for children, so that they often treat the pre-transformation and post-transformation questions as two different, unrelated, tasks.

This may be one reason why social context is so important: the social context may offer clues to the children as to whether to make a transitive inference; or to treat the post-transformation display as a new task.

Moreover, the traditional two-row number conservation task requires the child not only to understand invariance, but also to be able to compare the numerosities of two sets; and in particular to understand that one-to-one correspondence is a better cue than length for such comparisons. As we have already seen with regard to matching, young children tend to find comparing quantities a particularly difficult task: more so than other tasks requiring an understanding of quantity.

Bryant (1974) proposed that children fail the conservation task because they do not know that one-to-one correspondence and counting are better cues than length; so when there is conflict between the cues they rely on the most recent.

He found that if the rows in one-to-one correspondence:

0 0 0 0 0 0 0 0 0 0

x x x x x x x x x x

are transformed into a 'random' display:

0 0 0   0 0 0 0   0 0   0

  x x   x x x x x x x   x

children tend to conserve their correct judgement that there is the same number in each row.

If the rows in the misleading, length-biased display:

0 0 0 0 0 0 0 0 0 0 0

x x x x x x x x x x

are transformed into the 'random' display:

0 0 0   0 0 0 0   0 0   0

x x   x x x x x x x   x

children tend to conserve their incorrect judgement that the bottom row has more.

Thus, their problem may be more with resolving the conflict between different cues, and realizing that length is less reliable than some other cues, than with invariance as such.

This over-reliance on perceptual cues for comparing sets was also one of the characteristics observed by Piaget (1952, 1968) and seems to be one of the most consistent limitations found in young children's number under-standing. When asked to compare two rows, children under 6 rarely use counting spontaneously. Even when they are asked to count the rows, and do so correctly, they still say that the longer row has more, despite having just assigned the same count number to them (Gréco, 1962). Even when a puppet does the counting, thus removing the child's need to carry out the procedure, children under 5 or 6 seem not to recognize that counting the two sets is a suitable way of comparing them (Sophian, 1988).

Are Piagetian tasks related to arithmetic?

Until the early 1980s, much research on individual differences in young children's arithmetic was concerned with the relationships between per-formance on Piagetian tasks and in arithmetic. In general, significant but not enormous correlations have been found between number conservation and current or subsequent arithmetical performance (Brainerd, 1979; Hiebert & Carpenter, 1982; Young-Loveridge, 1987). However, correlation does not mean a necessary relationship; and in fact most studies also indicate that number conservation and success in other Piagetian logical tasks are not *necessary* for the development with arithmetic.

Number conservation is not equivalent to or a prerequisite for the understanding that counting establishes the quantity of a set (the cardinal word principle). This principle appears, as we have seen, in the fourth or, at latest, the fifth year. Success in standard conservation tasks is unusual before the age of about 6. Saxe (1979) found that children not only count to establish quantities, but even count to *compare* quantities before they pass number conservation tests. In his study, which involved both typically developing children and those with learning difficulties, all children who conserved number also used quantitative counting strategies, but some children used quantitative counting strategies without being able to conserve number (also see McEvoy & O'Moore, 1991). Rather than quantitative counting being dependent on conservation, it seems to provide an important basis for conservation. Young children perform a lot better in number conservation tasks when they are able to count than when they are prevented from doing so.

Many young children are able to carry out addition and subtraction without being able to conserve number (Hiebert, Carpenter, & Moser, 1982; Lemoyne & Favreau, 1981; Pennington, Wallach, & Wallach, 1980). However we interpret failures in the number conservation task, they cannot be seen as implying or causing an inability to do arithmetic.

Counting up or down by 1: Beginnings of arithmetic

> '*Armado*: It doth amount to one more than two.
> '*Mote*: Which the base vulgar call three.
> '*Armado*: True.' (William Shakespeare: *Love's Labour's Lost*, Act 1, Scene 2)

An important development occurs when a child can use knowledge of the counting sequence – for example, that 5 comes after 4 – to conclude that if you count a set of four objects, add a new object and then count again, you will get 5. Similarly, if you count five objects, take an object away and recount, you will get 4.

When does arithmetic, in the sense of addition and subtraction, begin? Formal written arithmetic does not usually develop before school; but other forms of arithmetic begin earlier. Some have even suggested that nonverbal arithmetic with very small quantities is present from infancy. Wynn (1992) found that 5-month-old babies showed the capacity to predict the results of addition and subtraction of objects, if the quantities involved were no greater than three; although these findings are still controversial. Some studies have replicated the findings (Kobayashi, Hiraki, Mugitani, & Hasegawa, 2004), but others have not (Cohen & Marks, 2002; Wakeley, Rivera, & Langer, 2000).

Starkey (1992) studied children's nonverbal understanding of addition and subtraction. Children from 18 months to 5 years old first put a number of balls into an opaque box. They watched as balls were then either added or subtracted from the initial quantity. They were then asked to take the balls out of the box one at a time. Most children from the age of 2 responded in ways that suggested that they realized that addition makes a quantity larger and subtraction makes it smaller. The number of reaches they made was fewer than the original quantity if items had been subtracted. It was more than the original quantity if items had been added. The number of reaches was more likely to correspond to the original quantity in the case of older children than younger children and if the original quantity was larger than if it was smaller. If the original number were three or less, even 2-year-olds often responded correctly. Subtraction problems were performed much better than addition problems.

Relationships between counting proficiency, the order irrelevance principle and early arithmetic

The order irrelevance principle, like conservation, involves the ability to discriminate irrelevant changes from relevant ones. Although the focus of such studies has been on children's recognition of changes in the order of counting, or in the perceptual appearance of the array, as irrelevant to the quantity, this is not sufficient for a true understanding of the concepts. If a child thinks that *all* recounts of a set of objects will give the same number, even if items actually are added or taken away, then (s)he does not have a full understanding of number (Cowan et al., 1996). Children have to realize that changing the order of counting, or the perceptual appearance of an array, will not affect the quantity, whereas addition and subtraction of objects will. This gives rise to the question: what effects do they think addition or subtraction of an object will have on the quantity? Predicting the effects of adding or subtracting an object from an existing set of objects is not merely a possible precursor or correlate of early arithmetic: it *is* a form of arithmetic.

Richard Cowan and I recently followed up our order irrelevance study (Cowan et al., 1996; discussed earlier in this chapter) by a study investigating the relationships between children's understanding of order irrelevance, their counting proficiency and their predictions of the results of addition and subtraction.

One hundred and fifty two children participated in the study: 72 boys and 80 girls. They were drawn from Oxford nursery classes and came from a wide variety of social backgrounds. Their ages ranged from 3 years 6 months to 5 years 2 months. The group consisted of 72 who failed to count a set of 10 objects accurately and 80 who succeeded. The successful and unsuccessful counters did not differ in age. All the children in the study could count to 3 without difficulty.

The children's counting predictions were then assessed with a set of 12 trials. For half the children, the initial numerosities were 2 and 3, for the remainder, sets of eight and nine objects were used. For each initial numerosity, there were two reverse-direction trials, two addition trials and two subtraction trials. Additions and subtractions took place in full view of the child.

All trials began with the child and experimenter counting the initial numerosity together. The two trials of each transformation type (reverse-direction, addition and subtraction) included one same-number trial and one specific-number trial. In the specific-number reverse-direction trial the child was asked, 'If we count them this way [pointing in the opposite direction], do you think we'll still get n [the initial number] or do you think we'll get another number?' For addition and subtraction trials the question was, 'Now I've put a new one here/ taken one away. If we count them now, do you think we'll still get n or do you think we'll get another number?' Children who did not expect n were asked to say what number they thought it would be. The same-number trials were similar except that the question was 'Do you think we'll get the same number or a different number?' Children who expected a different number were asked whether it was more or less.

Results showed that about 90% of the accurate counters and 77% of the inaccurate counters responded according to the principle that counting in the same direction would give the same number, while addition or subtraction would give a different number. On a stricter criterion, requiring that answers be ordinally appropriate (addition results in a larger number than before and subtraction results in a smaller number than before), 70% of the accurate counters and 49% of the inaccurate counters produced correct responses. All these percentages were greater than would be expected by chance alone and were not significantly influenced by whether the initial number of objects was large or small. Ability to give the exact number on a specific-number task *was* influenced by the size of the number, as well as by the children's counting proficiency. For small numbers (initial number 2 or 3), 79% of accurate counters and 57% of inaccurate counters gave the correct number. For larger numbers (initial number 8 or 9), 36% of accurate counters and 24% of inaccurate counters gave the correct number.

Thus, proficient counters performed better than less proficient counters on all tasks. This included tasks involving small numbers as well as large numbers, despite the fact that all the children in the study were able to count the small numbers. Thus, the association between counting proficiency and use of counting principles is not only because children deal better with numbers that they are able to count.

Nevertheless, there was considerable variability in both groups. Some proficient counters failed to respond correctly, while more of the non-proficient counters than would be expected by chance did respond correctly.

On all types of task, children performed better on subtraction than addition trials, and on addition trials than on reverse-direction trials.

As in the earlier study by Cowan et al. (1996), there was a very strong relationship between counting proficiency and task performance. In both Experiment 1 and Experiment 2, accurate counters performed considerably better than inaccurate counters. This finding was true for tasks involving the small numerosities as well as the large numerosities, despite the fact that even the inaccurate counters could count the small numerosities, although only the accurate counters could count the large numerosities. This result highlights the importance of checking accuracy of children's counting procedures in all investigations of their understanding of counting. Children of this age vary considerably as regards their counting proficiency and the conflicting results of different studies may in part reflect differences between the samples as regards this issue.

However, there were exceptions to this association and they occurred in *both* directions. There were some accurate counters who did not pass the experimental tasks and some inaccurate counters who did. Counting proficiency is closely associated with understanding order irrelevance principle and the foundations of addition and subtraction; but it is neither a necessary nor a sufficient condition for these skills.

Do principles precede procedures or vice versa – or does this vary across individuals?

One issue that has been extensively discussed is the relationship between counting principles and counting procedures: usually discussed from the point of view just of development rather than individual differences; yet highly relevant to both issues.

Researchers differ in how they view the relation between counting skill and knowledge of counting principles. Some see principles guiding children's learning to count (Gelman, 1997; Gelman & Gallistel, 1978; Gelman & Meck, 1983). Others see knowledge of principles developing from children's experience of counting (Briars & Siegler, 1984; Fuson, 1988; Siegler, 1991). Yet others propose a 'mutual development' theory whereby procedures and principles develop in tandem and reinforce each other during the course of development (Baroody, 1992b; Rittle-Johnson & Siegler, 1998; Sophian, 1997).

There have, however, been few studies that have looked directly at the relationships between counting proficiency and counting principles and the beginnings of arithmetic. Most studies, with a few exceptions to be described later, tend not to study such relationships directly, but to extrapolate them on the basis of the age at which children demonstrate a given counting principle. Early success on tests of counting principles and other arithmetical principles is taken as support for a principles-first theory; delayed success is taken as supporting a skills-first theory. While the age at which counting principles can be demonstrated is an important topic in itself, it is not a sufficiently direct measure of the relationship between counting skills and counting principles. In order to understand this relationship, it is necessary at least to investigate and correlate counting proficiency and the use of counting principles in the same children; and, better still, to carry out longitudinal studies to see the extent to which counting proficiency predicts the use of counting principles and/or vice versa.

To the best of my knowledge, there have been no such longitudinal studies, although I am in the early stages of carrying out such a study. However, we can draw certain conclusions from studies that have examined the relationship, in the same children, between counting proficiency and the use of counting principles.

Proficient counters tend to perform better than less proficient counters at tasks involving counting principles. This has been found in relation to the understanding of the cardinal word principle (Fluck & Henderson, 1996; Freeman et al., 2000); for the recognition of numerical equivalence between sets (Mix, 1999); and for order irrelevance (Cowan et al., 1996, and our follow-up study described earlier). Most studies do also show exceptions in both directions: proficient counters who do not show an understanding of the principles *and* non-proficient counters who do show an understanding of the principles. Such findings would seem to support the mutual development theory: procedures and principles develop together, but one does not inevitably precede the other. If the 'principles-first' theory were always true, then one would not expect to find children who demonstrated competent use of counting procedures but failed on tests of principles. If the 'procedures-first' theory were always true, then one would not expect to find children who demonstrated understanding of principles but were procedurally inaccurate.

It would be very interesting to carry out longer term longitudinal studies to investigate whether the order of development of procedures and principles in the preschool years would predict patterns of arithmetical performance in the school years. For example, would those preschoolers who master principles before procedures become schoolchildren who are better at arithmetical reasoning than calculation?

Counting in relation to arithmetic in school age children and adults

At an early stage, children add and subtract by counting (Carpenter, 1980; Steffe, Thompson, & Richards, 1982). For this purpose, they frequently use objects in the environment: often their fingers.

The most basic technique of addition by counting is what Carpenter (1980) has termed 'counting all'. If a child is asked, for example, to add 3 and 5, (s)he will first count three objects and then count five objects. In the earliest and most cumbersome version of this technique, (s)he will first count out three objects and then another five objects and will then recount the union of the two sets beginning from 1. A less time-consuming version of the same technique, sometimes referred to as 'Counting All from First' (CAF), is to perform a single counting sequence beginning with 1 and ending with the number representing the total of the two given quantities.

A more economical method, sometimes termed 'Counting On from First' (COF), is to begin with the first addend and count on from it, responding to 'What is 3 + 5?' with '3; then 4, 5, 6, 7, 8'. A still more efficient strategy is to count on from the *larger* addend: '5; then 6, 7, 8'.

Counting techniques for subtraction include:

1 initially counting out the larger quantity and removing the smaller quantity
2 initially counting out the larger quantity, then removing and setting aside objects until one is left with the smaller quantity; then counting the objects that have been set aside
3 starting with the smaller quantity and counting up to the larger
4 and putting out two sets of objects, representing the given numbers; matching them one to one; and then counting the unmatched objects.

The first of these strategies is the most common.

A more abstract type of strategy is to count backwards *mentally* from the larger number, either by the number of steps representing the smaller number (corresponding to the first object-counting strategy just examined) or until one reaches the smaller number (corresponding to the second object-counting strategy just given). This can be confusing, because it can be difficult simultaneously to combine counting backwards and keeping track of the number of steps involved, especially if the backward counting sequence has not been learned to the point of becoming automatic. Thus children often move to starting with the smaller addend and counting on until they reach the larger number (corresponding to the third object-counting strategy described earlier). The last procedure has rarely been taught in schools, but does seem to be frequently used by adults, especially shop assistants and others whose jobs involve giving people change (it was, of course, used more extensively in the days before calculators and automated tills).

Elements of counting-based strategies contribute to some of the derived fact strategies: for example, the $N + 1$ derived fact strategy (if $a + b = c$, then $a + (b + 1) = c + 1$) involves attention to the effects of counting on by 1 from a given number (Baroody, Ginsburg, & Waxman, 1983). In Chapter 6, I argue that the use of derived fact strategies has some of its roots in young children's ability to predict the results of counting under different conditions: for example, that if you add items to a set that has already been counted and count again, you will get a bigger number.

While the potential role of counting is most obvious in addition and subtraction, it also plays a role in multiplication and division: operations that can involve both counting the items within a group and counting the groups themselves (Anghileri, 1997).

One of the common stereotypes concerning school age children and adults with arithmetical difficulties is that they 'still need to count on their fingers'. This is an oversimplification. There are few people who never use finger counting and similar techniques as supplementary strategies, although more mathematically able people are probably more likely to use such strategies to assist in the enumeration of items, rather than for arithmetic. And not all people with arithmetical weaknesses do rely predominantly on counting strategies. Nevertheless, several studies (Geary, Bow-Thomas, & Yao, 1992; Gray & Tall, 1994; Ostad, 1997, 1998; Siegler, 1988) do suggest that children with arithmetical difficulties are more likely than other children of the same age to rely on strategies that are mainly based on counting, as compared with retrieval, written calculation procedures, or derived fact strategies. Moreover, their counting-based strategies are more likely to be of an immature nature: they may still use the counting-all strategy long after other children have acquired the counting-on strategy.

The reliance on counting strategies is likely to be, at least in part, the result of arithmetical difficulties: children may use counting-based strategies because they do not know how to use any other strategies. It may also be that over-reliance on counting strategies contributes to arithmetical difficulties by inhibiting the development of more sophisticated strategies. Over-reliance on counting strategies might also reflect a lack of abstract understanding of number, which, in itself, leads to arithmetical difficulties.

Moreover, sometimes the very children who over-rely on counting strategies are the very children for whom such strategies create the most difficulty. Children who have severe problems with the counting sequence – for example, some children with dyslexia – may become 'stuck' in the counting procedure (see Chapters 1 and 2). It takes so much of their attention that they are not able to concentrate on other aspects of arithmetic; to vary the counting strategies flexibly; or to develop alternative strategies. In extreme cases, the restriction to counting procedures, combined with the lack of efficiency of counting in this group may seriously inhibit both procedural and conceptual development (Yeo, 2001).

Gray (1997, p. 68) argues that: 'There are two main interpretations of arithmetical expressions such as 4 + 3. One makes use of numerical concepts and relationships, while the other triggers the use of counting procedures.' Children who understand arithmetical symbols as representing both concepts and procedures are able to use arithmetical strategies more flexibly than those who understand them only as representing procedures (Gray, 1991; Gray & Tall, 1994).

The need to integrate processes and concepts precedes the use of written symbolism. A child who interprets all 'How many?' questions merely as requests to count may ignore facts and numerical relationships that would preclude the need to count in that instance: for example, that they have already counted the objects in a different order and that the number must be the result of the previous count (order irrelevance principle). At the extreme, they may ignore what to an adult is the main point of counting:

the fact that, when one counts a set of objects, the last item in the count sequence represents the total number of objects in the set (cardinal word principle).

The last paragraph was deliberately ambiguous as to the reasons for children's failure to apply counting principles to guide their procedures. They may not *have* the principles. They may have the principles, but be distracted from using them by their difficulties of the counting procedures. Or they may have some knowledge of both procedures and principles but have difficulty in integrating them: in taking account of both principles and procedures at the same time.

Thompson (1997a, p. 61) argues that teachers:

> have to learn to distinguish those children whose relatively unsophisticated counting procedures are impeding their progress and those who are using counting as part of a network of strategies to help them derive new facts from unknown facts . . . Teachers need to listen to children's descriptions of their personal calculation methods so that they can identify those children who persist in using counting strategies as their sole strategy in all situations.

I would indeed suggest that the over-reliance on any single strategy or narrow range of strategies, whether based on counting or not, is likely to both reflect and contribute to arithmetical difficulties.

Counting difficulties in children with numeracy difficulties

Schoolchildren with numeracy difficulties need not have any difficulties in counting; and the majority do not have difficulty with basic counting. However, some do. Geary et al. (1992) found that 6-year-old children with mathematical disabilities were more likely than typical children to make procedural errors in counting; and some still showed conceptual difficulties, for example, assuming that a puppet is 'wrong' if it counts objects in non-adjacent order. Even children of 9 or 10 sometimes show difficulties in counting when this involves counting forwards and backwards from different starting numbers; and such children tend to have other arithmetical difficulties (Houssart, 2001).

In my own numeracy intervention study (Dowker, 2001, 2003c; Chapter 11 in this volume), it was possible to assess the counting and other numerical skills in a large group of children who had already been identified by their teachers as having numeracy difficulties. The counting abilities of the 146 children (aged 6 and 7) in my numeracy intervention group were assessed. All the children at this age could count verbally to 10 and showed evidence of understanding the cardinal word principle.

Tasks included:

- counting 10 objects
- understanding the order irrelevance principle, i.e. that the result of counting a set of items will not change if the items are counted in a different order, whereas adding or subtracting items will change the result of the count. After counting the 10 objects, they were then asked to predict the result of further counts:
  — in the reverse order
  — after the addition of an object
  — after the subtraction of an object
- *repeatedly adding 1*: children were shown a set of five items and then asked repeatedly, 'And how many will we have if we put one more there?'; this was repeated up to 15
- *repeatedly subtracting 1*: children were shown a set of nine items and then asked repeatedly, 'And how many will we have if we take one away?' This was repeated down to 0.

Of the 146 children, 27 had difficulties with at least one of the counting tasks. Thus, nearly 20% of a group of 6- to 7-year-olds, who had been selected for having arithmetical difficulties, demonstrated at least some basic level procedural and/or conceptual difficulties with counting. Examining this rather heterogeneous group of counting tasks separately showed the following.

Eight of the children had difficulty with the first task of counting 10 objects accurately: i.e. they had procedural counting difficulties with relatively small numbers of objects. (One may presume that a higher proportion of the children would have demonstrated such difficulties with larger numbers of objects.)

Of these eight children, three had difficulty only with the first of the four tasks and did not have any problem with order irrelevance or with addition or subtraction by 1: i.e. they appeared to have relatively 'pure' procedural difficulties with counting.

Ten had difficulty with the order irrelevance task; 8 had difficulty with repeated addition by 1 (which almost always showed itself even with numbers under 10, suggesting that the problem was not just with remembering the verbal counting sequence); and 12 had difficulty with repeated subtraction by 1. Five had difficulty with all three of the latter tasks, of whom two also had difficulty with the counting procedure.

The 27 children who had difficulties in any aspect of counting tended to perform poorly at standardized arithmetic tests, not only as compared with the general population, but even when compared with the other children who were selected for having arithmetical difficulties. Their median WISC arithmetic scaled score was 5, as compared with 7 for other children with arithmetical difficulties and 10 for the general population. Their median BAS Basic Number Skills scaled score was 85, as compared with 94 for other children with arithmetical difficulties and 100 for the general population. Their median WOND numerical operations scaled score was 84, as compared with 91 for other children with arithmetical difficulties and 100 for the general population. For all tests, the difference between the children who had difficulties with counting and the other children with arithmetical difficulties was significant, as shown by Mann-Whitney tests. Because of the relatively small numbers of children involved, it was not possible to investigate whether different patterns of counting difficulties were associated with different levels of performance on standardized arithmetic tests.

Nonetheless, it is possible for children to demonstrate weaknesses in counting and strengths in other areas of arithmetic. This seems to be particularly true of children whose weaknesses in counting are mainly procedural.

Bad at counting; better at arithmetic

There is a common sequence of development from object-based counting procedures and the mastery of the verbal counting string, through the use of verbal and finger counting strategies for simple arithmetic, to the use of more complex arithmetical strategies that do not appear to rely directly on counting. However, there are also sometimes individual exceptions.

Daniel, Emma, Mark and Martin are all children who, in various ways and for various reasons, performed rather poorly on certain apparently simple counting tasks and markedly better on some supposedly more difficult mathematical tasks.

Daniel had cerebral palsy and, at the age of 7, could not control his hands sufficiently well to co-ordinate pointing to objects with verbal counting. As a result, he could not count 10 objects reliably. This did not prevent him from performing very well on most arithmetical tasks, whether they involved word problem solving, mental calculation, or derived fact strategy use. He obtained a scaled score of 14 on the WISC arithmetic subtest (overall verbal IQ 127); and performed at the two-digit (carrying) level for addition and the two-digit (borrowing) level for subtraction. On the use of principles task (see Chapter 6), he used five out of six possible principles for addition and three out of seven possible principles for subtraction.

Emma was seen at the age of just 6. She had mild difficulties with counting procedures, which she herself described articulately: 'I find it difficult to count up to 10, because I do it too quickly and don't know where 10 is.'

In the test session, she counted verbally to 25 and also counted 10 objects correctly, but sometimes found it difficult to perform tasks that involved the counting sequence. She could perform hypothetical repeated additions and subtractions by 1, so long as the numbers involved did not exceed 12. However, she had problems when dealing with larger numbers:

She counted 10 counters correctly.
Researcher: If we bring one more here, how many will we have?

> *Emma*: 11
> *Researcher*: And another one?
> *Emma*: 12
> *Researcher*: And another one?
> *Emma*: I don't know.

She found it a struggle to work out the relative values of even small numbers. When asked which of two numbers was bigger, she thought hard and sometimes got the wrong answer: for example, she said that 7 was bigger than 9.

Yet she was able to say how many numbers there are between two single-digit numbers on Griffin, Case, and Siegler's (1994) Number Knowledge test:

> *Researcher*: How many numbers are there between 2 and 6?
> *Emma*: About 3
> *Researcher*: How many numbers are there between 5 and 7?
> *Emma*: If you ask me, there's about 1.

Mark was seen at 5 years 2 months. He had marked difficulty in dealing with the number sequence. He could count a set of 10 objects, and knew that he would get the same number if he counted them in the same order and a different number if items were added or taken away. However, he had a great deal of difficulty when asked the results of adding 1 repeatedly to a set of objects or subtracting 1 repeatedly from a set of objects. He also had difficulty in saying what number would come before or after a given number and in saying which was the bigger of two numbers. His score on the Number Knowledge Test was only 3: typical of a 2- to 3-year-old. Yet he could use and describe counting-on strategies for addition and even used the commutativity principle that if 6 + 3 is 9, 3 + 6 must also be 9. His performance on tasks that emphasized word problem solving was above average.

Martin has already been described (Dowker, 1998). At the age of just 6, he had considerable difficulties with counting procedures. He knew the verbal counting sequence at least to 20, but had trouble in co-ordinating verbal counting with pointing to objects. His counts of even quite small sets were often out by 1 or 2; for example, he counted four objects as five. He was reported by his teachers to have problems with language, motor skills and concentration – all of which could have contributed to his counting difficulties. At that time, he obtained a WISC verbal IQ of 77 and a performance IQ of 85, with an arithmetic subtest scaled score of only 1, which could have indicated a serious conceptual deficit with numbers or, alternatively, that his other difficulties were preventing him from demonstrating number concepts that he did have.

The latter was suggested by his performance on some number tasks. He could conserve number, understood the order irrelevance principle and could carry out simple concrete sums, giving the correct answer when asked what one would get if one added or took away one or two counters from a set which had been counted. On the occasion when he counted four counters as five, the researcher then added one more counter to the set, and he was asked how many there were now. He recounted correctly, getting 5 but 'corrected' himself: 'No, it's one more, it's 6.' This seems to show his arithmetical reasoning outrunning his counting.

Martin has been followed up over a long period. His ultimate progress both in arithmetic and more generally has been much better than would have been expected from his early test scores. At the age of 10, he obtained a verbal IQ of 101 and a performance IQ of 99. His arithmetic subtest score was now *11* (slightly above average). It is likely that some early deficits were largely resolved with age, partly as a result of maturation, partly as a result of home intervention. Perhaps his early demonstrations of counting principles and basic arithmetical reasoning were a good prognostic sign.

Thus, it is possible to have serious difficulties in counting objects, as Daniel does, and yet to be able to calculate two-digit arithmetic problems, solve word problems and use derived fact strategies. It is possible to be uncertain as to whether 7 is bigger or smaller than 5, as Emma is, and yet to realize that there is one number between them. It is possible to have severe difficulties with many aspects of the counting sequence, as Mark does, and yet to solve word problems accurately. It is possible to be unable to count four objects accurately, as Martin is, and yet to realize that re-arranging the objects or counting them in a different order will give the same number, while adding one object will result in the next number in the counting sequence.

Social and cultural influences on counting

The possible effects of the verbal counting systems in different languages on counting and other aspects of arithmetic will be discussed in Chapter 9. Other social and cultural factors, affecting the child's exposure to numbers at home or nursery school, may influence counting.

One explanation sometimes given for the very high level of performance by children in Gelman's studies is that most of the children came from highly educated family backgrounds. Social class differences seem on the whole to be much greater for counting procedures than counting principles. Nonetheless, social class does seem to have some influence on counting principles; for example, Wynn's (1990) middle-class participants acquired the cardinal word principle at a mean age of 3 years 6 months, while Fluck and Henderson's (1996) participants acquired this principle at a mean age of 4 years 6 months. Fluck and Henderson also observed significant influences of parental teaching and assistance on children's acquisition of counting.

Fischer (1981) studied a group of French children and found that they mastered counting procedures about one year later than the children studied by Gelman. Perhaps just because they were older than Gelman's participants with the same procedural counting ability, they seemed better able to reflect on their own counting. For example, they would say things such as 'I can't count more than 10', rather than producing an idiosyncratic counting sequence.

Counting and the brain

There is increasing evidence that some individual differences in counting and arithmetic are related to individual differences in brain functions, especially as regards the left parietal lobe. This issue is discussed at length in Chapter 10.

Conclusions

We may conclude from the many studies relating to these topics that counting and very early counting-based arithmetic are indeed not unitary processes, but are made up of many conceptual and procedural components. Individual differences can occur in any or all of these components and children can show marked discrepancies between the different components: they can also perform unexpectedly badly at some aspect of counting, while at the same time performing quite well at more advanced arithmetic.

We do not yet have a strong understanding of the underlying internal and environmental bases for these individual differences. Moreover, despite many years of research on the development of counting, surprisingly little is known about the longitudinal relationships between different aspects of counting or about the extent to which these predict later success in arithmetic.

5 Is arithmetic a foreign language? Representing numbers and arithmetical problems in different forms and translating between them

If one is to understand and deal with arithmetic, one must be able to understand how numbers and operations are represented by words and symbols. Some of these words and symbols are specific to arithmetic. For example, the numerals are used only to represent numbers and are distinct from the other symbols used in written language. Others may be used in different ways in contexts within and outside arithmetic. For example, the word 'times' refers to multiplication in the context of arithmetic, but in other contexts may refer to occasions ('I've gone there several times'); to an era ('The times are changing'); or even to the name of a newspaper.

Pimm (1987) considered that learning mathematics has a great deal in common with learning a new language. Although it is not a natural language, it can be described as a 'register': a set of meanings that is appropriate to a particular function of language. There are symbols, which have specific meanings, and rules about how to combine them and order them. As with a foreign language, there is the risk of miscommunications and misinterpretations. And as in learning a new language, one must realize that there can be more than one way of representing the same concept.

There are many different ways in which the same quantity or arithmetical operation may be represented. The number 3, for example, may be represented by three counters, three dots, three fingers, three drumbeats, the third step on a ladder, the third point from 0 on a number line, the Arabic numeral 3, the Roman numeral III, the English number word 'three' or the corresponding number word in other languages, e.g. *trois* in French or *drei* in German. The sum 'three plus two equals five' can be represented in words in English or other languages, by the written sum '3 + 2 = 5', by a word problem such as 'Jack had three sweets and he got two more so now he has five' or 'Joe had three boxes and Kerry had two more boxes than Joe so Kerry had five boxes', by adding two counters or bricks to three to produce a quantity of five, by putting up three fingers and then two more or by going two steps from the third point on a number line.

It is sometimes suggested that children find it difficult to understand how a quantity or arithmetical operation may be represented in more than one way. In particular, it has been suggested that translation between arithmetic problems presented in concrete, verbal and numerical formats is a crucial area of difficulty in children's arithmetical development. Some children (according to some studies, most children) do not understand that the same operation is being used in adding two counters to three counters; in solving a problems such as 'John had three sweets and his mother gave him two more sweets, so now he has five sweets'; and in doing the sum '2 + 3 = 5'. If a child who does understand translation is asked to show how to do the sum '2 + 3 = 5' using counters, then (s)he will put down two counters and then add three more to make five. A child who does not understand translation well will at best simply put out five counters to show the answer; may put out separate sets of two counters, three counters and five counters; or may put out an irrelevant number of counters. This is understandable for children who cannot yet cope with the sums at all or who have trouble with reading and writing numbers; but it occurs in children without these problems.

For example, Hughes (1986) reported that many primary school children demonstrate difficulty in translating between concrete and numerical formats (in either direction), even when they are reasonably proficient at doing sums in either one of these formats. For example, if 6- to 9-year-old children were shown two bricks being added to three bricks and were asked to write the sum for this, they tend to write just '5', but almost never wrote '2 + 3 = 5'. If they were shown the sum '2 + 3 = 5' and are asked to do this sum with bricks, they tended to show five bricks; sets of two bricks, three bricks and five bricks; or even to make the bricks form the numerals, rather than to show two bricks being added to three bricks to make five. There was little improvement between the ages of 6 and 9. Hughes has suggested that this difficulty in translation may be an important hindrance to children's understanding of arithmetic.

The ability to translate between arithmetical formats presented in different formats – e.g. numerical, verbal and concrete – is very important for several reasons. Without this ability, children's numerical understandings are limited, context bound and lacking in abstraction. Arithmetical strategy use is likely to be rigid and context specific; and a child will not be able to use arithmetical knowledge gained through one format to inform or check their strategies in another format: e.g. to use finger counting to check a written calculation. Moreover, a lack of translation ability is likely to impede communication of information between children and teachers, thus reducing the effectiveness of instruction (Munn, 1998). This is particularly important in view of the fact that much teaching involves presenting students with concrete materials and situations as an aid to understanding more abstract concepts. And throughout life, it is important to be able to apply abstract numerical rules and operations to concrete situations and often to interpret the numerical meaning of diagrammatic and pictorial representations (e.g. graphs, pie charts, bar charts, etc.).

Representations of number

Questions concerning the ability to translate between formats, and to understand the relationship between concrete and numerical representations, bring us to the fundamental issue: how *do* we represent numbers and arithmetic? Is it in words, numerical symbols, images of concrete materials, position and movement in space, tactile or motor images (e.g. of finger movements in finger counting) or something far more abstract?

There has been some discussion of the different ways in which arithmetical information and concepts are represented in the mind. For example, Goldin and his colleagues (Goldin, 1982, 1987; Goldin & Kaput, 1996) have proposed five major forms of representation: verbal/syntactic (language based); imagistic (based on mental images, which may be visual, auditory or tactile); formal notational; affective (emotional); and one based on planning, monitoring and executive control. Goldin and Kaput (1996) define a 'powerful' representational system as one that can be applied to many contexts; has meaning with respect to many other forms of representation'; results in efficient use of procedures; and encodes information efficiently. They stress (p. 426) 'the importance of powerful heuristic, imagistic and affective systems of representation'.

This is one of the most important and least understood aspects of mathematical thinking. Even with regard to babies' recognition of small quantities, there is disagreement as to whether this involves visual perception alone (Clearfield & Mix, 1999) or is more abstract (Starkey, Spelke, & Gelman, 1990; Wynn, 1992).

There is sometimes a tendency to assume that everyone's predominant modes of representation are similar. Some theories place a very considerable emphasis on the role of language in influencing our thinking. An extreme example is the strong version of the Sapir-Whorf hypothesis, which states that the language that we speak *determines* how we think: for example, English people cannot make as fine distinctions between different forms of snow as the Inuit, because the latter have more words for snow. Few researchers nowadays accept this theory in its strong form, although there is evidence that language can influence the ease or difficulty of certain forms of thinking. For example, the nature of the number words in a language influences the ease of some aspects of counting and arithmetic (see Chapter 9).

Other theories minimize the importance of language and emphasize the role of sensory images in thinking, including mathematical thinking. An old Chinese proverb, which became popular in educational circles in the 1960s and 1970s, stated: 'I hear and I forget; I see and I remember; I do and I understand.' While this may have been a valuable antidote to the view that mathematics requires nothing except the ability to recite number facts parrot fashion, it is also an oversimplified view. Not everyone remembers things better through seeing than hearing: insisting that a person with a poor visual memory should learn everything through seeing is just as self-defeating as insisting that a person with a poor verbal memory should learn everything through listening. And 'doing' does not invariably result in understanding that can be transferred to other activities than the one that has been practised (see Chapter 9).

More recent views, influenced by brain-based research, suggest that different forms of representation may be used for different forms of arithmetic. Dehaene (1997) suggests that exact numbers and arithmetical facts tend to be represented verbally, while approximate arithmetic and relative values of number tend to be represented more spatially, as though on a number line (see Chapters 7 and 10 for further discussion).

Many theorists, moreover, have proposed developmental shifts in the predominant forms of representations. Piaget's theory (1952) implies that young children's representations are predominantly based on sensory-motor imagery; verbal and symbolic representations are not important until much later. Piaget did not, in any case, consider verbal representations to be more important or powerful than other forms. Vygotsky (1962) ascribed a much more important role to language and other forms of symbolism in reasoning. He also considered that very young children do not reason verbally, but regarded this as a significant limitation on their thinking and considered the integration of language and reasoning at about the age of 7 to be an important breakthrough in their development. Bruner (1973) argued that children move from enactive (action-based) to iconic (imagery-based) to symbolic reasoning.

There are undoubtedly individual differences in the extent to which number and arithmetic involve verbal, visual or more abstract forms of representation (see Chapter 2). More research is needed on these individual differences, on their early origins, and how these may relate to developmental changes.

Recording quantities in written form

Most schooled adults take for granted that quantities can be recorded on paper. Many even regard written numerals as the most salient and appropriate way of representing numbers and find it hard to imagine the possibility of fully understanding or calculating with numbers without representing them as numerals. However, many people in the past and even today have been able to calculate without being literate or expressing quantities as numerals.

This is partly because arithmetic can be performed by purely mental means, without any written record. Also, and importantly, it is possible to record quantity in other ways than by means of words or numerals (Butterworth, 1999; Hughes, 1986). Tallying – making one mark per item in a set on paper, sticks, bones, string or whatever is available – is a very old and common method of recording number. Tallies were used in the Stone Age, before the invention of any other form of writing. Their history goes back at least 30,000 years.

It is, therefore, not surprising that children can develop methods of recording quantities on paper, even before they use written numerals. These can involve drawing the objects themselves or more symbolic forms of graphic representation such as circles and tallies. An early study by Vygotsky and Luria (1993) showed that preschool children tended to represent numbers by tallying methods such as piling objects or making knots in a rope, while school age children used numerals. Allardice (1977) asked children between the ages of 3 and 6 to represent sets of three and four objects (toy mice or buttons) to show a toy dog how many there were. Most of the 5- and 6-year-olds used numerals. The 4-year-olds sometimes used numerals, but more often used other appropriate forms of graphic representation. About half of the 3-year-olds made appropriate representations, which were usually graphic rather than involving numerals.

Hughes (1986) carried out a similar study with a larger group of children. Here the objects were bricks. He found only 12% of children under 5 used numerals or number words in such tasks. Just under one-third of them used idiosyncratic representations, which did not convey obvious numerical meaning and the rest were approximately equally divided between iconic representations such as tallies and circles and pictorial representations. About one-third of 5- and 6-year-olds used numerals or number words and most of the rest used correct graphic representations, which were usually pictorial rather than iconic. Presumably the older children's better representational drawing skills and greater concern for 'visual realism' in drawing were responsible for their greater use of this seemingly less abstract form of graphic representation. By the age of 7, most used numerals. It is interesting that the use of numerals for recording small quantities only became the predominant mode of representation at such a late age, given that the (British) children would have been reading and writing numerals at school from at least the age of 5 and many would have been familiar with numerals earlier.

Hughes also presented 3- to 5-year-old children with another task, where the practical purpose of representation was made clearer. The children were asked to play a guessing game, where they had to say how many bricks were in each of four identical, and repeatedly reshuffled, tins (which contained no, one, two and three bricks). After playing the game for a while, they were invited to label the tins so as to help them remember the numbers of bricks inside them. The results were very similar to the first task, except that iconic representations now outnumbered pictorial representations at all ages. This was presumably because the children now treated the task as one purely of *number* discrimination, and were less inclined to try to represent other aspects of the stimuli. As in the previous task, even the 5-year-olds made comparatively little use of numerals.

Cross-cultural research in countries with varying ages of school entry has given broadly similar results. Sinclair, Siegrist, and Sinclair (1983) gave Swiss children a task very similar to Hughes' first task. They obtained results to those of Hughes, but showed *greater* use of numerals by 6-year-olds, despite the fact that Swiss children begin formal education later than British children. Ewers-Rogers (2002) gave English, Japanese and Swedish children Hughes' 'tins' task, and obtained similar results, across the cultures, to those of Hughes.

Thus, the evidence is that most children of 4 and over, and some younger children, are able to represent small quantities quite effectively, although they often do not use conventional symbols even at an age when they are capable of doing so. There is, however, evidence for improvement with age in the extent to which the representations are used in tasks that involve recognizing changes in quantity. Munn (1998) presented 4- and 5-year-olds with a task similar to Hughes' 'tins' task and obtained similar results. She then introduced a game where a teddy bear was described as hiding an extra item in one of the tins and the children had to tell which tin contained the extra hidden item. On the whole, 5-year-olds were able to use their label to help them solve the task. They realized that if the number of objects in the tin no longer corresponded to that on the label, then it must have been changed. The 4-year-olds were typically unable to carry out the task successfully. There was a significant correlation between use of numerals and success on the task, although this could be just because both were related to age.

In any case it appears that while 4-year-olds can represent quantities, and can also detect changes in quantity (see Chapter 4), they do not readily use their representations to deal with the changes in quantity. This may mean that their representations are still fairly limited and inflexible. It may also reflect the general difficulty that 4-year-olds demonstrate in integrating number concepts with counting procedures, even when they can handle both separately (Chapter 4).

Effect of task on representation of quantities

Would children perform better in a task that appeared more socially relevant? Ewers-Rogers (2002) following up the 'tins' task by giving children a task that involved writing a note to a milkman to indicate how many milk cartons were wanted. Children performed *less* well on this task than on the tins task: even at 4, about half of the responses were idiosyncratic without obvious numerical relevance. Most of the English children had been exposed to the cultural practice of leaving notes for milkmen; most of those from other countries had not. Nonetheless, there were no cross-cultural differences. The problem was not only with written representation, as the children also performed poorly in an oral task of ordering quantities of fast food from a restaurant on a toy telephone. They tended either to make seemingly irrelevant idiosyncratic responses or to state what foods they wanted but not how many. Ewers-Rogers suggests (p. 139) that 'the act of communicating cardinal number to another person is unfamiliar to all young children and is . . . *less* meaningful than communicating or representing number to themselves for their own purposes'. Another possibility is that children are accustomed to communicating cardinal number to other people face-to-face, usually by counting in the other person's presence and/ or showing finger representations and become confused when this is not possible.

Finger counting and representations of number

Children and adults not only count on their fingers, but use fingers to represent quantities. It is not uncommon for a young child to respond to the question, 'How old are you?' by putting up the appropriate number of fingers: e.g. four fingers if (s)he is 4 years old. Primary school children often use strategies in arithmetic that are based not only on finger counting, but on using sets of fingers to represent numbers up to five without counting them (Brissiaud, 1992; Siegler & Robinson, 1982).

Finger representations of number have probably been frequent in adult counting systems for thousands of years, as suggested by the fact that typical counting systems are in base 5, 10 or 20: all readily represented by sets of fingers (and toes) (Butterworth, 1999; Menninger, 1969; Seidenberg, 1959). Such terms as 'digits' imply a relationship between fingers and counting.

There is some influence of culture and convention on the representations of number through finger gestures. Butterworth (1999) notes that most North Europeans and those from English-speaking countries such as the USA and Australia represent numbers as though they begin with the index finger: thus '3' is shown by holding up the index, ring and middle fingers. Most Mediterraneans, by contrast, represent numbers as though they begin with the thumb, e.g. '3' is represented by holding up the thumb, index and middle fingers. English and Chinese people count by starting with the fist and opening up the fingers; Japanese people begin with an open hand and close their fingers one by one. In mediaeval times there were manuals of instruction in finger counting and representations of number and their use in arithmetic (Menninger, 1969). These involved place value representation. Units were represented by counting on the little, ring and middle fingers of the left hand. Tens were represented by counting on the index finger and thumb of the left hand; hundreds by counting on the index finger and thumb of the right hand; and thousands by counting on the little, ring and middle fingers of the right hand. (See Chapter 3 for more extensive systems of using body parts in counting.)

Finger representations are often regarded as one form of visual image of quantity; and so they are. But they are not only visual. They involve motor and tactile representations as well. Brain studies suggest that the brain areas that deal with the tactile aspects of the fingers – the sense that we have of our fingers, whether or not we can see them – are important to number.

As discussed in Chapter 10, there is an association between developmental and acquired difficulties in finger awareness and arithmetical difficulties: the so-called Gerstmann syndrome. This association could be due to several possible factors. The actual representation of number could be affected; representations might be normal, but calculation strategies based on finger counting might be impaired; or the association could be coincidental due to simultaneous damage to, or abnormal development of, different parts of the brain.

There is evidence from brain-imaging studies that number representation and finger representation result in activation of different, but neigbouring, parts of the parietal lobes. Number representations are particularly associated with the inferior parietal sulcus and finger representations with the intraparietal sulcus (Chapter 10). The fact that these brain areas are near one another may simply increase the likelihood of their being simultaneously impaired, even though unrelated to one another. However, Butterworth (1999, pp. 249–250) suggests that there is a more fundamental relationship: that 'without the ability to attach number representations to the neural representations of fingers and hands in their normal locations, the numbers themselves will never have a normal representation in the brain'.

Further studies are needed to investigate how close and necessary such a relationship is. One possibility would be to investigate whether children who were born without fingers inevitably have problems in representing number. However, there is some evidence that even being born without fingers does not exclude the possibility of finger representations in the brain. It was once thought that the phantom limb phenomenon – experiencing sensation from a limb which is not there – was confined to adults who had had a limb amputated. This turns out not to be so. Poeck (1964) described several children with congenital limb deficiencies who experienced phantom limb sensations. One of these children was a girl born without hands who experienced strong finger sensations and who used her 'fingers' in counting and arithmetic.

It does, at any rate, seem likely that in most people there is a close relationship in the brain between finger representations and number representations. This leads to the question of whether some people represent number *predominantly* in terms of finger sensations and movements. This issue has not been greatly studied. It would seem particularly likely to be true of people with visual impairments.

How do visually impaired or totally blind people deal with numbers? The evidence suggests that, provided they are adequately taught and have no other disabilities, their early numerical abilities are not very different from those of sighted people. While some early studies suggested that blind children are seriously delayed in acquiring number concepts such as conservation (Gottesman, 1973), more recent studies suggest few such delays (Ittyerah & Samarapungavan, 1989; Iverson & Goldin-Meadow, 1997). Studies of mental arithmetic by blind children suggest that, despite some delays possibly due to delays in the onset of mathematics instruction, blind children, like sighted children, use a wide variety of appropriate strategies in arithmetic (Ahlberg & Csocsan, 1999; Lane, 1993). Lane (1993) found that 6- and 7-year-old blind children used broadly similar strategies to their sighted counterparts, including both finger-counting strategies and keeping track of objects by touching them. Ahlberg and Csocsan (1999) found greater differences in the strategies used: both blind and sighted children used estimation strategies and verbal counting on and counting down; but the blind children unlike the sighted children did *not* use finger-counting strategies. Interestingly, the blind children made greater use than the sighted children of derived fact strategies and of retrieval of facts from memory. Clearly, there is room for much more research on blind people's counting and arithmetic in general and their use of finger representations and finger counting in particular.

Visual imagery for numbers and synaesthesia

> 'Eye of man hath not heard; ear of man hath not seen.' (William Shakespeare: *A Midsummer Night's Dream*, Act 1, Scene 1)

It has been known for a long time that some people have unusual visual images for numbers (Calkins, 1892; Galton, 1880; Seron et al., 1992b). Usually, these involve either colours or spatial relationships: for example, numbers may be seen as positions on a ruler, or number line, or thermometer or along a journey. It is not extremely uncommon to have some form of consistent visual imagery for numbers. For example, such images, most commonly spatial ones, were reported by about one-quarter of a group of 194 students questioned by Seron et al. (1992). It is likely that many such images are the result of teaching or self-teaching and it is possible that they may increase in frequency in the future, due to increased use of number lines in schools.

A much smaller proportion of people have *extremely* strong and consistent images for certain numbers. Most recorded cases have involved colour imagery: e.g. 2 may be red and 3 blue. This is a form of synaesthesia (unusual connections between the different senses) and Ramachandran (2003) has shown by brain-imaging studies that at least some such people show unusual overlap between the areas of the brain that predominantly represent numbers and colours.

The relationship between number images and arithmetic is not clear. Seron et al. (1992) studied a few people who claimed to use their spatial number images in calculation, but obtained no clear results as to what *proportion* of people with number images use them in calculation; how *consistently* such people use them; and whether it is, in fact, beneficial to their arithmetical performance. We do not even know whether people with number images are better at numerical tasks than other people.

Another question is that of whether people with number images form a distinct group or form part of a continuum with the rest of the population (Seron et al., 1992b). There may very well be a spectrum from people who have absolutely no imagery for number relationships, through the majority who have some internal spatial representations for the relative values of numbers (Dehaene, 1997; see also Chapter 3), through those with much more distinctive visual number forms, to those with true synaesthesia.

Most research has concerned *visual* images for numbers. We do not know whether and to what extent some people may have distinctive *non*-visual images: e.g. auditory images of relative volume, pitch or quantity of sounds; motor images of finger counting; etc. We may note that Seron et al. (1992b) reported two people who associated numbers with sensations of temperature: one of them reported that odd numbers were cold and even numbers were warm.

Reading and writing numbers: Transcoding between numerals and words

Quite a lot of research on adult arithmetical cognition deals with the issue of 'transcoding': conversion of numbers from one form to another. Most of this work deals with conversions between numerals (4; 306) and words (four; three hundred and six), although a few studies have included alternative representations such as sets of dots. Most work on children's reading and writing numbers has focused on their understanding of the counting system and representations of place value. Much of this research involves mappings between the spoken and written number systems and is dependent on language and culture. It will, therefore, be mainly discussed in Chapter 9.

However, parallels must be noted between such studies of children and work on *adults'* reading and writing of numbers, which has focused on the *translation* aspect. In the words of Dehaene and Cohen (1998, p. 331):

> There is a domain of language in which we are all, in some sense, bilinguals: the domain of numbers . . . The human brain must contain mental representations and processes for recognizing, understanding and producing these various notations [verbal and numerical] of numbers and for translating between them.

Children tend to have considerable initial difficulty in reading and writing multi-digit numbers (Power & Dal Martello, 1997; Seron, Deloche,

& Noel, 1992a). Their difficulties tend to take a particular form: a tendency to represent hundreds and larger multiples of 10 as wholes, rather than as digits in their appropriate places. Thus, 123 is written as 10023; 2300 as 2000300; etc. It is less common for this to happen with two-digit numbers, e.g. 23 written as 203, but it can happen. For many children, there is, at least initially, a sharp distinction between two-digit numbers and larger numbers. Young children often *read* multi-digit numbers as concatenations of single-digit and two-digit numbers: e.g. 123 may be read as 'twelve-three'. Children tend, however, to make fewer such errors when reading than writing.

Similar difficulties have been noted in some adults with brain damage; for example, Cipolotti, Butterworth, and Warrington (1994) described a man who could *read* numerals adequately, but had difficulty in writing numbers; e.g. he wrote 1945 as 1000, 945.

There has been some debate as to whether transcoding between numerals and words involves attention to the *meaning* of the numbers. McCloskey, Caramazza, and Basili (1985) suggest that a stimulus problem, regardless of its format, is first converted into an abstract semantic representation, which is then translated into the required alternative format. Deloche and Seron (1987) have suggested that such an abstract representation is not necessary and that people can translate directly between formats without going to the meaning. More recently, researchers such as Dehaene (1992) and Cipolotti and Butterworth (1995) have proposed multiple routes in transcoding: an individual can either translate directly between numbers and words or does so through consideration of their shared meanings.

People can show better performance on one type of format than another: e.g. they may be better in doing arithmetic with words than numerals or, more usually, with numerals than words. There are several possible explanations for such differences. They may possibly be related to differences in the ways that their brains process numbers. People with brain damage can be impaired in arithmetic problem solving for one format but not another: e.g. words but not numerals or numerals but not words (Dehaene, 1992; McCloskey et al., 1985). It is possible for people without obvious brain damage to have 'digit dyslexia', where they have trouble in reading numerals but not words (Temple, 1991).

However, such differences in adults are likely in most cases to be related to experience. As a result of educational and other experiences, some people are more accustomed to dealing with number words than others. Most schooled people will have more experience in dealing with numerals than with number words. Hence, most adults are faster and more accurate at carrying out single-digit arithmetic problems with numerals than with number words (Campbell, 1994).

There are some children who seem to have more access to the meanings of numerals and/or number words than would be expected by their difficulties in translating between one and the other. For example, 6-year-old

Stephanie (Dowker, 1995) was erratic in reading and writing two-digit numbers (i.e. in translating between verbal and numerical representations of these numbers). She was not able to read any three-digit numbers accurately; for example, she read 306 as 'thirty six' and 215 as 'twenty one five'. But when she was shown 20 pairs of three-digit numbers, she was able to point with 100% accuracy to the larger number in each pair.

An 8-year-old, called Tony (Dowker, 1998), could read numbers up to 30, but often made reversals beyond that point: e.g. reading 69 as 96. He could not read any three-digit numbers correctly and his responses often seemed quite unrelated to the number presented: e.g. he read 125 as 22 and 213 as 85. Yet he was almost as successful as Stephanie in comparing three-digit numbers. He responded correctly to 18 of the 20 pairs, although he was less consistently successful in comparing pairs of two-digit numbers, responding accurately to only 25 out of 40 such pairs.

Stephanie and Tony showed a rather similar discrepancy between number pronunciation and number comparison. They were very different in many other respects, however. Stephanie performed adequately at the WISC arithmetic subtest, obtaining a scaled score of 11. Tony was unable to cope with it, obtaining a scaled score of 2. Stephanie was performing adequately, although unevenly, in schoolwork. Her Schonell reading age was 7 years 6 months, showing good word decoding ability, although her school regarded her as relatively weak in tasks that required language comprehension. Tony was performing very poorly in school and was virtually a non-reader, despite intensive reading instruction.

One thing that Tony and Stephanie did have in common, which may be relevant, was a very strong discrepancy between nonverbal and verbal abilities. Stephanie showed a 42-point discrepancy between verbal and performance IQ, obtaining a verbal IQ of 81 and a performance IQ of 123. Tony showed a 28-point discrepancy between verbal and performance IQ, obtaining a verbal IQ of 66 and a performance IQ of 94. His teacher considered that the fact that he performed comparatively well in a number comparison task may have been due to the fact that he did not need to use words in this task.

Christopher Donlan, and colleagues (Donlan, 1998, 2003; Donlan & Gourlay, 1999) have found that children diagnosed as having specific language impairments are often better than would be expected at comparing pairs of two-digit numbers, although they tend to be very weak at numeracy in general. Of a group of 8-year-olds with SLI, as compared with 83% of their typically developing contemporaries, 61% were able to compare pairs of two-digit numbers accurately, even when the unit value of the smaller number was larger than the unit value of the larger number (e.g. 21 versus 18). Those SLI children who succeeded on this task showed similar speed and efficiency to the typically developing children. One SLI child in the study was able to make such comparisons, but not to read two-digit numbers aloud.

It would be of interest to extend this study to other children with specific verbal weaknesses in general (e.g. deaf children of hearing parents) or in the language of the task (e.g. children speaking English as a second language and tested in English). A study by Nunes and Moreno (1998) does suggest that deaf children have some difficulties in representing tens and units through 10p and 1p coins, and that their performance on this task is closely related to their mastery of the counting sequence.

Word problems

> 'The fox, the ape and the humble-bee
> Were still at odds, being but three,
> Until the goose came out of door
> And stayed the odds by adding four.' (William Shakespeare: *Love's Labour's Lost*, Act 4, Scene 1)

> *Researcher (Delyth Lloyd)*: John had one boat. Then he bought another boat. How many boats did he have?
> *Child*: Noah's Ark.

> *Teacher*: If you buy a gun for two pence, and caps for a penny, how much do you spend?
> *Peggy*: My Mum says I can't buy guns.
> *Duggie*: Caps is three 'apence. You can't get none for a penny. (Joan M. Goldman, quoting the responses of her 6-year-old pupils in *Brave new school*, 1965)

Although word problems involve a multitude of skills, both verbal and mathematical, they are particularly demanding of the ability to translate between different formats: especially numerical and verbal, although concrete representations may also be important, especially for younger children.

Word problems (also sometimes known as 'story problems') constitute one aspect of arithmetic that creates difficulty for many children and adults. McLeod (1992) found this to be a particularly unpopular aspect of mathematics for secondary school pupils and adults. One of Gary Larsen's 'The Far Side' cartoons shows 'Hell's Library' as consisting of books with such titles as 'Story Problems'; 'More Story Problems'; 'Story Problems Galore', etc.

Word problems serve several functions in education. In particular, they are seen as important in teaching children to think about *when* and *why*, not just *how*, to use an arithmetical operation: to demonstrate 'utilizational' as well as 'procedural' competence. This is important for practical purposes: for example, knowing how to multiply is of limited use if the individual simply uses multiplication in all situations that involve numbers, even those that call for addition or division. Such a person will not even be helped by access to a calculator. Knowing when to use a given operation would also seem important from a somewhat broader point of view, in helping one to go beyond the rote memorization of facts and calculation routines and to gain an understanding of the nature and meaning of arithmetical operations.

Word problems are also used with the purpose of making arithmetic more realistic and meaningful to pupils and, therefore, easier to learn. It is questionable whether this is always, or even frequently, the case. Word problems, especially those used with older children, often feature situations that are unfamiliar and unrealistic to most pupils. Even what appears to be a 'realistic' problem may not seem so to all pupils. One professional mathematician remembered all his life how at the age of 7 he had been unable to do an arithmetic test, because all the problems dealt with how much people would get 'in cash' for certain arithmetical transactions and he did not know what the word 'cash' meant.

There is abundant evidence that the difficulty of word problems involving the same arithmetical operation can be greatly influenced by the type of situation that the problems portray. There have been several attempts to classify different forms of word problem in addition and subtraction (e.g. Carpenter & Moser, 1982; Fuson, 1982; Nesher, 1982; Riley, Greeno, & Heller, 1983). Although these classification systems differ in detail, they are broadly similar. The 1983 classification of Riley et al. will be used here.

The broad categories used by Riley et al., with some further subdivisions within each category, are:

1   *Change*. This type of problem involves an initial quantity that is then either increased or reduced.
    — **Addition example**: John had four sweets and his mother gave him two more. How many does he have now?
    — **Subtraction example**: Kate had five apples and she ate two. How many does she have left?
2   *Combine*. This type of problem involves two quantities that are combined to form a third.
    — **Addition example**: Sam has four books and Alice has three books. How many books do they have altogether?
    — **Subtraction example**: Jordan and Daniel have six pencils altogether. Jordan has four pencils. How many pencils does Daniel have?
3   *Compare*. This type of problem involves comparisons between two quantities.
    — **Addition example**: Michael has three biscuits. Louise has two more biscuits than Michael. How many biscuits does Louise have?
    — **Subtraction example**: Emma has five marbles. She has three more marbles than Mark. How many marbles does Mark have?

There are also other, less frequently used categories such as *equalize* problems (described by Fuson, 1992), which involve working out how to establish equality between two sets: e.g. 'Sam has five sweets and Joe has eight sweets. How many sweets does Sam need to be given to have the same number as Joe?'

On the whole, change problems and combine problems involving addition are solved more readily than compare problems, equalize problems or combine problems involving subtraction. Within the change category, problems with an unknown result set ('John has four sweets and his mother gave him two more; how many does he have altogether?') are easier than those with an unknown change set ('John had four sweets; then his mother gave him some more sweets, so now he has six. How many sweets did his mother give him?'), which are, in turn, easier than problems with an unknown initial quantity ('John's mother gave him two sweets, so now he has six sweets. How many sweets did he have altogether?'). Within the compare category, problems with an unknown difference set ('Emma has five marbles. Mark has two marbles. How many more problems does Emma have than Mark?') are easier than problems with an unknown compared set ('Mark has two marbles. Emma has three more marbles than Mark. How many marbles does Emma have?'), which are in turn easier than problems with an unknown referent set ('Emma has five marbles. She has three more marbles than Mark. How many marbles does Mark have?')

Addition word problems are more likely to be solved correctly than subtraction word problems, but this may be due not so much to the addition problems being easier for children, as to the fact that some children adopt a response strategy of 'When in doubt, add' (DeCorte & Verschaffel, 1987; Sowder, 1988). Hughes (1986) found that 4- and 5-year-old children, who are unlikely to have yet developed such response strategies, are if anything better at subtraction than addition word problems.

DeCorte, Verschaffel, Janssens, and Joillet (1984) found that in school children are mostly instructed on 'change' and 'combine' problems with the result unknown. This could result in mechanical solution strategies for the problem types that are over-represented and an inability to cope with those problem types that are under-represented or not represented at all. Nesher (1982) suggested that solutions to word problems are generally stereotyped, with children developing 'shortcuts' to identify the operation required on the basis of surface structure rather than understanding the underlying deep structure. Sowder (1992) described some of the strategies used by children to decide which operation is appropriate. These finding the numbers and adding them; guessing the operation; calculating all possibilities and selecting the most plausible; looking for a keyword to signal the correct operation (e.g. the word 'altogether' implies addition; the words 'how many are left?' imply subtraction); or inferring the operation from the size of the numbers. Such non-semantic strategies are often successful; e.g. Schoenfield (1992) found that in one textbook 97% of the problems could be solved by using a keyword strategy. Such superficial strategies, although successful at this early stage, may prove misleading and confusing later on. Studies have shown that giving children experience with unrepresented problem types can significantly improve performance and reduce the discrepancy between 'easy' and 'difficult' semantic problem types.

Representing word problems through numbers and concrete objects

Various studies have suggested that, although children have difficulty with many word problems, they are relatively good at translating simple word problems into other forms, as shown by their representations of addition and subtraction word problems with written sums or additions and sub-tractions of concrete objects (e.g. Bebout, 1990; Boulton-Lewis, 1993; Boulton-Lewis & Tait, 1994; Carpenter, 1985; Carpenter et al., 1981, 1988; Carpenter, Ansell, Franke, Fennema, & Weisbeck, 1993; DeCorte & Verschaffel, 1987; Fuson, 1986; Greer, 1987; Hiebert & Carpenter, 1982; Hone, 1990; Nesher & Katriel, 1977; Nesher & Teubal, 1974; Stetic, 1999).

These studies show that most children are indeed able to represent at least some kinds of word problems (especially change problems for addition and subtraction and combine problems for addition) with concrete objects (Carpenter & Moser, 1982; Carpenter, Hiebert, & Moser, 1981; Lindvall & Ibarra, 1982) and many can even represent them with written sums (Bebout, 1990; Carpenter, Moser, & Bebout, 1988; Ishida & Koyasu, 1989). Where they experience difficulty, this seems to be based more on failures to understand the word problems themselves than on difficulties with the concept of translating word problems into other forms. These studies indicate that, as with most tasks involving word problems, performance depends significantly on the semantic structure of the word problems.

If translation between numerical and concrete is so difficult, why does it seem relatively easy for children to translate from word problems to either concrete or numerical? One possible explanation could be that it is intrin-sically easier to translate from verbal to concrete or numerical than to translate between numerical and concrete. However, there is one fairly recent small-scale study, which, in contrast to the earlier results, found 5- and 6-year-olds to be relatively good at translating between numerical and concrete formats (Gifford, 1997).

Most studies have not, in fact, compared the same children's performance on different *types* of translation; e.g. verbal to numerical versus numerical to concrete. We now turn to a study that looks at young children's perform-ance on a variety of different translation tasks.

A study of young children's ability to translate between arithmetical problems in different formats

Mark Gent, Louisa Tate and I have carried out an investigation of the ability of 4-, 5- and 6-year-old children to translate between concrete numerical and verbal mathematical formats. In particular, we wished to investigate whether 6-year-olds do find such translations very difficult; whether younger children can carry them out at all; and whether there are significant differences in performance on different kinds of translation, depending on the presentation format and response format.

Method

Sixty children participated in the study. They included 20 4-year-olds from a nursery school, 20 5-year-olds from the first year of a primary school; and 20 6-year-olds from the second year of the state primary school. They were tested individually.

All were given tasks involving translations between word problem, concrete and numerical formats for additions and subtractions. The concrete formats involved the use of counters. Word problems included change, compare and combine problems for addition and subtraction (see earlier section on 'Word problems'). All six combinations of presentation and response domain were given, as the following demonstrated. No sum in any of these translation tasks included a number greater than 10. The order of tasks was varied systematically between participants.

Translation from numerical to concrete

Children were presented with written sums (e.g. '2 + 5 = 7'; '6 − 2 = 4') and were invited to 'show me how to do this sum with the counters'.

Translation from concrete to numerical

They watched the researcher perform arithmetical operations with counters (e.g. adding seven counters to two counters; subtracting six counters from nine counters) and then were then asked to 'write down the sum that goes with what I did'.

Translation from verbal to concrete

They were presented with word problems and asked to 'show me this story with the counters'.
    Examples included:

'Paul had 4 sweets; his mother gave him 3 more; so now he has 7 sweets.' (Addition: 'Change' semantic category)
'Susan has 5 books; Jill has 3 marbles; so they have 8 books altogether.' (Addition: 'Combine' semantic category)
'James has 3 marbles, and Fred has 2 more marbles than James, so Fred has 5 marbles.' (Addition: 'Compare' semantic category)

'Peter had 5 buns; he ate 3 buns; so now he has 2 buns.' (Subtraction: 'Change' semantic category)

'Jane and Tom have 8 toy cars altogether; Jane has 3 of the toy cars, so Tom has 5 toy cars.' (Subtraction: 'Combine' semantic category)

'Farmer John has 7 pigs and 5 cows, so he has 2 more pigs than cows.' (Subtraction: 'Compare' semantic category)

Translation from verbal to numerical

Children were presented with word problems (similar but not identical to those just described), and asked to 'write down the sum that goes with the story'.

Translation from numerical to verbal

They were presented with written sums (e.g. '3 + 6 = 9', '8 − 6 = 2') and invited to 'tell me a story that goes with this sum'.

Translation from concrete to verbal

Children watched the researcher perform arithmetical operations with counters (e.g. adding five counters to three counters; subtracting six counters from nine counters) and were then asked to 'tell a story to go with what I just did with the counters'.

In order to assess the effect of number size on performance, an additional test was given with larger numbers, for the 6-year-olds only. This involved similar tasks to those just described, but each sum included one number between 10 and 15: e.g. 'Sophie has 6 biscuits and Emma has 7 biscuits so they have 13 biscuits altogether'; '15 − 7 = 8'.

Each child in the study was also required to complete a standardized arithmetical reasoning test: the arithmetic subtest of the Wechsler Preschool and Primary Scale of Intelligence (WPPSI).

Classification of responses

The types of classification used for representations of addition are shown in Table 5.1.

A similar scheme was used for the classification of subtraction sums, although subjects who represented the subtraction process using by reciprocal addition (i.e. treating A − B = C as C + B = A) were treated as having given an incomplete correct response.

Table 5.1 Types of classification for responses given in the various mathematical formats [for *addition* sums A + B = C]

Format	Classification		
	Correct	*Incomplete*	*Incorrect*
Numerical Format	A + B = C	A + B C A B C A + B A, B or C	Subtraction Irrelevant sum Alphabet letter No response
Concrete Format	Representation	A B C $[A(+B) \rightarrow C]$ A B A, B or C	Subtraction Irrelevant sum Other No response
Verbal Format	Change Combine Other correct	Addend/result Embedded sum in story	Subtraction A + B + C Irrelevant story No response

Results

Age differences in complete, incomplete and incorrect representations

According to the classification just given, 44% of the 6-year-olds' responses, 3% of the 5-year-olds' responses and 1% of the 4-year-olds' responses were complete; further, 28% of the 6-year-olds' responses, 57% of 5-year-olds' responses and 40% of 4-year-olds' responses were incomplete; 28% of the 6-year-olds' responses, 40% of the 5-year-olds' responses and 60% of the 4-year-olds' responses were incorrect. Analyses of variance showed highly significant age differences for complete responses (which increased greatly with age) and for incorrect responses (which decreased greatly with age). Even *within* each year group, age in months correlated positively with number of complete representations and negatively with number of incorrect representations. Age and year group effects did not quite reach significance for incomplete representations, although these were more frequent at 5 than at 4 or 6.

Overall, 18 (90%) of the 6-year-olds, 10 (50%) of the 5-year-olds and 2 (10%) of the 4-year-olds produced at least one complete response in the course of the task. Thus, we see a very considerable increase in performance with age, and very clear indications that most 6-year-olds can translate between addition and subtraction problems in different formats.

Do different types of translation task differ in difficulty?

Children's scores on each task were assessed by assigning a score of 2 to each complete response, 1 to each incomplete response and 0 to each incorrect response or failure to respond. The scores were then divided by the number of items in each task. Statistical tests (matched pairs t-tests) across age groups revealed that translations from concrete to numerical resulted in significantly higher scores than translations from numerical to verbal or concrete to verbal. There was no significant differences in score between translations from numerical to verbal and those between concrete to verbal; or between the different types of translation that did not require a verbal response: verbal to concrete, verbal to numerical, numerical to concrete and concrete to numerical.

Thus, children find it relatively difficult to create story problems to fit numerical and concrete presentations. This is especially true for the younger children: 90% of the 4-year-olds' and 85% of the 5-year-olds' responses to tasks requiring the creation of story problems were incorrect or absent and only 5% of their responses to these tasks were complete. By contrast, 50% of the 6-year-olds' responses to such tasks were complete and 30% were incorrect or absent. Otherwise, translations between the different presentation and response formats seem to be relatively homogeneous in difficulty.

Comparisons between different types of word problem

When translating from word problems into concrete or numerical formats, children found it significantly easier to translate from change and combine problems than compare problems for addition; and from change problems than combine and compare problems for subtraction. In particular, they produced significantly more complete representations for change addition problems than compare addition problems and for combine addition problems than compare addition problems. They produced significantly more complete representations for change subtraction problems than combine subtraction problems, for change subtraction problems than compare subtraction problems and for combine subtraction problems than compare subtraction problems. These results are consistent with previous findings about the relative difficulty of the different forms of word problem (e.g. DeCorte et al., 1984; Riley et al., 1983).

6-year-olds' translation ability was not greatly affected by number size

The 6-year-olds performed just as well on translation problems involving larger numbers as smaller numbers. There were no significant differences between the two tests on addition, subtraction or overall. Thus, the 6-year-olds' ability to translate between formats is not strongly dependent on number size.

Relationship between arithmetical reasoning and translation

The main purpose of the WPPSI arithmetic test was to make sure that the different age groups had similar scaled scores and thus that any age differences in translation were unlikely to be due to extraneous differences in arithmetical ability. However, we also investigated whether WPPSI arithmetic subtest score was related to translation performance. The arithmetic score was indeed strongly positively correlated with number of complete representations and negatively with number of incorrect representations. It was not related to number of incomplete representations.

Thus, arithmetical ability seems to be related to translation ability. However, even some children who are quite weak at arithmetic can perform relatively well at translation tasks. A task similar to that of Dowker, Gent, and Tate (2001) was given to the 6-year-olds in my Numeracy Intervention group, who had been selected for being weak at arithmetic. At least one complete response was produced by 70%: certainly a smaller proportion than the 90% of an unselected group of 6-year-olds, but still a majority.

Some conclusions from the study of children's translations in arithmetic

The overall conclusion is that most 6-year-olds taught by contemporary methods can translate between numerical, concrete and word problem formats. Results are affected both by the nature of the task and by the children's arithmetical performance level; but are relatively good even in children with arithmetical difficulties.

However, children younger than 6 do experience considerable difficulty with all translation tasks, with 5-year-olds being much more likely to produce incomplete than complete translations and 4-year-olds finding such tasks very difficult and tending to produce incorrect or irrelevant responses or not to respond at all. This finding gives support to Munn's (1998) proposal that symbolic function develops rapidly at around school age.

It was predictable that tasks that required children to invent word problems would be more difficult than other translation tasks. What is really surprising is that so many 6-year-olds performed so well on the word problem creation tasks. This relatively good performance by 6-year-olds in creating word problems is impressive in view of the fact that few studies have even attempted to elicit word problems from children; and those that have made the attempt (Ellerton, 1986; English, 1998) have usually involved children over 8.

In any case, it does not appear that translation is a central problem for most primary school children over 6. In the future, longitudinal and training studies might aid the understanding of the factors responsible for becoming able to translate and establish the factors that create difficulty for the minority who do not make this step at approximately 6 years.

Why does translation ability increase with age and arithmetical ability?

It should not be taken as a truism that translation ability *must* increase with age. Hughes (1986) found few age differences in translation ability, at least after the age of 6. The more recent studies have shown more of an association with age and arithmetical ability. It may be useful, both practically and theoretically, to ask the question of why such associations should occur. An answer to this question may contribute to an answer to an even more basic question: what are the principal components of translation ability?

There are several possible reasons for the marked age differences and the difficulties demonstrated by the younger children in our study. One obvious reason is that the younger children were unfamiliar with written arithmetical symbolism. If a child has difficulty in reading or writing numerals or arithmetical signs, then they are likely to have difficulty in translating to and from written numerical formats. If they can read and write numerals but not operational signs, then their responses are likely to be incomplete. If they can read and write neither signs nor numerals, then their responses are likely to be absent or irrelevant. The incomplete nature of many 5-year-olds' responses seemed to be at least partly due to lack of familiarity with written arithmetic. For example, Craig (5 years 9 months) wrote '5 + 4 9' in response to a word problem that would have been correctly represented as '5 + 4 = 9'. He stated that this said 'Five plus four makes nine', and was aware that a bit was missing. Such difficulties were rare in 6-year-olds.

Unfortunately, this study did not include direct tests of the ability to read and write numerals and arithmetical signs; but ongoing research, which does include such tests, does suggest that they are related to translation.

However, difficulties with written representation are probably not the whole story, as the younger children also had difficulty in translating from verbal to concrete formats, where written numerals and signs were not involved.

A second explanation may be that increasing ability to understand the semantics of word problems, either through greater arithmetical experience or greater general verbal ability, is associated with improved arithmetical translation. This would be consistent with the relationship between translation performance and the WPPSI arithmetic test, which is predominantly a word problem-solving test. It is not surprising that proficiency at word problem solving should be associated with good performance at translation tasks that involve word problems. However, once again this does not explain why age and arithmetical performance are also linked to the ability to translate between concrete arithmetic and written numerals.

A third explanation is that greater ability at arithmetical procedures may lead to children being less 'tied up' with arithmetical procedures and more able to consider the wider aspects of the problem.

Another important possibility is that older children are better at translation due to more general cognitive factors. In particular, older and abler children may understand arithmetic at a more abstract level and be less bound to one format. This has two aspects. One is that greater arithmetical understanding may be associated with being less bound to the concrete;

more able to think in abstract and hypothetical terms. The other is that greater arithmetical understanding, with the increasing flexibility that it involves (Chapter 1) may be associated with being less bound to *any* specific type of presentation.

Information processing and translation: Simultaneously attending to more than one format

Chapter 8 discusses evidence that arithmetical difficulties are often associated with difficulties in working memory and attention. Usually, this is considered in terms of difficulties in keeping track of the different steps in an arithmetical procedure. Such working memory limitations might also cause or increase difficulties in keeping two or more forms of representation in mind at the same time.

Some researchers, such as Leslie (2000) have suggested that children under 4 have working memory limitations that prevent them from simultaneously considering two representations or dealing with conflict between a representation and a reality (e.g. an object and an out-of-date photograph of it). Whether or not such theories are correct, we are here mostly dealing with children who are past their fourth birthday. However, such working memory difficulties could still interfere with simultaneous attention to more than one representation, under circumstances where one or more of the representations is particularly abstract or difficult.

Educational factors and translation

> 'It has been observed before, that counting by realities, and by signs, should be taught at the same time, so that the ear, the eye and the mind should keep pace with one another.' (Richard and Maria Edgeworth: *Practical education*, London: J. Johnson, 1798, p. 257)

There are several methodological and sampling differences between our experiments and the earlier experiments by Hughes, which might explain the different results. However, I would suggest that one major factor is the changes in mathematical educational methods in Britain over the last 20 years. In recent years there has been far more emphasis than previously on teaching children how the same problem can be represented and/or solved in more than one way and that all these ways will achieve the same answer (DfEE, 1999).

If this interpretation is correct, then this would suggest that translation and abstraction are not intrinsic sources of difficulty, at least for children of 6 and over, but are heavily influenced by the extent to which teaching methods encourage integration versus compartmentalization of different arithmetical tasks and strategies. It is noteworthy that there appear to be cross-national differences in children's representational competence (Brenner, Herman, Ho, & Zimmer, 1999), suggesting that educational practices may be a factor.

A number of studies from the 1980s and earlier do indicate a greater tendency toward compartmentalization between different forms of presentation of arithmetic problems in schools. Erlwanger (1973) described an 11-year-old American boy, 'Benny', who had different methods of solving problems involving addition of fractions when these were presented in terms of concrete objects (e.g. portions of a ball of clay) and in terms of written numbers. When he used the concrete objects, he generally got the correct answer. When he dealt with written symbols, he used the common incorrect strategy of adding the numerators and denominators separately: e.g. $1/2 + 1/3 = 2/5$. Even when he saw that the different strategies resulted in different answers to the same problem, he did not conclude that one of the answers must be incorrect. He thought it possible for two methods to give different answers and considered that either method could be correct if it were required by a teacher or textbook at a particular time: the only way of telling whether an answer was correct was by seeing if it was the answer given in the answer book.

Hart (1989) studied a group of English middle-school children (between the ages of 8 and 13) who were being taught mathematical topics by the technique of first carrying out activities with concrete objects; then being encouraged to extract a general rule for these; and then doing problems on paper according to the rule. For example, they were taught to calculate the volume of a cube by first constructing a lot of big cubes out of little cubes; then, with the help of the teacher, extracting the rule that the volume of a cube is height × length × width; and then doing some pencil-and-paper calculations based on this formula. When Hart questioned them about two months afterwards, some remembered the formula and some did not; but even those who did remember it tended to say that the volume of a cube is height × length × width 'because that's what the teacher told us'. When they were asked if there were any relationship between the formula and their work with the little cubes, they usually said that there was not; and one child, when pressed, stated emphatically: 'Bricks is bricks and sums is sums!'

More recently, some researchers have found that – as suggested by the Edgeworths in 1798 – children tend to perform better if they are exposed *simultaneously* to different modes of representation: for example, numerals, words and concrete objects and are encouraged to make the links between them (Fuson, 1986; Fuson & Burghardt, 2003; Fuson, Fraivillig, & Burghardt, 1992; Hiebert & Wearne, 1992). This can take some weeks, but is more likely to lead to real links being made than approaches which involve starting with concrete objects and then moving on to numerical presentation, with only a very brief demonstration of the connections.

Use of concrete objects is not a panacea

'We may err either by accustoming our pupils too much to the consideration of tangible substantives when we teach them arithmetic or by turning their attention too much to signs [symbols].' (Richard and Maria Edgeworth: *Practical education*, London: J. Johnson, 1798, p. 248)

It is true that there is much evidence that arithmetical concepts and procedures are often aided by the use of concrete objects: most of all, perhaps, those 10 concrete objects that we have on our hands. It is also true that children are often confused by totally abstract, verbal teaching of arithmetic without reference to concrete objects or real-life situations and that such teaching can result in meaningless parroting, in a failure to see any point in arithmetic or in a complete misunderstanding of what the point is. Hollamby (1962) tells of a 6-year-old who thought that the 'two-times table' was the 'two-tons table': 'You know, like a ton of coal.'

It is not surprising that very young children perform better when carrying out additions and subtractions with objects than with number words or numerals. For one thing, as Hughes points out, the *language* of arithmetic is unfamiliar to young children: an issue discussed at greater length in Chapter 9. Children may not even be aware that 'two' and 'one' and other number words can be used on their own rather than as adjectives; witness the following conversation between Martin Hughes and 4-year-old Ram (Hughes, 1986, p. 45):

MH: How many is three and one more?
Ram: One more what?
MH: Just one more, you know?
Ram (disgruntled): I *don't* know.

However, it can be dangerous to assume that the use of concrete objects will of itself lead to a deep understanding of, or liking for, arithmetic. First of all, as some of the studies demonstrate, children do not always make the link between concrete and more formal arithmetic, even when they can learn to carry out both. Translation ability is essential if children are to be able to make this link; and, as we have seen, both individual and educational characteristics can influence the extent to which children are able to translate.

Second, some 'concrete' tasks may themselves be difficult or meaningless for some children. Lehr (1953) tells of a child who said that she 'didn't like arithmetic because she got tired of colouring rabbits'. Children who are poorly co-ordinated may find the procedures of dealing with concrete objects, especially under time pressure, so demanding that it distracts their attention from the concepts.

Back where we began: Individual differences in representation

It appears then that a better understanding of how children translate between formats and of how we can best encourage them to transfer their mathematical knowledge between different types of representation, will require a better understanding of individual differences in predominant modes of representation of number. This needs to be investigated across the age range. In particular, more research into number representation by deaf and blind people may help us to learn more about the different ways in which numbers may be represented.

6 Derived fact strategies

'If a child be required to divide a number of apples among a certain number of persons, he will contrive a way to do it, and will tell how many each must have. The method that children take to do these things, though always correct, is not always the most expeditious . . . To succeed it is necessary rather to furnish occasions for them to exercise their own skill in performing examples rather than to give them rules. They should be allowed to pursue their own method first, and then should be made to observe and explain it; and if it were not the best, some improvement should be suggested.' (cited by McIntosh, 1977)

Perhaps one of the most crucial aspects of arithmetical reasoning is the ability to derive and predict unknown arithmetical facts from known facts, by using arithmetical principles such as commutativity, associativity and the addition/subtraction inverse principle. For example, if we know that $44 + 23 = 67$, then we can use the commutativity principle to derive the fact that $23 + 44$ must also be 67. Without this ability, children will depend entirely on the facts that they have already learned and will be unable to go beyond them independently. Moreover, the complete inability to derive unknown arithmetical information from known information would seem, a priori, to imply a lack of understanding of the connections and interrelationships between individual number facts. By the same token, the ability to use derived fact strategies can compensate considerably even for quite severe calculation disabilities (Hittmair-Delazer, Semenza, & Denes, 1994; Hittmair-Delazer, Sailer, & Berke, 1995; Warrington, 1982). Derived fact strategies are probably of particular importance in mental calculation (Thompson, 1997a), although they are also used in written calculation.

The value placed on derived fact strategies varies markedly across countries and times. Some writings imply a sharp distinction between standard, 'school-taught', automatized, usually written strategies and non-standard, non-school-taught, often mental derived fact strategies. In fact, derived fact strategies and standard strategies can be best seen as parts of a continuum, rather than as totally distinct entities (Dowker, 2003a). Standard strategies for multi-digit arithmetic, when used with understanding, involve some of the same principles (e.g. associativity; distributivity) as derived fact strategies.

In the United Kingdom, recent changes in the curriculum (DfEE, 1999) with increased emphasis on mental rather than just written calculation, and on the flexible use of multiple strategies, have made the distinction less sharp from an educational point of view than was previously the case. 'Derived fact strategies' can also be school taught; and this will be discussed further in the section on 'Educational influences'.

Nevertheless, there are still important cognitive and educational distinctions to be made between the types of strategy: notably that standard strategies are far more dependent on memory and that derived fact strategies require far more explicit use of arithmetical principles. Developmental studies of children (Allardice & Ginsburg, 1983; Dowker, 1998; Ginsburg, 1977, 1997) and neuropsychological studies of patients (Hittmair-Delazer et al., 1994; Macaruco & Sokol, 1998; Warrington, 1982) demonstrate that very marked discrepancies frequently occur between the two.

Such strategies may involve:

1   *Decomposition.* This involves breaking up one or more of the terms in a sum or difference. For example, when asked to add $6 + 8$, a child may respond that $6 + 6 = 12$ and that $6 + 8$ is just 2 more, or 14. Such a child has decomposed 8 into $6 + 2$. Note that this strategy uses the associativity principle that $(a + b) + c = a + (b + c)$: in this case, $(2 + 6) + 6 = 2 + (6 + 6)$.

An example of a decomposition strategy for subtraction is to convert $12 - 5$ into $(12 - 2) - 3$ or $10 - 3$.

2   *Compensation.* At a slightly more sophisticated level, a child may use the fact that a change in one term is offset by a compensating change in another term: for example that $3 + 6$ must be 9, because $3 + 7 = 10$ and 6 is one less than 7. Again, the associativity principle is used.

3   *Regrouping.* When adding numbers with two or more digits, people may use such strategies as $21 + 32 = 20 + 30 + 1 + 2 = 5- + 3 = 53$. They may avoid the need for 'carrying' in this way: $34 + 47 = 30 + 40 + 4 + 7 = 70 + 11 = 81$. This strategy, which Pettito and Ginsburg (1982) found to be common among unschooled African Dioula children and adults, involves understanding place value and distributivity: $(a \times c) + (b \times c) = (a + b) \times c$. At least it involves understanding distributivity when $c = 10$. Such strategies are similar in some ways to the standard written algorithms, but differ from them in that the written algorithms generally involve adding from right to left, while informal regrouping strategies generally involve adding from left to right: first the tens and then the units. Adding from left to right is very rare as an informal strategy.

4   *Relationships between operations.* Children may use the fact that subtraction is the inverse of addition or that multiplication can usually be

represented as repeated addition to reduce subtraction or multiplication problems to addition, which may be easier for them.

To give a flavour, here are some examples of the use of derived fact strategies:

1   *Adult: How would you work out 23 + 44?*
    Joseph (aged 8): 'You would count on from 45, but you'd do one 10 and another 10 and then do a 3.'

2   *$7 \times 8 = ?$*
    Peter (7): '56 . . . I knew 10 8s, so I took away 8, that's 72, and another and another – 56.' (Plunkett, 1979, p. 2)

3   *23 – 17 = ?*
    Ross (aged about 10): '17 is 20 minus 3, and 3 and 3 is 6.' (Atkinson, 1992, p. 48)

4   *'How I worked out 6×8.'*
    'I knew that two eights were sixteen so I added another 8 on and that became 24 which was 3 eights. Then I added another 24 to that and it equalled 48 and that was my answer to 6×8.' (written account by James, aged about 7; reported by Proudfoot, 1992, p. 132)

5   *Adult: What is 6 – 3?*
    Julia (aged 4 years 9 months): 'Three. Because three and three are six.'

6   *Andrew (aged 5 years 10 months)* had a strong interest in number and performed at an 8- to 9-year-old level in standardized tests of arithmetic. When asked what was 7×7, he first multiplied 7×10 to get 70. He then worked out 7×3 by adding $7 + 7 + 7$ to get 21 and subtracted 21 from 70 to get 49. In other words, he realized that 7×7 is $(7 \times 10) - (7 \times 3)$.

7   *Agatha (aged 8 or 9)* and regarded as having difficulty with mathematics, was asked 'How much is 8×6?' She replied, 'The easy way to do it is 3×8 is 24. Then $24 + 24$ is 48.' And how much was 6×8? She said that the answer was 48 since 'the opposite is always the same'. (Ginsburg, 1989, p. 132)

8   *Hannah's (aged approximately 7)* account of how she did the sum 5 + 6: 'I looked back in my memory . . . six and six is twelve, so it's one less.' (Thompson, 1997a, p. 54)

9   *Adult: What is 11 – 3?*
    Louise (7 years 6 months): '11 is 2 lower than 13 so it's 8.' (obviously using the fact that $13 - 3 = 10$).

Early use of derived fact strategies

It has been clear for some time (Baroody, Ginsburg, & Waxman, 1983; Carpenter, 1980) that young primary school children often do use derived fact strategies, often without direct teaching. One of the earliest to emerge is the 'counting-on-from-larger' or 'min' concrete addition strategy, whereby the child adds two numbers (e.g. 2 + 6), by representing the larger number (e.g. with fingers) first and then 'counting on' the smaller number: '6, 7, 8 – it's 8!' This involves implicit use, with or without an explicit knowledge, of the commutativity principle (Baroody & Gannon, 1984; Cowan & Renton, 1996). By contrast, there are many sophisticated strategies involving the use of decomposition and decomposition for multi-digit arithmetic that appear late and appear to characterise unusually skilled mental calculators (Hope & Sherrill, 1987).

One of the earliest such strategies to emerge is probably the 'counting-on-from-larger' or 'min' strategy, whereby the child reverses the order of addends (for example, changing 2 + 8 into 8 + 2) so as to be able to count on from the larger rather than the smaller number, thus reducing the number of counting steps required. This is often used by children as young as 5 or 6.

Tests of derived fact strategies in young children have typically used variants of the technique of giving the children the answer to a problem and then asking them to solve another problem that could be solved quickly by using this answer, together with the property or relationship under consideration. Problems preceded by answers to numerically unrelated problems are usually given as controls, to test whether children calculate faster and/or more accurately when they have the opportunity to use the principle than when they do not.

One of the early studies to use this technique was that by Baroody et al. (1983). They studied 6- and 7-year-olds and investigated derived fact strategies involving three principles: commutativity (e.g. using the fact that 19 + 16 = 35 to help them solve the problem 16 + 19); the N + 1 principle (e.g. using the fact that 19 + 16 = 35 to help them solve the problem 19 + 17); and the addition/subtraction inverse principle (e.g. using the fact that 19 + 16 = 35 to help them solve the problem 35 – 16). More than half of the children used commutativity, even at the age of 6; and many 7-year-olds used the addition/subtraction inverse principle. Less than one-third even of the 7-year-olds used the N + 1 principle; but the study certainly provided evidence for the use of derived fact strategies by quite young children.

Derived fact strategy use by adolescents and adults

There has been surprisingly little research on the use of derived fact strategies by secondary school children or by adults. It is likely that such strategies continue to be important into adulthood and that there are extensive individual differences in the extent to which people use such strategies and the nature and variety of the strategies that they use. It would be desirable to investigate the extent of such individual differences and their relationship to individual differences in other aspects of arithmetic, such as mental and written calculation and estimation and in more abstract forms of mathematics such as algebra.

One of the few relevant studies in this area was carried out by Hope and Sherrill (1987). They investigated the self-reported mental multiplication strategies of 30 Canadian pupils from grades 11 and 12 (16- to 18-year-olds). Of these, 15 were classed as skilled calculators and 15 as unskilled calculators, on the basis of their performance on a calculation test. The unskilled pupils tended to solve the problems by using the same procedures as they would for written calculation. The most extreme case was probably a student's solution (p. 104) of the problem 20 × 30:

> 30 is on the top and 20 is on the bottom. 0 × 0 is 0. 0 × 3 is 0. Put down the 0. And 2 times 0 is 0, and 2 × 3 is 6. And then you add them together and you'd get . . . 6. 600?

By contrast, the skilled calculators rarely used such pencil-and-paper analogues and were more likely to use strategies based on the numerical properties of the particular numbers to be multiplied: distributivity-related strategies (e.g. 8 × 99 = 8 × 100 − 8 × 1), factoring and using fractional relationships (e.g. converting 25 to 25% or 1/4). Note that the strategies used by the skilled calculators in the mental multiplication task here have a considerable resemblance to those used by mathematically able adults in the estimation tasks described in Chapter 7.

A study of young children's derived fact strategy use, with particular reference to individual differences

This study investigated 5- to 9-year-olds' ability to use derived fact strategies, based on a range of principles, for both addition and subtraction. Part of this study was reported by Dowker (1998). It investigated explicit strategy use for relatively decontextualized arithmetical problems presented in numerical rather than concrete format. Therefore it may well provide a conservative measure of children's ability to apply arithmetical principles to the derivation of unknown facts.

The principles investigated in this study were selected for their apparent importance, combined with their applicability across a fairly wide range of difficulty. Some derived fact strategies, such as most counting-based strategies or those based on the use of doubles, are mainly applicable to single-digit arithmetic (Baroody, 1987; Carpenter & Moser, 1984); others, including certain decomposition strategies (Beentjes & Jonker, 1987; Beishuizen, 1993; Beishuizen, Van Putten, & Van Mulken, 1997; Carpenter, Franke, Jacobs, Fennema, & Empson, 1997; Fuson, 1990) are mainly applicable to multi-digit arithmetic. The strategies investigated in the study to be described were restricted to those that may be used for both single- and multi-digit arithmetic.

The principles investigated for addition were as follows:

1   The *identity principle* (e.g., if one is told that $8 + 6 = 14$, then one can automatically give the answer '14', without calculating, if asked 'What is $8 + 6$?'). This is the most basic of arithmetical principles: that if an arithmetical operation produces a given result, then the repetition of the same arithmetical principle will produce the same result. Its use in predicting the result of an arithmetical operation is properly speaking not a 'derived fact strategy' but a 'same-fact' strategy. Thus, its inclusion in the study is intended to investigate whether children possess the concept of using the result of an operation to predict the result of another at all, over and above the particular principles that they are able to use in such predictions.
2   The *commutativity principle* (e.g., if $9 + 4 = 13$, $4 + 9$ must also be 13).
3   The *N + 1 principle* (e.g., if $23 + 44 = 67$, $23 + 45$ must be 68).
4   The *N − 1 principle* (e.g., if $9 + 8 = 17$, $9 + 7$ must be $17 − 1$ or 16).
5   The *N × 10 principle* (e.g., if $26 + 72 = 98$, then $260 + 720 = 980$).
6   The *addition/subtraction inverse principle* (e.g., if $46 + 27 = 73$, then $73 − 27$ must be 46).

The principles investigated for subtraction were as follows:

1   The *identity principle* (e.g., if one is told that $12 − 5 = 7$, then one can automatically give the answer '7', without calculating, if asked 'What is $12 − 5$?').
2   The *minuend + 1 principle* (e.g., if $67 − 45 = 22$, $68 − 45$ must be 23).
3   The *minuend − 1 principle* (e.g., if $572 − 348 = 224$, $571 − 348$ must be 223).
4   The *subtrahend + 1 principle* (e.g., if $9 − 6 = 3$, $9 − 7$ must be 2).
5   The *subtrahend − 1 principle* (e.g., if $37 − 23 = 14$, $37 − 22$ must be 15).
6   The *addition/subtraction inverse principle* (e.g., if $681 − 214 = 467$, then $214 + 467$ must be 681).
7   The *complement principle* (e.g., if $11 − 3 = 8$, $11 − 8$ must be 3).

In the study, 291 primary school children ranging from 5 to 9 were tested individually. They included 20 5-year-olds; 121 6-year-olds; 60 7-year-olds; 52 8-year-olds; and 48 nine-year-olds). 115 were boys and 176 were girls.

In order to evaluate the children's competence in addition calculations, a mental calculation task was given to each child. This was the same test used in assessing children's mental calculation for the purpose of studying their estimation (Chapter 7); and consisted of a list of 20 addition sums graduated in difficulty from $4 + 5$, $7 + 1$, etc. to $235 + 349$. These sums were simultaneously presented orally and visually in a horizontal format. The

Table 6.1 Age and levels of arithmetical performance in addition

Level	Number of children	Mean age (years and months)	Standard deviation for age (months)	Problem just within range	Problem outside range
Beginning arithmetic	46	6; 4	5.1	2 + 2	5 + 3
Facts to 10	76	6; 9	11.85	5 + 3	8 + 6
Facts to 25	82	7; 2	14.7	8 + 6	23 + 44
2-digit (no carry)	24	7; 11	13.24	23 + 44	52 + 39
2-digit (carry)	43	8; 3	8.67	52 + 39	523 + 168
3-digit	20	8; 6	9.23	523 + 168	—
Total	*291*				

children's answers were oral. As in the estimation study (Chapter 7), the children were then divided into five levels according to their performance on the mental calculation task.

Table 6.1 gives brief descriptions of the levels, with numbers and children at each level, means and standard deviations for their ages and examples of the problems that could and could not be solved at these levels.

They were then given an arithmetical reasoning test involving use of arithmetical principles in derived fact strategies. The technique was used of giving children the answer to a problem and then asking them to solve another problem that could be solved quickly by using this answer, together with the principle under consideration (e.g. for the commutativity principle, children might be shown the problem 23 + 44 = 67 and then asked how much is 44 + 23). Problems preceded by answers to numerically unrelated problems were given as controls.

The exact arithmetic problems given varied according to the previously assessed calculation ability of the child and were selected to be just a little too difficult for the child to solve unaided. (Such a set of problems is referred to here as the child's base corresponding set.) Children of the highest (three-digit addition) level had no base corresponding set. They were given the same set as the next highest (two-digit addition; no carrying level). These were problems that they might have been able to solve by calculation and this fact must be taken into account when considering the results obtained from children at this level.

Each child was shown the arithmetic problems, while the researcher simultaneously read them to him/her. Children were asked to respond orally. The principles were those just listed for addition; and the children received three arithmetical problems per principle. On rare occasions, when there was serious ambiguity about the interpretation of their responses, they received a fourth problem.

A child was deemed to be able to use a principle if (s)he could explain it and/or used it to derive at least two out of three unknown arithmetical

Table 6.2 Percentages of children at each performance level using each of the principles for addition

	Beginning arithmetic	Facts to 10	Facts to 25	2-digit (no carry)	2-digit (carry)	3-digit	Total
Identity	22%	62%	75%	96%	84%	95%	68%
Commutativity	17%	45%	66%	96%	67%	90%	57%
N + 1	11%	29%	65%	88%	63%	75%	49%
N − 1	7%	24%	56%	75%	60%	70%	43%
× 10	0%	0%	13%	17%	19%	30%	10%
Inverse	0%	7%	10%	5%	14%	30%	9%
Number of children	46	76	82	24	43	20	291

Table 6.3 Age and levels of arithmetical performance in subtraction

Level	Number of children	Mean age (years and months)	Standard deviation for age (months)	Problem just within range	Problem outside range
Beginning arithmetic	36	5; 11	8.75	?	6 − 3
Facts to 10	62	6; 6	8.35	6 − 3	12 − 5
Facts to 25	54	7; 3	12.71	12 − 5	58 − 34
2-digit (no borrow)	27	7; 10	10.9	58 − 34	82 − 26
2-digit (borrow)	24	8; 5	10.06	82 − 26	893 − 515
Total	203				

facts, while being unable to calculate any sums of similar difficulty when there was no opportunity to use the principle.

Table 6.2 gives the means and ranges of the numbers (out of 6) of the arithmetical principles used by the children at each level.

Two hundred and three of the children were given a very similar test for subtraction. Once again, the children were given a calculation pretest, this time consisting of a list of 20 subtraction problems, ranging in difficulty from 6 − 2 to 572 − 148. Again, the children were then divided into five levels according to their performance on the mental calculation task.

Table 6.3 gives brief descriptions of the levels, with numbers and children at each level, means and standard deviations for their ages and examples of the problems that could and could not be solved at these levels.

The children were given a use of principles task for subtraction, which was similar to that used for addition. The principles were those listed earlier.

Table 6.4 gives the means and ranges of the numbers (out of 7) of the arithmetical principles used by the children at each level.

Most (91%) of children classed as using the principles were able to justify their answers.

Table 6.4 Percentages of children at each performance level using each of the principles for subtraction

	Beginning arithmetic	Facts to 10	Facts to 25	2-digit (no carry)	2-digit (carry)	Total
Identity	33%	66%	89%	85%	100%	73%
Minuend + 1: **Correct**	5%	39%	61%	63%	88%	48%
+1/−1 **confusion**	0	8%	20%	7%	0	9%
Minuend − 1: **Correct**	3%	23%	56%	59%	83%	40%
+1/−1 **confusion**	0	19%	24%	15%	0	14%
Subtrahend + 1: **Correct**	3%	6%	7%	19%	33%	11%
+1/−1 **confusion**	0	31%	74%	52%	58%	43%
Subtrahend − 1: **Correct**	3%	3%	7%	19%	25%	8%
+1/−1 **confusion**	0	32%	72%	52%	63%	38%
Inverse	0	6%	9%	26%	33%	14%
Complement	0	6%	2%	22%	25%	8%
Number of children	36	62	54	27	24	203

Typical justifications included:

> (*Identity*): 'It's the same!'
> (*Commutativity principle for addition*): 'Those numbers are just the same, but the other way round.'
> (*N + 1 principle for addition; minuend + 1 principle for subtraction*): 'It's just one more.'
> (*N − 1 principle for subtraction; minuend − 1 principle for subtraction*): 'It's just one less.'
> (*Subtrahend + 1 principle for subtraction*): (Correctly): 'That's one more, so the answer has to be one less.' (Incorrectly): 'It's just one more.'
> (*Subtrahend − 1 principle for subtraction*): (Correctly): 'That's one less, so the answer has to be one more.' (Usually, incorrectly): 'It's just one less.'
> ((× 10) *principle*): 'You just add on a 0.'
> (*Addition − subtraction inverse principle*): 'Because that [8] + 6 = 14, so 14 take away that [8] must be 6.'
> (*Complement principle for subtraction*): 'If that [12] take away that [5] = 7, then that [12] take away that [7] must be 5.'

Seventy of the children were also given the addition estimation task, described in Chapter 7.

The particular arithmetical performance measures included in the analysis were: (1) addition level; (2) use of addition principles for derived fact strategies; (3) subtraction level; (4) use of subtraction principles for derived fact strategies; and (5) addition estimation.

For the purpose of the analysis, these were defined in a simplified way by single numerical values. (2) and (4) were defined as the numbers of the principles (out of 6 for addition, and out of 7 for subtraction) that were accepted and used in derived fact strategies. (5) was defined as the number of estimates, within the base correspondence, that were reasonable. Reasonable estimates were defined (Dowker, 1989a) as those that were within 30% of the correct answer and that were also less than the larger addend (see Chapter 7).

The background and psychometric measures that were investigated were:

- gender
- social class
- age (in months)
- WISC verbal IQ
- WISC performance IQ
- WISC arithmetic scaled score
- WISC Digit Span scaled score.

Analyses of variance (see Dowker, 1998) showed that there was an overwhelming association between derived fact strategy use in addition and subtraction. If children used derived fact strategies for one operation, they tended to use them for the other.

Derived fact strategy use was not influenced by gender. In both addition and subtraction, calculation performance level was very significantly associated with derived fact strategy use. Children who had achieved a higher level of arithmetical calculation performance tended to make greater use of derived fact strategies. When calculation performance (which, of course, tended to increase with age) was controlled, age did not have any independent effect on use of derived fact strategies in addition, but older children did tend to use more derived fact strategies than younger children for subtraction. IQ also made an important independent contribution to derived fact strategy use, with verbal IQ being more important for addition, while both verbal and performance IQ were important for subtraction.

Verbal/performance IQ discrepancies *in either direction* were significantly related to extent of use of derived fact strategy use in addition, but not to their use in subtraction or to calculation performance. Thus, children who were either significantly better or worse at verbal than nonverbal tasks were also likely to be better at derived fact strategies than at calculation (at least as regards addition). One possible explanation (Dowker, 1998) is that children with uneven patterns of abilities learn in many situations to seek and adopt alternative strategies when 'standard' procedures do not work; and this may make them more likely to devise and use non-standard strategies in arithmetic.

A final important point is that there was a very strong independent relationship between estimation score and derived fact strategy use. This relationship was stronger than the relationship between calculation and derived fact strategy use.

Thus, derived fact strategy use was related to calculation ability; to IQ; to the existence of a verbal/performance IQ discrepancy, and most of all, to estimation.

Differential use of different derived fact strategies

So far, the use of derived fact strategies has been considered as a general skill or process, which varies quantitatively: some children use more derived fact strategies than others do. But it is also the case that some strategies are used much more readily than others. Although the main focus of this chapter is individual differences in derived fact strategy use, such individual differences cannot be fully understood without considering the relative difficulty of different strategies.

In the present study, sign tests for the whole sample of 291 children confirmed significant differences between the different types of derived fact strategy. Identity was used more frequently than commutativity; commutativity was used more frequently than the $N + 1$ strategy; the $N + 1$ strategy was used more frequently than the $N - 1$ strategy; and the $N - 1$ strategy was used more frequently than the $N \times 10$ strategy or the inverse strategy. The $N \times 10$ strategy did not differ significantly in frequency from the inverse strategy. The two last strategies were infrequently used by children in this age group.

Although some strategies were much easier overall than others, there was not a consistent hierarchy of strategies, such that the use of any given strategy was dependent on the use of another, easier, one. There were occasional dissociations in both directions between almost any two strategies. The only exception is that no child used the $N \times 10$ strategy without also using the identity strategy.

Despite this lack of a consistent hierarchy, it is notable that most children who used the identity strategy also used other strategies. When only children who used the identity strategy for addition were considered, at least one other strategy was also used by 55% of children at the beginning arithmetic level, 70% of children at the facts to 10 level, 93% of children at the facts to 25 level, 100% of children at the two-digit addition (no carrying) level, 92% of children at the two-digit addition (carrying) level; and 100% of children at the three-digit addition level.

Chi-square tests showed significant differences between children of the different calculation performance levels as regards their use of each of the addition strategy types. Every one of the strategy types was used more frequently by the more proficient calculators than by the less proficient calculators.

There were also significant differences between different types of strategy in the subtraction task. Identity was used more frequently than the minuend + 1 strategy; the minuend + 1 strategy was used more frequently than the minuend − 1 strategy; and the minuend − 1 strategy was used more frequently than the subtrahend + 1 strategy or the subtrahend − 1 strategy. The subtrahend + 1 strategy did not differ significantly from the subtrahend − 1 strategy. Both the last two strategies were used more frequently than the inverse strategy, but did not differ significantly in frequency from the complement strategy. The inverse strategy was used significantly more frequently than the complement strategy.

Once again, there was no consistent hierarchy of strategy use, except that the more advanced strategies (subtrahend + 1, subtrahend − 1, inverse and complement) were only used by children who also used the identity strategy. Once again, children who used the identity principle usually used other strategies as well.

When only children who used the identity strategy for subtraction were considered, at least one other strategy was also used by only 17% of children at the beginning arithmetic level, but 70% of children at the facts to 10 level, 88% of children at the facts to 25 level, 78% of children at the two-digit addition (no carrying) level and 92% of children at the two-digit addition (carrying) level.

Chi-square tests again showed significant differences between children of the different levels with regard to their correct use of each one of the strategies. There was also a significant increase with level in the incorrect subtraction strategies based on +1/−1 confusion. Thus, at least in this age group, erroneous use of subtraction strategies based on the addition or subtraction of 1 to a component of a problem were associated with a higher level of arithmetical performance than failure to use such strategies at all.

Some strategies in addition cannot be used in the same way for subtraction: notably subtraction is not commutative. But some strategies such as the N + 1, N − 1 and inverse strategies are very similar in addition and subtraction. Are children equally ready to use such strategies for addition and subtraction or are they readier to use them for the perhaps more familiar and congenial operation of addition than for subtraction? In the case of the 203 children given both tasks, sign tests were used to compare the following pairs of similar strategies:

1   identity for addition and identity for subtraction
2   N + 1 for addition and minuend + 1 for subtraction

3   N − 1 for addition and minuend − 1 for subtraction
4   addition/subtraction inverse and subtraction/addition inverse.

These were carried out for two groups of children: those who were at the same level for addition and subtraction and who were at higher levels for addition than subtraction. None of the sign tests proved statistically significant for either group. Thus, children are not readier to use any of these derived fact strategies for one operation than for the other. As has been seen, the nature of subtraction does, however, create complications that do not exist for addition as regards the decision as to whether adding to or subtracting from a component will increase or decrease the result.

There is, thus, no doubt that some arithmetical relationships are more readily used than others in derived fact strategies. There is, however, considerable individual variability in preference, such that almost any arithmetical principle may be used by an individual child in the absence of almost any other arithmetical principle.

The most basic principle, identity, was used with by far the greatest frequency and is the only strategy that seemed to be a prerequisite for some, although not most, of the other strategies. This was followed by commutativity of addition, supporting other studies that suggest the early use of this principle (Baroody et al., 1983; Cowan & Renton, 1996; Sophian, Harley, & Martin, 1995); and those strategies that involve adding, or (to a lesser extent) subtracting, 1 from a problem component and thereby to the result.

Strategies of the latter type could be, and often were, used incorrectly as well as correctly. For example, as we have seen, children are more likely, if told that $a - b = c$, to deduce that $a - (b + 1) = c + 1$, than correctly that $a - (b + 1) = c - 1$. In other words, when using this class of strategies, they often fail to make appropriate use of compensation. There are many possible explanations for such findings, ranging from working memory limitations to difficulties with reversibility in a Piagetian sense, but at least one major factor is likely to be that the arithmetical relationships most accessible to children are those appropriate to addition and that these are overextended to subtraction (see Chapter 2).

MacCuish (1986) found that slightly older children overextended the characteristics of addition to multiplication in a somewhat similar way. They tended to assume that $(a + 1) \times b = (a \times b) + 1$, rather than $(a \times b) + b$. For example, they assumed that if $31 \times 3 = 93$, then 32×3 must be 94: 32 is 1 more than 31, so (32×3) must be 1 more than (31×3).

In the present study, explicit use of the '× 10' strategy (here only tested for addition) was surprisingly rare and late in appearing, despite its fundamental importance to the understanding of multi-digit arithmetic. Further studies would be needed to establish whether the relative failure to use this strategy was due to the fact that it would have sometimes resulted in larger numbers than children at a given level could handle; to metacognitive limitations; or to real conceptual limitations in under-standing place value.

Strategies based on the inverse relationship between addition and subtraction: Are these particularly difficult?

The present study suggested that inversion strategies ($a + b - b = a$; if $a + b = c$, then $c - b = a$) are more difficult than many other derived fact strategies, and are rarely used by 5- to 9-year-old children. The same was true of the logically related complement principle: if $a - b = c$, then $a - c = b$.

The study was carried out before the introduction into Britain of the current National Numeracy Strategy, which has placed an increased emphasis on derived fact strategies in general and which encourages the use of the inverse relationship between addition and subtraction at the age of 6 or 7. Is this expectation unreasonable or would children now do better at using this principle?

Some primary school teachers have indeed remarked to me that children, especially those who are relatively weak at school arithmetic, find it difficult to understand and use this inverse relationship. Even with regard to older children, Lankford (1974) found that 7th-graders (12- and 13-year-olds) who had been taught about the inverse relationship between addition and subtraction made relatively little spontaneous use of this relationship in their arithmetic.

However, not all children have difficulty in acquiring the principle (we may remember Julia, who, before the age of 5, already realized that as $3 + 3 = 6$, $6 - 3$ must be 3).

Most studies concur with the present one in suggesting that the addition/subtraction inverse relationship is acquired quite late and is rarely used by children under the age of about 10 (e.g. Bisanz & Lefevre, 1990; Demby, 1993). However, it is noteworthy that Baroody et al. (1983) found that many 7- and 8-year-olds used this strategy and that it typically preceded the N + 1 strategy. Bryant, Christie, and Rendu (1999) found that, if the tasks were made sufficiently concrete, 6- to 8-year-old children understood that addition and subtraction cancel each other out and were able to use this principle to solve problems of the type $a + b - (b + 1)$.

It thus seems that the exact nature of the task, and perhaps individual differences in children's mathematical concepts or prior mathematical experience, can have a lot of influence on when and whether they use the addition/subtraction inverse relationship. It certainly need not be that all children, who failed to use such strategies necessarily lacked conceptual knowledge of the inverse relationship between addition and subtraction. However, whether they possessed this concept or not, most in the present study did not use their knowledge of addition facts to assist their subtrac-tion, or vice versa, and they sometimes explicitly referred to the distinctness of the two operations: 'It doesn't help, because that one's adding and that one's taking away.'

Further research might investigate whether there are any important characteristics that differentiate children who do and do not find this principle easy to understand.

Problem difficulty, estimation and use of derived fact strategies

Estimation studies (see Chapter 7) indicate that children are most likely to *estimate* effectively if the problems are just a little too difficult to be solved readily by mental calculation. Both activities involve deriving arithmetical facts (approximate in the case of estimation; exact in the case of derived fact strategies), which the individual cannot or does not calculate by means of standard algorithms. Thus, examining the interaction between the child's arithmetical knowledge and the difficulty of the problem domain is appropriate to both activities. It might be expected that children will make relatively little use of either estimation or derived fact strategies when problems are sufficiently easy to be readily calculated; although in the present study the children at the three-digit addition level did make extensive use of derived fact strategies for problems below their 'base correspondence'. It is also expected that derived fact strategy use, like estimation (Dowker, 1997; Chapter 7 in this volume), would deteriorate if children were presented with more and more difficult beyond the base correspondence.

There have already been a few studies relevant to the issue. Webb (1995) presented 40 children (20 6-year-olds and 20 8-year-olds) with addition and subtraction derived fact problems according to a procedure similar in most respects to that in the present study. Children were given problems requiring the derivation of arithmetical facts of varying levels of difficulty. Increased difficulty tended to result in 6-year-olds using more derived fact strategies for addition and fewer for subtraction, whereas 8-year-olds were more likely to show stable performance in the face of increasing difficulty. Surprisingly, within each age group, calculation performance level was not related to extent or direction of change in strategy use when difficulty was increased. However, caution is needed in interpreting these results because the sample size, range of problems and range of calculation performance levels within each age group were all relatively low.

Banks (1998) gave 5- and 6-year-olds, most but not all of whom were at the facts to 10 level for addition and subtraction, derived fact strategy problems, similar to Sets 1 and 2, in concrete (using blocks) and numerical formats. Children were more accurate for concrete than numerical presentations, but made similar use of derived fact strategies. They were somewhat more ready to use derived fact strategies for the more difficult problems, similar to Set 2, than for the easier problems, similar to Set 1, which for most participants were readily calculable without the use of such strategies.

So far, one may suspect that, at least within a broad general range of difficulty, children's use of derived fact strategies will be influenced by problem difficulty, but to a lesser extent than their estimation.

Derived fact strategy use and knowledge of arithmetical facts and procedures

Although rigid overemphasis on memorization and/or on the use of a few specific taught procedures is likely to inhibit the use of derived fact strategy use, it is certainly not the case that knowing the facts and procedures is in itself inimical to derived fact strategy use. In fact, the present study and some others (e.g. Canobi et al., 1998) suggest that, on the whole, children who are more competent at calculation also tend to use more derived fact strategies.

Access to known facts and automatized procedures actually facilitates the use of derived fact strategies. Since derived fact strategies require starting from known fact(s), some facts must be known by heart, presented to the child by teachers or others, obtained on a calculator or worked out by counting or the use of a calculation procedure before they can be used as the basis for derived fact strategies. If children know few facts and/or standard procedures, then their basis for use of derived fact strategies will be more limited.

Some recent researchers (e.g. Siegler & Jenkins, 1989) emphasize the complementary relationships between memory for facts and the ability to derive new facts on the basis of known facts.

It must be remembered, however, that the relationship between arithmetical ability and derived fact strategy use is likely to depend in part on which alternative strategies are being considered. Many studies (e.g. Renton, 1992) suggest that retrieval of facts from memory is positively associated with arithmetical ability; and, of course, if a child knows an arithmetical fact, (s)he does not need to derive it. Contrariwise, at least beyond the age of 6 or so, use of the counting-all strategy appears to be negatively associated with arithmetical ability; so that a more arithmetically able child might be expected to prefer derived fact strategies to counting all.

What children must understand in order to use derived fact strategies

The use of derived fact strategies involves several processes:

1　The understanding of the underlying principles on which they are based: e.g. commutativity of addition; the inverse relationship between addition and subtraction. These in turn may depend on broader arithmetical principles: e.g. part/whole relationships.
2　Strategy selection and implementation and the appropriate and flexible use of strategies.

3   The capacity for unknown fact derivation: i.e. the ability to cope with uncertainty and to realize that the absence of a memorized fact or well-learned procedure does not imply a lack of any knowledge at all about the arithmetical problem. This is relevant both to estimation, where the answers to unknown arithmetic problems are derived approximately, and to derived fact strategy use, where they are derived exactly but by 'non-standard' methods.

These processes will now be discussed further.

Knowledge of arithmetical principles

Most studies (Baroody et al., 1983; my study described earlier) have suggested that children do understand the principles behind the derived fact strategies that they use, in that they can frequently justify them. However, the studies have tended to assume that if children can use the strategy, they can understand the principle. This assumption has sometimes been questioned: for example, Baroody and Gannon (1984) have argued the counting-on-from-larger strategy in addition, in order to save mental effort, without really understanding commutativity. If asked to add 2 + 8, they may convert it to 8 + 2 because this is easier to solve; but may not truly understand that 8 + 2 must of necessity give the same answer as 2 + 8.

Renton (1992) studied 6- to 10-year-olds and found that most understood the commutativity of addition, both with numbers and with sets of concrete objects. There was, however, no relationship between understanding of commutativity and use of the counting-on-from-larger strategy.

In this context, particular emphasis has been placed by some researchers on the understanding of part–whole relationships. This was one of the concepts that Piaget considered that young children fail to understand adequately. Resnick (1983) considered that this is a prerequisite to the understanding and use of the commutativity of addition, since the latter implies awareness that the order of presentation of the parts does not affect their relation to the whole. Putnam, de Bettencourt, and Leinhardt (1990) extended this view to argue that there are two major components to the knowledge underlying derived fact strategies: mapping a problem onto the part–whole schema and making transformations to elements of the part–whole schema.

The relationship between understanding the principles, and the use of derived fact strategies, was the major focus of a study by Canobi, Reeve, and Pattison (1998). They gave 48 children between 6 and 8 two derived fact strategy tasks. In one of these, they were given problems that were preceded either by an arithmetically related or unrelated problem and their speed and accuracy were compared in the two conditions. They were also asked to say what strategies they had used. In the other task, they had to judge whether a puppet could use the arithmetical properties of one problem to solve the next problem. The arithmetical relationships studied were commutativity and associativity. In commutativity-based problems, the second problem included the same addends as the first, but in a different order: e.g. the sum 3 + 2 was immediately preceded by 2 + 3, and the sum 4 + 3 + 5 was immediately preceded by 5 + 4 + 3. Associativity-based problems involved either decomposing one of the terms of an immediately preceding two-term problem to form a three-term problem (e.g. 9 + 2 followed by 3 + 6 + 2) or adding the first two terms of an immediately preceding three-term problem to form a two-term problem (e.g. 7 + 4 + 5 followed by 7 + 9).

Children explicitly reported using commutativity on 48% of the occasions where it was possible to do so; but associativity on only 11% of such occasions. In support of these self-reports, they were significantly faster at solving commutativity-based problems than similar unrelated problems, but showed no differences in speed of solution of associativity-based problems and similar unrelated problems.

They were considerably better at judging and justifying the appropriateness of a puppet's use of such strategies than at using the strategies themselves. Even according to a strict criterion, requiring correct justification as well as judgement, 67% of their responses to commutativity-based problems and 46% of their associativity-based problems.

A particularly important aspect of this study is the finding that accurate performance on tasks that explicitly tested the understanding and use of commutativity and associativity was closely linked to the spontaneous use of arithmetical strategies based on these principles. Canobi et al. investigated children's self-reported strategy use on unrelated problems. They found that recognition and use of commutativity on the derived fact strategy tasks was closely related to the use of the 'counting-on-from-larger' strategy on unrelated problems. Recognition and use of associativity on the derived fact strategy tasks was closely related to the use of decomposition strategies on unrelated problems.

Multiple strategy use

Most children use a wide variety of strategies – including a large number of derived fact strategies – in arithmetic, at least if they have not been taught not to do so (Ginsburg, 1977). Siegler and his colleagues have found multiple and variable strategy use to be one of the most central features of children's arithmetical development (Kerkman & Siegler, 1997; Siegler, 1987; Siegler & Jenkins, 1989).

Multiple strategy use can be observed in almost *any* group of children, including educationally disadvantaged children (Baroody, Berent, & Packman, 1982; Jordan, Huttenlocher, & Levine, 1994a) and even some children with severe learning difficulties (Baroody & Snyder, 1983).

However, it is usually found that more successful calculators use a wider variety of arithmetical strategies, including a wider variety of derived fact strategies (see Chapter 1 for a discussion of the crucial role of strategy flexibility in mathematical talent). This is found for young children (Beentjes & Jonker, 1987); older children (Hope & Sherrill, 1987; Krutetskii, 1976) and adults (Dowker, 1992; Dowker et al., 1996b; Gilles, Masse, & Lemaire, 2001; Chapter 1 in this volume). Experience with using an arithmetical operation tends to increase the flexibility of strategy use for that operation (Kerkman & Siegler, 1995; Siegler & Jenkins, 1989).

A few studies have shown a less clear-cut relationship. Kerkman and Siegler (1993) found that 'good' and 'not-so-good' first- and second-grade pupils did not differ in their ability to adapt their strategies to the nature of a problem – e.g. using back-up strategies such as finger counting if the problem was too difficult for them to solve without such aids – though they did differ as to which problems were difficult for them and as to how efficiently they used their strategies. Ainsworth, Wood, and O'Malley (1998) found little relationship between 7-year-olds' mathematical ability and their production of multiple solutions and suggested (p. 156) that this might be because the mathematically more able children had 'already stabilised their notions about the nature of mathematics' (e.g. one correct answer per problem as quickly as possible).

As suggested in Chapter 1, there may be a U-shaped relationship between strategy variability and mathematical knowledge, with both novices and experts using more strategies than at an intermediate stage who have fixed on one or two strategies. It is possible that this U-shaped curve may explain the occasionally conflicting results from different studies.

Unknown fact derivation, estimation and the zone of partial knowledge and understanding

Chapter 7 discusses a 'zone of partial knowledge and understanding' for arithmetic, which is also applicable to other domains. My estimation studies indicate that people do not either 'know' or 'not know' how to do particular types of arithmetic of given levels of difficulty. Knowledge and understanding, even of very specific topics or skills, tend to be made up of many components and these components are not 'all-or-none' objects that one either has or does not have: they vary in degree with respect to the individual, with respect to the *difficulty of the problem relative to the individual* and often with respect to apparently random and unpredictable factors. Individuals frequently understand *some* but not all aspects of an arithmetical concept and/or can carry out *some* but not all aspects of an arithmetic procedure. The greater an individual's arithmetical expertise with respect to the problem space, the more components will be present and to a higher degree. The more difficult a problem with respect to an individual's performance, the fewer components will be present and the weaker the remaining components will be. But there is no strict hierarchy of components. Neither can we find any monotonic relationship between expertise, problem difficulty and level of knowledge or understanding of particular components that applies across individuals, across tasks or even necessarily to the same individual and task at slightly different times (see Chapter 2 for further discussion of this issue).

It is proposed here that derived fact strategies may characterize a region of the zone of partial knowledge and understanding where the problem cannot be solved readily by using retrieval or an automatized procedure, but can still be calculated exactly.

Use of derived fact strategies and estimation within the zone of partial knowledge and understanding do, however, both depend on the child's willingness to accept uncertainty: to use a procedure that is not automatized and may not work; perhaps to accept an approximate rather than an exact solution. This depends, in turn, on having a conceptual understanding, at least implicitly; that there is not only one correct solution process or in many cases even only one correct solution; and on not fearing uncertainty. This acceptance of uncertainty may be one important common factor that leads to close statistical associations between derived fact strategy use and estimation and between both of these processes and strategy variability.

Metacognition: The ability to reflect on strategy use – is this another cognitive factor in the use of derived fact strategies?

Although estimation and derived fact strategy use have several things in common, there seems to be one very important difference. Most young children are not able to describe or explain their estimation strategies effectively (Dowker, 1997) while they usually can describe their derived fact strategies.

Carr and Jessup (1995) found that second-grade (7-year-old) children's ability to describe the strategies that they used was positively related to successful use of decomposition strategies, but not to retrieval or counting-on-from-larger strategies. They argued that metacognition is important when a strategy that requires a lot of effort is in process of being acquired; but not for strategies that require less effort or have already been acquired. It might be added that verbal rehearsal is important when a strategy places particular strain of the use of working memory to keep track of and organize information (see Chapter 8).

Educational and environmental influences

There have been enormous variations across time and place in educational attitudes to derived fact strategies, ranging from active discouragement to explicit encouragement and teaching.

At the time when many of the relevant studies were done (the 1970s and 1980s) use of derived fact strategies was not strongly encouraged.

A number of researchers have commented on the fact that children often invent their own non-standard algorithms, but that adults have tended at best to ignore them, and often actively to discourage them. Cobb, Yackel, and Wood (1991, p. 104) summarize the conclusions of many researchers on mathematical development: 'It is generally accepted that . . . students' informal ways of making meaning are given little attention.'

Holt (1965) drew the distinction between the mathematical strategies of 'producers' and 'thinkers'. Producers were only interested in getting right answers and used rules and formulae uncritically, in the way that one might follow a recipe. Thinkers attended to the meaning of the problem. In Holt's view, most children and indeed teachers were 'producers': 'answer centred' rather than 'problem centred': 'They see a problem as some kind of announcement that, far off in some mysterious Answerland, there is an answer, which they are supposed to go out and find' (p. 95). Thinkers attended to arithmetical relationships and sometimes used derived fact strategies. Producers did not.

These last quotes come from the United States. In recent years, British education has probably tended to give more encouragement than much North American education to flexible strategy use in mathematics. However, this is a recent development. Dowker and Dowker (1979, p. 47) commented on mathematics education in the late 1970s:

> Most educators cannot imagine that there is such a thing as creative activity in mathematics. When a teacher says, 'That is not the right way to draw a house, this is the right way', she knows that she should not, or at least she knows that some educators believe that she should not. But when she says, 'That is not the right way to subtract, this is the right way', she is supported by educational theory . . . Too many educators and teachers and all too many textbooks for primary schools agree that for every question in mathematics there is only one right method, though they do not agree on which is the right method.

Recent educational approaches in some parts of Europe have, by contrast, come to emphasize the fact that the same problem can be solved in more than one way. The use of derived fact strategies is a central part of the current British National Numeracy Strategy. For examples, objectives proposed by the National Centre for Literacy and Numeracy for children in Year 1 (5- to 6-year-olds) include, among many others:

> Put the larger number first (i.e. the min strategy).
>
> Identify near doubles, using doubles already known (e.g. 6 + 5 is close to 5 + 5).

Add 9 to single-digit numbers by adding 10 then subtracting 1.

Use patterns of similar calculations (e.g. $10 - 0 = 10$; $10 - 1 = 9$; $10 - 2 = 8$).

Use the relationship between addition and subtraction.

Objectives proposed for children in Year 2 (6- to 7-year-olds) include:

Identify near doubles, using doubles already known (e.g. $8 + 9$; $40 + 41$).

Partition into 5 and a bit when adding 6, 7, 8 or 9; then recombine.

Add 9 or 11 by adding/subtracting and adjusting by 1; begin to add or subtract 19 or 21 by adding/subtracting 20 and adjusting by 1.

Use the relationship between multiplication and division.

Whether such teaching is indeed effective remains to be fully tested: although there have been several training studies in the area (Adetula, 1996; Markowits & Sowder, 1994; Steinberg, 1985; Thornton, 1978), which suggest that such training can be successful at least in the short term. It is notable, at any rate, that unlike the children studied by Baroody et al. (1983), none of those in my own more recent studies expressed the view that it was cheating to use shortcuts.

Environmental contexts that influence the use of derived fact strategies need not be scholastic (see Chapter 9 in this volume). There is much evidence (e.g. Carraher, Carraher, & Schliemann, 1985; Lave, 1988; Nunes et al., 1993; Schliemann et al., 1998) that some older children and adults, at least in certain cultures, develop such strategies despite – or perhaps because – of having limited or no formal education; and that even those who do attend school may use such strategies more readily and effectively in 'real-life' problem-solving situations than in school arithmetic. These strategies are sometimes associated with particular occupations that require arithmetical calculations: e.g. tailors, fishermen, street traders. In some cases, these strategies may be taught as cultural practices by experienced workers in these occupations. In others, they may be spontaneously acquired in a context that 'makes sense' to the individual, but may not be transferred to the school situation, even when the individual does attend school: perhaps because school mathematics is not seen as meaningful or because the school system in the country or region in question may actually discourage derived fact strategy use.

Derived fact strategies in mental and written arithmetic

It is often considered that derived fact strategies are more characteristic of mental arithmetic than of written arithmetic: both in the sense that children are more likely to invent derived fact strategies for mental arithmetic than for written arithmetic and in the sense that the 'standard' strategies for mental arithmetic are closer to derived fact strategies than are the standard strategies for written arithmetic. Mental arithmetic is more easily carried out than written arithmetic by processes that involve 'counting on' or 'counting down' from a given number: processes that are central to many derived fact strategies (Merttens & Brown, 1996). Moreover, multi-digit written arithmetic is usually carried out from right to left (units first) while multi-digit arithmetic is usually carried out from left to right (hundreds before tens and tens before units). When carrying out arithmetic from left to right, the overall magnitude of the number is more salient from the beginning, which is likely to make conceptually based strategies – and especially those that are related to estimation – more accessible (Baroody, 1987; Ginsburg, 1977). By contrast, when arithmetic is carried out from left to right, the size of the result may only become apparent when the calculation is completed. Children do sometimes use derived fact and other invented strategies in written multi-digit calculation (Bird, 1992; Clarke, 1992; Fuson et al., 1997; Ginsburg, 1977; Thompson, 1997a) but it appears more difficult to do so for written than mental calculation.

It is partly for these reasons that mathematics teaching in some parts of continental Europe has for some time emphasized mental more than written arithmetic in the early primary school years (Beishuizen, 2001; Bierhoff, 1996) and that the British mathematics curriculum has recently been changed in accordance with this approach (DfEE, 1999; Thompson, 1997b).

Strategies used by primary school children for mental addition and subtraction of numbers between 20 and 100 received relatively little attention in the past, with a few notable exceptions (Ginsburg, 1977; Holt, 1965) as the emphasis was on written calculation of such problems. They have received increasing attention in recent years (Anghileri, 1995; Beishuizen, 1997; Buys, 2001; Carpenter, Franke, Jacobs, Fennema, & Empson, 1998; Foxman & Beishuizen, 1999; Fuson et al., 1997; Thompson, 2000). One classification (Thompson, 2000) puts such strategies into the following broad categories:

1   The partitioning or split method ($37 + 25$ as $30 + 20 = 50$; $7 + 5 = 12$; $50 + 12 = 62$).
2   The mixed method, similar to the above but mixing additions and subtractions ($63 - 28$ as $60 - 20 = 40$; $40 + 3 = 43$; $43 - 8 = 35$).
3   The sequencing method ($63 - 28$ as $63 - 20 = 43$; $43 - 8 = 35$).
4   The compensation method, involving rounding strategies followed by adjustments ($37 + 25$ as 37 is 3 less than 40; $40 + 25 = 65$; $65 - 3 = 62$).
5   The complementary addition method, used for subtraction (for $63 - 28$: 28 to 30 is 2; 30 to 60 is 30; 60 to 63 is 3. $2 + 30 + 3 = 35$).

Further research is needed to establish the nature and extent of relationships between children's – and adults' – use of derived fact strategies that are applicable to small numbers, those that are applicable to larger numbers, and those that are applicable to both.

Foundations of derived fact strategy use

We have drawn certain tentative conclusions about individual differences in the use of derived fact strategies. Children are more likely to use derived fact strategies if they are reasonably good at calculation and, especially, if they are good estimators. They are also more likely to use them if they are cognitively uneven, so that their verbal reasoning is either much better or much worse than their spatial reasoning. Environmental factors are also important: they are more likely to use derived fact strategies if they are taught to do so, or, at least, if they are not discouraged from doing so. Such factors may also be important in adults; but there have been remarkably few studies of derived fact strategy use in adults, except for those with impaired calculation resulting from brain damage.

In order to gain a stronger understanding of derived fact strategy use, it would be desirable to investigate their foundations. Although there is some evidence that certain derived fact strategies have a link with counting (Baroody, 1987; Thompson, 1997a), there has been little or no research on early predictors of the later use of derived fact strategies.

I would propose the theory that the commoner strategies (those involving commutativity and the N + 1 and N − 1 principles) are ultimately derived from the ability to predict the results of a new count on the basis of a previous count. Chapter 4 in this volume describes research on young children's ability to understand that the result of a count will remain the same despite irrelevant changes in the appearance of the set being counted (number conservation) or in the counting procedure (order irrelevance principle). It also discusses the much smaller amount of research on children's ability to recognize that the result of a count will change in predictable ways if an item is added or taken away and to predict the result of the change (Chapter 4). Understanding that counting a set of items in a different direction will not change the result, whereas adding an item will cause the result to be one more than the previous count, may be a forerunner of the understanding that a sum will give the same answer despite the reversal of the order of the addends, whereas adding 1 to an addend will add 1 to the result.

There may be further parallels between younger children's use of counting principles in counting prediction tasks and older children's use of arithmetical principles in derived fact strategies. In Chapter 4, it is suggested that the theory of counting development, which is at this time most strongly supported by the evidence is Baroody and Ginsburg's (1986) 'mutual development' theory of the relationship between counting procedures and principles: that they develop in tandem, interact increasingly as time goes on and reinforce one another. Young children's use of principles may at first be limited due to a lack of integration between quantitative concepts and knowledge of counting procedures. At first, even if children may count relatively successfully as a rote procedure and have some knowledge about cardinality, these two aspects of knowledge may not be integrated.

Thus in certain situations, the counting procedure may actually distract children's attention from quantity. In order irrelevance tasks (Cowan, Dowker, Christakis, & Bailey, 1996; Chapter 4 in this volume), 4-year-olds perform better if asked directly about order irrelevance: 'If I count in this direction, will I get the same number or a different number?' than when they are asked, 'If I count in this direction, how many will I get?', since 'how many?' questions concerning specific numbers are often used to elicit counting, it is likely that they focus children's attention on counting procedures at the expense of quantitative concepts. As children get older, they are better able to integrate concepts and procedures in counting: most 5- to 6-year-olds will answer both types of order irrelevance question correctly.

The integration of concepts and procedures in arithmetic may take longer. There are numerous studies (e.g. Seo & Ginsburg, 2003) that suggest that children often regard the equals sign as an instruction to perform an arithmetical operation, rather than as a description of a numerical relationship. This may not be just a limitation in linguistic/symbolic understanding: children may perceive a sum as something they have to 'do', with the result that attention is focused only on procedures and these are not integrated with concepts. Gray and Tall (1994) have described number as a 'procept': simultaneously a process and a concept.

Once children begin to integrate the 'process' and 'concept' aspects of number, their arithmetic is likely to improve and to become more flexible. Children who do not make this integration, either as a result of inappropriate teaching or of their own cognitive limitations, are likely to find arithmetic difficult and to be restricted to the use of learned procedures, which they do not relate to concepts.

The present study showed that over half of children at the 'beginning arithmetic' stage fail to use the Identity principle. If they are shown the sum '9 + 4 = 13', and are asked if this tells them the answer to '9 + 4 = ', they guess or calculate a new answer, rather than realizing that it is the same sum and must give the same answer. This has parallels with the younger children (Cowan et al., 1996) who did not always predict that counting the same set of items in the same order would give the same answer. In both cases, such results may not stem so much from a lack of recognition of identity in counting and arithmetic, but from treating counting and arithmetic purely as procedures and not integrating them with concepts.

In this context, it would be particularly interesting to investigate whether early individual differences in preschool children's use of counting principles and procedures, and in the ability to integrate the two, are predictive of the ability to use derived fact strategies effectively at school age.

7 A good guess: Estimation and individual differences

Researcher: 'And about how much is five and two?'
Nasim (5 years 10 months): 'Lots!'

Jonathan (7): 'My brother says that 10 + 9 = 112! He only says that when it's his birthday. He likes teasing his birthday people.'

The ability to estimate an approximate answer to an arithmetic problem and the ability to evaluate the reasonableness of an arithmetical estimate are important aspects of arithmetical understanding. Estimation experience is likely to play a role in developing awareness of, and resourcefulness with, number relationships (Sauble, 1955). Estimation is also of considerable practical importance (Orton & Frobisher, 1996) and would seem essential to the appropriate use of calculators. Its educational importance has been increasingly emphasized in recent years, both in the United Kingdom (Cockcroft, 1982; DfEE, 1999) and in the United States (Kilpatrick, Swafford, & Findell, 2002; Sowder 1992).

Psychological and educational research indicates considerable individual variation in estimation performance by children (Dowker, 1997; Lefevre, Greenham, & Waheed, 1993; Lemaire, 2000; Sowder, 1992).

Estimation has also attracted increasing interest from neuroscientists, especially in view of findings that there are some brain-damaged patients whose estimation abilities are preserved in the face of severe calculation impairments. Recently, brain-imaging studies of 'normal' adults have suggested that different parts of the brain may be active in exact calculation and in some forms of estimation.

This chapter will review some studies of arithmetical estimation and discuss some of the possible reasons for the individual differences that have been found. In particular, it will look at the extent to which estimation is related to certain other arithmetical tasks. First, however, we must emphasize that estimation itself is not a single unitary process, but is made up of numerous components. In comparing and attempting to integrate different studies, it is important to remember that different aspects of estimation are emphasized in different studies: in particular, educational studies tend to emphasize aspects related to mental calculation, while brain studies tend to emphasize approximation.

What is arithmetical estimation?

Arithmetical estimation is not a single process. There are many processes that contribute to or could be described as arithmetical estimation. Consider the following examples:

1   In a study by Starkey (1992; see Chapter 4 in this volume), children as young as 2 were encouraged to put a number of balls into an opaque box. An adult then either added or subtracted balls from the original quantity. The children were then asked to take the balls out of the box one at a time. The number of times they reached into the box was used to indicate their expectation of the resulting quantity. When small numbers were involved, most 2-year-olds made an ordinally appropriate number of retrieval attempts: fewer than the original quantity if items had been subtracted; more than the original quantity if items had been added.

2   4-year-old Jack counted a set of eight counters. Another counter was then added, and Jack was asked how many there were now. He guessed, '6'. Paul, also 4, was passing by and commented, 'No, it's got to be more!'

3   5-year-old Michelle was asked to guess the answers to some single-digit addition problems. She consistently added 1 to the larger addend each time: $3 + 4 = 5$; $2 + 6 = 7$; $8 + 2 = 9$.

4   6-year-old Chloe could calculate or remember the answers to addition problems that added up to 10 or less. For larger sums, adding up to between 10 and 25, she did not calculate, but quickly guessed answers that were usually near to the correct answer: $8 + 6 = 12$; $12 + 13 = 21$. When she was given still larger sums, her answers were more erratic; and when invited to give the answers to three-digit addition sums, she alternated between replying 'A British billion' and 'A quadrillion'.

5   8-year-old Jordan is given two-digit addition sums to estimate. For each problem, he adds the tens and then adds a seemingly randomly chosen unit: '$23 + 39 = 54$'; '$71 + 18 = 86$', etc.

6   A class of 10-year-olds are being taught to use rounding strategies in estimation. Some of them consistently round the addends before doing the sum: e.g. $23 + 39$ is about $20 + 40 = 60$. Some, however, calculate the sums exactly and then round the *answer*: e.g. $23 + 39$ is calculated by a pencil-and-paper method to be 62, which is then rounded to the nearest 10 as 60. They understand estimation simply as producing a non-exact rounded answer (see Slater, 1990).

7   Some adult professional mathematicians are asked to estimate the answer to the problem 76 × 89. One rounds 89 to 90 and multiplies 76 by 90 by a standard procedure, obtaining the answer 6840. Another also treats 89 as 90, but treats 90 as (100 − 10); so that 76 × 90 must be about (76 × 100) − (76 × 10), or 7600 − 760, which is very approximately 6800. Another rounds both numbers in the problem and multiplies 70 by 90, obtaining 6300. Another treats 76 as about 75 and uses the fact that 0.75 is 3/4 to convert the problem into 100 × 0.75 × 88, or 100 × 3/4 × 88, which is 100 × 66 or 6600. This does not even begin to exhaust the strategies that they use, nearly all producing a reasonable estimate.

All these could be seen as demonstrating aspects of estimation or approximate arithmetic. The 2-year-olds in the first example were already demonstrating a nonverbal understanding of the fact that addition makes quantities larger and subtraction makes them smaller. Paul in the second example was demonstrating the same understanding on a more verbal, explicit level. Michelle in the third example was using a mechanical estimation strategy, consistent with the fact that addition increases a quantity. Chloe in the fourth example was able to provide reasonable estimate to arithmetical problems that were only a little too difficult for her to calculate. Jordan in the fifth example was using the fairly effective 'front-end strategy' (adding the left-hand digits), without yet using the convention of producing an estimate divisible by 10. The children in the sixth example had been taught to use the still more effective rounding strategy − but only some of them really understood its purpose. And the adults in the seventh example were using a wide variety of appropriate strategies, based on the properties of the specific numbers in the problem.

Thus, there are a wide variety of forms that estimation can take, from the toddler's dawning awareness that addition makes more, through the 5-year-old's mechanical strategies (Baroody, 1989b, 1992; Dowker, 1997) to the much more sophisticated strategies of the older child or adult.

Components of estimation

In an acknowledgement that estimation is not a single process, some of the researchers who have attempted to define estimation have divided it into components. This usually refers to the components of estimation as used by older children and adults. However, Dowker (2003a) has attempted to trace the emergence of the most basic components of estimation in 5- to 9-year-old children. These begin with the most basic principle: 'The answer to a numerical problem is a number'; and the only slightly less basic principle that the answers to sums of large addends are larger than those to the sums of small addends, before moving to the ability to use increasingly sophisticated strategies.

With regard to (mostly) older children, Sowder and Wheeler (1987, 1989) emphasized that arithmetical skills, concepts and attitudes were all important in influencing estimation ability. The concepts that they proposed to be most relevant to estimation ability were:

1   understanding of the role of approximate numbers in estimation
2   understanding that estimation can involve multiple processes and have multiple answers
3   understanding that context can influence the appropriateness of an estimate.

Case and Sowder (1990) and Lefevre et al. (1993) have emphasized the importance of *co-ordinating* different components of estimation. Case and Sowder (1990) have proposed that this need to co-ordinate the different components places intrinsic cognitive limitations to children's estimation competence before the age of 11 or 12, however they are taught. Their argument (p. 79) was that estimation:

> requires the coordination of two qualitatively different sorts of component activities: (a) using nearness judgment to select appropriate substitutes for the addends and (b) mentally computing the sum of the substitute numbers. According to Case's . . . theory of intellectual development, children are not able to achieve this sort of co-ordination until . . . about 11 or 12 years.

Lefevre et al. (1993) proposed a somewhat different componential model, consisting of three main processes: retrieval, calculation and reformulation. The first two of these are the processes also involved in exact arithmetic, where answers are either produced from memory (retrieved) or calculated. Reformulation, where the numbers in a problem are changed into 'simpler' or more 'convenient' numbers, is what differentiates estimation from exact calculation. Lefevre et al. considered that children's improvement in estimation between around 9 and 12 years is due not only to better co-ordination ability, but also to increased flexibility of strategy use (see also Lemaire et al., 2000).

It is likely that individual differences in these components are important; and that both children and adults may show marked discrepancies between the separate components. There has, however, been little or no research on individual differences in these specific components of estimation.

By the same token, there have been a number of studies looking at individual difference in estimation ability in relation to calculation ability and to flexibility of strategy use in both calculation and estimation and we shall now turn to these.

Arithmetical estimation and mental calculation

Arithmetical estimation is not the same as exact arithmetic: even mental arithmetic. Most studies do, however, suggest an association between estimation and exact calculation ability; and especially between estimation and the flexible use of non-standard strategies for exact calculation.

Much of the educational literature (e.g. Reys, 1984; Rubenstein, 1985) has emphasized the distinctions between arithmetical estimation and written calculation. Written calculation is seen as depending on standard, school-taught strategies, whereas estimation is more flexible, less dependent on any specific standard techniques and less likely to be taught in school. Moreover, in the case of multi-digit numbers, the two types of process differ with regard to the order in which units, tens, hundreds, etc. are calculated. Written calculations typically begin with the units, and continue from right to left, using carrying or borrowing procedures if necessary. By contrast, estimation typically begins, and sometimes ends, with the left-hand digits.

Some researchers treat estimation and *mental* calculation as closely related processes, to be treated together and contrasted with written calculation. It is true that some types of mental calculation do share the characteristics of estimation that differentiate it from written calculation. Thompson (1997b) points out that mental calculations, in contrast to written calculation, are usually carried from left to right: the same characteristic pointed out above for estimation. Plunkett (1979) argued that mental calculation differs from written calculation in being flexible, variable and usually not generalizable. These are the characteristics that my research has indicated to be particularly important to estimation (Dowker, 1992; Dowker et al., 1996b).

Most studies have shown a relationship between mental calculation ability and estimation. The reasonableness of young children's estimates increases with their mental calculation ability, even when the problems that *all* the children are given to estimate are adjusted to be just a little too difficult for them to calculate accurately (Dowker, 1997, 1998). The same is true of older children: Rubenstein (1985) found that 8th-graders' (13- to 14-year-olds') performance on a variety of arithmetical estimation tasks was predicted by their calculation ability, especially by their ability to operate with tens.

Studies of children's estimation in relation to calculation

An addition estimation task was given to 213 children between 5 and 9 (Dowker, 1989a, 1997, 2001). In order to evaluate the children's competence in addition, a mental calculation task was given to each child. This consisted of a list of addition sums, graduated in difficulty from 4 + 5, 7 + 1, etc. to 235 + 349 (Dowker, 1997, gives the full list of sums). These sums

Table 7.1 Summary of addition performance levels

Level	Code	Problem just within range	Problem outside range
Beginning arithmetic	A	Counts to 10	5 + 3
Addition to 10	B	5 + 3	8 + 6
Simple addition	C	8 + 6	23 + 44
2-digit (no carry)	D	23 + 44	52 + 39
2-digit (carry)	E	52 + 39	523 + 168

were simultaneously presented orally and visually in a horizontal format. The children's answers were oral and were recorded on a taperecorder.

The children were then divided into five levels according to their performance on the mental calculation task. The criteria for assignment to the different levels are described in more detail elsewhere (Dowker, 1997, 1998). Table 7.1 contains a brief summary of the levels, with the code letters that were used for them in the tables and with examples of the problems that could and could not be solved at these levels.

Four sets of estimation problems were devised. Each set contained nine items. The sets were designed to be progressively more difficult to solve. The four sets of estimation problems are described by Dowker (1997). An example of a Set 1 problem was 5 + 4; an example of a Set 2 problem was 9 + 8; an example of a Set 3 problem was 18 + 59; and an example of a Set 4 problem was 217 + 285. In this study, each child was presented with the set of addition problems within their base correspondence as defined earlier. One hundred and eight of the children were also asked to estimate answers to sums more difficult than the base correspondence. The main results of this study were that:

1   Children, at least from the time when they can calculate addition problems adding up to between 5 and 10 (addition to 10 level), possess good intuitive estimation abilities: a majority of their estimates are reasonable estimates (defined as those that are within 30% of the correct answer and that are also greater than the larger addend).
2   Estimation performance improves with calculation performance level. Within the base correspondence, the proportion of estimates that were reasonable increased with calculation performance level. The greatest differences were between children at the beginning arithmetic level and higher levels. This is not just because older children tend to be better than younger children at both estimation and calculation. When age and calculation performance level were included separately in a multiple regression, it became clear that age had no effect on number of reasonable estimates, after controlling for calculation performance level.
3   Within each performance level estimation accuracy deteriorated as problem difficulty increased. Both for groups and for individual children,

there was a marked diminution in the proportion of reasonable estimates and marked increase in unreasonable estimates (especially those less than the larger addend) as children moved further and further from their base correspondence.

Thus, mental calculation performance level is closely linked to estimation performance; but it has to be considered in relation to the difficulty of the problems given. It is the interaction between mental calculation level and problem difficulty that determines estimation performance, far more than either of these two factors on its own.

Subsequent research (Dowker, 1998; Chapter 6 in this volume) demonstrated a strong independent relationship between estimation and derived fact strategy use.

Thus, there is a strong relationship between the use of arithmetical reasoning to derive exact unknown facts (derived fact strategies) and to derive approximate unknown facts (estimation). Although this association is strong, the two processes cannot be reduced to a single process, as there were individual children who showed strong discrepancies between the two processes, in both directions.

Do children who have difficulty in arithmetic demonstrate a particular difficulty in estimation? Of course, one would expect them to have some difficulties in estimation simply because of the association that is usually found between calculation and estimation. But do they have estimation difficulties over and above what would be expected from their calculation performance level?

The Numeracy Recovery intervention project (Dowker, 2001, 2003a; Chapter 12 in this volume) has made it possible to investigate this issue. Estimation performance for addition was investigated in 128 6- and 7-year-olds who had been selected by their teachers as being weak at arithmetic and in need of intervention. The number included children at the beginning arithmetic level for mental addition; the addition to 10 level; and at the addition to 25 level. Their estimates at the base correspondence were compared with those found for unselected children at the same performance levels (Dowker, 1997). As it turned out, children at the two lower levels performed very similarly to other children at these levels. However, children at the addition to 25 level, who had been identified as weak at arithmetic, were much worse estimators than others at the same level. Only about one-third of their estimates were reasonable, as compared with about two-thirds of the estimates by unselected children at the same level.

Why would this be? The most likely explanation is that children who are weak at arithmetic are not necessarily disproportionately bad at estimation. However, there are some children who are performing at an average level at some forms of mental calculation, but whose estimation skills are poor. Such children, despite their relatively adequate mental calculation, will often have difficulty with some other aspects of arithmetic and be identified by their teachers as arithmetically weak. Thus, among the children who were seen as experiencing arithmetical difficulty, it was those children, whose mental addition skills were the *least* weak, who showed disproportionately poor estimation performance.

Estimation in adults: The difficulty it can present

Estimation performance in adults is quite variable and can be very weak.

Levine (1982) gave 89 American college students, who were not majoring in mathematics, her Computational Estimation Test. This test involved estimating the approximate solutions to a set of multiplication and division problems: (e.g. 11.6 × 12.4; 648/22.4). She studied both the accuracy of their estimates and the strategies used. Her scoring system gave three points to each estimate that was no more than 10% away from the exact product or quotient, three points were scored. If the percentage of error was greater than 10% but no more than 20%, two points were scored. If the percentage of error was greater than 20% but no more than 30%, one point was scored. Zero points were scored if the percentage of error was greater than 30%. She found that the general standard was quite low, with a mean score of 25.9 out of a potential maximum of 60. Moreover, many students used only a narrow range of strategies and relied just on school-taught rounding strategies or often just on proceeding algorithmically (i.e. using some form of a standard algorithm to calculate roughly, estimate and then combine all partial products or quotients: for example, responding to the problem 424 × 0.76 by approximate long multiplication of 424 by 70 and then 6 to give about 32,000, followed by division by 100 to give 320).

Estimation and strategy variability

I gave Levine's estimation task to 44 academic mathematicians (Dowker, 1992). In that study the mathematicians were shown to be very accurate estimators, although few obtained perfect scores. The mean score was 51 out of a possible 60. The most striking result there was the great variability of strategy use by the mathematicians, with many different strategies being used for each problem. A subsequent study (Dowker et al., 1996b) compared the mathematicians with accountants, psychology students and English students. The mathematicians were more accurate than the psychology students or accountants, who were, in their turn, more accurate than the English students. Although the participants were not given other tests of mathematical ability, estimation accuracy was greater in the groups that had most arithmetical experience. Strategy use was very variable between individuals; within individuals for different problems; and, in the case of 20 mathematicians and 18 psychology students who were retested a few months later, within individuals for the same problems on different occasions. Within each group, strategy variability was positively associated with accuracy.

Thus, once again we see that people who are mathematically able tend also to be good estimators. We also see that variability of strategy use correlates with estimation ability. As discussed in Chapter 1, such findings have implications beyond the area of estimation. They imply that high levels of expertise and/or ability in mathematics and perhaps also in other domains are not associated so much with the ability to home in accurately on a single 'best strategy' but with the flexible use of an extremely wide variety of strategies.

Discrepancies between calculation and estimation

Despite these strong associations, dissociations and discrepancies between computational estimation and calculation do occur quite frequently. Dowker (1998) reported a number of children who did show marked discrepancies between calculation and estimation; and also found similar discrepancies among adults (Dowker, 1994).

Macaruso and Sokol (1998) gave calculation and estimation tasks to a group of developmentally dyslexic children and young people, ranging in age from 12 to 20, who were regarded by their teachers as having basic weaknesses in mathematics. They found that some individuals had difficulty with calculation but not with computational or quantitative estimation, while others showed the reverse pattern.

Adults with mild specific calculation difficulties: How do they fare at estimation?

The Adult Group described in Chapter 2 was investigated with regard to estimation abilities. Specifically, 38 adults (16 men and 22 women), who claimed to have relatively specific problems with arithmetic, were studied and compared with 12 adults (8 men and 4 women) who did not report specific calculation difficulties. Most of the adults, with a few exceptions, were university students and few had extremely severe difficulties. On the whole, the subgroup with specific difficulties performed at a roughly average level at arithmetic, while performing at an above average level at many other tasks, and the comparison subgroup performed at an above average level at arithmetic as well as at other tasks.

They were given the following tasks:

1   All subtests of the verbal scale of the Wechsler Intelligence Scale for Adults, including the arithmetic subtest.
2   All subtests of the performance scale of the Wechsler Intelligence Scale for Adults.
3   Graham Hitch's (1978) Numerical Abilities Scales. These are written tests for adults, first standardized on a group of industrial apprentices:

Table 7.2 Characteristics and scores of the Adult Group

	Main group (N = 38)	Comparison group (N = 12)	Total (N = 50)
Men	16	4	20
Women	22	8	30
Verbal IQ	120.81	123.54	121.52
	(7.36)	(11.47)	(8.36)
Performance IQ	110.49	119.19	111.96
	(12.83)	(10.61)	(12.99)
WAIS arithmetic	10.84	15.0	11.78
	(2.28)	(5.55)	(3.69)
Numerical abilities scales			
Test 1	91.49	128.64	101.18
(basic arithmetic)	(27.48)	(26.88)	(32.83)
Test 2			
(fractions and decimals;	24.11	37.91	27.27
maximum 40)	(9.72)	(2.39)	(10.73)
Test 3			
(reasoning and approximation;	31.46	36.73	32.67
maximum 40)	(10.74)	(2.94)	(9.7)
Computational estimation task	25.16	41.45	28.55
(maximum 60)	(15.39)	(14.28)	(16.52)

— Test 1 (basic arithmetic). This test comprises six parts: (a) three-digit addition without carrying; (b) three-digit addition with carrying; (c) three-digit subtraction without borrowing; (d) three-digit subtraction with borrowing; (e) single-digit multiplication; and (f) single-digit division.

— Test 2 (fraction and decimal arithmetic). This test includes fraction and decimal arithmetic; conversions between fractions, decimals and percentages; and long multiplication and division of whole numbers.

— Test 3 (arithmetical reasoning and magnitude comprehension). This test includes approximation; magnitude comparison; comprehension of arithmetical expressions (e.g. the use of brackets); and arithmetical reasoning problems involving ratio, proportion and percentage.

4   Levine's (1982) Computational Estimation Test.

The mean scores of the two subgroups on these tests are shown in Table 7.2.

Analyses of variance revealed significant subgroup differences for WAIS arithmetic, performance IQ, computational estimation and the first two of the numerical abilities tests: basic arithmetic and decimals and fractions. For all of these, the comparison subgroup did better than the main subgroup. They did not show significant differences on either verbal IQ, or the third of the numerical abilities tests.

Estimation turned out to be independently influenced by only two factors besides subgroup. One was gender. Males were better estimators than females. Overall, males obtained a mean score of about 37 out of 60; females obtained a mean score of about 24 out of 60. Further analyses revealed that estimation was the *only* measure here that showed a gender difference. Also, the second of the numerical abilities tests – the test involving fractions and decimals – contributed significantly to estimation. The other number tests did not contribute independently to estimation.

The importance of this particular test is not very surprising, since this particular estimation task did include a number of items relating to multiplication and division of decimals and some of the strategies used frequently by participants involved the perception and use of fractional relationships, e.g. that multiplying by 0.76 is similar to multiplying by 3/4.

The gender difference is more surprising, since there were no gender differences in other aspects of arithmetic and my other estimation studies, both of young children and of adult professional groups, did not reveal significant gender differences. It may reflect the tendency found in some studies for males to be more confident than females about mathematics: they may therefore be more willing to estimate. This may be particularly relevant to a group which is to some degree self-selected for perceiving itself as having arithmetical weaknesses – although the gender difference seemed to be as great in the rather small comparison subgroup as in the main subgroup.

What is perhaps most striking is the relative independence of estimation of other measures: it is not related either to the WAIS arithmetical reasoning test, to the basic arithmetic part of the numerical abilities tests, or to the arithmetical reasoning/approximation part. This seems to support the view of a certain independence between calculation and estimation.

Discrepancies between calculation and estimation: Two contrasting individuals in the Adult Group

Rose is in her mid-20s and is a graduate student in an arts subject. James is in his early 30s and is a research technician. On the WAIS, Rose obtained a verbal IQ score of 126 and a performance IQ of 114, while James obtained a verbal IQ of 118 and a performance IQ of 110. Rose's arithmetic subtest scaled score was 13 (well above average) while James' score was 9 (somewhat below average).

One very striking difference is, however, shown on their performance on the estimation task. James obtained a score of 50 out of a potential 60: very similar to the mean for the group of mathematicians. Rose obtained a score of 13: i.e. she performed very much less well than any of the professional groups studied or even than Levine's (1982) less able student group. Moreover, James used a wide range of strategy types: including fractional relationships, rounding, factorization and others. By contrast, Rose *only* used the strategy termed proceeding algorithmically: i.e. doing the standard calculation. This is a somewhat limiting strategy for anybody and especially for someone who has some trouble with mental calculation. Her confusions when performing mental calculation led to many errors. There were indeed some other people in the Adult Group who made numerous calculation-based errors in the estimation task and obtained similarly low scores. Rose, however, stood out even among these. When others were given computationally simpler estimation problems, such as quickly estimating the sums of two- or three-digit numbers, they performed extremely well, using efficient rounding strategies. Rose certainly performed better on such problems than on the more arithmetically difficult problems of the estimation task. But she still showed significant limitations. In particular, she sometimes tended to make a rather rigid use of front-end strategies involving adding the left-hand digits, without regard to the other digits. For example, she estimated that 198 + 201 as about 300, while better estimators estimated it as about 400.

How might this contrast relate to their performance on other arithmetic tests? As we have seen, Rose is actually better at a test of arithmetical word problem solving. But might she be weak at arithmetical fact retrieval?

James' score on Hitch's basic arithmetic test (Test 1) was very slightly above the mean for Hitch's less highly educated participants: probably a little less good than would be expected for his educational level; certainly less good than that for some other people in the Adult Group who were much less good estimators. His outstanding estimation performance cannot be due to very superior knowledge of arithmetical facts.

Rose's arithmetical fact retrieval did indeed appear to be relatively poor. She scored well below the average of Hitch's less highly educated participants on his basic arithmetic test (Test 1). She scored below average on all subtests except the division subtest, on which she obtained a score one standard deviation *above* the mean. Rose's fact retrieval difficulties are, however, not severe enough to be the main explanation for her estimation difficulties. Several better estimators performed less well on Hitch's Test 1.

Given the general association between estimation ability and decimal and fraction arithmetic (Hitch's Test 2), one possible explanation for the discrepancy between James and Rose is that Rose could have conceptual or procedural difficulties in dealing with multiplication and division of multidigit numbers or with fractions and decimals; while James could be particularly capable in this area. In fact, in written tests Rose's performance on such problems is exceptionally good. On the decimal and fraction arithmetic test (Test 2), she obtained an overall score nearly two standard deviations *above* the mean for controls. James once again performs at a fairly average level: slightly above the mean for Hitch's less highly educated participants and considerably less well than Rose.

What about arithmetical concepts? On Hitch's Test 3, which emphasizes conceptual aspects of arithmetic, both obtained almost perfect scores, with one important exception. Rose performed poorly on the approximation subtest, again indicating a poor grasp of arithmetical estimation.

Could it be that James is much better than Rose at *mental* calculation? In fact, *both* James and Rose claimed to be worse at mental calculation than written calculation; and both indeed made a number of errors in mental calculation tasks. In addition to being given all of Graham Hitch's arithmetic tests in written form, both were given some problems from his basic arithmetic test orally. These included three three-digit addition problems without carrying, three three-digit addition problems with carrying, three three-digit subtraction problems without borrowing, and three three-digit subtraction problems with borrowing. They were also given four problems, involving multiplication of pairs of two-digit numbers. James gave correct answers to the addition problems without carrying and the subtraction problems without borrowing, but replied, 'Sorry, I've lost it' to most problems with carrying and borrowing. Rose gave correct answers to the subtraction problems without borrowing, but became confused and miscalculated the answers to the problems involving carrying and borrowing and also to two out of three addition problems without carrying.

On the multiplication problems, both subjects gave correct answers to two problems and nearly correct answers to the other two. Thus, James and Rose performed quite similarly on tasks involving mental calculation.

I would here suggest one contributory factor to Rose's estimation difficulties. What after all do the terms 'estimation' and 'approximation' imply in an arithmetical context, if not the ability to reduce relatively complicated arithmetic problems to a simpler form? For Rose (possibly due to much better secondary than elementary school teaching) the difference between 'complicated' and 'simple' arithmetic problems is much less than for most people. She is better than average at the former; less good than average at the latter. There is thus less reason for her than for most people to attempt to reduce complicated problems to a simpler form and the skill may not have developed.

And James? He is an intelligent man with excellent arithmetical reasoning ability and some limited occupational experience of estimation. However, so are many other people with much less good estimation ability. We do not have any single pat explanation for his superior estimation performance.

What we can say is that James and Rose demonstrate that marked discrepancies between estimation and calculation can and do occur in educated people without brain damage. People's estimation abilities can be much better than would be expected from their calculation abilities: witness James with his relatively poor mental calculation and his below average WAIS arithmetic score, who estimates like a professional mathematician.

Or their estimation abilities can be much worse than would be expected: witness the severe estimation problems shown by Rose, whose mental calculation is no worse than James'; whose WAIS arithmetic score is well above average and who performs outstandingly well on written tests involving fraction and decimal arithmetic.

Estimation and evaluation of other people's estimates

> 'How silly is silly? If it's ten out, is that silly?' (9-year-old David, a statistician's son, when asked whether a guess was good or silly)

Estimation and *evaluation of other people's estimates* are often treated as essentially two sides of the same coin. Cockcroft (1982) treats the ability to say whether an estimate is reasonable or not as one aspect of general estimation ability. Reys (1984) emphasizes the importance of, for example, being able to say whether an answer obtained on a calculator is reasonable or not and treated this as equivalent to estimation ability. There are certainly reasons why one might expect that there would be a close relationship between the ability to estimate and the ability to evaluate other people's estimates. However, it is not, a priori, impossible that there could be discrepancies between the two. Evaluation of other people's estimates could be easier than estimation, because the latter may involve some ability to use arithmetical procedures, while the former may rely more purely on approximation.

By the same token, evaluating other people's estimates might actually be more difficult, especially for children, because it may require them to *reflect* on a cognitive procedure, rather than simply carrying it out. There is considerable evidence that metacognition – the ability to think about thinking – poses difficulties for children (Brown, 1987; Piaget 1952; Schoenfield, 1987). Moreover, as 9-year-old David implied, evaluating an estimate as good or bad requires the setting of some sort of criteria, implicit or explicit, for 'a good guess'. There are no universal criteria for a good estimate; and setting such criteria could make heavy demands on number sense. Moreover, most people probably have more experience with making estimates than with evaluating other people's estimates.

I investigated the relationships between children's estimation ability and their ability to judge the *degree* of reasonableness of an estimate. This was inspired by children's responses to the questions in the addition estimates task (see earlier) when asked whether Tom and Mary's estimates were 'good' or 'silly'.

Children often made comments such as: 'Pretty close'; 'Not too good and not too silly'; 'Not bad for a *guess*'; 'A bit silly. But is this their first try? Then it's not bad'; 'Very very silly'; 'Stupid! How *old* were Tom and Mary?'

Such comments revealed a quite unexpected ability to make discriminations between different degrees of 'goodness' and 'silliness'.

The subsequent study used the same materials and the same estimates by 'Tom and Mary'. Eighty four children took part: 20 at the beginning arithmetic level (A); 20 at the addition to 10 level (B); 24 at the addition to 25 level (C); and 20 at the two-digit (carry) level (E). In this study, the children were invited to rate each guess on a five-point 'smiley faces' scale from 'very good' (the very smiley face) to 'very silly' (the very frowny face). In this study, all children were given all sets, including those below their base correspondence.

Results demonstrated that children's ratings for estimates below their base correspondence were closely related to the extent to which the estimate deviated from the correct answer: the further from the correct answer it was, the worse it was rated. However, children's ratings within and above their base correspondence were not correlated with the actual accuracy or reasonableness of the estimates. Moreover, the accuracy of children's ratings (as measured by the rank correlations between their ratings and the deviations of the estimates from the correct answers) was not associated significantly with the proportion of reasonable estimates that they themselves produced.

Arithmetical estimation is not identical to all other forms of estimation

One might think that quite similar processes would be involved in estimating the answer to a sum; in estimating the number of dots on a piece of paper or the number of apples in a basket; in estimating a person's height or the length of a parking space; or in estimating the population of a country. After all, all of these tasks involve working with approximate quantities. Some textbooks and curriculum guides group such activities together, under a general heading of 'estimation'.

But arithmetical estimation seems to be far less closely related to other forms of estimation than it is to other forms of arithmetic. As we have seen, it is possible to be much better at exact calculation than at arithmetical estimation or at arithmetical estimation than at exact calculation. Overall, however, those who calculate well tend also to estimate well and there are some calculation processes that are particularly strongly associated with estimation. By contrast, it turns out that there is *very little relationship* between arithmetical estimation and other forms of estimation. For instance, in a study of older secondary school pupils, Paull (1971) found no significant correlations between arithmetical estimation, length estimation and weight estimation.

Lisa Hook (1992) studied 35 of the psychology students who took part in the study of arithmetical estimation strategies in different professional groups (Dowker et al., 1996b). As well as the Computational Estimation Test, she gave them Shallice's shortened Quantitative Estimation Task, and her own test of estimating lengths of string. None of these three tests correlated significantly with any of the other tests.

Moreover, factors such as age and arithmetical calculation ability, which have been shown to affect computational estimation, do not always have the same influence on other forms of estimation.

All studies (e.g. Case & Sowder, 1990; Lefevre et al., 1993; Sowder & Wheeler, 1987, 1989) that have compared children of different ages have shown an improvement with age in *arithmetical* estimation. By contrast, Forrester and Pike (1998) and Forrester, Latham, and Shire (1990) found that age did not affect length or area estimation. In a further study, Pike and Forrester (1998) found that 'number sense' tasks involving mental computation, derived fact strategy use and comparison of numerical magnitudes did not correlate significantly with length estimation, although they did correlate with area estimation.

Arithmetical estimation and numerosity estimation

If arithmetical estimation is not strongly related to measurement estimation, might it be more closely related to numerosity estimation: estimating the number of items in a set? After all, since arithmetical estimation involves understanding and manipulating *numbers*, perhaps it would be facilitated by an ability to represent the quantities associated with these numbers. Moreover, numerosity estimation does seem to improve with age, at least as regards numbers greater than 5 (Crites, 1992; Huntley-Fenner & Cannon, 2000; Peak & Dowker, 1995; Siegel, Goldsmith, & Madson, 1982).

To my knowledge, relationships between arithmetical estimation and numerosity estimation have not been much investigated in children. Some results have, however, been obtained with regard to adults.

The Adult Group, as well as being given the Computational Estimation Test, WAIS verbal and performance IQ scales, and Hitch's numerical abilities tests, were also given Elizabeth Warrington's test of numerosity estimation. In this test, the participants were required to state or estimate the number of black dots randomly arranged on sheets of white paper. There were 20 stimulus arrays: consisting of 2–10 dots, 15, 20, 25, 30, 40, 50, 60, 70, 80, 90 and 100 dots.

Two seconds of inspection time were permitted per stimulus. Reaction times were not otherwise measured in this task. I used four measures of estimation accuracy for each protocol:

1   correlation between the log of the estimated number of dots and the log of the actual number of dots
2   lowest number of dots that elicited the wrong answer

Table 7.3 Means and standard deviations for scores for measures on dot
          number estimation task

	Main group (N = 38)	Comparison group (N = 12)	Total (N = 50)
Correlation	0.99 (0.01)	0.99 (0.006)	0.99
Lowest error	10.08 (4.9)	14.72 (12.51)	11.15
Median deviation	0.08 (0.09)	0.02 (0.04)	0.07

3   median percentage deviation of the estimated number from the correct
    answer
4   highest percentage deviation of the estimated number from the correct
    answer.

The means and standard deviations for each of these measures are shown
in Table 7.3.

As can be seen, there seems to be something of a ceiling effect for the first
measure – the correlation between the log of estimated number of dots and
the log of the actual number of dots, which is very close to 1 – the highest
possible correlation. In other words, whether or not the participants' estimates were numerically accurate, they were usually ordinally appropriate.
The participants exhibited far more variability on the other measures. For
example, although all participants were accurate in estimating quantities up
to 6, the lowest number that they got wrong varied quite a bit. It varied from
7 to 20, except for one participant in the comparison group, whose estimates
were accurate for all arrays below 50 dots, which he estimated as 60.

Analyses of variance revealed no significant differences between the
groups for any of the numerosity estimation accuracy measures. It may
look as though the comparison group were performing better than the main
group as regards the lowest number of dots that elicited the wrong number,
but that seemed to be due to the one outlier who could estimate accurately
up to 50. It was not significant.

There were also no significant gender differences or any significant interaction between gender and group, as regards any of the numerosity
measures.

Multiple regressions did reveal associations between some of the arithmetic measures and the numerosity measures. The third numerical abilities
measure, which deals with arithmetical reasoning and magnitude appreciation, was a predictor of both the correlation between the logs of the
estimated and actual numbers of dots and of the highest percentage deviation of the estimated number from the correct answer. Perhaps this is
because this test includes measures of magnitude appreciation and approximation. More puzzlingly, the second numerical abilities measure, which
deals with decimals and fractions, was a significant predictor of the median
percentage deviation of the estimated number from the correct answer.

What was notable for its absence was any statistical relationship between the computational estimation task and any of the measures of numerosity estimation.

Estimation and context

Much of the research discussed in this chapter has looked at estimation in relation to the understanding and manipulation of numbers and the relationships between them. It is important not only to consider the numbers themselves, but the contexts in which they are encountered.

We may consider the old joke about the lecturer who estimated that the world would end in 'about 50 billion years' and was asked by a member of the audience to repeat the sentence. 'Thank God!', exclaimed the member of the audience, after hearing the estimate repeated. 'I thought you said only *15* billion years!' In fact, if considered only in terms of numerical relationships, there is quite a large difference between 15 billion and 50 billion. According to the criterion that a reasonable estimate is within 30% of the correct answer, it is definitely 'unreasonable' to confuse the two numbers. But in this particular context, to regard the difference between the two numbers as very important is so inappropriate as to be funny.

The topic of context is relevant to estimation in two ways: first, different types of estimates and strategies can be differentially appropriate to different contexts; and second, people are likely to estimate better in contexts that make sense to them (Koloto, 1995).

The *context* in which estimation occurs can be an important determinant of the type of estimate that is suitable and therefore of the type of strategy that is desirable to use. Sowder and Wheeler (1989) proposed that one important component of estimation ability is the ability to recognize that whether a particular estimate is acceptable will depend in part on the context: both as regards the size of the numbers involved and as regards the practical or educational situation in which the estimate is made. Some situations permit greater deviation from the exact answer than do others. Moreover, in some contexts, the *direction* of the deviation from the exact answer is unimportant: it does not matter whether an estimate is too high or too low. In other contexts, an underestimate can be preferable to an overestimate, or vice versa. For example, when budgeting it is usually safer to overestimate ones likely expenses than to underestimate them.

In many areas of mathematical cognition, there has been considerable recent emphasis not only on the role of context in determining the strategies that are used; but also on the fact that different contexts may have differential validity to different people, depending on their prior experiences (Carraher, Carraher, & Schliemann, 1985; Nunes, Schliemann, & Carraher, 1993).

The effects of contextual relevance, although generally considered to be important for estimation, have not been studied with regard to estimation to the same extent as, for example, with regard to counting (Saxe, 1982); place value and derived fact strategies (Carraher et al., 1985; Nunes et al., 1993) or word problem solving (Resnick, 1983). However, a few studies have explored the role of estimation in different cultures (e.g. Koloto, 1995, discussed the traditional estimation methods of Tongan weavers) and have indicated that people do indeed make better estimates within contexts that are personally and culturally relevant to them. For example, Kearins (1991) found that Australian Aboriginal children were better than non-Aboriginal children at estimating direction, which was traditionally very important in this group. Contrariwise, non-Aboriginal Australian children were better than Aboriginal children at estimating age, which is very important in western culture but much less so in Aboriginal culture (see Chapter 9).

The effect of cultural context has been explored more with regard to measurement estimation than to arithmetical estimation. There is still considerable room for investigating the role of context in the latter case, especially as there are many occupations where estimation is important. These include, to mention but a few: cooks; tailors; scalers in the lumber industry; financial consultants; and, of course, contractors and their customers.

Educational influences on estimation

As with other areas of arithmetic, individual differences in estimation are likely to be influenced in part by differences in educational experiences and in part by interactions between the prevailing educational practices and the cognitive characteristics that children bring to school.

For many years, researchers and educators have argued that school mathematics education focuses too exclusively on exact calculation and does not give appropriate emphasis to estimation (e.g. Carpenter, 1980; Reys, 1984; Sauble, 1955; Slater, 1990; Sowder, 1992). Moreover, both Slater (1990) and Baroody (with Coslick) (1998) point out that even when estimation is encouraged, it tends to take the form of asking children to estimate the answer to an arithmetical problem, before doing the calculation. In practice, children tend to respond to such requests by calculating first and then rounding their answer to a multiple of 10. Such instruction may fail to convey to children the purposes of estimation, which is rarely used when one *can* and *intends to* get an exact answer (although it may still be useful in checking the reasonableness of such answers).

There has, in fact, been considerable historical and cultural variation as to the extent to which estimation is encouraged in schools and the stage at which it is introduced. In Britain, measurement estimation has been encouraged for some time. Recently, the government's recommendations for increased emphasis on mental calculation have included an increased focus on estimation. For example, children from Year 3 (approximately age

7) onwards are expected to learn to check the results of calculations by using rounding strategies.

There have been relatively few studies focusing directly on the effects of educational practices and teaching techniques on estimation. Most of the studies that have investigated this issue have done so mainly with regard to measurement estimation (Forrester & Pike, 1998; Koloto, 1995); and, as we have seen, there appear to be important differences between computational and measurement estimation.

There is evidence for some cultural differences in estimation, which may reflect educational practices. For example, Reys, Reys, Nohda, Ishida, Yoshikawa, and Shimizu (1991) found that Japanese fifth- and eighth-grade pupils were better at mental calculation than their American counterparts, but that 'their tendency to use pencil-and-paper procedures mentally often interfered with the estimation process'. This probably reflects a strong emphasis in Japanese schools on exact mental calculation.

Estimation and the brain

As pointed out throughout this book, educators and developmental and cognitive psychologists have been obtaining increasingly strong evidence that arithmetical ability is not unitary but is made up of numerous components. Converging evidence is coming from the work of neuropsychologists and neuroscientists, who have been investigating evidence that different parts of the brain are responsible for different aspects of arithmetic. One issue that has received considerable attention from this point of view is the evidence for dissociations between estimation and exact calculation.

One of the first papers that discussed this issue was Warrington's (1982) seminal study. Warrington studied a patient who suffered a stroke affecting the left posterior parieto-occipital region of the brain. This patient, known in the literature as DRC, was selectively impaired in the retrieval of number facts and, as a result, was inefficient and inaccurate at calculation. His arithmetical reasoning was essentially unaffected. He obtained a very low score on Hitch's Test 1, involving whole-number arithmetic, but performed at the same level as controls on his Test 2 – involving fraction and decimal arithmetic – and Test 3 – involving numerical reasoning and appreciation of the magnitude of numbers. In particular, he was unimpaired in tasks involving arithmetical estimation.

Since then, several researchers, especially Dehaene and his colleagues, have used both studies of patients and, more recently, brain-imaging studies to examine discrepancies between calculation and approximation.

Dehaene and Cohen (1991) studied a patient 'Mr N' with a left subcortical lesion, who had much more severe calculation deficits than Warrington's patient. He could not perform *any* exact calculations reliably, even adding 2 + 2. Yet, he could still carry out approximations. He could locate numbers approximately on a number line; could usually say which was the larger of a pair of two-digit numbers; and could reject wildly wrong answers to addition sums. For example, he was prepared to accept the sum $5 + 7 = 11$ as correct, but rejected $5 + 7 = 19$ as wrong. Another patient, with a left inferior parietal lesion, had difficulty with such approximation tasks, but was still able to carry out some exact calculations through preserved rote knowledge of some addition and multiplication facts.

Dehaene and his colleagues later carried out functional MRI and ERP studies with normal individuals (Dehaene, Spelke, Pinel, Stanescu, & Tsivkin, 1999; Cohen, Dehaene, Chochon, Lehricy, & Naccache 2000; Stanescu-Cosson, Pinel, Van de Moortele, Le Bihan, Cohen, & Dehaene, 2000). They found that these resulted in different patterns of brain activation. In particular, parietal and frontal areas were more active during approximation than exact calculation. Conversely, a distributed set of areas, including a left anterior inferior frontal region and the bilateral angular gyri, showed greater activation during exact calculation. They argued that verbal coding is important for exact arithmetical facts, while approximate numerical information is coded non-linguistically.

These are fascinating findings and support behavioural findings that estimation and calculation abilities can dissociate considerably. However, the question arises: how do we explain the fact that, although normal individuals do sometimes show strong discrepancies between arithmetical estimation and exact calculation, calculation and estimation do tend to correlate with one another, both in children and adults?

It is important in this context to remember two things: (1) most arithmetical estimation tasks involve more than just approximation; and (2) exact arithmetic involves more than just the memory for rote-learned facts. I would propose that numerical and arithmetical tasks can be placed at various points along a continuous spectrum, according to the extent to which they require the retrieval of learned information versus the derivation of unknown facts. At one end of the scale is the retrieval of overlearned facts, such as multiplication tables. Then comes arithmetical calculation involving well-learned procedures. Next comes the use of non-standard, non-automatized calculation procedures: for example, derived fact strategies, whereby arithmetical principles such as commutativity and associativity are used for the exact derivation of unknown arithmetical facts from known facts.

Next comes arithmetical estimation, which, as we have seen, is closely related to derived fact strategy use in children. Arithmetical estimation, as proposed by Case and Sowder (1990), involves two components: using nearness judgements to carry out approximations and then performing calculations with the approximate numbers. In fact, this seems to describe only some forms of arithmetical estimation and is probably more relevant to secondary school children than either to younger children or to mathematically knowledgeable adults. But it does emphasize that arithmetical estimation typically has both approximation and calculation components. The work both with children and adults suggests that the calculation components often involve non-standard, derived fact strategies, rather than only the retrieval of known facts.

At the final end of the continuum we find approximation without calculation: the process that was found to be preserved in Dehaene and Cohen's severely dyscalculic patient, who demonstrated the preservation of some numerical cognitive processes in the absence of any access to known facts.

Fascinatingly, one of the most recent papers from Dehaene and his colleagues could be seen as giving some brain-imaging evidence for this idea of a continuum, rather than a clear-cut dissociation, between calculation and estimation. Stanescu-Cosson et al. (2000) found, in a functional MRI study, that the patterns of brain activation elicited by exact calculations with large numbers were more similar to those elicited by approximations than to those elicited by exact calculations with small numbers. The exact calculations with small numbers activated primarily left-literalised regions, especially in the frontal cortex. Both approximation and exact calculation with large numbers put heavier evidence on the left and right parietal cortices. One would presume that exact calculation with small numbers would typically involve the retrieval of learned facts, while calculation with larger numbers would involve the use of strategies for deriving unknown facts. To my knowledge, no brain-imaging studies have yet been carried out on the distinction between the use of standard, relatively automatized calculation strategies and the use of non-standard derived-fact strategies, although Delazer (2003) has demonstrated dissociations between these types of strategies in patients.

It would be particularly interesting to investigate whether there are individual differences in brain activation patterns of normal participants, according both to their overall calculation ability and the relative strength of different components of calculation and estimation. This would be likely to require a rather larger sample than typically takes part in brain-imaging studies.

8 Arithmetic facts, procedures and different forms of memory

'For Christopher remembers up to twice times ten,
But I keep forgetting where I put my pen.' (From *Now we are six*
© A. A. Milne. Published by Egmont UK Limited)

'How would you do five and five?'
'I'd count, you know. But it's noisy in the room, so while I was counting, I'd
think, I'd concentrate.' (Sonya, aged about 6, quoted by Ginsburg, 1977)

It has already been emphasized that arithmetical knowledge is often divided
into three broad categories: factual, procedural and conceptual knowledge.
Some chapters in this book emphasize aspects of conceptual knowledge.
This chapter will place greater emphasis on factual and procedural knowledge and on certain influences on these. We have already considered how
these may be associated with certain aspects of brain function and how they
may be influenced by aspects of language and culture. This chapter will
emphasize one important influence on factual and procedural knowledge:
memory, and some related cognitive functions. Rather, one could say that it
will emphasize several important influences on factual and procedural
knowledge, since, like many cognitive functions, memory has several components and these influence factual and procedural knowledge in different
ways and to different degrees.

Individual differences in memory, attention and 'executive function' have
sometimes been invoked to explain individual differences in arithmetic.

Of course, 'memory' is a term with many meanings, both in everyday life
and within psychology. Are we referring to long-term memory – e.g. for
arithmetical facts such as multiplication tables or procedures such as
borrowing in subtraction? Are we referring to short-term memory: to the
ability to keep the components of the arithmetic problem in memory long
enough to arrive at the solution? Are we referring to working memory: the
ability to *use* short-term memory efficiently in carrying out a cognitive task?

The question then arises of what exactly these aspects of memory involve.
In particular, 'working memory' has several overlapping meanings: for
example, the ability to use memory to guide problem solving; to organize

information in short-term memory; and to keep track of one operation while carrying out the next. There is much debate as to what lies at the core of working memory, and there is room for even more debate as to which aspects of working memory are most important in arithmetic.

There is also room for argument as to the extent to which the processes involved in memory are the same for different types of material. Memory has been studied extensively and is probably best understood with regard to verbal material: words, sentences and texts. Visual memory has also been studied, albeit to a lesser extent, and there are a number of specific tests for visual memory; e.g. the Benton Visual Retention Test for abstract patterns and the Warrington Face Recognition Test for unfamiliar faces.

What is memory?

Research on the nature and components of memory is discussed in detail elsewhere; e.g. Baddeley (1986) and Parkin (1993). The following is a brief account of some of the more relevant aspects.

Memory is usually regarded by psychologists as divided into two stores: short-term memory and long-term memory. The short-term memory store keeps information for a very short time. It is limited to a small number of items (typically around 7). Unless the items in this store are rehearsed, they are lost after a few seconds. Long-term memory has a seemingly unlimited capacity and keeps information for periods lasting from a few hours to a lifetime. It is, however, less good than the short-term memory store at keeping lists of unrelated items in their exact order.

Psychologists further divide long-term memory into two main categories: episodic memory and semantic memory. *Episodic* memory includes memories for particular events that we have experienced or observed. We usually have at least an approximate idea of when and where these events happened. *Semantic* memory includes our general knowledge of facts about the world: knowledge of words; knowledge of who people are; school-taught information, etc. Most people have little *episodic* memory for things that happened before the age of 3 or 4; but much important information in our *semantic* memory (notably including the foundations of language) was acquired before that age. In other words, much of what we need to know we learned *before* kindergarten; we just don't remember learning it.

Moreover, adults who develop amnesia as a result of brain damage usually lose episodic memory for recent and many past events, but retain much of their semantic memory.

At first sight, it would appear that the main aspect of memory that would influence arithmetic would be long-term semantic memory: specifically, long-term memory for arithmetical facts and procedures. This form of memory is certainly considered to be important in arithmetic. However, many researchers also consider short-term memory to be very important in arithmetic. This reflects the current view that short-term memory is not just a store, but acts as a *working memory*. In other words, it is important in keeping track of relevant information while problems are being solved; and in particular keeping track of one step in solving the problem while the next step is being planned or carried out. In other words, it is important in keeping track of relevant information while problems are being solved; and in particular keeping track of one step in solving a problem while the next step is being planned or carried out. For example, in arithmetic, it may be important to keep track of the units while adding the tens (see next section); or to keep track of the meanings within a word problem – is Fred *adding* to his store of sweets or *eating* them – while at the same time manipulating the numbers?

Thus, long-term memory may be particularly important in memory for arithmetical facts and for remembering *how* to carry out arithmetical procedures. Working memory may be particularly important in carrying out the procedures accurately, in the right order, without becoming confused or sidetracked.

Most studies suggest that many aspects of memory are related to success in arithmetic. For example, Fei (2000) found that Taiwanese children who were low achievers in mathematics were worse than high achievers of similar overall IQ in a variety of tasks involving short-term memory, long-term memory and working memory.

Multi-step arithmetic procedures and working memory

> 'Edward shifts his focus of attention so slowly that when he has figured out what he was *supposed* to be doing, he has forgotten what he *was* doing, and vice versa. I sometimes imagine him dialling a phone number. He has it written before him. He looks at it, and begins to dial. By the time he has dialled two or three digits, he has forgotten the rest of the number. He looks back at the paper, and reminds himself of the number; but by now he has forgotten how much of the number he has dialled, and must begin again. Maybe Edward doesn't do this with phones, but this is exactly how he does his maths. I can often hear him muttering to himself, "Now, where was I?"' (Holt, 1966, p. 103)

This passage describes the problem that many people experience when they carry out arithmetic problems that involve more than a single step. Multi-step arithmetic, especially multi-step mental arithmetic, can present particular difficulties for anyone who has a problem with working memory. It is more difficult to work out that $7 + 5 + 6 = 18$ than to work out that $12 + 6 = 18$. Multi-digit arithmetic is difficult not only because of its demands on place value concepts, but because it usually involves several steps. The addition sum $18 + 49$ may be solved in more than one way; e.g. '$10 + 40 = 50$; $8 + 9 = 17$; $50 + 17 = 67$'; or '$8 + 9 = 17$; put down 7 and carry the 1;

1 + 4 = 5; add the 1 that I carried so that makes 6; the answer is 67'; or '18 + 50 = 68; subtract 1 as 49 is 1 less than 50; 68 − 1 = 67'. All these strategies, however, have in common that they include more than one step and that it is necessary to keep track of the result of one step while carrying out the next step. This keeping track is an important function of working memory (Adams & Hitch, 1998).

It is relatively difficult for anyone to keep track mentally of the results of intermediate steps in an arithmetic problem. Presumably this is an important reason for the invention of written methods of recording the steps in a calculation. Hitch (1978) found that adults' calculation accuracy was dramatically reduced by any delays in opportunity to use the results of intermediate steps. Such interim information was forgotten if not used immediately.

Keeping track of multi-step arithmetic is thus likely to be a severe problem for people with memory disorders. Indeed, people in the early stages of Alzheimer's disease perform worse at many aspects of arithmetic than healthy elderly people; but in *particular* they have extreme difficulty with *multi-step* arithmetic (Santana, 2001).

Problems with using working memory in arithmetic can, however, be specific to arithmetic in some people who do not have general memory disorders. Takayama, Sugishita, Akiguchi, and Kimura (1994) found that three patients with isolated acalculia following damage to the left parietal lobe had particular difficulties with multi-step arithmetic. They could remember basic arithmetical facts; understood the basic processes of calculation; were able to align arithmetic problems on the page and deal with place value; and had no problem with immediate memory for calculation problems. But they experienced difficulty when they had to keep track of more than one step in arithmetic simultaneously. Takayama et al. concluded that isolated acalculia results from the disruption of working memory for calculation. One must be cautious about drawing such a conclusion: as will be discussed in Chapter 10, there are many forms of acalculia. But it is certainly striking that some patients do seem to have this specific problem.

The fact that individual differences in working memory are associated with arithmetical performance does not mean that working memory efficiency *causes* arithmetical success or that weaknesses in working memory *cause* arithmetical difficulties. For one thing, researchers disagree on the precise definition of working memory. (Debates on this issue are outside the scope of this book; the reader can refer to Andrade, 2001; Baddeley, 1986; etc.)

Working memory itself is not unitary. It involves several processes: holding information in short-term memory; using this information to guide action; keeping track of the order of steps in solving a problem or carrying out an activity; keeping track of the results of one of these steps while carrying out the next. Also, most current theories imply that working memory takes at least two forms: *verbal* and *visual-spatial* and that these can work in somewhat different ways and over different time periods; although there is considerable debate as to whether they are fully independent, or are 'slave systems' to a common 'central executive'.

It is not clear whether different domains tap the same forms of working memory. Would a boy like Edward indeed have more problems than others in dialling phone numbers, as well as with arithmetic? If so, would this be just because phone numbers are also in the category – numbers – with which he has difficulty; or would he have the same trouble in keeping track of words, pictures or landmarks on a journey? Does working memory for words involve the same processes as working memory for numbers? Does working memory for words *or* numbers involve the same processes as working memory for pictures, locations or other visual-spatial material?

The question marks in the previous paragraph are indeed question marks. It does indeed seem to be the case that arithmetic is closely associated with tasks that involve working memory *for numbers*. There is, however, much conflicting evidence as to whether arithmetical performance is associated with individual differences in working memory within all domains or just with individual differences in working memory for numbers.

Working memory for numbers: How it affects arithmetic

Digit span and arithmetical performance are quite highly correlated (Geary, Brown, & Samaranayake, 1991; Jackson & Warrington, 1986). My research (Dowker, 1998) has indicated that children's digit span does correlate with their performance on arithmetic tests, but that it has a much stronger independent relationship with *estimation* than with exact calculation.

Digit span on its own may not, however, be the best test of the sort of working memory needed for arithmetic, as it includes relatively little requirement to simultaneously keep in mind one step of a problem while carrying out the next. Some techniques have been devised which do involve this requirement.

An example of such a technique is the 'counting span' task, devised by Case, Kurland, and Goldberg (1982). In this task, children are presented with progressively longer series of cards showing different numbers of coloured spots on each card. At the end of each series, the child attempts to recall the results of all the counts. The counting span corresponds to the longest series of cards for which the child can remember the results of all the counts. Similar span tasks have since been devised for other types of material. For example, Hitch and McAuley (1991) and Henry and Maclean (2003) measured listening span by presenting children with increasingly long series of four-word sentences, and asking them to remember the last word of each sentence.

Maybery and Do (2003) devised 'running span' tasks for both verbal and spatial material. These contrast with traditional fixed span tasks, such as digit span, where the requirement is to recall a set number of items from start to finish. In running span tasks, children are presented with series longer than they could be expected to store in short-term memory (e.g. 12 letters) and are asked to recall a specified number of items from the *end* of the sequence. This number of items is progressively increased during testing, until the child ceases to be able to respond correctly.

Studies that show a specific relationship between arithmetic and working memory for numbers

Children with arithmetical difficulties have generally been found to have a lower counting span than children without such difficulties (Hitch & McAuley, 1991; Siegel & Ryan, 1989). Is the relationship to arithmetic specific to counting span or are other types of span also weak? Results are very contradictory in this area. Siegel and Ryan (1989) and Hitch and McAuley (1991) found that if children's arithmetical difficulties were specific and not combined with reading difficulties, then they were impaired *only* on *counting* span and not on similar tasks involving words.

Such results could mean that there are some processes specific to numerical working memory and that these processes in their turn have a specific effect on arithmetic. However, another explanation could be that the causal relationship is in the other direction. Facility with arithmetic and numbers could *cause* numerical working memory to be more efficient. This could be due to arithmetical facts and/or procedures being automatized, i.e. so well learned that they do not require a lot of thought and attention, thereby reducing the load on working memory.

Hitch and McAuley (1991) did indeed find that counting was slower and more effortful in their group with arithmetical difficulties and suggested that this may have contributed to the differences found in counting span.

It is likely that both 'vicious' and 'virtuous' circles may be present. For example, facility with counting procedures may contribute to efficiency of working memory for numbers, which may contribute to greater competence in arithmetic, which, in turn, may facilitate working memory for numbers. Several studies indicate that children with arithmetical difficulties are often slower and less efficient at using counting-based strategies in arithmetic (Geary, Widaman, Little, & Cormier, 1987; see also Chapter 4). This is likely to contribute to their difficulties in arithmetic. Whether as a result of their difficulty with counting-based strategies, or for other reasons, such children tend to be hampered in their progress toward using other types of strategy in arithmetic. This means that the very children who have most difficulty in using counting-based strategies are often those who rely most exclusively on such strategies, compounding their problems with arithmetic.

It could also be that people who have more arithmetical knowledge have a wider network of associations, which facilitate the organization of information in working memory: for example, one individual was aided in remembering a telephone number which included the numbers '8864' by associating it with her knowledge that $8 \times 8 = 64$. Moreover, better arithmetical knowledge may facilitate the *choice* of suitable strategies for remembering, organizing and handling numerical information.

Arithmetic and other forms of working memory

Not all results show a specific relationship between arithmetic and *numerical* working memory. Some studies (e.g. Fei, 2000; Jarvis & Gathercole, 2003; Keeler & Swanson, 2001; Swanson & Sachse-Lee, 2001) suggest that arithmetical performance is *not* only related to a specific working memory for numbers, but is related to both verbal and visual-spatial working memory span.

Moreover, Baddeley's theory of working memory states that there are not only visual-spatial and verbal working memory systems, but that these are controlled by a domain-general 'central executive'. According to this theory, any task that requires working memory, whether verbal or visual-spatial, will place demands on the central executive. It can be unclear where to draw the line between demands on the central executive and demands on one particular working memory system. Some researchers (e.g. Gathercole & Pickering, 2000; Henry & Maclean, 2003) consider that those tasks that do emphasize keeping track of a multi-step sequence of items, actions or events (rather than emphasizing just the short-term storage of information) should be seen as involving the central executive.

It is certainly true that arithmetic tends to be disrupted by (and to disrupt) the simultaneous performance of any cognitive task that requires attention and planning; and that some aspects of arithmetic are more difficult than others to combine with such tasks. Furst and Hitch (2000) found that carrying in addition was particularly hard to combine with a Trails task and suggested that this implies that carrying is particularly dependent on the central executive.

Findings about whether arithmetic is more closely related to verbal or spatial working memory and/or to a domain-general 'central executive' are even more conflicting than those concerning the relationships between arithmetic and verbal and spatial ability in general (see Chapter 2). Some studies show arithmetic to be more strongly associated with verbal working memory tasks than with visual-spatial working memory tasks (Wilson & Swanson, 2001), while others show the reverse (Gathercole & Pickering, 2000; Maybery & Do, 2003; McLean & Hitch, 1999).

The conflicting findings with regard to the effects of different forms of working memory on arithmetic may reflect the fact that people use different strategies for arithmetic. As pointed out elsewhere in this book, different people often solve the same problem in different ways and the same person may solve the same problem in different ways at different times. Some of these strategies are predominantly verbal; some are predominantly spatial;

some are abstract. Some individuals have a general tendency to learn and reason through words and others through visual imagery (e.g. Riding & Watts, 1997).

Riding, Grimley, Dahraei, and Banner (2003) have found that measures of working memory capacity are more strongly associated with the general school performance of children who rely on verbal rather than visual strategies. They also found that working memory interacts with other aspects of cognitive style and strategy preference. Measures of working memory capacity are more strongly associated with the school performance of children with an analytic than a holistic cognitive style (see Chapter 2). Clearly, there is much work to be done on the relationships between different types of working memory, individual differences in cognitive style and strategy preference and mathematical performance.

Moreover, it is sometimes suggested (Dehaene, 1997) that some arithmetical operations, such as multiplication, place more demand on verbal strategies; others, such as subtraction, on spatial or abstract strategies. If this is true, it would mean that the relative importance of verbal and visual-spatial working memory would also be different for different operations.

Relative importance of verbal and visual-spatial working memory at different ages

Most research seems to indicate that different forms of working memory are differentially associated with arithmetic at different ages.

There has been quite a lot of research on both verbal and visual working memory in *adults*. One way of assessing the role of verbal or visual-spatial working memory in performing a task is to ask people to perform that task (Task A) at the same time as another task (Task B) that requires either verbal or visual-spatial processing. If the simultaneous performance of Task B interferes with the speed and accuracy of performing Task A, then this could imply that the two tasks are making demands on the same form of working memory. Hitch and colleagues found that mental arithmetic is significantly impaired by the simultaneous performance of a verbal task (e.g. saying the word 'rhubarb' repeatedly), while it is much less disrupted by a task that does not involve speech, such as tapping a foot repeatedly. This is true both of adults (Furst & Hitch, 2000; Hitch, 1978) and of children (Adams & Hitch, 1998). When the numbers are *visible*, the simultaneous verbal task has a far less disruptive effect (Furst & Hitch, 2000). This indicates that people use subvocal speech when keeping track of the steps of a mental arithmetic operation; but that this becomes less necessary when the information is visually present.

Lee and Kang (2002) found that holding a visual image in the mind slowed down adults' subtraction but not their multiplication, while verbal rehearsal of unrelated material slowed down their multiplication but not their subtraction. This gives some support to the view that multiplication makes more demands on verbal working memory and subtraction on visual-spatial working memory: perhaps because multiplication emphasizes retrieval of verbally learned facts (multiplication tables) while subtraction is a form of calculation that may enlist spatial strategies, such as the use of imagined number lines.

Hecht (2002) found that disrupting adults' working memory by requiring them to carry out verbal tasks at the same time did not influence the strategies that they used for verifying the correctness of simple addition statements (e.g. $4 + 2 = 6$; $4 + 3 = 8$). It only disrupted arithmetical performance if people were using a counting-on strategy.

Does this mean that people who rely more on counting-on strategies will be more dependent on verbal working memory when doing arithmetic than people who do not? This would imply that children's arithmetical performance should be more dependent on verbal working memory than that of adults and that people who are relatively poor at remembering arithmetical facts should be more dependent on verbal working memory than those who are better at remembering arithmetical facts.

A few studies suggest that the relationship between working memory and arithmetical ability does *not* vary much with age. Wilson and Swanson (2001) found a stable relationship between arithmetical ability and working memory across a broad age span including both children and adults. In all age groups, arithmetic was more closely related to verbal working memory than to visual-spatial working memory.

However, many other studies give different results. For example, McKenzie, Bull, & Gray (2003) found that visual-spatial interference disrupted 6-year-olds' arithmetic more than verbal interference did, while the reverse was true of 8-year-olds. By contrast, some other studies suggest increasing involvement of visual-spatial working memory as children grow *older*. Henry and Maclean (2003) found that 7- and 8-year-olds' arithmetical reasoning was best predicted by 'central executive' tasks, with some added contribution from word and digit span. 'Central executive' tasks were also the best predictors of arithmetic in intellectually impaired 11- and 12-year-olds with mental ages of 7 or 8. However, the arithmetical reasoning of typical 11- and 12-year-olds was best predicted by visual memory, with some additional contribution from word and digit span.

One may make some sense of these results, by assuming that different strategies are particularly emphasized at different ages. Younger children may rely on finger- and object-counting strategies, which are significantly related to visual-spatial working memory (Kyttala, Aunio, Lehto, Van Luit, & Hautamaki, 2003). Somewhat older children may rely most on mental calculation (especially in the United Kingdom, where mental calculation is typically taught before written calculation). This would be expected to require verbal memory and, in particular, to involve the ability to keep mental track of one step while performing the next: an ability supposedly measured by 'central executive' tasks. Yet older children may have more experience with written arithmetic and with diagrams and may rely more on visualizing written sums and/or diagrams.

Set size and working memory

There is overwhelming evidence that people, especially very young children, tend to perform better at tasks that involve small numbers than those which involve large numbers. This is true for counting; quantity estimation (Huntley-Fenner & Cannon, 2000; Starkey & Cooper, 1995); number conservation (Cowan, 1979; Gelman, 1982); the cardinal word principle (Munn, 1997); word problem solving (Hughes, 1986) and nonverbal arithmetic problem solving (Klein & Bisanz, 2000). There are several reasons why this should be the case – greater familiarity with small numbers; the fact that very small numbers may be recognized without counting; but it has sometimes been suggested (Klein & Bisanz, 2000) that one important reason is that smaller set sizes may place less of a load on working memory.

Different aspects of working memory

'Working memory' covers not only several modalities but several processes and the term is used with a different emphasis by different researchers. The meaning ascribed to the term may range from being almost identical to the term 'short-term memory' to implying a much wider range of cognitive processes, overlapping closely with such terms as 'attention' and 'executive function'. It can refer to the processes involved in organizing and rehearsing information to keep it in short-term memory and to select parts of it for transfer into long-term memory. It can refer to the amount of information that can be temporarily stored from one task while carrying out the next task. It can refer more broadly and deeply to the cognitive processes involved in selecting and maintaining strategies for carrying out mental tasks.

Sometimes it is explicitly treated as a combination of several specific processes: notably, the influential model proposed by Baddeley and Hitch (1974) includes three major components: the phonological loop, which maintains and processes verbal material by means of overt or covert verbal rehearsal; the visuospatial sketchpad, which stores and manipulates spatial or visual information; and the central executive, which stores and manipulates visual and spatial information.

Differences between the results of different studies may be due to differences in the aspects of working memory that are emphasized and in the ways that they are measured. For example, Passolunghi and Siegel (2001) found that children who were poor at arithmetical word problem solving had a poorer memory span than others for numbers, but not for words. However, they were worse than others at all tasks, whether numerical or not, that involved inhibiting irrelevant information: i.e. ignoring it in favour of relevant information.

The inhibition of irrelevant information may be more important for word problem solving than for other arithmetical tasks, as word problem solving makes much greater demands on the ability to sift through a passage and decide what is relevant (see Chapter 4).

Bull and her colleagues (Bull & Johnston 1997; Bull & Scherif, 2001; Bull, Johnston, & Roy, 1999; McKenzie et al., 2003) investigated the relationship between 6- to 8-year-old children's mathematical skills and their performance on several different measures of working memory and 'executive function'. Mathematical ability did not correlate significantly with auditory verbal short-term memory, with visual sequential memory or with dual task performance: the ability to attend to two tasks at once. However, it was independently related to measures of processing speed; to a test of the ability to attend specifically to relevant information and to inhibit irrelevant information (the Stroop Task); and to a test of solving a multi-step problem where a strategy had to be worked out and followed, including the use of intermediate steps that were appropriate to achieving the long-term goal but seemed superficially discordant with it in the short term (the Wisconsin Card Sorting Test). These relationships persisted, even after controlling for IQ and reading ability. The researchers concluded that mathematical difficulties are associated with speed of retrieval of facts and also with problems in switching between strategies, evaluation of inappropriate or ineffective strategies and evaluation of new strategies.

Some aspects of executive function seem to be more impaired in children with arithmetical difficulties than in children with other academic difficulties. Sikora, Healey, Edwards, and Butler (2002) found that children with arithmetical difficulties were worse than those with reading difficulties at the Tower of London test: a test that, like the Wisconsin Card Sorting Test, requires people to devise and follow a long-term strategy and not to be deflected by superficial conflicts between intermediate steps and the final goal.

Strategies for helping children with working memory difficulties

El-Naggar (1996) points out that one consequence of working memory difficulties is that children may have difficulty in following multi-step instructions. Children with such problems may only be able to keep one instruction in mind at the same time. El-Naggar suggest that teachers may help such pupils by sitting the pupil near the teacher so that reminders may be given more easily; checking written work frequently so that the child has not forgotten the task by the time the corrections are made; building 'rehearsal' of familiar facts into the programme; assisting children to create and use mnemonics; and permitting the use of memory aids, including calculators.

McKenzie et al. (2003) have suggested that visual-spatial working memory should be assessed in the early school years, and that children who have difficulties in this area should be encouraged to use alternative, e.g. verbal, strategies.

Memory for arithmetical facts

> *Researcher*: 'Do you like maths?'
> *Nick (8)*: 'Yes, when it's about times tables!'

In the early 20th century, some behaviourist psychologists, notably Thorndike (1921), placed a great emphasis on the storage of arithmetical facts; on the formation of correct associations between sums and their answers; and on developing habits of producing the correct responses. Few researchers or educators would now consider that arithmetical thinking consists solely of memory for arithmetical facts. Indeed, as discussed in Chapter 2, this has not been the *only* available viewpoint for a very long time, if ever. However, although memory for arithmetical facts is only one component of arithmetical cognition, it is one that has received a lot of attention. People who have difficulties in retrieving arithmetical facts, such as multiplication tables, often describe themselves on this basis as 'no good at maths'. People who consider that educational standards have declined over the years often justify this opinion with reference to younger people's allegedly reduced knowledge of arithmetical facts: 'Children nowadays don't learn their tables.'

There is much evidence that individual differences in arithmetical fact retrieval are closely related to individual differences in general measures of arithmetical performance (Gray & Mulhern, 1995). In particular, children with mathematical difficulties are more consistently weak at retrieving arithmetical facts from memory than at other aspects at arithmetic and often rely on counting strategies in arithmetic at ages when their age mates are relying much more on fact retrieval (Cumming & Elkins, 1999; Fei, 2000; Fleischner, Garnett, & Shepherd, 1982; Geary & Brown, 1991a, 1991b; Ostad, 1997, 1998; Russell & Ginsburg, 1984; Siegler, 1988; Yeo, 2001).

There have been fewer studies of the extent to which high levels of arithmetical talent are associated with prowess in fact retrieval. Certainly, fact retrieval is not *all* that is associated with arithmetical talent (see Chapter 1); flexibility of strategy use and the ability to spot, understand and use arithmetical patterns and relationships are very important. Arithmetically talented people tend to be better than others at arithmetical fact retrieval, but they also seem to be quicker and more efficient at using *any* arithmetical strategy, whether based on counting, retrieval or other forms of calculation (Dark & Benbow, 1990; Geary & Brown, 1991a, 1991b).

As with many correlations, it is hard to establish direction of causation: which comes first, the chicken or the egg? Do children develop mathematical difficulties because they find it hard to remember arithmetical facts or do they find it hard to remember arithmetical facts because they have other mathematical difficulties?

Part of the reason for the associations between number fact retrieval and more general arithmetical performance lies in the ways in which arithmetical performance is often assessed. If arithmetical tests and assessments emphasize fact retrieval, then those who are poor at fact retrieval are likely to do badly in the tests and be classed as having arithmetical difficulties. If arithmetical fact retrieval is emphasized in the school curriculum, then those who are weak at this aspect of arithmetic will struggle with their school arithmetic lessons and assignments, even if they have no difficulty with other aspects of arithmetic. Similarly, those who are particularly good at fact retrieval are likely to be classified as 'good at maths' if this is an important criterion in assessments.

There does, however, seem to be more to the problem than this. If people have trouble in remembering 'basic' arithmetic facts, then they will have to calculate these facts by alternative and usually more time-consuming strategies. Even if they are able to do so accurately, this means that they must devote time and attention to obtaining facts that someone else might retrieve automatically; and this will divert time and attention from other aspects of arithmetical problem solving, resulting in lower efficiency.

Some adults with acquired dyscalculia as a result of brain damage have been found to be selectively impaired in memory for arithmetic facts, despite seemingly unimpaired procedural and conceptual knowledge (Cohen & Dehaene, 1994; Warrington, 1982). This pattern is often found in people in the early stages of Alzheimer's disease and related conditions (Duverne, Lemaire, & Michel, 2003). (See Chapter 2 for more extensive discussion of discrepancies between factual, conceptual and procedural knowledge; and Chapter 10 for discussion of their possibly different representations in the brain.)

Some forms of arithmetic typically depend more on fact retrieval than others. For example, people are more likely to be trained to memorize multiplication facts (tables) than addition facts and are more likely to memorize addition facts than subtraction or division facts. Therefore, multiplication is likely, for most people, to depend more on factual knowledge and subtraction and division more on procedural knowledge. Roussel, Fayol, and Barouillet (2002) found that presenting the operation sign (+ or ×) before presenting the numerals had a stronger effect for addition than for multiplication. They suggested that this may be because addition requires more use of calculation strategies, whereas multiplication is more dependent on direct retrieval of facts.

It is usually found that adults are quicker and more efficient than children at retrieving arithmetical facts (e.g. addition combinations and multiplication tables) and that they use retrieval as a strategy more often than children do (Kaye, Post, Hall, & Dineen, 1986). Among children, efficiency of retrieval increases with age (Ashcraft & Fierman, 1982; Lemaire, Barrett, Fayol, & Abdi, 1994).

Increases in memory for number facts with age will result from several cognitive factors, including improvements in the various aspects of memory discussed in this chapter. Specific practice effects may also be important. School arithmetic textbooks devote different amounts of space to different arithmetic facts (Ashcraft & Christ, 1995). Practice effects may begin early. Siegler and Shrager (1984) found that at least some parents give pre-schoolers practice in simple addition, and that they tend to concentrate on problems with 1 or 2 as the addend. Are they simply responding to their children's emerging ability to add small but not large numbers (Hughes, 1986; Chapter 4 in this volume); or does the children's ability to add small numbers develop partly in response to the practice that they receive? (See Chapter 9 in this volume for a discussion of the effects of culture and experience on arithmetic.)

The rote learning of arithmetical facts has been emphasized in some intervention programmes. Some earlier programmes did so because factual knowledge was seen as the essence of arithmetic. Some more recent programmes do not subscribe to this view, but still emphasize fact learning because, once children have learned the facts they can deal with them automatically and devote more attention to higher order mathematical thinking (Cheng, 1985; G. Mulhern, personal communication; Pellegrino & Goldman, 1987; Thornton, 1978).

Fox (1995) carried out a training study, where 3rd-graders (8- to 9-year-olds) were given computer drill on addition facts. The children who were given the drill did indeed become faster and more accurate at retrieving addition facts than children who had played a mathematical board game that did not emphasize the memorization of facts or who had not received any training. However, this improvement in arithmetical fact retrieval did not lead to any improvement in performance on higher level mathematical tasks. It also did not affect mathematical motivation, either positively or negatively.

Selecting the relevant facts

Retrieval of arithmetical facts depends on the actual knowledge of the arithmetical facts: an aspect of long-term memory. It also depends on the ability to select the relevant arithmetical fact and inhibit competing alternatives, which may be seen more as a function of working memory. The latter is important, since many quite similar arithmetical facts are stored together and may be readily confused with one another (Campbell, 1987; Murray, 1941). For example, addition facts may be confused with multiplication facts involving the same digits (e.g. '2 + 3 = 6', through confusion between 2 + 3 and 2 × 3) and multiplication facts may be confused with other multiplication facts that belong to the same multiplication table and especially those that immediately precede or follow them in the same table (e.g. '8 × 3 = 32', by confusion between 8 × 3 and 8 × 4).

Studies of such confusions – termed 'associative interference' – have, for example, consistently revealed that the multiplication errors of children, adolescents and adults tend to belong to the table of one of the operands (Barouillet, Fayol, & Lethuliere, 1997). Barouillet et al. (1997) found that 13- and 14-year-olds with mathematical difficulties are particularly inclined to make such errors and that they are also more likely than others to select the wrong answer in multiple-choice tasks where the correct response was presented along with three distractors. Barouillet et al. concluded that these adolescents may have had difficulty not so much with knowledge of the multiplication facts as with the inhibition of related but incorrect responses.

Although memory for facts increases with age, interference also increases with age (Lemaire et al., 1994). The more facts we know, the more facts we can confuse.

Retrieval strategies in arithmetic: Dangers of oversimplifying the issues

It is important to avoid oversimplifying the issues.

It is oversimplified to imply that the only types of strategy that can be used are those based on counting and those based on retrieval. Indeed, two of the key issues of this book are the fact that people use *a wide variety of strategies* in arithmetical problem solving and that there are many forms of arithmetical knowledge, which can be broadly grouped in the categories of *factual*, *procedural* and *conceptual* knowledge. Retrieval comes into the category of factual knowledge (including appropriate access to this knowledge). Counting-based strategies are based on a combination of simple concepts and simple procedures (see Chapter 4). There are many aspects of procedural and conceptual knowledge that are not covered by retrieval and counting-based strategies. In particular, once arithmetical problems involve numbers of more than one digit, retrieval becomes difficult and calculation procedures become increasingly important. Derived fact strategies – involving knowledge of and reasoning about arithmetical properties such as commutativity and associativity to work out arithmetical facts that are not known from memory – are very important in arithmetic, and have been given an entire chapter in the present book (Chapter 6).

Svenson and her colleagues (Svenson & Broquist, 1975; Svenson, Hedenborg, & Lingman, 1976) gave children between the ages of 9 and 12 single-digit addition problems with a sum smaller than 13. Reaction time measures were supported by the children's verbal reports of their strategies in suggesting that about one-third of the responses involved direct retrieval from memory. The rest involved heuristics that were only partly based on memory. The three commonest heuristics were counting on from the larger added by single steps; counting in larger units, e.g. counting by 2s; and reference to ties, i.e. converting the problem into one that involves doubling an addend, e.g. $4 + 5 = 4 + 4 + 1 = 8 + 1$. Only the first of these heuristics would normally be described as a counting strategy. When children in special classes for those with learning difficulties were compared with typically developing children, they were slower in responding to all tasks, but also showed difficulty in selecting the most efficient strategy.

Steel and Funnell (2001) studied the learning of multiplication facts by a group of children between the ages of 7 and 12. These children had been taught by 'discovery methods', which did not place great emphasis on rote learning of multiplication tables. Children used a variety of strategies, including counting in series (e.g. '5, 10, 15, 20'); retrieval on its own; and retrieval combined with calculation. Retrieval was the fastest and most accurate of the strategies, and counting in series the slowest and most error prone. Older children were more likely than younger children to use retrieval; and retrieval was, not surprisingly, used more for problems including small numbers than large numbers.

It is oversimplified to assume that adults always use retrieval strategies, even for small-number arithmetic. Several studies have indicated that even educated adults sometimes use counting-based strategies for single-digit addition: most commonly, the counting-on-from-larger strategy (Groen & Parkman, 1972; Lefevre & Kulak, 1994; Lefevre, Smith-Chant, Hiscock, Daley, & Morris, 2003), and that there are individual differences in this respect.

Where numbers of two or more digits are to be added, adults rarely rely solely on retrieval. Thevenot, Barouillet, and Fayol (2001) carried out a study where adults had either to add a pair of two-digit numbers or to compare them and say which was larger. They were then given a recognition task where they were shown a number and had to say whether it was one of the pair that they had already seen. The addition task interfered with the recognition task, while the comparison task did not. Thevenot et al. suggest that this brings into question the view that adults have developed automatic, necessary associations between operands and answers in arithmetic.

As discussed in Chapter 1, variability of strategy use is an important characteristic of arithmetical thought and performance in both children and adults. Self-reports by adults of the procedures that they use for simple subtractions (Daley & Lefevre, 1997) and multiplications (Smith, 1995) indicate that retrieval is only one of many strategy types that they use: they also reported frequent use of repeated addition, derived fact strategies, counting strategies and rules about the numbers 0 and 1 ($n \times 1 = n$; $n \times 0 = 0$; $n - 0 = n$). Several studies indicate that adults combine other strategies with retrieval even for quite simple problems. For example, Lemaire and Fayol (1995) found that both adults and children were quicker in rejecting an answer to a multiplication problem as wrong if it disobeyed rules about odd and even numbers: i.e., if an odd number was given as the product of two even numbers or an even number as the product of two odd numbers. Thus, the participants were using their knowledge of arithmetical relationships to judge the plausibility of an answer before 'deciding' whether they needed to retrieve the facts from memory.

It is oversimplified to assume that retrieval is *always* 'better' than other strategies. There is a lot of evidence that retrieval is indeed faster and more efficient and less error prone than other strategies for addition, multiplication (Steel & Funnell, 2001) and other arithmetical tasks. However, it does not necessarily indicate or inculcate better understanding of the arithmetical concepts involved. In some ways, access to a large number of arithmetical facts for easy retrieval is rather like access to a calculator: it makes arithmetical computation less effortful and more efficient and enables the individual to attend to the meaning of the problem, rather than needing to focus attention on the laborious calculation of each arithmetical fact. However, over-reliance on either calculator use or retrieval as the *only* important process in arithmetic could, at least in theory, inhibit the development of number sense and arithmetical reasoning. Moreover, the memorization of arithmetical facts is something that presents difficulty to a significant number of children and adults; and overemphasizing its importance, and discouraging other strategies, could encourage 'learned helplessness' about arithmetic and an assumption that because one has difficulty with the memorization of facts, one is, globally, 'no good at maths'.

It is oversimplified to go to the other extreme and assume that learning arithmetical facts is always 'bad for you', or intrinsically unpleasant, and that memorization of addition or multiplication facts will of itself prevent real learning. Despite the many discrepancies that can be found, factual knowledge is positively, rather than negatively, correlated with conceptual aspects of arithmetic such as estimation and derived fact strategy use (see Chapters 6 and 7). Some children, like Nick who was quoted earlier, positively enjoy collecting and repeating arithmetical facts. On several occasions, when visiting schools, I have been stopped by children wanting to impart such facts to me: 'Did you know, ten times one is ten, and ten times two is twenty, and ten times three is thirty . . .'

Cultural influences on facts and procedures

There is much evidence that people in some cultures are better at arithmetical fact retrieval than those in other cultures (see Chapter 9, section on 'International comparisons'). In particular, Chinese, Korean and Japanese people tend to be better than North Americans. Campbell and Xue (2001) compared three groups of university students: Chinese students; Canadian students of Chinese descent; and Canadian students with no Chinese connection. The Chinese students were better than either Canadian group at multi-digit arithmetic. The Chinese and Chinese-Canadians were equally good and better than the non-Chinese Canadians, at single-digit arithmetic.

Chinese adults rely more exclusively than Canadian adults on retrieval rather than other strategies for single-digit multiplication problems (Penner-Wilger, Leth-Steenson, & Lefevre, 2002).

Arithmetical fact memory and other aspects of long-term memory

Is the ability to memorize, store and retrieve arithmetical facts associated with the ability to memorize, store and retrieve other forms of information? In other words, are some people just good at remembering facts?

The evidence so far does not suggest a strong specific relationship between memory for arithmetical facts and other aspects of long-term memory. There do seem to be some people with particular *difficulties* in remembering facts, especially of a verbal nature. People with dyslexia and related specific learning difficulties frequently experience difficulty with long-term memory for various forms of information, which include, but are not restricted to, arithmetical facts and formulae (Chinn & Ashcroft, 1998; Miles, 1993; Chapter 2 in this volume). The same is true of children with specific language impairments (Fazio, 1999). However, Watkins (1998) found that children with any form of specific learning difficulty tended to be worse at long-term memory tests than those without such difficulties, but those with specific learning difficulties in arithmetic did not differ greatly from those with specific learning difficulties in other areas.

When memory and arithmetic do not go together

Although memory plays an important role in arithmetic, it is possible to be competent in arithmetic despite having a very bad memory for most kinds of material. There are several striking examples of dissociations between arithmetic and most forms of memory.

First of all, people with acquired long-term memory disorders (amnesia) are often unimpaired at arithmetic (Delazer, Ewen, & Benke, 1997; Schnider, Bassetti, Gutbrod, & Ozdoba, 1995). Even when amnesia begins in childhood, it is possible to end up with average arithmetical ability (Benedict, Shapiro, Duffner, & Jaeger, 1998). This is not quite as surprising as it seems at first sight. As stated earlier, amnesia tends to affect episodic memory (for events) more than semantic memory (for information); and arithmetic probably makes greater demands on the latter.

Can semantic memory be impaired, while arithmetic is preserved? This is a difficult issue to study, since it is almost impossible for semantic memory to be globally impaired in isolation from other intellectual functions. Severe developmental global impairment of semantic memory is associated with low IQ and general learning difficulties; severe acquired global impairment of semantic memory is associated with dementia. Nevertheless, some people do show good arithmetical competence, despite severe problems with other aspects of semantic memory. This would appear to be true of at least some of the 'savant' calculators, who are very good at some or all aspects of arithmetic, despite having very low IQs and limited general knowledge about the world. Perhaps even more strikingly, Butterworth (1999) describes a man, 'Monsieur Van' who was suffering from Alzheimer's disease or a similar disorder. He had severe impairments in almost every intellectual function that might be seen as possibly relevant to arithmetic: logical reasoning, episodic memory and semantic memory. Yet he performed at least an average level on standardized test of arithmetic, and was able to tell reliably whether a given 3- or 4-digit number was a square or not.

Monsieur Van's *working memory* was relatively unimpaired, at least when measured by the usual tests, such as digit span. Could it be that working memory is essential to arithmetic? The answer may depend on how one defines working memory. It would seem that *some sort* of ability to keep track of the steps involved in solving a problem *must* be essential to some types of arithmetic.

However, good performance on standard measures of working memory is not essential to arithmetic. Butterworth, Cipolotti, and Warrington (1996) studied a man who, following a stroke, was unable to repeat more than two digits. (The average adult can repeat 7 digits.) Yet he had no difficulty in carrying out mental additions and subtractions involving three-digit numbers: for example, $128 + 149$ or $119 - 35$. This was despite the fact that he could not *repeat* these sums.

Moreover, people with schizophrenia often show signs of frontal lobe impairment and have difficulties with many aspects of working memory; but arithmetical disabilities are not a usual feature of the disorder. Kiefer, Abel, and Weisbrod (2002) found that schizophrenic patients showed impaired performance in several working memory tests including backward digit span and some verbal fluency tests; but they performed similarly to controls on tasks that required them to verify the correctness of single-digit multiplications and divisions.

Monitoring one's own thinking

> 'Most of us have very imperfect control over our attention. Our minds slip away from duty before we realize that they are gone. Part of being a good student is learning to be aware of the state of one's own mind and the degree of one's own understanding. The good student may be the one who often says that he does not understand, simply because he keeps a constant check on his understanding. The poor student who does not, so to speak, watch himself trying to understand, does not know most of the time whether he understands or not.' (Holt, 1966, p. 23)

Being aware of one's own thought processes (metacognition) is often seen as one of the important factors in arithmetic (Schoenfield, 1987, 1992). If one is aware of one's own thought processes, this makes it possible to notice when we are failing to remember; when our attention is wandering; when we are failing to understand. It makes it easier to plan a strategy and keep track of whether we are following this strategy correctly. Metacognition is related to many aspects of arithmetic, but is included in this chapter because metacognition during arithmetical problem solving would seem to depend on working memory.

Especially during the last 20 years, there has been much discussion and research concerning the general importance of metacognition in psychology and in education (e.g. Palincsar & Brown, 1987). Most of this research is outside the scope of this book. However, there is a significant amount of research that indicates that many people do not reflect effectively on the arithmetical strategies that they use and that this may interfere with their arithmetical performance (Schoenfield, 1987, 1992).

Individual differences in achievement in arithmetic has been found to be related to been found to be worse than higher achievers at metacognitive aspects of arithmetic, including describing arithmetical rules explicitly, predicting results of arithmetical operations, planning their strategies, monitoring their use of these strategies and evaluating their answers (Carr, Alexander, & Folds-Bennett, 1994; Lucangeli, Coi, & Bosco, 1997; Lucangeli, Cornoldi, & Tellarini, 1998; Montague & Bos, 1990; Slife, Weiss, & Bell, 1985). One study even found arithmetical word problem solving by 5- and 6-year-olds to be more strongly related to arithmetical metacognition than to IQ (Mevarech, 1995).

As always, association does not mean cause and it could be that better arithmetical performance is leading to better metacognition, rather than the other way around. Those who are more experienced at arithmetic may be better at monitoring their own strategy use; and some metacognitive skills such as predicting and evaluating results would seem to depend in part on such arithmetical abilities as estimation and number sense. Moreover, some apparent differences in metacognition between high and low achievers in arithmetic could be due not to differences in accuracy in reflecting on ones arithmetical strategies, but to differences in the strategies themselves. For example, Lucangeli et al. (1997) found that low achievers in fifth grade (10- and 11-year-olds) attributed disproportionate importance to the size of the numbers in a problem as an indicator of difficulty. In fact, however, number size does strongly influence young children's ability to solve an arithmetical problem (see Chapters 3 and 6) and slightly older low achievers may resemble younger children in this respect. As we have seen, lower achievers rely far more than higher achievers on counting-based strategies; and one would expect these to be particularly affected by number size.

However, there is some evidence for metacognition leading to better arithmetic, inasmuch as training people to analyze arithmetical problems explicitly and to monitor the strategies that they are using in arithmetic, seems to improve their arithmetical performance. This is true of children between the ages of 8 and 13 (Cardelle-Elawar, 1992; Lucangeli et al., 1998); older teenagers (Maqsud, 1998); children through the secondary age range (Adey & Shayer, 1994); and adults (Nietfield & Schraw, 2002).

Attention

Arithmetic may depend more than some other activities on continuous, focused concentration and attention. In many verbal and spatial tasks, if the attention wanders for a short time, it is often possible to compensate by attending to other cues or to reconstruct what was missed by 'common sense', for example, by reference to what usually happens in similar situations. In the case of arithmetic, a number or arithmetical step that has been lost may not be so readily reconstructed and its absence may prevent subsequent steps from being carried out.

It is nowadays difficult to discuss individual differences in distractibility or in the ability to pay focused attention, without becoming involved in the debates as to the existence, nature, incidence or treatment of 'attention deficit disorder'. Such debates are outside the scope of this book. For the purposes of this discussion, relatively high distractibility certainly need not imply the presence of any specific disorder.

Attention may not be a unitary process: people may differ in their ability to attend to different types of information (e.g. verbal versus spatial). It is undoubtedly influenced by the level of difficulty of a task for an individual. On the whole, moderately difficult tasks will elicit the greatest amount of attention: very easy or well-practised tasks may be performed in an automatic fashion, requiring and eliciting little attention, and excessively difficult tasks may lead to 'switching off'. The individual's interest in the subject matter and/or motivation to perform well in a task will, of course, also influence attention. So will the individual's emotional and physical state and sometimes external physical conditions: for example, many of us will have experienced difficulty in attending to a lecture in a room that was excessively hot or cold.

Attentional skills require both the ability to pay attention to appropriate stimuli and to ignore inappropriate stimuli. People with attentional difficulties are often not simply 'switched off' or 'half asleep'. They may be distracted by stimuli irrelevant to the task or information to which they wish, or are required, to attend, as in the following exchange:

> *Researcher*: How much is two and five?
> *Imran (aged 6, looking at the school bell)*: There's the bell! It goes ding-dong!

Do children with serious arithmetical difficulties have particular problems in paying attention? As often, the evidence is somewhat conflicting. Shalev, Manor, Kerem, Ayali, Badichi, Friedlander, and Gross-Tsur (2001) found that 'attention deficit disorder' was not a risk factor for dyscalculia. By way of contrast, Ehlers et al. (1997) found that children with a diagnosis of attention deficit disorder performed worse on the arithmetic (and coding) subtests of the WISC IQ test than on the other subtests. Lindsay (2001) found that children with a diagnosis of dyscalculia performed worse than controls on a test of continuous attention and that arithmetic scores were associated with attention scores in both groups.

Arithmetical word problems often require the ability to sort out relevant from irrelevant information and this aspect might be expected to create particular difficulties for individuals with difficulties in selective attention.

There is indeed evidence that children rated as inattentive by their teachers have more difficulty than other children in solving word problems that contain irrelevant information, while performing equally well for word problems that contain only relevant information (Marzocchi, Lucangeli, DeMeo, Fini, & Cornoldi, 2002). Irrelevant verbal information was more distracting to them than irrelevant numerical information. This may be because children who fail to select relevant *verbal* information are more likely to demonstrate attentional difficulties in a variety of classroom tasks, as these often involve attending to verbal information (written or oral) and following verbal instructions. It may also be because interpreting verbal information is precisely what makes word problems difficult for most children.

Conclusions

Thus, it appears that long-term memory, working memory and attention are all important in arithmetic. However, it is still a matter of debate whether these should be seen as global, domain-general processes; or whether they are much more dependent on the particular domain. In other words, it may really be just long-term memory, working memory and attention *for numbers* that are important in arithmetic. Moreover, some people who appear to have weaknesses in any or all of these processes can still be good at arithmetic and some people have problems with arithmetic without noticeable weaknesses in memory or attention. Nonetheless, individual differences in these cognitive processes do seem to have a significant impact on individual differences in arithmetic.

9 Effects of culture, language and experience

Learning and development are influenced by culture and experience from birth: indeed, even earlier. As discussed in Chapter 10, not only does the brain influence what we can experience, but experience also influences the development and organization of the brain. For human beings, experience is intrinsically influenced by culture. Culture influences the language that we speak; the social organization of the community in which we grow up; the practical and economic activities that we pursue and the age at which we begin them; whether we go to school or not and the form that our schooling takes. It influences the existence and nature of the monetary system that we use and the major preoccupations of the society. For example, age and birthdays are important concerns within most western cultures, but not in certain other cultures.

Skills that do and do not depend on culture

Some numerical skills appear to be much more dependent on culture than others. Not surprisingly, the skills that are most dependent on culture tend to be those that are taught formally in schools, those that are closely related to specific occupations and those that are highly dependent on language.

The ability to compare quantities does not vary much with culture. Young children are fairly good at selecting which of two quantities is 'more', e.g.:

```
0    0    0
   0    0
0  0    0   0
```

is more than

```
0   0

0  0  0
```

They can do this fairly well even when the quantities involved exceed their counting span (Binet, 1969) or when they are prevented from counting (Estes & Combs, 1966). What does drastically reduce their performance is any discrepancy between the numerical difference between the quantities involved and the difference between the lengths or areas covered. As discussed in Chapter 4, Piaget (1952) found that children tend to rely on length and area cues when comparing quantities, so that for example they assume that the longer row always has more. Binet (1969) and Estes and Combs (1966) found that, if children are shown a more numerous set of small objects and a less numerous set of larger objects that takes up more space, they tend to select the latter set as having more.

Ginsburg and Russell (1981) found that, within the United States, social class, race and culture had little or no effect on young children's strengths or weaknesses in such tasks. Posner (1982) extended these findings to schooled and unschooled children in the Ivory Coast: they differed little from one another or from American children. Regardless of culture, country, schooling or parental level of education, children tend to do reasonably well, at least from the age of 2 or 3, in comparing quantities where there are no misleading perceptual cues. Older children do better than younger, but it does not depend on starting school. Moreover, children under the age of 6 or 7 rely excessively on perceptual cues and tend to judge the set that occupies the larger area as having more; and this too is relatively independent of culture.

However, there are many areas of arithmetical knowledge and understanding that depend very significantly on social class, culture and experience.

Social class differences in arithmetic

Parental social class is an important predictor of children's academic performance in all subjects, including mathematics. British adults with severe persisting numeracy difficulties are far more likely than those without such difficulties to have come from 'working-class' backgrounds and to have been poor. For example, far more qualified as children for free school meals, which are only provided for children from low income families (Basic Skills Agency, 1999). In countries with greater social inequalities, such as Brazil, social class effects on academic performance are even greater (Nunes, Schliemann, & Carraher, 1993).

There are many possible ways in which social class could influence academic performance, including mathematical performance. Better off parents are can afford more books and toys for their children. On average, they may have more time to talk to and interact with their children (although this is not always the case). The children are likely to attend schools with better resources. The parents are more likely to be able to keep the children at school beyond the official school leaving age and to support them through higher education. Moreover, they are usually better educated themselves and therefore more able to help their children to learn academic subjects. Also, the culture of the school is likely to be less alien to a child from a highly formally educated family than one from a less formally educated family (Biddle, 2001; Brooker, 2002).

For example, in school mathematics, as in other school subjects, children need not only to learn the subject matter but also to the 'rules of the game': what is expected of them. For example, they must learn that adults often ask them questions in order to find out what they know, rather than in order to learn the answer. This will probably be a familiar experience to children from school-oriented families, whose parents will have asked them such questions from an early age: 'What's that?' 'What colour is this?' 'How many apples have we got here?' However, many people will think it strange to ask children questions to which they themselves know the answer. Heath (1983) reports that working-class African-American adults in Trackton in the Carolinas found it strange when white middle-class adults asked children such questions as 'What's that?' The adults presumably knew what 'that' was so did not need to ask and the children were not going to know anything that they had not known before just because someone asked them. Children brought up by adults with this attitude may find it bewildering when teachers ask them questions about simple arithmetic.

When do social class differences become important to children's mathematical development? Some studies suggest that they are relatively unimportant to the acquisition of number concepts in the early years and only affect the learning of formal mathematics in school. For example, Ginsburg and Russell (1981) looked at some other early-developing numerical tasks: number conservation, verbal counting, enumeration of objects, concrete addition and writing numbers. Middle-class children performed slightly better than working-class children on these tasks, but differences were not very large.

Social class is not always found to have a large effect even on primary school children's understanding of arithmetic. As reported in Chapter 4, Dowker, Gent, and Tate (2001) found no differences between children from a predominantly middle-class and a predominantly working-class school as regards their ability to translate between problems presented in numerical, concrete and word problem formats. Dowker (1998) found that, while social class did have some effect on children's use of derived fact strategies in addition and subtraction, this effect ceased to be significant after controlling for IQ. Even without controlling for IQ, social class had little effect on arithmetical estimation.

By way of contrast, many studies show a greater social class influence, even in the early years. For example, Davie, Butler, and Goldstein (1972) found that even at the age of 4, there was a year's difference on intellectual tasks, including numeracy tasks, between working-class children living in a deprived area and middle-class children living in a comfortable area.

Evidence suggests that (1) early influences of social class are much greater on verbal than nonverbal aspects of mathematics; and (2) that the crucial difference at this stage may not be so much between 'middle class' and 'working class' as between children from extremely disadvantaged backgrounds and those from less disadvantaged backgrounds (including the majority of 'working-class' children in developed countries).

As regards the verbal/nonverbal distinction, Jordan, Huttenlocher, and Levine (1992, 1994a) found that there were no social class differences in preschoolers' ability to do nonverbal addition and subtraction problems; but middle-class children were better than working-class children at verbal arithmetic. It would seem that middle-class children have more experience than working-class children with conventional mathematical language, which gives them an advantage in verbal arithmetic, but not necessarily in nonverbal arithmetic.

As regards the effects of severe disadvantage, work in several countries by Ginsburg, Choi, Lopez, Netley, and Chao-Yuan (1997) indicated there was not a very great difference between the basic numerical skills of middle-class and working-class preschool children, but that those from *very* disadvantaged backgrounds performed much worse than the rest. Disadvantaged children from Mexico performed worse than low SES children in countries where poverty was less likely to be severe.

International comparisons

International comparisons (e.g. TIMSS, 1996) tend to show considerably better arithmetical performance by children in some countries than in others. In particular, children from countries in the Far East, such as China, Japan, Korea and Singapore tend to perform better in arithmetic than do children in Europe and, even more so, in America. Stevenson, Lee, Chen, Stigler, Hsu, and Kitamura (1990) found that Japanese and Korean children outperformed American children to a greater extent in mathematics than in reading. They concluded that there must be cultural differences that particularly favoured children from the Far East in the mathematical domain (one might, however, argue that their relatively lesser advantage in reading could reflect intrinsically greater difficulties in learning to read oriental languages as compared with English).

There are several reasons why culture and nationality might influence arithmetical development. They include:

1 *Cultural differences in attitudes to mathematics.* Some cultures may value arithmetic more than others do (see Chapter 11 for further discussion of this issue).
2 *Amount of time devoted to arithmetic in school.* In English schools, for example, primary school children study a wider variety of subjects than children in some other countries, so that mathematics represents a

smaller proportion of the total. Even within mathematics, English primary school children probably study a wider variety of topics than those in some other countries: e.g. shape; space; measurement; recording data, e.g. in graphs and charts; applying mathematical knowledge to real-world problems, etc. as well as arithmetic. This could lead to English children being less good at arithmetic, but better at some other aspects of mathematics, than those elsewhere. Indeed one international comparison did indicate that English children were worse at arithmetical calculations but better at applying mathematics to real-world problems than those in most other European countries.

3   *The economic and political situation of a country.* On the whole, the international comparisons for mathematics have not included the poorest countries. One would expect standards, at least in school-taught arithmetic, to be particularly low in such countries, even among those pupils who do attend school. This might be expected as a result of poorer health and nutrition; more time devoted to both paid and unpaid work; longer and more difficult journeys to school resulting in poorer attendance; and fewer resources for the schools themselves. Of the 25 countries involved in the 1995 study by TIMSS (1996), the country with the lowest mathematics scores was Iran. It is probably relevant that Iran had experienced serious internal political turmoil and had been involved in war in the Middle East shortly before the period of the study. The 1999 study included several new countries: of these, Morocco, the Philippines and South Africa performed even less well than Iran. All these countries had serious problems of poverty and inequality and had experienced political instability. In the case of South Africa, the lowest scoring country, the non-white majority had suffered the effects of several generations of apartheid.

Educational methods

Particular attention has been paid to the ways in which *methods of teaching* may affect arithmetical development. The issue can only be considered relatively briefly within the scope of this book. One should be careful not to interpret cross-national educational differences too simplistically, as they occur in the context of many other cultural differences. However, it is important to examine ways in which educational methods might contribute to better mathematical learning in some countries than in others. There may, of course, be considerable variation in educational methods within the *same* country. This may be particularly true of the United States, which has featured in many of the comparisons, as it is a very large and diverse country with no national curriculum.

James Stigler and his colleagues have discussed aspects of Japanese and Chinese educational methods, which might explain the better mathematical performance of children in these countries (Stevenson & Stigler, 1992;

Stigler & Perry, 1988; Stigler, Fernandez, & Yoshida, 1996). Stigler, Fernandez, and Yoshida (1996) suggest that one of the main differences between mathematics education in the United States and Japan is that Japanese schools place a greater emphasis on pupils' *thinking*.

For example, Japanese lessons tend to begin by posing a problem and then having pupils try and work it out for themselves. Only after that does the lesson move toward a whole-class discussion of the pupils' solution strategies. In US schools, the lesson starts with the children being taught rules and formulae and only after that do the children begin to solve problems on the basis of these rules and formulae. Moreover, Japanese children are given more 'time to think': fewer problems are covered per lesson in Japanese than US schools, but they are covered in greater depth.

Also, US schools tend to emphasize the learning at any given time of one strategy, which is prescribed by the teacher and textbook. By contrast, Japanese schools encourage children to present and discuss alternative strategies. It is made clear to them that there can be many reasonable solution strategies for the same problem: not just the 'one in the book'. The strategies are evaluated predominantly by the other pupils in group discussion, rather than by the teachers. Admittedly, there are some potential problems in over-reliance on peer evaluation, just as there are in over-reliance on adult evaluation or an answer book. For example, Kinoshita (1989) found that a majority of Japanese, but not English, 11-year-olds considered that the correct answer to a multiplication problem could be determined by democratic vote: possibly reflecting the Japanese emphasis on group discussion and evaluation. Nevertheless, the Japanese methods do seem to have far more potential for encouraging flexibility in strategy use (see Chapter 6) and also for encouraging children to reflect on their own strategies. It is noteworthy that the National Numeracy Strategy, which was introduced in Britain in the late 1990s, also places considerable emphasis on group discussion of alternative strategies.

Ma (1999) pointed out some similar differences between China and the United States: Chinese schools placed more emphasis on thinking about the strategies being used. In addition, the teachers in Chinese schools organized sessions where they discussed mathematics with one another, which may have encouraged a deeper understanding of and interest in mathematics for the teachers and thereby for their pupils.

Mathematics in the 'real world': The importance of cultural practices

'The summer term of [my] last year at school did produce an improvement in my ability to add up and subtract. This advance was not due, however, to my classroom activity but to the fact that I became scorer to the cricket eleven.' ('Balaam': *Chalk gets in your eyes*, London: Benn, 1955, p. 72)

'Counting sheep
When you're trying to sleep,
Being fair
When there's something to share,
Being neat,
When you're folding a sheet,
That's mathematics!

'When a ball
Bounces off a wall,
When you cook
From a recipe book,
When you know
How much money you owe,
That's mathematics! . . .

'When you choose
How much postage to use,
When you know
What's the chance it will snow,

'When you bet
And you end up in debt,
Oh, try as you may,
You can't get away
From mathematics!' (from: Tom Lehrer: *That's mathematics*, In Tom Lehrer:
The remains of Tom Lehrer, © 1993 Tom Lehrer, used by permission)

Cultural differences in arithmetic should not be ascribed just to school-related factors. Calculation skills are often acquired elsewhere than in school. People whose cultural practices require them to buy, sell, trade and use money often develop calculation strategies suitable for such activities, even if they have limited or no schooling. Even if they do have schooling, the strategies used in school and in the workplace or marketplace often seem to have little in common.

Important studies of the strategies of child street vendors in developing countries have been carried out by Carraher, Carraher, and Schliemann (1985) in Brazil and by Saxe (1985, 1990) in Papua New Guinea.

Carraher et al. (1985) studied Brazilian child street traders between 9 and 15 years. All attended school, although not all did so with great regularity. They were given the same arithmetic problems in three different contexts: a 'street' context, where the researchers approached them as customers and asked them about prices and change; a 'word problem' context where they were given school-type word problems dealing with prices and change in hypothetical vending situations; and a numerical context, where they were given the problems in the form of written sums. They performed much better in the street context than on word problems and much better on word problems than on written sums. In fact, they solved almost all – 98% – of the problems correctly in the street context; 74% of the same problems were solved correctly when presented in the form of oral word problems; whereas only 37% were solved correctly when presented in the form of written sums. Moreover, the same children used different strategies in the three conditions.

Saxe (1985, 1990) studied the arithmetical strategies of children in Papua New Guinea. Some were street vendors with little or no schooling; some attended school but had no vending experience; and some had both types of experience. They were all given word problems based on the prices and profits for selling sweets. Those with more schooling relied more on written numbers and place value notation, whereas those with little or no schooling referred more to the specific features of the currency. Among children with equal amounts of schooling, children with vending experience used more derived fact strategies, whereas those without vending experience relied more on well-learned, school-taught algorithms.

Posner (1982) found that the Dioula, a mercantile group of people on the Ivory Coast, learned to use rather complex calculation strategies for trading and selling purposes. Even those merchants who had never been to school were adept at calculation. Baoule people in the same region, who were farmers rather than merchants, tended not to demonstrate such high-level calculation abilities, presumably because their cultural practices did not require them.

It is not only people with limited schooling who may perform better, and use different strategies, when performing activities that are of personal relevance to them than when carrying out textbook exercises. Lave, Murtagh, and de la Rocha (1984) studied a group of Californian house-wives, all of whom had received at least secondary education in mathe-matics. They were observed on shopping expeditions, where they sometimes had to use proportional reasoning strategies to work out which was the 'best buy'; e.g. whether two boxes at price Z were better value than three boxes at price Y. They were able to perform the necessary calculations efficiently and well. However, when given the same problems in school textbook form, some claimed that they were unable to carry them out and the rest carried them out much more slowly and laboriously than in the shopping context.

There are many anecdotal reports of people failing in school arithmetic who were able to carry out arithmetical tasks quite well in recreational contexts, e.g. as scorers for darts games. This book has referred in several places to Claire, an adult who had relatively mild specific difficulties in arithmetic and had experienced severe mathematics anxiety from childhood onwards. Yet between the ages of about 11 and 15, she was very keen on playing Monopoly, a game that requires a significant amount of mental calculation, and showed little hesitation or anxiety when carrying out the relevant calculations.

In many cases, individuals tend to regard their out-of-school mathematical activities as something quite separate from, irrelevant to and perhaps inferior to the 'real maths' that they do in school. For example, DeAbreu (1994) found that Brazilian children were reluctant to use the calculation skills that they used in the marketplace in a school context and did not regard these as examples of 'proper' mathematics.

The most crucial difference between the 'informal' or 'marketplace' strategies used outside of school and those used within a school setting is that the former are largely mental and the latter are written, or, even when carried out mentally, are closely based on written algorithms. Pettito and Ginsburg (1982) found that American undergraduates and Ivory Coast Dioula merchants used very similar strategies when carrying out mental arithmetic; and showed similar implicit use of arithmetical principles in derived fact strategies. Both groups made extensive use of the base 10 structure of their counting systems. The Americans additionally made use of algorithms based on written place value.

Thus, real-world cultural practices are extremely important to arithmetical development. However, regarding mathematics education *purely* as a matter of transmitting cultural practices by apprenticeship carries the same dangers as regarding mathematics education *purely* as any single issue. Theoretically it is an oversimplification; and from an educational perspective it risks encouraging a relatively narrow and inflexible form of learning. Children can be trained in unchangeable, inflexible routines outside a school environment as well as within it. The child in a school environment that emphasizes examinations risks being trained to answer examination questions, rather than to understand the subject more broadly; the child who is learning how to pursue a culturally valued activity risks being trained to follow specified methods prescribed by tradition without considering alternative possibilities (Greer, 1996).

Experience of handling money: A changing cultural practice

> *Researcher (giving the WISC information subtest)*: 'Can you tell me the names of two kinds of coins?'
> *Adam (aged 6)* looks blank.
> *Researcher*: 'Can you tell me the names of two kinds of money?'
> *Adam* still looks blank.
> *Researcher (trying to work out where the difficulty lies)*: 'If you go to a shop and you want to buy something, what do you have to give the shopkeeper?'
> *Adam (without any hesitation)*: 'A credit card!'

It is sometimes suggested that contemporary children in 'developed' countries may be less good at some aspects of arithmetic than children of a generation ago, because they have less direct experience of handling money.

This is partly because most western children nowadays are less independently mobile than in the past: a situation aggravated, with respect to
shopping, by the fact that corner shops have been increasingly replaced by
large town-centre stores. As recently as the 1960s, 80% of English 4-year-
olds had some experience of going into shops on their own and making
independent purchases (Newson & Newson, 1968); nowadays, children are
rarely permitted to do so until they are much older. Moreover, the shopping practices that children, especially in middle-class families, observe in
their parents have become more abstract, with less direct handling of
money and goods. People are more likely to buy in bulk and to pay by
credit card, as just noted by Adam. An increasing number of people shop
on the internet, still further reducing the amount of directly observable
handling of goods and money.

Whether or not children's decreasing experience of shopping and handling money actually reduces their arithmetical skills, it is likely to make
'money sums' less relevant to them. Schools have frequently encouraged
young children to play 'shopping' games with pretend money and have
given children of all ages word problems that feature financial exchanges.
This has been partly for the purpose of direct training in financial
calculations and partly because it has been assumed that this will provide
children with a relevant and familiar context in which to acquire calculation
techniques. It is necessary to take into account that such contexts may be
less relevant to children nowadays than 30 or 40 years ago.

An important cultural issue: Age and date

'Soon I will be eight, but now I'm three.' (Russian child quoted by
Chukovsky, 1983)

'I was two yesterday. My Daddy says I'll be five in a minute.' (Richard,
actually aged 4 years 3 months)

'I am not six and a half! I am six and three quarters!' (Rosemary, correctly
and indignantly)

'Fifteen is like a very tall Dad! It's up to the sky!' (Ken, aged 4 years
6 months)

*Julia (6 years 8 months; on being asked to define 'ancient' as part of the
WISC vocabulary test)*: 'When you get to be about seventy you're ancient,
and nobody is supposed to mess around with you!'

Eva (5 years 8 months): 'Is it true that when you're a hundred, the Queen
writes to you?'
Adult: 'I think so.'
Eva: 'Will the Queen ever get to be a hundred years old?'

> *Adult*: 'I don't know. Maybe. We'll have to wait and see.'
> *Eva*: 'Oh, won't she be tall!!!'

When considering important cultural influences on mathematical concepts, researchers have tended to focus on marketplace and other workplace issues. However, there are other important cultural practices that may influence mathematical performance, but that have been less studied.

For instance, it would be of interest to investigate whether children who live in countries with very cold winters understand negative numbers earlier than those who live in warmer climates. In countries with cold winters, conversations often centre around how many degrees it is 'below zero' and it is emphasized that, for example, 20 below is colder than 10 below.

One of the most striking culture-specific preoccupations is that in many, but not all, cultures with *age* and to some extent with dates, especially with regard to birthdays.

In many cultural groups, especially in the West, children's lives at home and especially in the highly age-stratified society of school are dominated by considerations of age. In their relations with one another, children are very concerned about who is older than whom and tend to associate superior age with superior status (some readers may remember the popular song about 'Big Valerie Wilkins' who was able to boss her neighbour around because she was six and a quarter and he was only six years old). Like Ken and Eva earlier, children tend to associate age with size and often assume that size increases with age, even in adulthood. At least from the age of 4, children are implicit developmental psychologists, associating increasing age with increasing ability in a variety of domains from reading to running, although they may not always be accurate about the actual age when a skill is likely to be attained (Dowker, Heal, Phillips, & Wilson, 1994).

In England, fractions are likely to be encountered with regard to age earlier and more frequently than in many other situations. Rosemary (earlier) was well aware that six and three-quarters was more than six and a half. It would be interesting to investigate whether children perform better on arithmetical problems that relate to age than on those that relate to many other issues. It would also be interesting to investigate whether English children have a better concept of halves and quarters than children who speak languages where age is not so frequently discussed in terms of fractions.

It is notable that among 'savant' calculators (see Chapter 1), a high proportion are *calendrical* calculators: they can tell you on what day of the week a given date will fall. They tend to be relatively good at arithmetic in general, but better when this is expressed in terms of dates (Cowan, O'Connor, and Samella, 2003; O'Connor, Cowan, and Samella, 2000). At the other end of the scale, Nicola, the 19-year-old 'developmental dyscalculic' mentioned in Chapter 1, finds arithmetic much more meaningful when expressed in terms of ages or sometimes in terms of dates and often spontaneously rephrases an arithmetic problem in such terms, so as to make it more understandable to herself: '19 + 14 is 33, so I've got 14 years to go before I'm 33'; '54 – 31 = 23, so if you're 54, 31 years ago you were 23'; '83 – 5 = 78, so 5 years before I was born was 1978'. Thus, it seems that a tendency to see mathematical relationships in terms of age and time can be readily found in typical children, in those with a specific arithmetical talent and in at least one individual with a specific arithmetical disability.

Compared with other cultural influences on arithmetic – e.g. workplace activities, money and shopping and, of course, schooling – age and birthdays have received rather less attention. This may be partly because the importance of age and birthdays is so embedded in many western cultures that it is not always instantly seen as a cultural issue. I have noticed that even many students and others who are highly aware of cultural influences on mathematical development are sometimes startled when reminded that people in some cultures do not celebrate birthdays or have a sharp awareness of their own ages.

In any case, it would be well worth carrying out investigations into the importance of age concerns to arithmetical development and thinking in those cultures that emphasize age and whether this leads to any differences in arithmetical strengths and weaknesses from cultures that do not emphasize age. One of the few studies that examines related issues was carried out by Kearins (1988), who found that Australian Aboriginal children, even once they had been exposed to schooling, were far less aware of their exact ages than were non-Aboriginal children. This appeared to be due to the fact that 'correct-to-the-day age was not seen as important by Aboriginally oriented children even if their parents, and, in many cases, grandparents had some Western schooling, and though almost all of them lived in a modern town' (Kearins, 1988, p. 252). By contrast, the Aboriginal children were much better than the non-Aboriginal children at estimating direction, reflecting the importance of navigation in Aboriginal culture.

Technology and arithmetic: Effect of mechanical aids to arithmetic

One aspect of contemporary culture that may affect arithmetic is the use of technology: computers and, especially, pocket calculators.

The use of 'technology' to facilitate arithmetic is in fact nothing new. Long before calculators, people used slide rules to facilitate calculation. And one technological aid – the abacus – has been in use since mediaeval times. Even earlier, people used counting boards, tallies and such tokens as pebbles.

The abacus is still used by many people in Japan, China and elsewhere. This involves the use of beads on strings, where the strings represent place value. As mentioned in Chapter 1, many Asians become very adept and fast at using an abacus: often outstripping calculators in their speed.

Experienced abacus users can often use a 'mental abacus': visualizing operations on an abacus, even when there is none present (Hatano, Miyake, & Binks, 1977; Stigler, 1984). The effects of abacus use on general arithmetical development are a little unclear. Again as discussed in Chapter 1, expert abacus calculators do not always transfer their abacus skills to other arithmetical contexts. It is unlikely that the use of the abacus on its own can explain the superior arithmetical skills of people in Pacific Rim countries. However, it appears that any effects of abacus use are positive: certainly, it does not atrophy arithmetical skills.

Much controversy has surrounded the question of whether allowing children to use calculators promotes an 'unthinking' approach to mathematical problems. Some educators distrust calculators in general. Others consider that they are useful for older children and adults performing advanced calculations, but can interfere with the development of number sense if introduced too early. Dehaene (1997, p. 135) expresses a contrary view:

> I am convinced that by releasing children from the tedious and mechanical constraints of calculation, the calculator can help them concentrate on meaning. It allows them to sharpen their natural sense of approximation by offering them thousands of arithmetic examples . . . The mere observation of a calculator's behaviour is an excellent way of developing number sense.

Most studies of the effects of calculator use have shown few strong effects in either direction on arithmetical calculation or reasoning than might be expected. A meta-analysis of over 80 studies (Hembree & Dessart, 1992) indicated that calculator use had little effect on the development of arithmetical computation skills. Problem solving was better when pupils used calculators than when they did not. Experience with calculators had no effect, or only a weak positive effect, on problem solving when calculators were not available.

These studies included children who were introduced to calculators at a wide variety of ages. There have been a few studies of children enrolled in programmes that use calculators as a central part of the mathematics curriculum from the age of 5 or 6 (Brolin & Bjork, 1992; Ruthven, 1998; Shuard, 1992). These have shown no negative effects on calculation and some positive effects on attitude and arithmetical reasoning. It should be noted that these studies involved children who were exposed to calculators deliberately as part of their mathematics curriculum; taught how to use them appropriately; and encouraged to use them to investigate large numbers and discover arithmetical patterns. It cannot be assumed that very early exposure to calculators would have the same positive effects under other circumstances. However, there is little evidence that calculators are damaging in themselves.

Some recent work (Dowker, Huke, & Morris, 1999) has looked at the immediate effects of calculator use on two specific aspects of arithmetical reasoning: (1) the use of derived fact strategies; and (2) arithmetical word problem solving.

The first study, carried out by Katherine Huke, investigated whether allowing 8-year-old children to use a calculator to work out addition and subtraction problems reduced their use of derived fact strategies: i.e. the derivation of unknown number facts from facts that they already knew.

Twenty children were included in the study. The methodology used for assessing the use of derived fact strategies was that devised by Dowker (1998; also described in Chapter 6 in this volume). Children were first given tests of mental calculation, in both addition and subtraction, to establish the level of difficulty of problems that they could solve unaided by mental calculation. They were then given problems just above this level of difficulty. In practice, only two problem-difficulty levels were needed for each operation in this study: two-digit arithmetic without carrying/borrowing and three-digit arithmetic with carrying/borrowing.

The main tasks involved the child seeing or calculating (by written arithmetic or with a calculator) the answer to a problem and then being presented with a problem that could be solved easily using the previous problem plus an arithmetical principle.

Each child received three conditions, in randomized order: (1) they just looked at the previous problem, together with its answer (as in Dowker's 1998) study; (2) they worked out the answer to the previous problem using the pencil-and-paper method that they had been taught in class; and (3) they solved the previous problem with a calculator.

The arithmetical principles involved were those described in Chapter 6.

Children were assessed as demonstrating use of a principle, if they obtained the correct answer, while being unable to calculate the correct answers mentally to control problems of similar difficulty; and/or if they provided justifications for their answers in terms of the principle. Most correct answers were correctly justified.

An ANOVA showed no significant difference between the total number of derived fact strategies used in the 'Written calculation', 'Calculator', and 'Just looking' conditions. Moreover, the mode of problem presentation also did not affect the frequency of use of *any* one of the principles.

The second study concerned the understanding of word problems and was carried out by Eve Morris. Forty children participated in the study: 20 were in Year 3 (7 to 8 years) and 20 in Year 4 (8 to 9 years). They were given arithmetical word problems, which were presented to them visually, and were also read aloud orally. The problems comprised included addition problems in the 'Change' semantic category (e.g. 'John had 25 pounds and then he earned 31 more pounds; how much money does he have now?'); in the 'Combine' semantic category (e.g. 'Bill had 28 marbles and Jane had 33 marbles; how many marbles did they have altogether?') and in the

'Compare' semantic category ('Sam had 24 books, and Susan had 21 more books than Sam; how many books did Susan have?'). It included subtraction problems in the 'Change' semantic category ('There were 58 birds and 23 flew away; how many were left?'); in the 'Combine' semantic category ('Jack and Helen had 56 crayons altogether; Jack had 29 crayons; how many did Helen have?') and in the 'Compare' semantic category ('Jim has 35 toys, and Judy has 18 toys; how many more toys does Jim have than Judy?'). Within each semantic category for each operation, there were four problems: two involving carrying for addition or borrowing for subtraction; and two not involving carrying or borrowing. Thus, each child received 24 problems: 12 for addition and 12 for subtraction.

Half of the children solved the problems with a calculator and half with pencil and paper.

Not surprisingly, an analysis of variance showed that the 'calculator' group got significantly more sums correct than the 'pencil and paper' group. Children in the pencil-and-paper group performed significantly better on the addition problems that did not involve carrying than on those that did and on the subtraction problems that did not involve borrowing than on those that did. No such effects were found in the calculator group. Both groups performed better in addition on the change and combine problems than on the compare problems and in subtraction on the change problems than on the combine and compare problems; thus replicating the results of many previous studies. The semantic category effects were the same for the pencil-and-paper group than for the calculator group. Thus, using a calculator did bypass the difficulty of carrying and borrowing, but had no apparent effect on the ways in which children dealt with the semantics of word problems.

The combined results of the two studies suggest that using a calculator does not *of itself* encourage an unthinking approach. It facilitates calculation; but does not inhibit (or in these studies facilitate) arithmetical reasoning. The similarity between arithmetical reasoning strategies with and without calculators was quite striking.

This study relates to the immediate effects of calculator use, rather than the long-term effects; but concurs with those studies that have indicated that the effects of calculator use are far less strong than is sometimes assumed.

Language of mathematics

> '"Two and two makes four", says the tutor. "Well, child, why do you stare so?"'
> 'The child stares because the word "make" is in this sentence used in a sense which is quite new to him; he knows what it is to make a bow and to make a noise but how this active verb is applicable in the present case, where there is no agent to perform the action, he cannot clearly understand . . . We have

chosen the first simple instance we could recollect, to show how difficult the words we generally use in teaching arithmetick must be to our pupils. It would be an unprofitable task to enumerate all the puzzling technical terms which, in their earliest lessons, children are obliged to hear, without being able to understand.' (Richard and Maria Edgeworth: *Practical education*, London: J. Johnson, 1798, pp. 245–246)

'Math is like learning a foreign language, Marcie . . . No matter what you say, it's going to be wrong anyway.' (character in Charles Schultz' 'Peanuts' cartoon strip)

'Now X multiplied by Z would make this zerox of a hyblernonic, extranonic, excromblonomic Y, it would make it a C. A C minus an extramonic chimernomic exclusionomic hyblonic chimblonomic would make it true. Now if you take three minutes of a quarter of a scivernomic minute of an extranomic b of a chimblomonic g, it's quite simple. Now the values of extramonic Zs are quite simple . . .
'Now if you B plus minus a minus zerox scivernomic three, then it would *obviously* make a Y. Call it a Y. It would be a one or a zerox. This is an actual equation. Zerox could be anything. It could be anything, but you've got to figure out what the Y is.' (Sarah, aged 9, a mathematician's daughter, talking on the taperecorder and pretending to be the 'world's greatest mathematician'.)

One important influence on arithmetic, which varies both between cultures and between the home and school context in most schooled societies, is that of mathematical language. Mathematical language can be confusing. Some terms, even in early arithmetic, are technical and are rarely used outside of an arithmetical context. If they are not explained, or correctly deduced by the child, they may lead to the idea that mathematics is bewildering and strange: full of incomprehensible mumbo-jumbo. Amy, for example, was frightened of mathematics in her first year at school because she did not know what the word 'add' meant and it did not occur to anyone to explain it to her.

Other words can be confusing to children because they *are* used both in arithmetic and in other contexts, but the arithmetical usage is slightly different. Hughes (1986) tells of a child who was asked 'What is the difference between 11 and 6?' and gave the answer, '11 has two numbers'. After this was marked wrong, she tried again: '6 is curly'. Note that her understanding of the word 'difference' was perfectly correct for most purposes: it just happened to be used in a different way in this particular arithmetical context. I remember that, at the age of 11 or 12, I was rather puzzled, as were some of my classmates, by a request to 'evaluate' a certain sum: it sounded as though we were expected to judge the moral or aesthetic qualities of the sum. ('This is a very beautiful sum!')

Durkin, Shire and their colleagues (Durkin & Shire, 1991; Durkin, Crowther, & Shire, 1986; Shire & Durkin, 1989) have described children's difficulties with such terms as 'big number' and 'high number'. Children sometimes assume that such terms refer to the physical and spatial characteristics of the numerals. A big number is one that is written large; a high number is one that is high up on the page.

The use in English, and some other languages including French, of the same words for fractions and ordinal terms (e.g. 'third', 'troisième') can create stumbling blocks for children in their interpretation of fractions (Bergeron & Herscovits, 1987).

Misunderstandings are particularly likely to occur when there are unrecognized discrepancies between a pupil's mathematics-related terminology and that of the teacher or textbook. This is particularly likely to happen if a pupil uses a different dialect from that used in school. Orr (1989) discusses some of the linguistic misunderstandings that can occur between teachers who speak standard American English and pupils who use 'Black English vernacular'. For example, when making partitive comparisons, the former use fractional terms: 'half of', 'one third of', 'half as old as', 'half the number', while the latter make use of multiplicative terms: 'two times less than', 'three times less than', 'two times younger than', 'twice smaller the number'. Such differences in usage are likely to increase the confusions between multiplication and division, especially when dealing with fractions, that are pervasive at the best of times (Bergeron & Herscovits, 1987).

Number words and counting systems

One of the cultural characteristics that could influence children's arithmetical development is the way in which numbers and arithmetical relationships are expressed in a language.

The possible importance of this factor has been recognized for a very long time indeed, although systematic research was not carried out until quite recently. Locke (1690) argued that small numbers can be represented without words by showing numbers of fingers, but words are needed to keep track of larger numbers. Thus, speakers of languages without number words will be restricted to the understanding of numbers that can be represented through fingers (10 to 20 or so, depending on whether they are with someone else whose fingers can be counted together with their own). Edgeworth and Edgeworth (1798) pointed out that English speakers may be at a disadvantage compared with speakers of some other languages due to their relatively irregular English counting system.

The linguistic characteristics that may be relevant are:

1   Whether the language includes number words at all; and whether, if it does, there is an upper limit to what is counted. Most languages have

number words at least up to 10. There are some exceptions. Some Australian Aboriginal languages, e.g. Aranda, have only words corresponding to 1, 2, 3 and many. A rather larger number of languages have limits on how far one can count; for example, some of the languages of Papua New Guinea count by pointing to body parts and use the names of these body parts for their counts (Butterworth, 1999; Lancy, 1983). For example, in the Kewa language '1' is represented by the right little finger and '34' by the nose. The upper limit of the Kewa counting system is 68, while that of the somewhat similar Oksapmin system is 19.

The complete or near complete lack of a verbal counting system is likely seriously to constrain the development of arithmetic. It need not prevent it altogether: we see from many studies of pre-verbal infants and of individuals with language impairments that quantities and even arithmetical operations can be represented nonverbally.

If there is an upper limit on the counting sequence in a language, then this may not only interfere with arithmetic and quantity representation beyond that number, but may limit the ability to understand one of the central mathematical concepts: that of infinity; of the fact that a quantity can in theory be increased indefinitely, without limit.

There is little published research on the effect on mathematical understanding of growing up in a culture with no verbal counting system or a counting system with an upper bound. Such research would seem to be extremely important, both from the point of view of understanding cultural influences on mathematics and on understanding the extent to which language and number concepts are interrelated

2   *The base of the counting system.* The counting system generally used today is base 10. In the past, bases have included base 5, base 20 and base 60. Base 12 has its survivals in the terms 'a dozen' and 'a gross'; and in the tendency for some items such as eggs to be sold in 'dozens' or 'half dozens'. The French verbal counting system is still partly in base 20: for example, 70 is *soixante-dix* (sixty-ten); 80 is *quatre-vingts* (four-twenties); and 90 is *quatre-vingt-dix* (four-twenties-ten).

Some current or recent currency and measurement systems use bases other than 10 and often more than one base within the same system. Until 1971, the British currency system operated on the principle of 12 pennies in a shilling and 20 shillings in a pound. The Imperial measurement systems are typically not of a decimal structure (e.g. 12 inches in a foot; 3 feet in a yard; 16 ounces in a pound; 14 pounds in a stone). These measurement systems are still used in many parts of the world. Britain changed officially to the metric system in the 1970s and children learn only the metric system in schools; but there is still frequent use of the older measurement systems in everyday practical contexts; and many parents still think predominantly in terms of the older systems. Perhaps as a result of the division between within-school and out-of-school measurement systems, Clayton (1988) found that children tended to use the metric system for exact measurement and the older systems for estimates. It is not yet clear whether and when this will change, now that many of the first generation to learn the metric system in school have become parents themselves.

Once again, there has been little research into the effect of using different bases. It would in theory be interesting to know whether the use of a base 10 system is intrinsically easier to acquire and use than other systems, due to the fact that we have 10 fingers. Such a study would be difficult, however, as there are few groups who use a system that is *exclusively* in a base other than 10. However, it would be much easier to carry out a study of the effects of exposure only to base 10 versus exposure to other bases as well. This could be done by comparing individuals in countries that use only the metric system of measurement with those in countries with other measurement systems, which use bases other than 10. It would also be desirable to compare standard French speakers, whose verbal counting system still contains number words from an earlier base 20 system with Belgian or Swiss French speakers, whose counting system is exclusively in base 10. Seventy in these versions of French is *septante* and 90 *nonante*.

The effect of exposure to more than one base could be either positive or negative. On the one hand, it could be confusing and could reduce the salience of the currently dominant base 10 system. On the other hand, it might permit a more flexible approach to number and give children some idea of the abstract nature of all bases. Indeed, arithmetic in different bases was an important part of the 'new math' teaching in the 1960s and 1970s, although it is rarely taught nowadays.

3   *Whether there is a written number system.* Some languages still do not have a written form and this includes the number system. The extent to which the existence of a written number system affects arithmetical understanding is not clear. A written system not only makes it possible to keep permanent records, but also reduces the load on memory during arithmetical calculations. By the same token, as already pointed out in Chapter 6, many people think that excessive concentration on written calculation at an early age may interfere with the development of deep mathematical understanding and flexible strategy use and that it is better to begin with mental calculation.

It is difficult to study the effects of the existence of a written number system, due to the confounding factors of exposure to schooling; literacy within the culture, etc.

4   *Whether, if there is such a written system, it is 'regular' in terms of giving a clear and consistent representation of the base system (usually base 10) used in the language.* The Arabic number system that is almost universally used in writing today is highly regular: representing place value in a consistent fashion. However, some written number systems have

not been. Roman numerals were far less consistent. Although there were separate symbols for units (I), tens (X), hundreds (C) and thousands (M), there were also special symbols for numbers involving multiples of 5: V for five; L for 50; D for 500. Moreover, numerals sometimes represented addition to a salient number (VI as 5 + 1, i.e. 6; XIII as 10 + 3 or 13) and sometimes subtraction from a salient number (IV is one less than 5, i.e. 4; IX is one less than 10, i.e. 9).

Calculation would appear to be far more difficult in Roman numerals than Arabic numerals (Butterworth, 1999; Flegg, 1989). Some historians have argued that the use of Roman numerals was one contributory factor to the low level of arithmetical skills in the Middle Ages and that arithmetical skills improved when Arabic numerals came into greater use (Flegg, 1989); although is difficult to establish the exact level of arithmetical skill at different periods in history.

5   *The regularity of the spoken number system: the degree to which it gives a clear and consistent representation of the base system (usually base 10) used in the language.*

6   *The degree and consistency of conformity between the spoken and the written number system.*

Since most languages currently use the highly regular Arabic written number system, there is in fact little distinction between 5 and 6; and they are generally not distinguished in research. It is, however, important to bear in mind that the degree of regularity of an oral counting system could be important *either* because the base system that it uses is made explicit *or* because the oral counting system is consistent with the written counting system; and that the two need not be exactly the same.

East Asian languages such as Chinese, Japanese and Korean have very regular oral counting systems according to both of these criteria. They correspond closely to the written number system and they make the relationship between units, tens and higher powers of 10 very explicit. For example, in these languages the number word for 12 is the equivalent of 'ten-two'; and the number word for 23 the equivalent of 'two-tens-three'. Irregular number words such as the English 'twelve' and 'twenty' do not occur in these languages.

It is sometimes suggested that the relative regularity of Asian counting systems is a major contributory factor to the superior performance of Pacific Rim children in most aspects of arithmetic. Learning number names may be easier in systems where new numbers may be inferred rather than having to be learned by rote. Therefore, a regular counting system would make it easier for young children to count to higher numbers at an earlier stage than those who have to cope with a more irregular counting system and that this might give them a head start in manipulating numbers. One might also expect that the concept of place value would be easier to comprehend and use in a regular counting system. Essentially, place value *means* the representation of the base 10 system by written symbols. It is very difficult for English-speaking children to acquire (Askew & Brown, 1997; Thompson, 2003).

Indeed, there is considerable evidence that speakers of Asian languages perform better than speakers of less regular counting sequences, both in learning the counting sequence and in learning to represent tens and units.

Miller, Smith, Zhu, and Zhang (1995) studied counting in Chinese and American 4- and 5-year-olds. The two groups performed similarly in learning to count up to 12, but the Chinese children were about a year ahead of the American children in the further development of their counting.

As regards the development of the understanding of tens and units, Irene Miura and her colleagues studied 6-year-old children of different nationalities (Miura & Okamoto, 2003; Miura, Kim, Chang, & Okamoto, 1988; Miura, Okamoto, Kim, Steere, & Fayol, 1993). These included three groups who used regular counting systems – Chinese, Japanese and Korean – and and three groups who used less regular counting systems – French, Swedish and US. The tasks involved representation of two-digit numbers with base ten blocks (unit blocks and tens blocks; the latter are blocks with 10 segments shown of them). None of the children had previous experience with base 10 blocks. The users of regular counting systems were far more likely than the users of irregular counting systems to represent the tens and units by means of the blocks: e.g. to represent 42 by four tens blocks and two unit blocks. The American, French and Swedish children tended to attempt to represent the numbers as collections of units: e.g. to represent the number 42 as 42 unit blocks.

Quite similar results have been obtained with Korean children (Fuson & Kwon, 1992; Song & Ginsburg, 1988).

However, it is difficult to draw firm conclusions on how such results should be interpreted (Towse & Saxton, 1998), because there are so many other cultural and educational differences between Asian and western children.

The Welsh language and numeracy

The Welsh language can offer important insights here. Historically, there has been more than one Welsh counting system and an older system is still used for dates (Roberts, 2000). However the main counting system in current use is, like the counting systems used in Pacific Rim countries, completely regular (Roberts, 2000). The number words are easily constructed by knowing the numbers 1 to 10 and the rule for combining them. For example, 11 in Welsh is 'un deg un' (one ten one), 12 is 'un deg dau' (one ten two), and 22 is 'dau ddeg dau' (two tens two).

Wales provides an unusual opportunity for research on linguistic influences on mathematics, since it is a region in which languages with both regular and irregular counting systems are used. In Wales, children receive either an English- or Welsh-medium schooling within the same country, educational system, curriculum, and cultural environment. In some cases, Welsh- and English-medium education even takes place in different streams in the same school. Children whose parental language is English may still receive their education from age 4 entirely in Welsh. This makes it possible to compare groups with varying levels of exposure to the regular and irregular number systems: (1) children whose first language is Welsh, have a Welsh home environment and a Welsh-language schooling; (2) children who receive a Welsh-language schooling, but have English speaking parents and home environment, and for whom English is their first language; (3) children whose first language is English and who receive an English medium education. Any extraneous cultural or educational differences between these groups will at any rate be far less than those between, for example, English and Chinese children.

Moreover, speakers of Asian languages might be advantaged not just because their counting systems are regular, but because their number words are short and take up relatively little space in working memory. By contrast, Welsh number words are actually longer than their English counterparts. Ellis and his colleagues (Ellis, 1992; Ellis & Hennelly, 1980) found that the length of Welsh number words does indeed appear to increase load on working memory and to have an adverse effect on some aspects of number processing. Bilingual adults have shorter digit spans in Welsh than in English and some aspects of calculation are slower in Welsh. Thus, any mathematical advantages that one does find in the Welsh counting system are much more likely to be due just to its regularity.

Maclean and Whitburn (1996) found that children in Welsh-medium schools performed better than those in English-medium schools on certain numerical measures: in particular, they could count higher. Comprehension and use of multi-digit numbers was hard to assess in their study, as most of the children were 6-years-old or under and had not been much exposed to oral and written representations of tens and units.

Delyth Lloyd carried out a study with me (Dowker & Lloyd, in press), looking at Welsh 6-year-olds who had just begun dealing with such representations and 8-year-olds who had greater experience.

A total of 60 children drawn from three junior state schools in south Wales (in areas of similar socioeconomic status), participated in the testing. There were 10 6-year-olds and 10 8-year-olds from each school. One was a Welsh-medium school in a predominantly Welsh valley. Welsh was the first language for the children; they all received a Welsh-medium education, and also came from Welsh-speaking homes. This school is henceforth referred to as *WW*. The second was a Welsh-medium school in a predominantly *English-speaking* area of Wales (henceforth referred to as *WE*. The children attending school WE spoke English as a first language, but received education entirely through the medium of Welsh. School 3 was an English-medium school in the same town as school WE. Although situated in the same education system, country and cultural environment as the Welsh-medium schools, school 3 is an English-medium school in an English area (henceforth referred to as *EE*). The English-educated children of school EE were compared to those educated through the Welsh medium in schools WW and WE.

The children were given three standardized tests: the British Abilities Scales Basic Number Skills test, which measures written calculation; the WISC arithmetic subtest which measures mental arithmetical reasoning, especially word problem solving; and the WISC block design subtest which measures nonverbal reasoning. They were also given a number comparison task, based on that used by Donlan and Gourlay (1999).

In the number comparison task, 24 pairs of two-digit numbers were presented to children in a flip booklet. There were three types of number pair: transparent, misleading and reversible. Transparent word pairs required judgement between numerals that either had different number of tens but the same number of units (decade comparisons; e.g. 73 and 63) or contained repeated digits, e.g. 11 and 99. In misleading number pairs the smallest numeral always contained a digit that was larger than the sum of the digits in the target item, e.g. 51 and 47; 19 and 21. Reversible pairs included, for example, 76 and 67; 25 and 52.

Twenty-four numbers were presented in all, eight of each type, in a random order. All participants were required to read the numbers aloud before pointing to which was the biggest.

Hesitations (where children nearly pointed at the incorrect answer and then changing to the correct one at the last second); misreadings; and incorrect answers were recorded.

A *comparison errors* score indicated overall performance on the task: the total number of hesitations, misreadings and incorrect answers added together.

Children were tested individually. For schools WW and WE all communication was in Welsh and for school EE it was in English.

It was important to check that the groups did not differ in overall ability. The WISC block design subtest was used as a measure of nonverbal reasoning. An analysis of variance showed that the scaled score on this test did not differ significantly either between schools or between age groups.

The schools also turned out not to differ in terms of overall arithmetical reasoning or calculation ability. No significant differences were found between schools or age groups on the standard score on either the WISC arithmetic subtest or the British Abilities Scales Basic Number Skills subtest. This suggests that the counting system on its own does not have an impact on global arithmetical ability in otherwise culturally similar groups.

However, one of the central tenets of this book is that, in any case, there is no such thing as global arithmetical ability! Might counting system have an effect on some more specific aspects of arithmetic? It appeared that this was, indeed, the case. There were group differences in more specific areas of arithmetical ability: notably, in the ability to read and judge number pairs, as shown by the number comparison task. Although almost all children performed at ceiling level for correct answers, they varied in the mis-readings of numbers and hesitations in judgement.

A comparison error score was constructed as a composite measure of children's hesitations, errors and misreadings in the number comparison tasks. Analyses of variance showed that older children obtained significantly better comparison error scores than younger children and that children in WW schools performed significantly better than those in WE schools, who, in turn, performed significantly better than those in EE schools.

Thus, there are some differences between the mathematics skills of children who learn mathematics in Welsh and English. These were revealed in specific areas of children's performance, but not on more general arithmetical performance as measured by WISC arithmetic and BAS Number Skills tests. Welsh-speaking children find it easier than English-speaking children to read and compare two-digit numbers. This suggests that they are better at using the principles of place value.

It is important to emphasize that, in contrast with most studies of linguistic effects on mathematics, cultural and educational differences were not strong confounding variables in this study, which means that linguistic differences were more likely to have, indeed, been causal factors.

The limited but significant advantages of speaking Welsh appeared to hold, even if it were not the child's first or only language. Children who had no preschool knowledge of a regular counting system, but who attended a Welsh-medium primary school, appeared to benefit from the introduction of this knowledge during their primary education. Children in the WE group gained to the extent that they outperformed monolingual English children in number reading and number comparisons when tested in what is their second language after just 2 years of Welsh education, at age 6, supporting somewhat similar findings for Korean-English bilingual children (Song & Ginsburg, 1988). Miller et al. (1995) found linguistic differences in counting ability between English and Chinese speaking 3- to 5-year-olds; the present study indicates that differences in number skills continue beyond the preschool years, well into primary education.

The study also indicates that the effects of language on mathematics, although important, are quite specific. Children who use a regular counting system are not thereby better at all aspects of calculation. The globally better performance of Pacific Rim children must be attributed not only to linguistic factors, but also to other cultural factors, such as attitudes to mathematics and amount of time devoted to it in the school curriculum. But linguistic factors *do* appear to influence the ability to use place value in reading, comparing and manipulating two-digit numbers. Further studies, involving larger numbers of children and a wider age range, would be desirable in order to confirm the generality of these findings.

It should be noted that very few children learn *only* Welsh. Children who attend Welsh-medium schools do also learn English; so ultimately they will learn two counting systems. In fact, most learn three counting systems. Ultimately, they become exposed not only to the contemporary regular decimal counting system, but also to an older vegesimal (base 20) system, which, although it is not used in schools or in mathematics instruction, still has some place in the culture (Roberts, 2000). Thus, Welsh-speaking children start out by being exposed to a simple, regular counting system; but eventually are exposed to the complexity of multiple counting systems. The advantages and disadvantages of such exposure to multiple systems remain to be studied.

How aware are children of cultural differences in number representation?

Awareness of the fact that the same number may be expressed in more than one way is one indication of an abstract understanding of number. It is one aspect of the ability to represent numbers and arithmetic in different ways, which is discussed in Chapter 5.

How good are children at understanding this? Bilingual children – and adults – are relatively good at it. They learn to count in both of their languages and to keep these straight, although they may have a preference for counting in one of the languages: usually the one that they have learned first?

There is some evidence that bilingual children, who count in more than one language, do have an advantage in being able to focus selectively on those aspects of a stimulus that are relevant to number. Bialystok and Codd (1997) investigated 4- to 6-year-old bilingual (French/English) and mono-lingual children's ability to say which of two towers contained more blocks. Sometimes the taller tower had more blocks; sometimes the shorter tower did. As is generally found (Piaget, 1952; Chapter 4 in this volume), it was difficult for children to disregard the perceptual cues and focus on the number relationships: they tended to say that that the taller tower had more. The bilingual children, however, were better at this task than the monolingual children. Perhaps knowing that the same number could have two names, but that this did not change the quantity, had made them more able to extract and abstract just the information that was relevant to number.

What about monolingual children? How aware are they that numbers can be represented in different ways by different cultures? Obviously, there will be individual differences and differences based on experience. However, there is a lot of admittedly anecdotal evidence to suggest that many chil-dren, at least by early primary school age, are not only aware that different cultures might represent numbers differently: they are fascinated with the subject.

Opie and Opie (1969) pointed out that primary school children frequently use nonsense syllables for 'counting out' to decide who will play a specific role in a game; and that these are sometimes dignified by such terms as 'Chinese counting' (in Britain) or 'Indian counting' (in America). Common examples, at least in the 1960s, were variations on:

> *Eeni meeni macaraca,*
> *Rare, ri, domeraca,*
> *Chiceraca,*
> *Rom pom push.* (version collected from Ipswich)

Some rhymes used by 19th-century children had a somewhat greater resemblance to English counting; e.g. the following from Surrey, quoted in Jamieson's *Scottish dictionary*, Supplement, Vol. II, 1825, p. 169:

> *One-erie, two-erie, tickerie, seven,*
> *Allabone, crackabone, ten or eleven;*
> *Pot, pan, must be done,*
> *Tweedle-come, twaddle-come, twenty-one.*

However such verses may have originated, they are of interest here because they indicate that many children are aware of and interested in the fact that counting is different in different languages; and that different words can be used to express the same numbers.

One child who showed a striking interest in cultural differences in both verbal and nonverbal representations of number was Michael, a mono-lingual white English working-class 6-year-old boy in my intervention study, who was regarded as having difficulty in arithmetic. He was very interested in demonstrating the ways in which numbers could be counted and written in 'African'. He would count on his fingers in unusual orders: for example, the third finger, then the first, then the fourth, then the second, then the fifth; and describe this as 'African counting'. He would draw shapes and patterns that were labelled in an apparently arbitrary way as the 'African' for certain numbers; for example a triangle was '5 in African'. It is unlikely that any of his representations corresponded to any actual African (or other) counting or writing system: they were presumably his own invention. What is of interest is that he realized and was interested in the fact that the same numbers *could* be represented in different ways by different cultures and that they were still the same numbers.

Such cases, although anecdotal, give support to the view expressed already in this volume that many young school age children *can* represent a number in multiple ways, translate between different types of representation and recognize that the number remains the same number through such translations.

Conclusions

There is overwhelming evidence that culture has a strong influence on the ways in which numbers and arithmetical operations are represented and used and on level of performance in arithmetic. These cultural influences include language; teaching methods; economic factors; technology; and cultural practices and preoccupations (e.g. work activities; money and trading; concerns about issues such as age).

However, there do appear to be some core numerical abilities that vary relatively little with culture. These are those number perceptions and concepts that develop in infancy or early childhood: especially those that depend relatively little on words.

Moreover, the cultural variations in themselves demonstrate a universal potential for arithmetical reasoning. This may never be realized if there is never any need or opportunity for such reasoning: either because no arithmetic is required or because it is taught in ways that make it appear meaningless. But arithmetical reasoning can develop in a very wide variety of contexts: in a family with an interest in number; in school; in games; in the context of shopping and financial planning; in jobs ranging from street trading to carpentry; in cooking and other domestic activities; and in dealing with cultural preoccupations such as age.

It is particularly interesting that at least some children seem to be aware of, interested in, and able to reason about cross-cultural variations in counting and arithmetic. This reflects both the importance of culture to arithmetical thinking and the fact that arithmetical thinking is not *totally* culture bound.

10 The brain and individual differences in arithmetic

A lot of work, both with 'normal' individuals and with patients, supports the view that there are areas and networks in the brain that are particularly important for arithmetic. Two recent books, Stanislas Dehaene's *The number sense* (Macmillan, 1997) and Brian Butterworth's *The mathematical brain* (Oxford University Press, 1999), have dealt extensively with the ways in which the brain is specialized for number and arithmetic. The focus of the present chapter is the possible role that individual differences in brain functions might play in individual differences in arithmetic. There has so far been rather little direct research on this topic, at any rate as regards 'normal' individuals, although this is an important goal for future research.

Brain damage and dissociations between different components of arithmetic

Some of the most striking evidence for the componential nature of arithmetic, and the possibility of individual differences in the relative levels of functioning of the different components, comes from studies of patients who have become dyscalculic (unable to cope with some or all aspects of arithmetic) as the result of brain damage. This evidence is gained from the study of what are commonly termed *dissociations* in such patients: i.e. impaired functioning of one component while another is preserved. *Double dissociations* where one patient shows impaired performance in one component but not in another (e.g. can add but not subtract) while another shows the reverse (e.g. can subtract but not add) are particularly important for establishing the potential independence of different components.

Patients can indeed demonstrate single and double dissociations between different arithmetical operations – addition, subtraction, multiplication and division – (Cipolotti & Delacycostello, 1995; Dagenbach & McCloskey, 1992; McNeil & Warrington, 1994; Van Harskamp & Cipolotti, 2001); between oral and written presentation modes (Campbell, 1994; McNeil & Warrington, 1993); between number comprehension and production (Campbell, 1990); and between transcoding (reading and writing numbers) and calculation (Caramazza & McCloskey, 1987; Cipolotti & Butterworth,

1995). There are even claims that some patients may have particular problems with specific numbers. Wedell and Davidoff (1991) reported a patient with selective impairment in processing the numbers 7, 9 and 0.

On a still more abstract level, the study of patients with brain damage provides evidence for the broad distinction that the developmental psychologists Greeno, Riley, and Gelman (1983) proposed between three major components of mathematical knowledge: factual, procedural and conceptual knowledge (see Chapter 2). Double dissociations have been reported between factual and procedural knowledge (McCloskey, 1992; Warrington, 1982) and between factual/procedural and conceptual knowledge (Delazer, 2003; Delazer & Benke, 1997; Girelli & Delazer, 1996; Hittmair-Delazer, Semenza, & Denes, 1994; Hittmair-Delazer, Sailer, & Berke, 1995; Luchelli & Derenzi, 1993; Warrington, 1982). Another important form of dissociation, discussed extensively in Chapter 7 is that sometimes found between exact calculation and estimation (Dehaene & Cohen, 1991; Warrington, 1982).

Functional brain imaging and the components of arithmetic

Recently, the evidence from patients has received increasing support from functional brain-imaging studies of people without brain damage. Different aspects of arithmetic seem to make different demands on different parts of the brain. Dehaene and his colleagues (Dehaene, Tzourio, Frank, Raynaud, Cohen, Mehler, & Mazoyer, 1996) found that the left parietal cortex is particularly involved in exact calculation, while approximation and estimation seem to depend more on the right hemisphere.

In a functional MRI study, Chochon, Cohen, van de Moortele, and Dehaene (1999) found that the parietal, prefrontal and anterior cingulate areas of the brain are active in a variety of number-processing tasks, with greater activation of the right hemisphere in a number-comparison task, of the left hemisphere in a multiplication task and equal activation of both hemispheres in a subtraction task.

While different studies disagree as regards the details of brain organization for arithmetic, most suggest that the parietal cortex is involved bilaterally, with a bias toward the right, in magnitude comparison and approximation; while exact calculation is a predominantly left hemisphere function, involving the parietal (especially inferior parietal) cortex, prefrontal cortex, and basal ganglia. Some studies (e.g. Rickard, Romero, Basso, Wharton, Flitman, & Grafman, 2000) suggest bilateral and symmetrical involvement of the hemispheres, even though different *regions* are differentially activated by different numerical tasks; others (e.g. Chochon et al., 1999; Dehaene et al., 1996) suggest greater hemispheric specialization. The results of several studies suggested that the left parietal cortex is particularly important in the verbal retrieval of learned facts, such as the multiplication tables, whereas other parts of the brain play a greater role in tasks which require more arithmetical reasoning (Cohen, Dehaene, Chochon, Lehrichy, & Naccache, 2000; Kazui, Kitagaki, & Mori, 2000). However, it is necessary to be careful in making assumptions about the form of processing required in any given task, since quite different strategies may be used for the same task by different individuals or even by the same individual at different times (Dowker, 1992; Lefevre, Bisanz, Daley, Buffone, Greenham, & Sadesky, 1996a; Lefevre, Smith-Chant, Hiscock, Daley, & Morris, 2003; Siegler & Jenkins, 1989).

Functional brain-imaging studies typically involve larger and perhaps more representative samples than studies of patients. Nonetheless, due to practical constraints, they usually involve smaller samples than would be deemed ideal in most experimental studies (more than 10 in a single experiment is unusual). For this reason among others, it has been difficult so far to study individual differences in brain organization using such methods, although this has been recognized as an important potential area of study (Haier, 2001; Yeo, 1989). It will be of great interest to discover whether individual differences in brain organization for different components of arithmetic are correlated with individual differences in performance levels and strategies for these components.

The brain and arithmetic in children

Most studies directly relating to the brain have involved adults. They are more likely to suffer the accidents and diseases, such as strokes, that can cause localized brain damage. It is easier, and less ethically and practically controversial, to use brain-imaging techniques to test adults than children.

However, arithmetical disabilities do sometimes result from brain damage or brain abnormality in children. It is known that children with certain specific genetic conditions tend to have specific difficulties in arithmetic. This is particularly true of children with Turner syndrome (Butterworth, Grana, Piazza, Girelli, Price, & Skuse, 1999; Mazzocco, 1998, 2001; Temple & Marriott, 1998). Specific or disproportionate arithmetical difficulties are also characteristic of some other conditions; notably Williams syndrome; fragile X syndrome occurring in girls without major learning difficulties (Mazzocco, in press); and the chromosome 22q11.2 deletion syndrome (Bearden et al. (2001)). This genetic component might imply that the arithmetical difficulties are linked to unusual brain characteristics. Shalev, Manor, Kerem, Ayali, Badichi, Friedlander, and Gross-Tsur (2001) recently obtained results that suggested that developmental dyscalculia, even when not linked to a known genetic disorder, has a strong tendency to run in families.

Arithmetical difficulties can also occur in children with known early brain damage. Studies of children with unilateral early brain damage have given conflicting results as to which hemisphere is most associated with arithmetical difficulties. Some studies (Aram & Ekelman, 1988; Kiessling,

Denckla, & Carlton, 1983; Van Hout, 1995) have obtained results which suggest that right hemisphere damage is more associated with arithmetical difficulties, while others (Ashcraft, Yamashita, & Aram, 1992; Martins, Parreira, Albuquerque, & Ferro, 1999a) found that, as is typical for adults, left hemisphere damage caused greater arithmetical difficulties. Martins et al. (1999) pointed out that most of the studies showing greater effects of right hemisphere damage involved younger children than those in their own study. They suggested that the right hemisphere may be crucial in the development of early number concepts in preschoolers, while the left hemisphere may be more important in the development of calculation skills in somewhat older children.

It is always necessary, however, to be cautious about extrapolating from atypical development in genetically impaired or brain-damaged children to normal development. As has recently been pointed out (Karmiloff-Smith, 1998; Paterson, Brown, Gsoedl, Johnson, & Karmiloff-Smith, 1999), typical and atypical brains may differ at multiple levels, making it difficult or impossible to attribute cognitive differences to damage to a specific neuro-psychological module. Moreover, the patterns of such differences may change with time. For example, infants with Williams syndrome show good recognition of numerical quantities, but poor word comprehension, while in later childhood and adulthood they tend to show the reverse type of pattern: very poor arithmetic and relatively good language (Ansari & Karmiloff-Smith, 2002).

Interaction between inborn and environmental factors in neurological and cognitive development

'Could you talk if you didn't have a brain?'
'Yes, but you wouldn't know the words.' (overheard conversation between two children of about 8-years-old)

Localization of brain function for different components of arithmetic – whether by studies of patients or by brain-imaging studies – provides supporting evidence for the existence and functional separability of these components. It does not prove that these components are 'innate' or uninfluenced by environmental factors.

There is no doubt that physiological and environmental factors interact in all aspects of cognition and behaviour. Nearly a hundred years ago, the issues were stated clearly by Kirkpatrick (1908, pp. 8–9):

Unlike other machines, the brain is always in process of construction, always being modified and never completed . . . Every time the mind does a thing it becomes a different mind; hence the factors of nature and nurture are almost inextricably mingled in psychical development

. . . The question is often asked whether certain characteristics are native or acquired. The answer might be in nearly every case, 'They are both'.

Much research since that time has confirmed this view of the brain (e.g. Elman, Bates, Johnson, Karmiloff-Smith, Parisi, & Plunkett, 1996; Johnson, 2000; Morton & Frith, 1995). Not only do characteristics of the brain affect development and behaviour, but experience affects the brain. For example, children with squints that are not corrected before the age of about 3 may never have good binocular vision, even if the surgery is subsequently performed and even if vision is good in each eye. This is because the areas of the brain responsible for binocular vision have failed to develop due to lack of experience during a critical period.

Language acquisition is an area that demonstrates the importance and complexity of these issues. Virtually all children acquire language, whatever their environment. The environment determines whether they acquire English, French, Chinese, British Sign Language, or any other of the world's many languages. But it is generally accepted that all these languages share universal grammatical characteristics. Moreover, studies of brain-damaged patients and brain-imaging studies of typical adults converge in demonstrating that most people use the same specific parts of the left hemisphere of the brain in producing and comprehending language; and that this is essentially independent of the particular language that they speak or even of whether it is a spoken or a sign language (Hickok, Bellugi, & Klima, 1998).

Nevertheless, a child who has most or all of the left hemisphere surgically removed in infancy may still acquire near normal language (Ogden, 1996); while a child without brain damage who is not exposed to language before puberty will probably always have a serious grammatical impairment (Newport, 1990).

Less dramatically, Castro-Caldas, Petersson, Reis, Stone-Elander, and Ingvar (1998) have reviewed evidence that suggests that adults who are illiterate for purely environmental reasons tend to show less strong left hemisphere lateralization for language than do literate adults. A functional brain-imaging study by Paulesu et al. (2000) suggested that there are even subtle differences between people who read very regular orthographies such as Italian, which follow strict letter-to-sound correspondence rules, and those who read less regular orthographies such as English, with regard to the activation of brain areas during certain language tasks.

'Normal' individual differences in arithmetic: Are they related to brain differences?

'I, in particular, felt convinced that I was about to undergo some fearful operation that would show to all the world the big hollow places in my brain where the knowledge ought to be. As to that cavity where the mathematics

> should have grown – I trembled to think of it.' (Maude Forsey: *Mollie Hazeldene's Schooldays*, London: Nelson, 1924. Every effort has been made to trace copyright holder and obtain permission to reproduce this extract. Any omissions brought to our attention will be remedied in future editions)

The findings that different arithmetical tasks make demands on different parts of the brain do not necessarily mean that individual differences in 'normal' people's performance in these tasks are related to differences in the functioning of these parts of the brain or the ways in which they are connected. It is, however, noteworthy that both children and adults in the general population can show discrepancies between different aspects of arithmetic, which are almost as great as the dissociations found in some patients. Sometimes these occur in individuals who have severe arithmetical deficits and are describable as having 'developmental dyscalculia'. For example, Sokol and McCloskey (1991) and Temple (1991) describe some such children who show dissociations between the ability to deal with facts and procedures.

In some other cases, the overall arithmetical deficits are rather less severe, although still troublesome. Some examples of such people showing marked discrepancies between different components have already been described: for example, Rose and James who showed discrepancies, in opposite directions, between estimation and exact calculation.

I will here discuss the case of Claire, a member of the Adult Group described in Chapter 2. She is a woman in her late 20s, who experienced a lot of difficulty with school mathematics and at the age of 10 was described by her school as being of 'remedial' standard in this subject. At that age, she was given the Stanford Binet IQ test and almost solved the Superior Adult arithmetical reasoning problem about the yearly growth of a tree – except that, after working out a correct solution strategy, she calculated 37 + 13 as 39. When given the WAIS IQ test as an adult, she obtained a verbal IQ score of 132 and a performance IQ of 110. Her scaled score on the arithmetic subtest was 13, suggesting above average arithmetical reasoning. Her definitions of arithmetical operations are very sophisticated; e.g.:

> [Addition is] sort of self-explanatory. It's to make more of something by adding something to it. Unless you're adding minus numbers. If you add a minus number, you make less of the positive number.

> [Division is] to take a number and to split it into the number of parts that you're dividing by, and the answer will show how much is in each part.

However, she performed considerably less well than Hitch's (1978) less highly educated control subjects in most of his tests of whole-number, fraction and decimal arithmetic. Her score for Test 1 (whole-number arithmetic, including three-digit addition and subtraction and single-digit multiplication and division) was 93. Her performance on the division test was above average, but her scores on tests of subtraction with borrowing and subtraction without borrowing were over one and a half standard deviations below the mean of the controls; and she could not add with carrying at all, earning a score 2.65 standard deviations below their mean.

Her score on Test 2 (decimal and fraction arithmetic and long multiplication and division) was 11 out of a possible 36: more than a standard deviation below the mean for the controls. Her score on Test 3 (magnitude, approximation, rules of expression and proportional reasoning) was 29 out of 36: similar to that for controls.

In these respects – good arithmetical reasoning and definitions of arithmetical operations, combined with poor calculation – her performance was quite similar to that of Warrington's (1982) dyscalculic patient, DRC, who underwent many of the same tests; although his performance on decimal and fraction arithmetic was better than hers. Warrington used this case to demonstrate that calculation and arithmetical reasoning can be markedly discrepant in patients. Claire, and many others in the Adult Group, shows that such discrepancies also occur in individuals without brain damage. It is not clear to what extent they are caused by internal factors versus environmental factors: there is likely to be an interaction between these. Certainly there seems to be such an interaction in Claire's case. She has always found memorization of facts relatively difficult. This contributed to her being labelled as a child as being bad at arithmetic; and this labelling in turn contributed to her developing a strong anxiety about mathematics, which may have impeded her subsequent progress.

Indeed, some adults show even more specific and marked weaknesses within the domain of arithmetic. Alice, in her early 20s, was a member of the Adult subgroup *without* arithmetical difficulties. She was not considered to have any arithmetical weakness and had indeed obtained an A-grade in mathematics A-level. She obtained a WAIS arithmetic subtest scaled score of 14 (considerably above average) and performed outstandingly well on all parts of Graham Hitch's numerical abilities tests – except for the test of subtraction with borrowing, which she could not perform at all. She claimed that she 'always forgot' the rule for borrowing. Such specific deficits in patients would usually be taken as a demonstration of the neuropsychological modularity of specific arithmetical operations and processes: for example, Martins, Ferreira, and Borges (1999b) report an 11-year-old patient who experienced specific difficulty with subtraction, and especially with borrowing, in association with a left temporo-parietal tumour. Can Alice's specific difficulty in this area reflect subtle weaknesses in the functioning of a specific area or network in the brain? Is it more plausibly attributed to poor teaching of this topic? But then why are other aspects of numeracy not affected? In any case, the existence of such cases gives some support to Dagenbach and McCloskey's (1992) argument that the possibility of pre-morbid individual differences in the relative strength of different arithmetical operations must be taken into account when interpreting dissociations between the operations in brain-damaged patients.

It appears that a significant degree of functional independence, not only between arithmetic and other abilities but between different components of arithmetic is not confined to patients with neurological damage, but is readily observable in the general population (Dowker, 1998; Ginsburg, 1977). As suggested by cognitive neuropsychology, different cognitive functions, even within the same domain, can show considerable functional independence. Thus far, the view that they are 'modular' is strongly supported. However, the evidence contradicts the view sometimes implied by cognitive neuropsychology that these functions are modules that one either does or does not have and that most people do possess but some patients lack. Rather, they show continuous variation in the general population, both in children and adults.

As larger scale functional brain-imaging studies become more practicable, it will become increasingly possible to investigate the relationships between such variations in performance and variations in brain function (see earlier section, 'Functional brain imaging and the components of arithmetic').

There has been one study that compared highly accurate and less accurate arithmetical problem solvers in the general population. Menon, Rivera, White, Eliez, Glover, and Reiss (2000) carried out an fMRI study of 16 healthy young adults, and compared those who performed perfectly on a simple arithmetic test and those who occasionally made errors. The focus was on discovering whether there were differences either in the overall functioning of the left parietal lobe or in any of its subregions. The main difference was that perfect performers showed *less* activation of the left angular gyrus. This may be due to greater automatization resulting in less need for rehearsal.

Similarities between mathematical difficulties in people with and without brain damage

Some of the evidence for such continuous variation in the components of arithmetic comes from the fact that, when tested, supposedly normal adults can show considerable individual differences even in apparently very simple components of arithmetic. Deloche and his colleagues (Deloche et al., 1994; Deloche, Souza, Willadino-Braga, & Dellatolas, 1999) gave 180 normal adult subjects the EC301, a standardized testing battery for the evaluation of brain-damaged adults in the area of calculation and number processing. Although most of the normal subjects performed well, there were significant individual differences even in such components as written and oral counting, and transcoding between digits and written and spoken number words. Normal adults also show significant individual differences both in reaction times and in strategy choice for single-digit addition and multiplication (Geary & Widaman, 1987; Lefevre & Kulak, 1994; Lefevre et al., 1996a; Lefevre et al., 2003).

Moreover, children with developmental difficulties in arithmetic often show very similar deficits to those found in people with some forms of brain damage. Many researchers have pointed out such similarities (Delazer & Butterworth, 1997; Dowker, 1998; Geary, 1990, 1993; Geary & Hoard, 2001; Geary & Widaman, 1992; Jordan & Hanich, 2000; Jordan & Montani, 1997; Jordan et al., 2003; Kosc, 1974; Neumarker, 2000; Rourke, 1993; Sokol & McCloskey, 1991; Temple, 1994, 1997; Von Aster, 2000). Some have used the components that are found to dissociate in brain-damaged patients to devise tests, assessments and classification systems for children with developmental difficulties in arithmetic (Shalev, Manor, Amir, & Gross-Tsur, 1993; Shalev, Weirtman, & Amir, 1988).

It has also been pointed out that the development of arithmetical strategies in children has quite a lot in common with the re-emergence of arithmetical strategies during the rehabilitation or spontaneous improvement of patients with brain damage (Siegler, 2001; Siegler & Engle, 1994).

How might differences in brain function affect arithmetic?

Relevant differences in brain functioning may involve (1) differences in functioning of brain areas specifically related to arithmetic; or (2) differences in functioning of brain areas that involve non-numerical skills that are related to arithmetical performance. The latter could include areas involved in verbal ability, spatial ability, memory; attention; planning and flexible use of strategies, etc. The distinction between areas specifically related to arithmetic and those that are involved in other functions that facilitate arithmetic may not be completely clear cut. Many brain-imaging studies suggest that arithmetic and even its more delimited subcomponents are represented in the brain by networks rather than by single localized areas and such networks may include areas related to numerous different functions.

Different researchers have expressed somewhat different views as to the extent to which the areas of the brain that subserve arithmetic are in fact specialized for arithmetic, as opposed to subserving functions that are important for other cognitive processes besides arithmetic. For example, Butterworth (1999) emphasizes the existence of a 'number module', while Dehaene (1997) places greater emphasis on the role of verbal ability in calculation and spatial ability in magnitude comparison and approximation.

Gruber, Indefrey, Steinmetz, and Kleinschmidt (2001) used functional MRI to compare the areas of the brain that are active in calculation and in non-arithmetical tasks that make demands on language, visual-spatial processing, attention or memory. They concluded, on the basis of similarities between areas activated by arithmetical and non-arithmetical tasks, that most of the cortical areas that subserve arithmetic 'do not exclusively represent modules for calculation but support more general cognitive operations that are instrumental but not specific to calculation'. However, there were also brain areas that were more specifically activated by arithmetical tasks: the left dorsal angular gyrus and the medial parietal cortices.

It is likely that individual differences in arithmetic may often stem from differences in the functioning of brain areas other than those directly involved with arithmetic. As Dowker (1998) points out:

> Few if any of the children [with arithmetical difficulties] appeared to have a selective and specific disruption of a global arithmetical 'module', in the sense that *all* arithmetical abilities and *only* arithmetical abilities were affected. Rather, most children who had some arithmetical difficulties appeared to have deficits in *some* but not all components of arithmetic. The affected components varied from child to child. When numerous components were simultaneously disrupted, this was usually associated with difficulties that extended beyond the domain of arithmetic.

More specific disruptions of one or two components in arithmetic may also be associated with difficulties and unevennesses beyond the domain of arithmetic.

How might differences in brain function affect specific non-mathematical domains in ways that could affect arithmetical performance? So far, when individual differences have been considered in relation to brain function, this has usually been considered in terms of specific or general learning difficulties. It is, however, a central thesis of this book that such learning deficits, even when they result from brain damage, can be most usefully investigated as the extreme ends of continua through varying levels of normal function, with exceptional talents at the other ends. This does not mean that differing levels of normal functioning, and exceptional talents, need to be related to differences in functioning of the same brain areas whose injury leads to specific deficits; but they may be. Studies of people who combine extreme specific talents with general learning difficulties – the 'savant syndrome' – may shed interesting light on this topic and will be discussed later in the chapter.

This chapter will now discuss how differences in arithmetical functions might be related to brain-related differences in processes that are not specifically mathematically; and then at whether they may be related to differences in brain functions that are more specifically related to number.

Non-mathematical functions that may be related to individual differences in arithmetic are discussed in Chapter 3. They include motor control and co-ordination, especially as these affect counting; awareness of the fingers and their position; language; spatial ability; and attention, working memory and so-called 'executive function'.

Individual differences in these functions are unlikely to be exclusively caused by differences in brain function; but brain differences may contribute to them. This issue will be discussed here with particular regard to language.

The brain and individual differences in non-mathematical domains relevant to arithmetic: The case of language

There is little doubt that arithmetical difficulties can be associated with language difficulties (see Chapter 3). It appears that unusual patterns of brain functioning may contribute to many language difficulties are often due to unusual patterns of brain functioning, but the extent and nature of the contribution are still unclear. Following current practice, the term 'specific language impairment' will here be used to refer to marked delays or abnormalities in the production or comprehension of spoken language that cannot be explained by low nonverbal IQ, hearing impairment, emotional problems or environmental deprivation. 'Dyslexia' will be used to refer to difficulties in reading or writing that are similarly unexplainable by other factors. The use of the terms does not necessarily indicate acceptance of brain-based explanations for the difficulties.

To what extent are brain differences responsible for differences in linguistic functioning? The significant genetic contribution to specific language impairment (Bishop, 1997) and to dyslexia (Pennington, 1995) suggests that a physiological factor may be involved. While some cases of specific language impairment are clearly associated with abnormal functioning of certain brain areas, in other cases no abnormality can be detected. Very few cases of developmental dyslexia are associated with brain damage or obviously atypical brain functioning. However, there have been some studies suggesting subtle differences in brain functioning between people with and without dyslexia. People with dyslexia are more likely than non-dyslexics to be left-handed or ambidextrous and are less likely to have a left hemisphere that is clearly larger than the right hemisphere. However, none of these characteristics is exclusive to or defining of people with dyslexia. Most people with dyslexia are right-handed; many people without dyslexia are left-handed or ambidextrous; and 25% of people do not show a clear size difference between the two hemispheres, while only 5 to 10% of people are dyslexic.

Also, recent brain-imaging studies (e.g. Paulesu, Frith, Snowling, Gallagher, Morton, Frackowiak, & Frith, 1996) have suggested that people with and without dyslexia show different patterns of brain activation when reading. Both groups show activation of language areas of the left hemisphere; but those with dyslexia show less simultaneous activation of different parts of the left hemisphere and, in particular, show less activation of the insula, which connects visual and language areas. These differences may be related to dyslexics' generally poorer reading or to their emphasizing different reading strategies: it is usually found that dyslexics are less sensitive to rhyme and alliteration in speech and to phonics in reading, and that they tend to use whole-word strategies rather than phonic strategies when reading. It is not, however, clear whether the differences in brain functioning are the *cause* or the *result* of differences in reading strategies. In some ways, the differences between dyslexics and non-dyslexics in this study parallel the differences between English and Italian readers in the 2000 study by Paulesu et al. English people show less activation of the insula when reading than do Italians. Perhaps the level of activation of the insula depends on the extent to which individuals use phonic strategies in reading, rather than phonic strategies depending on activation of the insula.

There is, indeed, some evidence that the brain activation differences between dyslexics and non-dyslexics are a *result*, as well as, or instead of, a *cause* of strategy differences and that they can be influenced by learning and experience.

Posner and McCandliss (1999) recently carried out some fMRI scans of 10- to 12-year-olds with and without dyslexia. Again, the children showed reduced activation of the left angular gyrus. The researchers found that, after training in phonological awareness, the dyslexics not only improved in their reading, but their brain scans when reading became more similar to those of good readers: in particular, they showed greater activation of the left angular gyrus. These results were supported by Temple, Deutsch, Poldrack, Miller, Tallal, Merzenich, and Gabrieli (2003), who found that 8- to 12-year-old children with dyslexia showed not only improved reading, but also changes in their brain scans during a rhyming task, after training that involved auditory processing and oral language. In particular, they showed increased activation of their left temporo-parietal cortex and left inferior frontal gyrus: thus showing an increased resemblance to non-dyslexic controls in this study and in other studies.

Moreover, the comparatively small samples in the studies so far makes it difficult to assess individual differences *within* groups and to investigate whether the difference between dyslexics and non-dyslexics is one of degree or one of kind.

Role of the frontal lobes in arithmetic: Planning and control

Other chapters have emphasized the importance in arithmetic of flexible and appropriate choice and use of strategies and the ability to remember, monitor and reflect on the procedures involved. Since the frontal lobes of the brain are important in working memory, self-monitoring, planning and strategy choice, one might expect them to be important in arithmetic.

There is indeed some evidence from brain imaging studies (e.g. Prabhakaran, Rypma, & Gabrieli, 2001) that the frontal lobes of the brain are active in arithmetical tasks, especially those that cannot be solved purely on the basis of memory, but require some arithmetical reasoning.

Patients with frontal lobe damage are often particularly bad at the estimation of quantities (Shallice & Evans, 1978), making very unreasonable estimates such as that it is 10 miles from London to Paris, or that 500 people can fit on a double-decker bus.

Semenza, Miceli, and Girelli (1997) have suggested that some deficits in arithmetical procedures result from lack or loss of *knowledge* of the procedures, while others result from difficulties in *monitoring* the procedures.

Dehaene (1998) suggests (pp. 122–123) that:

> Innumeracy results from the difficulty of controlling the activation of arithmetic schemas distributed in multiple cerebral areas . . . (N)umber knowledge does not rest on a single specialized brain area; but on vast distributed networks of neurons, each performing its own simple, automated and independent computation.

Different networks control different functions: e.g. intuitions about numerical quantities; verbal counting; manipulation of number symbols; rote memory for number facts.

> Innumeracy occurs because these multiple circuits often respond autonomously and in a disconcerted fashion. Their arbitration, under the command of the prefrontal cortex, is often slow to emerge. Children . . . focus on calculation routines and fail to draw appropriate links with their quantitative number sense . . . (I)nnumeracy reflects one of the fundamental properties of our brain: its modularity, the compartmentalization of mathematical knowledge within multiple partially autonomous circuits. In order to become proficient in mathematics, one must go beyond these compartmentalized modules and establish a series of flexible links among them.

This characteristic is seen by Dehaene as resulting from immaturity of the prefrontal cortex, which is particularly involved in 'implementing and controlling nonroutine strategies'. The problem is likely to be aggravated by educational techniques that compartmentalize different parts of arithmetic and discourage the use of nonroutine strategies.

This is extremely relevant to the themes presented in other chapters of this book: flexibility and variability of strategy use as discussed in the Chapter 1 and integration of procedures and concepts as discussed in Chapter 4. In these chapters it is emphasized that children's failure to link different aspects of arithmetic could be due to their being taught arithmetic in a compartmentalized fashion; to a lack of abstract understanding of arithmetic; to difficulty with some of the procedural aspects of arithmetic, so that these take up a child's attention, leaving little room for other matters; or to a difficulty in integrating and forming links between different cognitive processes. It is the last that seems to be implicated in Dehaene's theory.

Brain areas specialized for number itself: Their possible role in individual differences

As we can see, there are many skills and processes involved in arithmetic; and many of these are important for other domains as well as arithmetic. Nevertheless, as Butterworth (1999, pp. 166–167) points out, the existence of patients with severe but seemingly localized deficits in arithmetic supports a view that there is an area or network in the brain that is specialized for arithmetic itself. Number understanding cannot be explained *only* in terms of language, spatial ability, logical reasoning or memory.

Some of the strongest evidence comes from the patient 'Signora Gaddi', described by Cipolotti, Butterworth, and Denes (1991). She suffered a stroke affecting the left parietal cortex. She had severe difficulties with all aspects of number. She could deal with numbers up to 4, but only if she was permitted to count them: unlike most individuals, including young babies, she was not able to distinguish two dots from three without counting. She could not count beyond 4, or in any way deal with numbers beyond that point. Yet she had no lasting problems with language, spatial ability, memory, reasoning or any other non-mathematical abilities that could explain such a deficit.

There are also a few reports of patients who show the reverse pattern to Signora Gaddi. They suffer from dementia affecting most cognitive functions, but have a spared capacity to do arithmetic. Rossor, Warrington, and Cipolotti (1995) described the patient 'Mr Bell', who had Pick's disease and had profound deficits in language and memory, but could still add, subtract and compare the sizes of two- and three-digit numbers. It turned out that the left parietal lobe – the area damaged in the case of Signora Gaddi – was one of the few areas in the left hemisphere that was *un*damaged in Mr Bell's case.

This suggests that the left parietal lobe, or certain areas within it, may be particularly and specifically crucial to number understanding and arithmetic. Does this mean that individual differences in arithmetic might be at least partly linked to individual differences in the functioning of the left parietal lobe?

An early study by Genkin (1960, reported by Krutetskii, 1968) suggested that electrophysiological responses of the inferior parietal lobes during a mathematical task were less strong in children with mathematical difficulties than in children who were performing normally in mathematics. He suggested that the inferior parietal lobes were less well developed in children with pronounced mathematical difficulties. The EEG techniques available at that time were far less precise and reliable than the brain-imaging studies that are now available; but the results are interesting, especially given their convergence with other findings.

Isaacs (2001) studied a group of children who had been born very prematurely and weighed less than 3 pounds 2 ounces at birth. A relatively high proportion of these children had specific arithmetical difficulties. Within this group, those who were experiencing difficulty in arithmetic had smaller left parietal cortices than those who were not experiencing any such difficulty. This finding suggests that the size and functioning of the left parietal lobe could indeed be a factor in individual differences in normal arithmetical development. However, very premature babies, even if they have not experienced actual brain damage, may be an unusual group with regard to brain development (for example, left-handedness is much commoner in very premature babies than in full-term babies). The degree to which such findings can be extended to children who were not born very prematurely still remains to be discovered.

Bearing this caution in mind, how might such differences in the left parietal lobe affect arithmetical development? Would children whose left parietal lobes are relatively small be expected to show weaknesses just at calculation or at a wider variety of numerical abilities? In particular, are their weaknesses, like those of Signora Gaddi, linked to an inability to recognize even very small quantities?

There does seem to be evidence that some people with developmental difficulties in arithmetic may demonstrate difficulties in small number recognition. Butterworth (1999) studied one adult without known brain damage, who claimed to have always had difficulty with arithmetic. He did indeed have difficulty with many aspects of arithmetic; but, in addition, he could not recognize two or three dots without counting them. Such difficulties have also been seen in some children with Turner's syndrome (Butterworth et al., 1999) and in some cases of severe developmental dyscalculia (Ta'ir, Brezner, & Ariel, 1997).

Although more research in the area is desirable, it does not appear likely that most individual differences in arithmetic in the general population are caused by differences in ability to recognize small numbers. There are very few people who cannot recognize quantities up to three, without needing to count them. Despite some controversy over the matter, it appears likely that even babies under 6 months can distinguish between one item, two items and three items (see Chapter 4). Among 146 children who were selected for my Numeracy Intervention programme – i.e. children who were considered by their teachers to be particularly weak at arithmetic, and who usually performed poorly on standardized tests – none showed an inability to distinguish between such small quantities. However, this need not mean that individual differences in functioning of the left parietal lobe have no important implications for slightly more difficult aspects of counting and arithmetic.

Arithmetical talent and the brain

Most studies of arithmetic and the brain have involved either brain-imaging studies of typical individuals or studies of patients with calculation impairments following brain injury. As discussed earlier there have been studies of exceptionally skilled calculators (Binet, 1894; Hope & Sherrill, 1987; Hunter, 1962; Krutetskii, 1968; Smith, 1983), including some mostly autistic 'savants' with preserved arithmetical ability in the face of low overall IQ (Heavey, 2003; Hermelin & O'Connor, 1991). The savants provide further evidence for the potential separability of arithmetical abilities from language and other abilities. However, most such studies have not looked directly at brain function and organization in arithmetically talented people, especially as most were carried out before the advent of functional brain imaging.

One 'calculating prodigy' (of good overall intelligence) did, however, recently take part in a PET brain-imaging study (Butterworth, 2001; Pesenti, Seron, Samson, & Duroux, 1999). This talented calculator had not been exceptional at arithmetic as a child, but had, as an adult, developed his calculation skills to the point of being able mentally to calculate ninth powers and fifth roots with great accuracy. When compared with controls, he did not show obviously different levels or types of activation of brain areas previously shown to be specifically associated with number, but did show much more activation, during arithmetic tasks, of areas of the brain associated with episodic memory: the right medial frontal cortex, the right parahippocampal gyri and the right upper anterior cingulate gyrus. This might be consistent with a particularly efficient and extensive use of long-term memory for arithmetical information when carrying out arithmetic tasks.

A larger number of talented calculators, both among savants and those of normal intelligence, must be studied before firm conclusions can be drawn about the brain characteristics that may be associated with their talent. Indeed, there is likely not to be a single answer. Just as there are many types of dyscalculia, so there are likely to be many types of exceptional talent at calculation.

Some as yet rather inconclusive conclusions

Although far more is known than a few years ago about the ways in which the brain is specialized for arithmetic, much remains to be learned about whether and how this specialization relates to individual differences. We know that certain parts of the brain, most notably the left parietal lobe, are particularly active in calculation tasks and that damage to this area may result in calculation disorders. We know that different components of arithmetic can be selectively damaged in brain-damaged patients; and that brain-imaging studies can show different brain areas being predominantly activated for different types of arithmetical task. We also know that certain brain areas, which are not exclusively specialized for arithmetic, support cognitive functions that are important for arithmetic as well as for certain other functions.

We know that children with developmental arithmetic disorders can show selective deficits in specific arithmetical components, which can parallel the deficits found in brain-damaged patients. Some children experience arithmetic disorders as part of genetic syndromes or early acquired brain damage. Although such causes are rare, there appears to be a genetic component to many developmental arithmetical problems that are not caused by specific syndromes. All of this would suggest a physiological, probably brain-based contribution to developmental arithmetical deficits (this does *not* mean that they are caused *exclusively* by physiological factors). There is evidence for an association in some groups of children between arithmetical deficits and reduced size of the left parietal lobe.

What we do not know is the extent to which all this relates to individual differences in arithmetic within the 'normal' range and especially to individual differences in specific components of arithmetic. Some of the individuals discussed in this and other chapters in the book provide evidence that selective strengths and weaknesses in different components of arithmetic are not found only in patients, but also in 'normal' people, including some who would not usually be described as bad at arithmetic. The extent to which these differences are due to differences in parts of the brain specialized for arithmetic, differences in other parts of the brain, environmental and educational factors and/or motivational factors is not at all clear; neither is the timescale in which such possible causal factors may operate. It is likely that all of these factors interact and reinforce each other. Certainly the existence of a neurological component to an arithmetical, or other, weakness does not mean that the weakness is not amenable to improvement through environmental intervention or even that the neurological factor itself might not have been caused or affected by environmental influences. Perhaps brain-imaging studies with larger groups of people will lead to a greater understanding of the role of the brain in individual differences in arithmetic along the 'normal' continuum.

11 'Maths doesn't like me anymore': Role of attitudes and emotions

'Multiplication is vexation.
Division is as bad.
The Rule of Three it troubles me
And Practice drives me mad.' (traditional rhyme; versions go back to the 16th century)

'I am now going to tell you about the horrible and wretched plaege that my multiplication gives me. you cant conceive it – the most devilish thing is 8 × 8 and 7 × 7 it is what nature itselfe cant endure.' (written at age 7 by Marjorie Fleming, 1803–1811)

'What do you minus
and from where?
I ask my teacher,
but he don't care.

'Ten cubic metres
in square roots,
Or how many toes
go in nine boots?

'Change ten decimals
to a fraction.
Aaaaaaaahhhhhhhhhhhh!
is my reaction.' (from Deepak Kalha: *Tall thoughts*, London: Basement Writers, 1976, written at the age of 15)

Maths
'I've tried counting in my head singing tables in my bed
Multiplying till I'm red till I'm most sure
Maths doesn't like me anymore.

'Subtract and take away and minus in one day there isn't time to play and I'm quite sure
Maths doesn't like me anymore.

'Number lines and magic squares all that jumping here and there
Doesn't get me anywhere

So I'm positively sure
Maths doesn't like me anymore.

'But for drawing I've a flair so I really shouldn't care
but painting numbers that's not fair now I'm absolutely sure
Maths doesn't like me anymore.' (David Woodrow, aged 9, in *Cadbury's sixth book of children's poetry*, London: Beaver, 1988, p. 19)

For many generations, arithmetic has aroused strong emotions: too often, highly negative ones. It is not possible fully to understand arithmetical difficulties without taking into account fear of arithmetic; not possible to understand individual differences in arithmetical ability and performance without taking into account individual differences in attitudes to arithmetic. As pointed out by Krutetskii (1968, p. 345): 'Without an inclination for mathematics there can be no real capacity for it. If a pupil feels no inclination for mathematics, even good abilities would scarcely provide an entirely successful mastery of it.' More negatively, some of the people in my study of adults with mild arithmetical difficulties spontaneously rephrased the description of the study in more emotional terms: 'I would like to take part in your study of people who are terrified of maths!'

Dehaene (1997, p. 235) points out that even research on the neural bases of mathematics must take emotion into account: 'Cerebral function is not confined to the cold transformation of information according to logical rules. If we are to understand how mathematics can become the subject of so much passion or hatred, we have to grant as much attention to the computations of emotion as to the syntax of reason.'

Mathematics anxiety

'I had nightmares about maths . . . I really did . . . Numbers and figures would go flashing through my head. Times tables, for example. I especially had nightmares about maths tests.' (student teacher quoted in D. Haylock: *Mathematics explained for primary teachers*, 2nd ed., London: Chapman, 2001, p. 4)

Most research on attitudes to mathematics has emphasized the more negative attitudes that people have toward mathematics. Many people feel an extreme dislike, even fear, of mathematics including arithmetic. These negative attitudes can have very deleterious consequences (Cockcroft, 1982; Richardson & Suinn, 1972). People who fear mathematics are seriously restricted in their choice of occupation. They may experience difficulty and anxiety in managing their finances and, if the fear is severe, even in such activities as reading train and bus timetables. Parents and teachers may pass on their dislike of mathematics to the next generation; or at least may be inhibited by their own anxiety from giving children adequate support in their mathematical learning. Fear of mathematics is in fact quite common in primary school teachers (Briggs & Crook, 1991; Haylock, 2001).

Although some people have a general fear and dislike of academic activities, and/or serious performance anxiety about tests and evaluations in such subjects, mathematics probably elicits fear more frequently than do most other school subjects. Whole self-help books have been written on the subject; e.g. Buxton's (1981) *Do you panic about maths: Coping with math anxiety* and Tobias' (1993) *Overcoming math anxiety*. There are few or no books with titles such as *Do you panic about reading?* or *Overcoming spelling anxiety*.

A considerable amount of research has been carried out on the topic of mathematics anxiety: anxiety stimulated by mathematical cues, usually especially by requirements to perform arithmetical tasks. Richardson and Suinn (1972, p. 551) defined mathematics anxiety as 'feelings of tension and anxiety that interfere with the manipulation of numbers and the solving of life and academic situations'. Richardson and Suinn (1972) estimated that 28% of 400 undergraduates exhibited extreme levels of tension associated with mathematical situations or number manipulations; and Richardson and Suinn (1972) estimate that 11% of university students show high enough levels of mathematics anxiety to be in need of counselling. Betz (1978) concluded that about 68% of students enrolled in mathematics classes experience high mathematics anxiety. In one British study, 50% of people approached for a survey of performance on simple arithmetical tasks refused on the grounds of dislike for and/or self-perceived incapacity at mathematics (Cockcroft, 1982).

There are several assessment instruments for measuring mathematics anxiety in adolescents and adults. The best known pure test of mathematics anxiety is probably the Mathematics Anxiety Research Scale (MARS) (Richardson & Suinn, 1972). Measures of anxiety also play a part in most broader attitude measures such as the Fennema-Sherman Mathematics Attitude Scales (Fennema & Sherman, 1976).

There have been many studies of the relationships between mathematics anxiety, as measured on the MARS and other variables (Ashcraft, Kirk, & Hopko, 1998; Hembree, 1990). Mathematics anxiety, as rated on the MARS, seems to be more closely related to other measures of anxiety, especially test anxiety, than to measures of academic ability and performance. Nevertheless, mathematics anxiety scores did correlate negatively with high school and college grades in mathematics and scores on tests of mathematical aptitude and achievement, while they showed no significant correlation with verbal aptitude and achievement.

Can mathematics anxiety be treated or prevented?

Like other phobias, severe mathematics anxiety has sometimes been treated by 'systematic desensitization', whereby individuals are exposed, usually in imagination, to gradually increasingly frightening stimuli, while carrying out relaxation exercises. It has also sometimes been treated by cognitive therapy, which involves trying to change an individual's beliefs ('I am no good at maths'; 'Everybody will think I'm stupid if I don't answer this question correctly') and to reduce intrusive thoughts during mathematical tasks ('I'm doing so badly'; 'I will fail this test'). Such treatments have a modest but significant effect on measures of both mathematics anxiety and mathematical performance (Hembree, 1990). Systematic desensitization and cognitive therapy seem to be more effective in combination than separately (Hembree, 1990). Training in basic arithmetical skills and in relevant study skills such as note taking can also reduce mathematics anxiety (Hutton & Levitt, 1987); although, of course, the most anxious individuals may refuse to participate in such training.

Clearly, it is better to prevent mathematics anxiety from developing in the first place than to treat it once it has developed. From this point of view, it is important to study the extent and development of mathematics anxiety in young children.

Mathematics anxiety in young children: A pilot study

Gemma Thomas and I carried out a study (Thomas & Dowker, 2000) concerning relationships between mathematics anxiety, attitudes to mathematics, self-ratings, mathematics anxiety and actual arithmetical performance in younger children. The study included 20 6-year-olds and 20 9-year-olds. Each age group was equally divided between girls and boys. Children were asked about the following aspects of maths lessons: maths in general, written sums, mental sums, easy maths, difficult maths, maths tests and understanding the teacher. For each item, children were asked to rate (a) their self-perceived performance; (b) their attitude (liking versus disliking the topic); (c) their unhappiness if they did badly; and (d) their anxiety.

The children were given four pictorial 5-point rating scales for each item. The self-perceived performance scale was used to show how good/bad the children thought they were at each aspect of maths. It ranged from two ticks (very good) through one tick (quite good); empty space (don't know); and one cross (quite bad) to two crosses (very bad).

The attitude scale measured children's liking for each aspect of maths and ranged from two wasps (hate very much) through one wasp, empty space and one sweet, to two sweets (like very much).

The 'unhappiness at poor performance' scale measured children's level of unhappiness if they performed poorly at each aspect of maths. It ranged from a very frowny face (very unhappy) through a moderately frowny face, a flat mouth and a moderately smiley face to a very smiley face (very happy). The anxiety scale was used to show how worried or relaxed the children would feel if they couldn't do something in a maths lesson. It was also a scale of facial expressions, ranging from a face based on the 'Mr Men' character Mr Worry (very worried) to the 'Mr Men' character Mr Happy (very relaxed).

Children's responses were recorded on a scale of 0 to 4, where 0 was the most negative response (i.e. very bad, hate very much, very unhappy, very worried) and 4 was the most positive response (i.e. very good, like very much, very happy, very relaxed). With seven items, the maximum total score on each scale was 28 and the minimum 0.

The children's overall attitudes to mathematics were considerably less positive than those generally reported in this age group (mean 8.85 out of a possible 28; s.d. 5.85). Their self-ratings concerning their own mathematical performance were also relatively low (mean 8.4; s.d. 4.8). These relatively low ratings may have reflected the particular school that the children attended or may have resulted in part from the fact that the study placed some emphasis on 'failure' situations and their power to provoke anxiety and unhappiness. Most of the children, however, did not express strong anxiety at inability to do something in maths (mean 15.48; s.d 5.34) or unhappiness at poor performance (mean 16.58; s.d. 5.27).

There were very strong correlations between liking for mathematics, self-ratings of mathematical performance and actual performance. Mathematics anxiety correlated strongly with unhappiness at poor performance, but neither measure correlated with liking for maths, self-rating or actual performance. Thus, at this age, mathematics anxiety does not seem to be either a cause or a result of poor mathematical performance, low self-esteem at mathematics or dislike for mathematics. This could indicate that such relationships only become manifest at a later age. It could also be that mathematics anxiety needs to reach a certain level of severity in order to have deleterious effects and that mathematics anxiety is rarely sufficiently strong in young children to produce such effects.

Enjoyment and pleasure in arithmetic

'For me, the refuge at first was in numbers. My father was a whiz at mental arithmetic, and I, too, even at the age of six, was quick at figures – and, more, in love with them. I liked numbers because they were solid, invariant; they stood unmoved in a chaotic world . . . I particularly loved prime numbers, the fact that they were indivisible, could not be broken down, were inalienably themselves.' (Oliver Sacks: *Uncle Tungsten*, London: Picador, p. 26)

'I love working with logs, I love messing with tables, I really enjoy that . . . (H)aving a formula and working it out, I love doing that sort of thing . . . the idea, the sheer pleasure of doing that is just really very nice.' (Harriet, a 28-year-old mature student with comparatively little previous mathematical background; quoted in Evans, 2000, p. 200)

'I've got a calculator at home, and I learn quickly. I like doing sums more than anything in the world!' (Elizabeth, aged 7)

Not surprisingly, given the prevalence of mathematics anxiety, studies of attitudes to mathematics have tended to emphasize their negative side, sometimes implying that a positive attitude to mathematics merely implies an absence of negative emotional reactions. Nonetheless, enthusiasm for mathematics characterizes many people. It is most clearly seen in those who are very gifted at mathematics and/or have chosen to pursue it seriously.

Krutetskii (1976) studied over 100 mathematically gifted Russian school children between the ages of about 8 and 16. He commented (pp. 346–347) that:

All the gifted children . . . were marked by a profoundly emotional regard for mathematical activity . . . Without exception . . . all the children possessed . . . a keen interest in mathematics, an inclination to be occupied with it, and an insatiable striving to acquire information about mathematics and to solve problems.

Personal accounts by professional mathematicians frequently express intense aesthetic enjoyment of the subject; and sometimes mention aesthetic factors as contributing to their mathematical judgements. The mathematician Poincaré (1908) remarked:

It may be surprising to see emotional sensibility invoked à propos of mathematical demonstrations which, it would seem, can interest only the intellect. This would be to forget the feeling of mathematical beauty, of the harmony of numbers and forms, of geometric elegance. This is a true esthetic feeling that all real mathematicians know, and surely it belongs to emotional sensibility.

Hadamard (1945, p. 31) comments on this and other remarks by Poincaré:

That an affective element is an essential part in every discovery or invention is only too evident, and has been insisted upon by several thinkers; indeed it is clear that no significant discovery or invention can take place without the *will* of finding. But with Poincare, we see something else, the intervention of the sense of beauty playing its part as an indispensable *means* of finding. We have reached the double conclusion: that invention is choice; that this choice is imperatively governed by the sense of scientific beauty.

More recently, Silver and Metzger (1989) found that research mathematicians often evaluated solutions to mathematical problems from an aesthetic point of view: they referred to the elegance, harmony and coherence of solutions to problems.

Such enthusiasm for mathematics can also be observed in children. Although there has been relatively little research on young children's mathematical enthusiasms, there is little doubt that some children do have strong enthusiasms about mathematics; and that counting and numbers can be a source of fascination to them. For example, Court (1920) describes a child who, '(e)ver since he began to talk . . . showed immense interest in numbers . . . He always delighted in counting, and whenever there was any danger of his becoming impatient with the process of combing his curls, or dressing him, he would be kept quiet by either a story, or a verse, or "counting".'

In my experience with research with young children, it has been striking that very few refuse to co-operate on the grounds that they 'don't like maths'; and that many welcome the opportunity to come and do the mathematical tasks. Some of this enthusiasm may be due to a desire for a break from regular class work; or the chance of individual attention from an adult. But liking for mathematics as such seems to play a significant role: 'Can I have a go – I'm ever so good at maths!'

Personal relationships with numbers

> 'Don't bother me now, Daddy; I'm thinking about my favourite numbers.'
> (Elaine, aged 2 years 10 months)

> 'For there is a mystery in numbers.
> For One is perfect and good being at unity in himself.
> For Two is the most imperfect of all numbers.
> For everything infinitely perfect is Three . . .
> For Three is the simplest and best of all numbers.
> For Four is good being square.
> For Five is not so good in itself but works well in combination.
> For Five is not so good in itself as it consists of two and three.
> For Six is very good consisting of twice three.
> For Seven is very good consisting of two compleat numbers.
> For Eight is good for the same reason . . .
> For Nine is a number very good and harmonious . . .' (from Christopher Smart: *The Poetical Works of Christopher Smart, Vol. 1: Jubilate agno*, 1980, by permission of Oxford University Press)

Children and adults alike can have very strong likes and dislikes for particular numbers. There are certain numbers that tend to be regarded as 'lucky' or 'unlucky' within a particular culture: for example, superstitions in the English-speaking world treat the number '7' as lucky and '13' as unlucky. Individuals can have their personal 'lucky' and 'unlucky' numbers.

Dowker and Dowker (1979) describe mathematically gifted children as tending to have a 'Pythagorean' attitude of ascribing personalities to particular numbers.

Such personal feelings for numbers are most often recorded in those who deal most with numbers: professional mathematicians and, even more, talented calculators (Smith, 1988). For example, Weinland (1948) reports that Salo Finkelstein, a clerk by occupation and a lightning calculator who gave public performances, described 214 as 'beautiful', 8337 as 'very nice', and zero as his 'pet aversion'. Hans Eberstark, another such lightning calculator, spoke, for example, of the 'sinister' 64, the 'arrogant smug self-satisfied' 36, and the 'helpful' 37 (Smith, 1988).

Calkins (1892, pp. 454 and 462–463) discussed individuals who had unusual visual (e.g. colour) or auditory associations with numbers. Several of the participants in her study also gave articulate descriptions of more emotional, evaluative associations with particular numbers, for example:

> 1, 2, 4, 7 and 8 are reliable, quiet, well-disposed but not brilliant numbers. 3 is a sharp, shrewd disagreeable number, always making as much trouble as possible . . . For 13, I always have a great antipathy. It has all the disagreeable qualities of 3 added to a pertness and aggressiveness which make it repugnant to all the other numbers, with which it seems never to associate. I never wanted to be 13 years old . . . I always feel a great respect for 16.

It would be desirable to investigate the prevalence of such a tendency to attribute personality to numbers in unselected samples of children and adults and whether this has any relationship to other individual differences in attitudes toward and performance in arithmetic. One might expect that such attributions would be commoner in people who are positively disposed toward arithmetic in general and consider numbers to be important and interesting. Most of the existing reports on personal relationships with numbers do indeed involve people who are unusually interested in numbers, but it may be that such people are just more likely to discuss their reactions to numbers spontaneously. Systematic investigation is needed to supplement the existing anecdotal reports.

Cultural influences on attitudes to mathematics

Most studies of attitudes to mathematics have taken place in one country: the United States. Given the extensive evidence for considerable cross-national and cross-cultural differences in mathematics education and mathematical performance (see Chapter 9), there are some dangers in extrapolating from one country to others.

Although there have been relatively few studies of cross-cultural differences in attitudes to mathematics, there have been some studies (e.g. Stevenson, Chen, & Lee 1993) have reported cross-cultural differences in parental attitudes by parents to mathematics teaching. American parents tend to be more satisfied than Chinese parents with their children's mathematical achievement. Moreover, Chinese parents are more likely to attribute their children's failures in mathematics to lack of effort, while American parents are more likely to attribute such failures to factors beyond the children's control: innate ability and/or poor teaching. Such differences could lead to American children being put under less pressure to achieve than Chinese children.

It is important, here as elsewhere, not to equate country with culture or to view 'cultures' in too monolithic a way. Stevenson, Hofer, and Randel (2000) studied over 6000 15- and 16-year-old pupils in China, Taiwan, Canada, Hungary and Germany, and investigated their attitudes to mathematics, self-evaluations and attributions of mathematical successes and failures to ability versus effort. They found that differences within a country – notably between schools in Beijing and Taipei in China – were often greater than those between different countries.

Gender differences in attitudes to mathematics

It has often been found that girls and women have more negative attitudes than boys and men to mathematics (Hyde, Fennema, Ryan, Frost, & Hopp, 1990b; Wigfield & Meece, 1988); and in particular that they are more likely to experience fear and anxiety in connection with mathematics (Ashcraft & Faust, 1994; Hembree, 1990; Lefevre, Kulak, & Heymans, 1992; Levitt & Hutton, 1983; Tobias, 1993); although some recent studies (Evans, 2000; Nyangeni & Glencross, 1997) have not shown very strong gender differences in attitudes to mathematics as a whole.

A wide variety of explanations have been proposed for such findings: poorer spatial ability making some mathematical tasks more difficult; self-fulfilling cultural expectations that girls will not be good at mathematics (and, in some communities, that being good at mathematics will make them less attractive to boys); generally lower confidence and greater performance anxiety in females; domination by boys in co-educational classrooms; greater attention by mathematics teachers to girls than to boys, etc.

As pointed out in Chapter 1, gender differences in mathematics are not as great in contemporary Britain as in many countries or as in Britain at an earlier time. Indeed, until the age of 16 *girls* tend to do somewhat better at mathematics, in contrast to many countries where boys do better at mathematics from the age of about 11 or 12. One might guess from this that there should also be less of a gender difference in attitudes to mathematics in contemporary Britain; but this awaits testing.

Young children's attitudes to mathematics

The relatively few studies that have looked at younger children's attitudes to mathematics have usually shown positive attitudes. For example, Tizard, Blatchford, Burke, Farquhar, and Plewis (1988) asked 7-year-olds to rate their liking for mathematics on a rating scale showing faces ranging from a broad smile to a deep frown: 80% of the boys and 62% of the girls expressed a positive attitude towards mathematics.

Unfortunately, there is some evidence that children's liking for mathematics declines with age. In an early study by Blatchford (1966), children aged 11 and 16 years, respectively, were asked to name their three most favourite school subjects. Two-thirds of the 11-year-olds, but few of the 16-year-olds, chose mathematics as their first most popular subject. More recently, Mortimore (1988) found a decline in children's liking for mathematics in children between the ages of 8 to 10.

An international study of primary school children's attitudes to mathematics

There have, however, been relatively few studies of young children's attitudes to mathematics, as compared with those of older children. Alice Gregory, Jessica Snell and I have recently studied the attitudes of a large and international group of primary school children to a wide variety of aspects of mathematics (Gregory, Snell, & Dowker, 1999).

The sample consisted of 548 school children from 11 different countries: England (75), France (42), Germany (43), Greece (18), Iran (30), Israel (23), the Netherlands (20), Sweden (36), Taiwan (101), Thailand (96) and the United States of America (64). Most of the children came from co-educational state schools. An attempt was made to gain samples from comparable schools and areas from each country, although sampling was to some degree constrained by practical considerations.

Approximately half of the children were boys and the other half were girls. Ages ranged from 5 to 10, but most children were 7- or 8-years-old and in the second or third year of primary school.

The questionnaire included 36 items. An adult read each of the 36 items on the questionnaire to the participants. The children were asked to indicate on an answer sheet their attitude to the item by choosing one of five 'smiley faces' on a separate sheet (the same as those used in Gemma Thomas's study). They were labelled A-E, with A being the happiest face, and E the most sad.

The need to convert facial expressions to letter symbols and to write these down made the task more demanding than just pointing to one of the faces, as in some other attitude studies involving 'smiley faces' scales. Therefore, in order to check whether children could understand and cope with the rating scale and procedure, they were asked two control questions: 'If someone gave you three sweets how would you feel?' and 'If you had three sweets and someone took them away, how would you feel?' Almost all the children demonstrated an understanding of the task, giving A or B ratings to the question about being given three sweets and D or E ratings to the question about having them taken away.

The questionnaire consisted mainly of questions both about mathematics as a whole and about specific mathematical activities. The latter included: doing written sums; doing sums in your head; listening to the teacher talk about maths; counting with one's fingers or blocks to do sums; doing maths with a calculator; doing maths on a computer; weighing and measuring; telling the time; working with shapes; and playing games involving maths. For mathematics as a whole, and for each of the specific activities, children were asked to rate both how much they liked it and how good they thought they were at it.

They were also asked to rate how good they thought boys were at maths; how good they thought girls were at maths; how much they thought that boys liked maths; and how much they thought that girls liked maths. They were also asked about how they felt about getting the right answer to a hard sum; getting the right answer to an easy sum; getting the wrong answer to a hard sum; and getting the wrong answer to an easy sum.

Four questions concerned how much the children liked reading and science and how good they thought that they were in these subjects; these were included so that we could see how attitudes to mathematics compared with those to other academic subjects.

Main results

Most children liked mathematics reasonably well, giving a mean rating of 2.05 (like moderately) for the question about liking mathematics. This was similar to the rating for liking science (1.9) but lower than the rating for liking reading (1.66).

Among the specific activities, the most popular were written sums (1.78), listening to the teacher talk about maths (1.85), telling the time (1.89) and weighing and measuring (1.9). The least popular were doing sums on a calculator (2.33), using a computer to do mathematics (2.37) and using fingers and blocks to do sums (2.39). The relative unpopularity of this last activity was probably due to the fact that children sometimes perceive, or are led to perceive, the use of fingers and concrete objects as being only for very young children or low achievers in arithmetic. Thus, the use of such aids may be inimical to their self-esteem. Nevertheless, it should be noted that all activities were given mean ratings that were at least higher than the neutral rating of 3.

Children tended to rate themselves as relatively good at maths (mean rating 2.05). This was higher than their self-rating for science (2.22) but lower than their self-rating for reading (1.81).

The specific aspects of maths on which they rated themselves most highly were written sums (1.76), using fingers or blocks to do maths (1.79); listening to the teacher talk about maths (1.9) and using a calculator to do maths (1.96). Those at which they rated themselves lowest were using a computer to do maths (2.48), doing sums in their head (2.18) and using shapes (2.18).

There were no gender differences in liking for maths, but boys tended to rate themselves higher at maths than did girls (1.93 versus 2.19). There were no gender differences in self-ratings for either reading or science, suggesting that the difference for maths was not just one of boys being generally more confident or less reluctant to 'boast'.

There were no gender differences in liking most of the specific aspects of maths; but boys expressed significantly greater liking than girls for doing maths in their heads and doing maths on a calculator while girls expressed significantly greater liking than boys for listening to the teacher talk about maths.

Girls rated themselves higher than did boys at listening to the teacher talk about maths. Otherwise, there were no significant differences in self-ratings for the specific aspects of maths.

Overall, children tended to give girls higher ratings than boys for being good at maths (mean 2.11 for girls versus 2.24 for boys) and for liking maths (1.95 for girls versus 2.35 for boys). However, there was a strong tendency for both boys and girls to favour their own gender: e.g. girls gave girls a mean rating of 1.79 and boys a mean rating of 2.55 for being good at maths while boys gave girls a mean rating of 2.43 and boys a mean rating of 1.92 for being good at maths.

Children did not like to get wrong answers in maths, but their aversion was not extreme: their mean attitude rating for getting the wrong answer to a sum was 3.67 (with 5 as the most negative possible rating) and it did not differ for hard and easy sums. They were very happy to get sums right and getting a hard sum right gave them more satisfaction (mean rating 1.25) than getting an easy sum right (1.5). There were no significant gender differences here, but there was a trend for girls to dislike getting a hard sum wrong more than boys did.

Differences between countries must be interpreted with great caution, given the relatively small sample sizes in some countries and especially the fact that most countries were represented by only one or two schools, leading to the danger of confounding differences between countries and differences between schools. Thus, the most interesting result is that broad patterns were similar across countries. Nevertheless, there were significant differences between countries for most of the items.

Notably, children in all countries had a positive attitude to maths, in the sense that they liked it more than they disliked it; but this ranged from the extremely positive in Iran (mean rating 1.1) and Thailand (mean rating 1.68) to the nearly neutral in Taiwan (mean rating 2.55) and Germany (mean rating 2.74). Children in the United States (mean rating 2.1) and England (mean rating 2.24) came in between.

Children in Greece, Sweden, Iran, Israel, the USA and Thailand all rated themselves as very good at maths with mean ratings between 1 and 2. English children gave themselves a mean rating of 2.1, and children from Germany, Holland, Taiwan and France gave themselves somewhat lower ratings. The lowest mean ratings were still above average: 2.53 for Taiwanese children and 2.6 for French children. It is interesting that Taiwanese children should have rated themselves particularly low, given that Taiwanese children usually do especially well in international comparisons; but of course they would have been comparing themselves with others of the same country.

Ratings for liking and self-perceived performance at reading were more consistently positive and differed less between countries, than ratings for liking and self-perceived performance at reading. Children of all countries liked reading very much (mean ratings from 1.1 to 1.97) with the striking exception of the Israeli children, who gave a completely neutral mean rating of 3.04. Ratings of self-perceived performance in reading ranged from 1.27 (Iran) to 2.07 (Germany). Liking for, and self-ratings in, science varied to a rather greater extent; but it must of course be noted that the meaning of 'science' as a school subject varies a lot between countries: in some countries, the only form of science studied at primary school level is nature study, while in Britain physical sciences are taught quite early.

Children in the UK, Sweden, France, Israel and Germany gave higher ratings to boys' performance in maths than to girls' performance in maths. Those in Greece, the Netherlands, Iran, Taiwan and Thailand rated girls higher, while those in the USA gave them exactly equal ratings (mean 2.38). The most striking difference in favour of boys was in Israel (mean rating for boys 1.82; mean rating for girls 2.78) and the most striking differences in favour of girls were in Thailand (mean rating for boys 2.7; mean rating for girls 1.65) and in the Netherlands (mean rating for boys 3; mean rating for girls 1.94).

There were significant declines with age both in children's liking for mathematics and in their self-perceived performance in mathematics. Children's liking for work with computers increased with age, while their liking for finger and block counting, for doing sums in their heads and for listening to the teacher talk about maths all showed strong declines with age.

Thus, the overall finding is of a positive attitude to most aspects of mathematics and of a rather high self-rating for most aspects of mathematics. There is a decline with age in both attitudes and self-ratings. Gender differences are only noticeable for self-ratings; boys and girls at this age do not seem to differ in their liking for mathematics. There was no overall tendency for this group of children to consider boys to be better than girls at mathematics; if anything, the reverse was the case.

To what extent are attitudes to *specific* aspects of mathematics related to attitudes to mathematics in general? Regression analyses showed that liking mathematics was predicted by rating oneself as good at mathematics; liking reading; considering that boys like mathematics; considering that girls are good at mathematics; liking to do written sums; rating oneself as good at written sums; liking to hear the teacher talk about mathematics; liking to play mathematical games; rating oneself as good at working with shapes; and liking to learn to tell the time.

Rating oneself as good at mathematics was predicted by liking mathematics; rating oneself as good at reading; liking science; considering that boys like mathematics; considering that girls like mathematics; liking to do written sums; rating oneself as good at written sums; liking to hear the teacher talk about mathematics; and rating oneself as good at playing mathematical games.

In particular, liking mathematics was extremely closely correlated with rating oneself as good at it. Both were very closely associated with liking to do written sums, suggesting that children may see written sums as a core aspect of mathematics.

Relationships between attitudes and actual performance

'I've learned a little tiny bit,' said Bruno. *'Can't* learn no more!'
'Oh, Bruno! You know you *can*, if you like.'
'Course I can, if I *like*,' the pale student replied; 'but I can't if I *don't* like.'
(Lewis Carroll: *Sylvie and Bruno concluded*, 1893)

Studies over many years in many countries from the United States to Japan to South Africa have shown that actual performance in mathematics tends to be related positively to liking for mathematics and to high self-ratings in mathematics and negatively to mathematics anxiety (Abed & Alkhateeb, 2000; Aiken & Dreger, 1961; Ashcraft & Faust, 1998; Ho et al., 2000; Ma & Kishor, 1997; McLeod, 1991; Satake & Amato, 1995; Suinn, Taylor, & Richards, 1988). There are a few contrary findings: for example, Cain-Caston (1993) failed to find a significant relationship between attitudes and achievement in a group of 8- and 9-year-old American children and Kolubya and Glencross (1997) found little relationship between mathematics performance and either anxiety or attitudes in a group of senior secondary school pupils in Transkei (South Africa). On the whole, however, the evidence is very consistent. In older children and adults, mathematics anxiety is negatively related to self-ratings in mathematics and related subjects (Onwuegbuzie, 2000); although as stated earlier, Thomas and Dowker (2000) failed to find such a relationship in 6- and 8-year-olds.

For example, Young-Loveridge (1991) found that 9-year-old children were more likely to choose mathematics as their favourite subject if they were good at it (32% of high-scoring children chose arithmetic as their favourite subject) than if they were not (18% of low scoring children choose mathematics as their favourite subject). Aiken (1972) found that 13-year-olds who have positive attitudes towards mathematics tend to achieve higher grades in the subject than do those with less favourable attitudes. The international study of young children by Gregory, Snell, and Dowker (1999) included performance measures (WISC arithmetic scores) for the English children only: these were positively associated with liking for and self-rated performance in mathematics.

An important question is the direction of causation of the positive relationship between attitudes and performance. Do positive attitudes lead to better performance or does better performance lead to more positive attitudes? There are plausible reasons for expecting relationships in both directions. If an individual likes mathematics, they are likely to devote more time, effort and practice to the subject, leading to better performance. If they dislike mathematics, they are likely to avoid it where possible, thus reducing the opportunity for practice. Adolescents and adults who score high on mathematics anxiety measures are less likely than their less anxious peers to take optional mathematics courses in high school and college (Ashcraft, Kirk, & Hopko, 1998; Hembree, 1990) or to plan careers in science, even after controlling for scores on quantitative tests (Chipman, Krantz, & Silver, 1992).

Moreover, extremely avoidant or panicky reactions to mathematics are likely to have an immediately adverse effect on performance. For example, Ashcraft and Faust (1994) found that people with high levels of mathematics anxiety solved mathematics problems more quickly and less accurately than those with less anxiety. Far from making people more careful and vigilant, mathematics anxiety seems to result in people rushing to get through the unpleasant task as fast as possible, even at the cost of accuracy. There may also be an element of feeling under pressure to come up with an answer – any answer – to a problem that one has been set. Right answers, if one can get them, are better than wrong answers, but even a wrong answer may be better than no answer at all (Holt, 1966).

Also, anxious people are likely to have intrusive thoughts about how badly they are doing, which may distract attention and thereby necessary working memory resources from the mathematical problems themselves (Ashcraft, Kirk, & Hopko, 1998). Ashcraft and Kirk (2001) found that people with high maths anxiety demonstrated smaller working memory spans than people with less maths anxiety, especially in tasks that required any sort of calculation. In particular, people with high maths anxiety were much slower and made many more errors than others in tasks where they had to do mental addition at the same time as keeping numbers in memory. Ashcraft and Kirk concluded that maths anxiety does indeed disrupt working memory in mathematical tasks.

It is also possible that people who have working memory limitations in arithmetic for other reasons are more likely to experience mathematics anxiety as a result. The difficulty of determining whether mathematics anxiety is the cause or result of poor performance is a pervasive issue in research on this topic. It is likely that it both affects and is affected by performance: i.e. there is a vicious circle, whereby anxiety leads to worse performance, which, in turn, leads to greater anxiety.

Certainly, people tend to experience more enjoyment of activities at which they are successful. Difficulties with mathematics are likely to lead to a dislike of the subject, both for external reasons (fear of humiliating failures in the classroom and at examinations and of criticisms by teachers, parents and fellow pupils) and for internal reasons (frustration and bewilderment at what appears to be an incomprehensible subject). Some children – and adults – end up expecting mathematics to make no sense (Holt, 1966). Brown (1981) tells of a 12-year-old girl who was given an arithmetic problem, which she solved not only wrongly, but also in a way that could not have been correct on logical grounds. When this was explained to her, she understood the explanation, but commented: 'I wasn't thinking logically – I was thinking mathematically', implying that for her, logic and mathematics were virtually incompatible.

A similar question relates to the direction of causation of the positive relationship between self-rating of ability in mathematics and actual performance (Abed & Alkhateeb, 2000). This may just mean that children are relatively accurate in their self-ratings and are aware of how well or badly they are performing in class. It may also be that high self-esteem in mathematics contributes to children's willingness to practise the subject and perhaps in particular to their willingness to take the risks and make the experiments that contribute to the development of a wide range of arithmetical strategies and a deep understanding of the subject (see Chapters 6 and 7). Adolescents and adults with high mathematics anxiety tend to be less flexible in their strategy use than those with low mathematics anxiety.

There is some evidence (Ma & Kishor, 1997) that relationships between attitudes to mathematics and actual performance increase with age. This could be, in part, due to increasing variability with age in attitudes to mathematics, with increasing prevalence of severe antipathies and anxieties concerning mathematics. If there is greater variation in attitudes in older children and adolescents than in younger children, then there is more scope for significant links to performance in the older age groups. Such trends could also reflect either increasing longitudinal effects of attitudes on performance or performance on attitudes – or both. Since most studies have not been longitudinal, it is hard to draw firm conclusions.

In particular, it is hard to draw firm conclusions on the basis of current evidence about one particularly important question: to what extent do attitudes at a given time predict and influence the level of subsequent improvement in mathematics?

On the whole, one would expect that a positive attitude toward one's own abilities in mathematics should be associated with a tendency toward improvement. Thus, if two children are currently performing at the same level, one who thinks that (s)he is 'good at maths' should perform better than one who thinks that (s)he is 'bad at maths'. Beyond a certain point, this may break down: a child who grossly overestimates his or her own mathematical abilities and/or underestimates the difficulties of the subject may not see the need to develop appropriate strategies for improvement. It is known (Flavell, 1979) that very young children often overestimate their own memory spans and therefore do not use appropriate rehearsal strategies and it is at least possible that similar issues can occur in mathematics.

Indeed, the findings about consistent negative relationships between mathematics anxiety and achievement may reflect the fact that most such studies include a large proportion of people with rather severe mathematics anxiety. Perhaps mild mathematics anxiety – involving concern about performance rather than true fear – might be associated with higher achievement than complete indifference. Indeed, Evans (2000) found that an inverted U best described the relationship between mathematics anxiety and mathematics test performance in a group of British mature students in higher education, suggesting that there may be an 'optimum' level of anxiety, rather than that all anxiety is deleterious.

Attributions for good and bad performance in mathematics

'ARITHMETIC
'Arithmetic is easy when you know how to do it.
Adding up, taking away, multiply and divide.
All very easy when you know how.' (poem by Margery, aged 10, in Hourd, M.L. & Cooper, C.J. (1959). *Coming into their own*. London: Heinemann. Copyright © 1959. Reproduced by permission of Elsevier Ltd.)

Attitudes to mathematics include not only degrees of liking for mathematics, but ideas about mathematical ability and reasons for good or bad performance in mathematics.

There have been a number of studies of people's attributions for the causes of their successes and failures. Attributions may be external (e.g. the quality of the teaching that they have received) or internal (e.g. their own ability); stable or unstable (e.g. ability versus motivation); and controllable (e.g. lack of practice) versus uncontrollable (e.g. intrinsic difficulty of mathematics). Some studies have indicated that females tend to attribute success in mathematics to effort and failure to lack of ability, while males tend to attribute success to ability and failure to lack of effort (Fennema, 1989; Fennema & Peterson, 1985).

As stated earlier, other studies have suggested that Chinese and other Asian families tend to attribute level of or performance to effort, while

American families tend to attribute it to innate factors or quality of teaching (Stevenson et al., 1993).

The emotional overtones of attributing performance – and especially failures – to ability or effort may be quite complex and may vary with age, culture and social group. It may also be related to the extent to which individuals perceive mathematical ability is perceived to be related to other abilities.

The individual in a culture that places a strong value on mathematics may be very distressed at the thought that (s)he lacks mathematical ability. The individual whose culture does not greatly value mathematics may be unconcerned about or even somewhat proud of mathematical weaknesses. For example, in Britain, it is not uncommon to joke or even boast about innumeracy, whereas illiteracy is far more likely to lead to feelings of shame or distress.

Moreover, individuals who see mathematics as closely linked to general intelligence may be very distressed by mathematical failures that could indicate that they are 'stupid'. Those who see mathematics as a specific and perhaps unusual talent may be far less distressed. There is anecdotal evidence that some people regard mathematics as negatively correlated with certain other abilities ('People are usually good at maths or English but not both'; 'Creative people are usually bad at maths') and such attitudes would certainly be likely to prevent or reduce distress at the thought of not being mathematically able.

Effort attributions may have a strong negative emotional content in a context where effort in academic subjects is demanded of children and real or perceived failures to make sufficient effort can result in parents and teachers displaying anger or disappointment at the child's 'laziness'. This may have a particularly distressing effect on pupils who are in general academically capable and motivated, but experience difficulties with specific subjects: in this case, mathematics. Haylock (2001, pp. 4–5) reports this to be a common theme in self-reports by student primary teachers who experience anxiety about mathematics: 'Teachers expect you to be good at maths if you're good at other things. They look at your other subjects and just can't understand why you can't do maths. They say to you, "You should be able to do this".'

Contrariwise, effort attributions may have little or no emotional content in a situation where individuals are seen as having a choice as to what interests and activities to pursue ('I could have kept up more with my maths, but I chose to concentrate on languages instead'; 'I've forgotten all my algebra – never needed to use it after I left school!'). Among some groups of children, adolescents and even adults, academic effort may actually lead to social disapproval: it may be seen as 'not cool'; the mark of socially unskilled and unpopular 'swots' and 'nerds'. This is perhaps even more marked with regard to mathematics and related activities than to verbal or artistic pursuits.

Thus, attributions need to be examined within a wider context. The effect of attributing failure to effort versus ability may be very different for a child who thinks that lack of effort deserves and may receive a severe punishment, whereas lack of ability entitles one to be left alone, as compared with a child who thinks that lack of mathematical ability means that you're stupid, but that you only need to make an effort in it if you are planning a career that specifically involves numbers.

The ability/effort dichotomy may not fully explain attributions, especially those by young children. Studies of young children's spontaneous explanations for good or poor performance in mathematics and other subjects (Dowker, Cameron, & Grech 1995; Dowker, Dye, & Lowe, 2000) have tended to suggest that children of 7 and under tend to attribute levels of performance to the amount of *practice* that one has had. In their view, being good at something is due to having practised it a lot; being bad at it is due to lack of practice. As children get older, they are more likely to attribute good and bad performance to ability. Practice could be seen as an effort attribution, but it also depends on opportunity. People cannot practise an activity to which they have little or no exposure.

Moreover, there is one aspect of attributions that may have a crucial influence on their impact on actual performance. This is whether mathematics, and thereby success or failure at it, is seen as global versus specific. If a child or adult sees themselves as globally 'bad at maths', they are likely to become discouraged and avoid the subject. If they see themselves as being 'better at adding than multiplying', 'better at doing sums in writing than in my head' or 'better at logic than at memorization' this may lead to working out strategies for using relative strengths to overcome relative weaknesses. Similarly, an attribution of failure to global lack of effort is likely to be associated either with guilt for 'laziness' or with a dismissal of maths as 'boring' or 'not worth bothering about'. Focusing on a particular area where more effort needs to be made ('I need to practise long division a bit more'; 'I need to take more time to think about what word problems mean') is far more likely to lead to appropriate strategies for improvement. One of the central messages of this book is indeed the deleterious effect of regarding oneself as globally 'bad at maths' or maths as globally 'boring', because of difficulty with or lack of interest in a particular component of the subject.

There are some findings that do indeed suggest that attitudes to different aspects of mathematics may be specifically related to performance in these particular aspects. Nankeen and Glencross (1997) gave 278 senior secondary school pupils separate questionnaires about their attitudes to mathematics in general and to geometry and gave them tests in algebra and geometry. Attitudes to mathematics correlated with performance in algebra but not geometry, while attitudes to geometry correlated with performance in geometry but not algebra. Moreover, boys showed both more positive attitudes and better actual performance than girls in geometry, while the genders did not differ either in attitudes to mathematics in general or in actual performance in algebra. Evans (2000) found that, among a group of mature students, anxiety about mathematics tests and courses could be distinguished from anxiety about using numbers in everyday contexts. He also found that the former was more related to school mathematics performance and the latter to practical mathematics performance.

Conclusions

Mathematics arouses very strong positive and negative emotional reactions: possibly more so than other school subjects. Young children, from a wide variety of countries, tend to like mathematics; negative attitudes and mathematics anxiety appear to increase with age. Most studies show more negative attitudes and greater anxiety in females than in males, although this tendency is not so clearly shown in the most recent studies.

On the whole, there tends to be a positive relationship between liking mathematics and performing well at it and a negative relationship between being anxious about mathematics and performing well at it. However, there are many questions still to be answered about the direction of causation between attitudes and arithmetic.

Since most studies have been cross-sectional rather than longitudinal, it is difficult to interpret findings about the relationships between attitudes and arithmetical performance. Do some people dislike or fear mathematics because it is an area in which they perform poorly; or do they perform poorly at it because they dislike or fear it? In order to begin to answer this question, it is important to carry out longitudinal studies to investigate the predictive relationships between attitudes and performance. This is an important next step for research.

12 Implications for helping children with their arithmetical difficulties

Note: Some of this material has appeared in: Dowker, 2003c.

The previous chapters have dealt with individual differences in various components of arithmetic and with some of the factors that contribute to these individual differences. Can our knowledge about the characteristics and causes of such individual differences in arithmetic tell us how to help the many people who have difficulties in these areas?

The findings indicate that individual differences are large. They also suggest that simple explanations in terms of nature alone or nurture alone are misleading and counterproductive. Children with apparently similar environments can perform very differently in arithmetic. A child's poor performance in arithmetic is not necessarily due to the child's lack of effort or to failings on the part of parents or teachers. By the same token, difficulties in arithmetic are not purely innate or immutable. There are very large differences in performance between children in different countries, suggesting a very important influence of environment. Such findings suggest that successful interventions are *possible*.

The findings also suggest that arithmetic can be acquired or improved at *any time*. There is no 'critical period' or rigid timescale for learning. Age of starting formal education has little impact on the final outcome. People who, to varying degrees, lacked opportunity for or interest in learning arithmetic in school may learn later as adults.

Nonetheless, there is one important potential constraint on the timescale for learning arithmetic and other aspects of mathematics (apart, of course, from the practical constraints imposed by school curricula and the timing of public examinations). Many people develop *anxiety* about mathematics, which can be a distressing problem in itself and which also may inhibit further progress in the subject (see Chapter 9). This is rare in young children and becomes much more common in adolescence. Intervening to improve arithmetical difficulties in young children may reduce the risk of later development of mathematics anxiety. In any case, interventions are easier and less painful if they take place before mathematics anxiety has set in. Therefore, while it is *never too late* to intervene to help people with their arithmetical difficulties, interventions may be particularly effective if they are *early*.

Perhaps most crucially, there is by now overwhelming evidence that arithmetical ability is not unitary: it is made up of many components, ranging from knowledge of the counting sequence to estimation to solving word problems. Moreover, although the different components often correlate with one another, weaknesses in any one of them can occur relatively independently of weaknesses in the others. Several studies have suggested that it is not possible to establish a strict hierarchy whereby any one component invariably precedes another component.

The componential nature of arithmetic is important in planning and formulating interventions with children who are experiencing arithmetical difficulties. Any extra help in arithmetic is likely to give some benefit. However, *interventions that focus on the particular components with which an individual child has difficulty are likely to be more effective than those that assume that all children's arithmetical difficulties are similar* (Keogh, Major, Reid, Gandara, & Omari, 1978; Keogh, Major, Omari, Gandara, & Reid, 1980; Weaver, 1954).

There have been far fewer intervention programmes for children with arithmetical difficulties than, for example, for children with literacy difficulties. In the area of reading skills, there has been considerable emphasis on early identification of individual patterns of strengths and weaknesses and their use in compensatory education for backward readers; for example, the Reading Recovery programme set up by Clay (1985) and reviewed and evaluated by Sylva and Hurry (1995). Such approaches have been less widespread and less publicized with regard to arithmetic.

Nevertheless, there have been more such programmes, and over a longer historical period, than is often realized. This chapter will endeavour to review some important intervention work. It will start out by discussing some group-based intervention programmes, and will then discuss individualized component-based programmes. It does not claim to be a comprehensive review of *all* significant intervention programmes.

Preschool intervention programmes for children at risk

Some intervention programmes target children who are perceived to be members of high-risk groups: usually children living in poverty. Such programmes may or may not involve individualized assessment. Often they involve preschool children and are not always restricted to numeracy. For example, the Head Start program in the United States includes significant emphasis on number concepts, among other aspects of early intervention (Arnold, Fisher, Doctoroff, & Dobbs, 2002).

One example in Britain is the Peers Early Education Partnership (PEEP) programme (Roberts, 2001). This programme is based in a disadvantaged area of Oxford and works with parents of children from birth to school age.

It offers materials, group sessions and home visits to parents. The focus is on parents and children talking, singing and playing together, and on parents sharing books and similar materials with their children. The central focus of this programme is preparation for literacy; but numeracy activities are also incorporated. These involve counting games; as well as encouraging parents to discuss numbers with children in the context of practical activities such as shopping and preparing meals and also to discuss numbers in the environment, such as house and bus numbers.

Recently, the British government instituted 'family literacy' and 'family numeracy' programmes, where parents with limited education improve their own basic skills, while their preschool and early primary school age children are exposed to activities relating to language and number.

Three major American intervention programs with preschool children that focus specifically on mathematics are the Rightstart program (Griffin, Case, & Siegler, 1994), the Berkeley Maths Readiness program (Starkey & Klein, 2000) and the Big Math for Little Kids program (Ginsburg, Balfanz, & Greenes, 1999).

The Rightstart program has been used in some inner-city kindergartens in the United States and Canada. It focuses on assisting children to acquire the 'central conceptual structure' of a mental number line. A child who has this conceptual structure will be able, at least for relatively small numbers, to tell which of two numbers is larger; to count backwards or forwards from a given number (e.g. to say which number comes two numbers after 7); and to use the addition strategy of counting on from the larger addend; (e.g. if asked to add 2 and 5, will start with 5 and count on '6, 7'). Research on the subject (Case & Griffin, 1990; Griffin, Case, & Sandieson, 1992; Resnick, 1983) has indicated that children under 5 usually do not appear to use such a mental number line, while children over 5 generally do. However, some 5- and 6-year-old children, especially those from low income backgrounds, demonstrate difficulty with the mental number line tasks.

The Rightstart program includes 30 games to be played by small groups of four or five children, as well as some whole-class activities. The predominant mode of work with the children involves 20 minutes a day of small-group activities. The games and activities used in the programme involve counting; quantifying sets of objects; matching sets to written numerals; and predicting the result of adding 1 to or taking 1 away from a given set.

In an initial evaluation (Griffin, Case, & Siegler, 1994), 23 kindergarten children from the programme and 24 controls from similar backgrounds were followed up into first grade. Those who had been in the programme improved significantly more than the others on tests of oral arithmetic and word problem solving. They also did better on number line knowledge and on written arithmetic problems of the sort taught in school; but differences here were not significant, because children in both groups tended to do well at these tasks. The children who had been in the Rightstart group also received significantly better ratings from teachers on most aspects of number understanding and arithmetic.

Another project is the Berkeley Maths Readiness Project (Starkey & Klein, 2000). This project is funded by the US Department of Education and is being carried out by Prentice Starkey and Alice Klein at the University of California at Berkeley. The researchers are developing and evaluating a pre-kindergarten mathematics curriculum including eight topical units:

1   enumeration and number sense
2   arithmetical reasoning
3   spatial sense
4   geometric reasoning
5   unit construction and pattern sense
6   logical reasoning
7   measurement
8   computer mathematics.

For example, the arithmetical reasoning unit includes a division activity (dividing a set of concrete objects into two equal subsets) and addition and subtraction activities such as using finger counting to solve problems such as 'Three bears and one bear make how many bears altogether?'.

Both preschool teachers and parents deliver the curriculum. The teachers attend two workshops to learn about the curriculum and the materials. They then teach the curriculum in their classrooms and also demonstrate related activities to parents and children in a series of home visits. The parents are given advice sheets and materials for use with their children.

The mathematical progress of children in demonstration classes using the curriculum is being compared with that of children in other classes and children from the same classes a year before the project was implemented. Improvements in performance have already been demonstrated both in middle-class children and in disadvantaged children in Head Start and California State Preschool programs. Evaluations are still in progress.

Ginsburg et al. (1999) introduced the BigMath intervention program. Like the Rightstart program, it introduces mathematical games and activities into the general curriculum in preschool and kindergarten programmes in disadvantaged areas. Whereas the Rightstart program emphasizes certain specific number skills that appear to be important to the development of numeracy, the BigMath program emphasizes introducing children early to a wide variety of important mathematical concepts: not necessarily relating to number.

The development of the programme reflects the view that mathematics education in the early years has often been limited to counting, shape identification and some simple measurement comparisons. Where more sophisticated ideas are introduced, they have often been dealt with too briefly and not revisited. The BigMath program is aimed at helping children to explore 'big' mathematical ideas over lengthy periods of time. It includes activities designed for individuals, small groups and the whole class. There are six major strands:

1   Use of numbers, involving counting procedures and principles, the use of numbers as labels (e.g. house numbers) and the different ways in which numbers may be represented.
2   Shape, involving not only recognition and naming of shapes, but exploration of their characteristics (e.g. number of sides and angles), symmetry and ways of partitioning them into other shapes.
3   Measurement, involving comparison, seriation and iteration (repeated use of a measurement unit) with regard to a wide variety of quantities: length, weight, capacity, area, time, temperature and money.
4   Working with numbers, including grouping of objects, adding and subtracting and the relationships between sets and their subsets.
5   Patterns, involving the systematic repetition of elements in the context of number, shape, colour, and sound (e.g. rhythm). Children copy patterns; extend them (e.g. adding 2 repeatedly to make 1, 3, 5, 7 . . .); describe them; and create their own.
6   Spatial relationships, involving describing and mapping positions and routes.

The programme includes a wide variety of games, stories and pictures. For example, one of the tasks involving line symmetry involves presenting children with pictures of halves of faces and asking them how to complete the faces. Some of the spatial tasks include 'treasure hunts' where children attempt to locate an object from clues about its position relative to other objects. One of the number activities involves listening to a story, 'So Many Fives', about children who represent the number 5 through number words in different languages, the written numeral and various types of tally. The children are then encouraged to think of a wide variety of ways of representing other numbers.

The programme is still in its initial stages and has not yet undergone full evaluation. However, results so far are promising and suggest that young children are far more ready to engage in mathematically challenging activities, and to go beyond very simple counting, than some traditional views have suggested.

The programmes described so far target children who are at risk for mathematical difficulties for socioeconomic reasons, rather than children who have been directly assessed as having actual or likely mathematical difficulties. Van Luit and Schopman (2000) carried out such a study in the Netherlands. They examined the effects of early mathematics intervention with young children attending kindergartens for children with special educational needs. The participants were 124 children between the ages of 5 and 7. They did not have sensory or motor impairments or severe general learning disabilities. Most had language deficits and/or behavioural problems. All had scored in the lowest 25% for their age group on the Utrecht Test for Number Sense, a test of early counting skills and number concepts. Sixty two underwent intervention and the other 62 served as a control group, who underwent the standard preschool curriculum. The intervention programme was the Early Numeracy Programme, designed for children with special needs, which emphasizes learning to count. The programme involved the numbers 1 to 15, which were represented in various ways, progressing from the concrete (sets of objects) through the semi-concrete (tallies) to the abstract (numerals) sets of objects, and tally marks. Patterns of 5 were particularly emphasized and were represented by 5 tally marks within an ellipse. The number activities were embedded in games involving families, celebrations and shopping. The children had two half-hour sessions per week in groups of three for six months. At the end, the intervention group performed much better than the control group on activities that had formed part of the intervention programme, but unfortunately did not transfer their superior knowledge to other similar but not identical numeracy tasks.

How schools have dealt with individual differences in arithmetic

Before discussing intervention programmes, we may consider the ways in which schools may deal with individual differences in arithmetic. One possibility is, of course, simply to disregard them: to teach all pupils the same curriculum by the same method. This has the advantages that it requires relatively few resources and avoids the potential problems of labelling children as 'good' or 'bad' at arithmetic and of reduced expectations for pupils who are considered as 'bad' at the subject. However, ignoring the existence of individual differences (whatever their sources) is not going to make them disappear. Individual differences are not created solely by the school environment, although they may be exaggerated by it. Unless expectations are reduced for *all* pupils, some pupils will struggle and become discouraged, if not 'math phobic', if their difficulties are not taken into account. Unless expectations are raised to the point of creating difficulty for a large number of pupils, some other pupils will find the tasks too easy and become bored. Pupils who are much better at some components of arithmetic than at others will not be helped to use their strengths to overcome their weaknesses. (None of this is to say that mathematical weaknesses are innate, fixed or immutable: merely to say that ignoring or disregarding them, or demanding that pupils perform at a higher level of ability, is not necessarily going to make them overcome their weaknesses.)

Another possible approach, which has often been taken in practice, is to divide children into ability groups, thus reducing the level of individual variation in any given class. This may involve children being placed in separate schools or classes according to supposed overall ability or in 'sets' specifically for mathematics. This avoids many of the problems that occur when individual differences are totally ignored, but can create its own problems. Some children may be labelled as 'failures' or 'no good at maths' and live down to expectations. Resources may be concentrated on pupils who are regarded as more able and the 'less able' classes or sets may be assigned to weaker or less experienced teachers.

Research on the effects of streaming and setting has yielded somewhat complex and equivocal results (Harlen & Malcolm, 1999; Ireson & Hallam, 2001). Overall, streaming and setting do not influence school performance overall or in most subjects. However, several studies suggest that they do have a deleterious effect specifically on the performance of low achievers in *mathematics*, who perform less well than similar pupils in mixed ability groups (Boaler, 1997; Hoffer, 1992; Ireson & Hallam, 2001).

Boaler (1997) carried out interviews with pupils in schools that used either mixed ability groups or sets for mathematics. The setted pupils of all ability levels expressed greater dissatisfaction. Their major source of concern was that they were required to follow a standard pace and that individual differences were not taken into consideration as they had been in primary school mixed-ability classes. Thus, setting may sometimes increase the very problems that it seeks to avoid, because teachers and curriculum planners assume that the classes are homogeneous and that individual differences can be ignored whereas in fact individual differences are still marked even within a set. Streaming and setting, as commonly used, may have deleterious effects on low achievers' performance, not because they take too much account of individual differences, but because they lead to taking too *little* account of individual differences.

Moreover, in view of the componential nature of arithmetical thinking, the construction of homogeneous 'sets' may not even be possible: where, for example, do we place a child who is excellent at mental arithmetic but poor at using written symbolism or one who has difficulty in remembering arithmetical facts but is an accomplished user of derived fact strategies?

Another approach is to enable some independent individualized or small-group work within a class (El-Naggar, 1996). Individualized work within a class usually involves progressing through a textbook at one's own pace; the use of individualized worksheets; and/or (in recent years) the individualized use of educational computer software. Such approaches are very variable. They include the component-based approaches discussed later under the heading 'Could interventions be useful for children without arithmetical difficulties?' as well as approaches which treat arithmetical ability as a more global unitary ability. Small-group approaches may take a similar form or may involve group projects where several pupils work together on the solution or solutions to a problem.

Such approaches are far more flexible and have more potential for taking account of the componential nature of arithmetical ability than the approaches previously mentioned. Their potential disadvantages include the risk that, even within one class, some pupils may be labelled as 'low attainers' and live down to expectations; and the risk that work will become so individualized that pupils will not benefit from mutual discussion and exploration of ideas.

Lou, Abrami, Spence, Poulsen, Chambers, and d'Appolonia (1996) carried out a meta-analysis of ability grouping and small-group work *within* classes, in a variety of school subjects. In contrast to most findings with regard to setting, this study indicated that *within*-class grouping had a positive effect on the performance of low achievers; but only if it was accompanied by provision of appropriate materials and activities.

Askew, Bibby, and Brown (2001) developed a small-group intervention technique that involved the use of *derived fact strategies* (see Chapter 6). The researchers pointed out that there are some children who do not develop such strategies. Often (although not always) these are among the children who know relatively few arithmetic facts and rely on counting strategies. Their failure to use derived fact strategies may further impede their developing a store of known facts, which, in its turn, may interfere with the development of derived fact strategies.

Their programme emphasized working out strategies for deriving new facts on the basis of known facts. Teachers worked with small groups (four per group) of Year 3 children (7- to 8-year-olds) who had performed below average in National Curriculum tests at age 7. The children underwent intervention once a week for 20 weeks. The interventions emphasized devising strategies for working out new arithmetical facts on the basis of known facts. There were 48 children in the intervention group, who were compared with 48 matched controls. All children were given a diagnostic test of arithmetic problem solving, devised by the researchers, just before intervention and again shortly after completing the intervention. The children in the programme improved significantly more than the controls, both in accuracy and in their use of known and derived facts rather than needing to resort to counting strategies.

In Britain in the 1990s, the pendulum swung back from an emphasis on individual and small-group work toward greater emphasis on whole-class work. In particular, teachers have been recommended to engage in whole-class teaching during the 'daily mathematics lesson'. Whole-class teaching avoids some of the pitfalls that have been discussed with regard to individualized, small-group and selective teaching; but it carries the potential risk of returning to the pitfalls of ignoring individual differences and teaching all pupils in the same way, regardless of their particular pattern of strengths and weaknesses.

To reduce this problem, the National Numeracy Strategy (DfEE, 1999) now incorporates some intervention techniques for children who are struggling with arithmetic. The main intervention programme is the Springboard programme, used with children in Years 3 to 7 (7 to 12 years).

The target group is children with relatively mild arithmetical difficulties. The Springboard programme provides additional tuition for small groups of six to eight children as a supplement to the daily mathematics lesson that they undergo with the whole class. Typically, it provides two 30-minute sessions that consolidate the work currently being taught in the daily mathematics lessons.

Some materials for individualized interventions in mathematics have been piloted since June 2003 in 25 local education authorities across the country (Marie Heinst, personal communication). They are still in draft form and await full evaluation. They emphasize individualized diagnosis of the errors and misconceptions shown by children with significant difficulties, specific or non-specific, with mathematical learning.

The children in the pilot study are given diagnostic interviews to determine conceptual and procedural difficulties in coping with the major areas of the mathematics curriculum materials are being developed for use with children to correct the errors and misconceptions that have been spotted. For example, children who have difficulty in understanding the values of digits may be shown three-digit numbers made out of arrow cards. The teacher then replaces one of the digits (e.g. changing 233 to 203) and asks the child how it has changed.

The materials can be used within or outside the daily mathematics lesson and are used individually by the child with the class teacher, a teaching assistant or a special needs teacher. The child typically undergoes one 20-minute individual session per week and five-minute 'spotlight' sessions on each of the following days, in addition to following the mathematics curriculum with or without specialist support.

At present, there are no similar government-sponsored intervention programmes for children under 7 in Britain. This younger age group seems particularly important from this point of view, as the first two years of school are when much of the foundation is being laid for later mathematical learning; and identifying and intervening with difficulties at this stage has the potential to prevent children from developing inappropriate arithmetical strategies that may handicap them in later work and from developing negative attitudes toward arithmetic.

Peer tuition and group collaboration

One way in which schools can deal with individual differences is by encouraging children to teach one another. This can involve older children teaching younger children; more able classmates teaching less able classmates; or collaborative learning between peers of similar ability. All these techniques have been used extensively in general teaching. Collaborative group projects have been common in schools for many years and have their adult counterparts in the classes, workshops and seminars that occur in higher education and professional development. The teaching of younger children by older children has a very venerable history, going back at least to the early 19th-century 'monitorial' system, where older children became teachers as well as learners as a means of coping with the enormous class sizes and high teacher/pupil ratio of Britain's earliest free schools. The present discussion will be confined to the use of such techniques with regard to arithmetic.

The commonest forms of peer teaching involve collaborative group work, where several children co-operate in solving a mathematical problem. This can serve several purposes: increasing motivation; in encouraging children to put their mathematical ideas into words and to reflect on the strategies that they use; and in enabling children to transmit mathematical knowledge and ideas to one another. The possible disadvantages of such approaches are that their success may depend on the dynamics of a particular group. There is the risk that a dominant child, or one who is perceived as 'clever', may do most of the work, while the others simply accept his or her decisions and are 'carried' along without really learning anything new. If we are specifically considering low achievers in mathematics, this is a particular danger. Such children may be ignored or dismissed in group discussions and decisions. However, some studies have indicated that collaborative learning can be beneficial to children with arithmetical difficulties.

Davenport and Howe (1999) looked at the effect of collaborative learning on children's ability to solve addition and subtraction word problems. Children worked in groups, using problem-solving guidelines that they had been given to solve the problems, and then 'taught' their problem to a fellow pupil. The children in this collaborative condition were compared with children who solved the same problems individually. The children in the collaborative condition performed better than those who worked individually and, in particular, children who were *below average* in arithmetic benefited from being the 'learners' who listened to peers.

More intensive forms of peer tutoring involve one-on-one tuition of one child by another: often following some form of explicit training of the child 'teacher' (FitzGibbon, 1981; Levin, Glass, & Meister, 1984; Topping & Bamford, 1998; Vosse, 1999). Usually, older children teach younger children. Studies tend to show benefits both for the tutors – perhaps due to their need to reflect on the arithmetical concepts and procedures that they teach – and for the tutees.

One recent meta-analysis has, however, suggested that, while peer tutoring interventions are beneficial for children with arithmetical difficulties, they are less so than some other forms of intervention (Kroesbergen & Van Luit, 2003). This result needs to be interpreted cautiously, as the criteria for including children in peer tutoring programmes may be less strict than those involving other forms of intervention. Thus, children involved in peer tutoring may show less improvement just because they tend to have less serious problems in the first place.

Games as an aid to arithmetical intervention

> 'When the weather's bad, I've been learning him to play cards; I thought to myself, well, this'll help him with his numbers, it'll learn him them, it'll help him know how to exchange money, you know . . . When we first started to play, he knew some of the numbers but he didn't know 'em all. Well, now he knows, and he knows which not to put down, and he can change his money. So we're helping him there on that. He thinks it's a game, but it's an education really.' (mother quoted by John and Elizabeth Newson: *Perspectives on school at seven years old*, London: Allen & Unwin, 1976, p. 128)

Teachers and parents have also often used games as a means of improving children's arithmetical performances; and games form a part of many intervention programmes, both group based and individual.

Many children enjoy playing table and other games that include arithmetical activities. Playing cards show numbers both in terms of numerals and quantities and most card games are based on these numbers. Dominoes involve number recognition and matching. Board games with dice and counters involve counting; addition and often subtraction; and matching between different modes of presentation of numbers (e.g. translating the number of dots on a die into number of moves on a board). Some games, of which the best known is probably Monopoly, involve complex imaginary financial transactions.

The role of numbers is most immediately obvious in games that include such materials as playing cards, dominoes, dice and boards with numbered squares. However, they are used in many other games. Any game that requires score keeping will provide further need for arithmetic. Children's playground games often involve numbers as part of the game (e.g. counting up to a certain number while players hide in 'Hide and Seek') and/or in scoring; but most of all, perhaps, in some of the elaborate counting-out rituals that are used to assign the roles in a game.

Some children and adults who perform poorly at or dislike school arithmetic may enjoy and perform well at apparently similar activities in a game context. Herndon (1971) writes of a pupil with seemingly poor mathematical abilities, who earned money as a darts scorer. Claire, whose mathematical difficulties and anxieties are described in Chapter 9, was, at the age of 11 or 12, very fond of playing Monopoly, and performed the arithmetical manipulations involved with relatively little trouble. (See Chapter 8 for other examples.)

A number of teaching and intervention programmes have used games as an opportunity for practising arithmetical skills (Ainley, 1990; Kirkby, 1992; Rowe, 2001). Some have used existing games; others have devised their own games for the purpose (e.g. Ainley, 1990; Straker, 1996). An example is Straker's (1996, p. 68) game 'Snake'. In this game, a snake made out of eight circles is portrayed on a page. Each player rolls two dice in turn and writes the total number in one of the circles. A number may only be written once and the numbers in all the circles must be in order. If there is no space for a number, the player misses a turn. The player who has written the most numbers when all the circles are full wins the game.

Ainley (1990) points out that one of the reasons for inventing games especially for the purpose of mathematics teaching is that in most games, many of the associations between numbers and game rules and moves are arbitrary from a mathematical point of view – e.g. 'If you throw a six, you will get another turn.' In specially designed mathematical games, it is possible to place a greater emphasis on intrinsic arithmetical properties and rules.

Cognitive enhancement interventions

Some mathematical intervention techniques involve attempts to increase children's global cognitive performance, by teaching particular strategies or concepts. A detailed discussion of such techniques, especially when they do not relate specifically to arithmetic, is outside the scope of the present book. However, two important methods of this nature must be mentioned: training in Piagetian operations and training in metacognition.

Training in Piagetian operations

At certain times in the past, training in Piagetian operations (see, especially, Chapter 3) was considered an important form of intervention to improve children's arithmetic. The basis for this approach was that understanding the underlying number concepts is a necessary prerequisite to arithmetic.

This approach in its pure form is susceptible to criticism on more than one front. Those who consider Piaget's theory flawed or inadequate will consider intervention approaches based on Piaget's theories to be inadequate. By the same token, some who agree substantially with Piaget's theory consider that training in Piagetian operations is inappropriate, because such operations are developed through maturation and experience rather than direct training and because it seems unnecessary to train children in concepts that develop universally (Ginsburg, 1977).

Some approaches that have emphasized Piagetian training have been relatively unsuccessful in improving arithmetical performance (Snorre Ostad, personal communication). Contrariwise, some approaches that have combined Piagetian training with other forms of intervention have led to significant improvement (e.g. Van de Rijt & Van Luit, 1998).

So far, 'Piagetian training' has referred mainly to the number concepts that are acquired relatively early and which, in Piaget's theory, are dependent on the attainment of *concrete* operations. The acquisition of *formal* operations (involving the manipulation of symbols and abstractions) in adolescence may be more susceptible to and dependent on training. There are considerable individual and cross-cultural differences as regards whether and when formal operations are attained and they seem to depend highly on schooling. There has been some research involving training older children in formal operations. So far, this has been aimed at groups of children of all abilities, rather than specific interventions for children with difficulties. Research by Adey and Shayer (1994) indicates that training in formal operations does indeed appear to have a positive impact on the mathematical development of older children and adolescents. This research was predominantly aimed at improving performance in science; improvement in mathematics was a by-product. More recently, Adhami, Johnson, and Shayer have used training in formal operations more specifically to enhance mathematical learning (cognitive acceleration in mathematics education (CAME)) (Adhami, Johnson, & Shayer, 1998).

Training in metacognition

Metacognition – awareness of one's own mental strategies and level of knowledge – is often regarded as particularly important to arithmetic (see Chapter 8). Current mathematics education in Britain and other countries has placed increasing emphasis on encouraging children to reflect on and discuss their mathematical ideas and strategies. Several intervention projects have involved training children, with and without arithmetical difficulties to reflect on their knowledge and plan and monitor their arithmetical strategies (Adey & Shayer, 1994; Desoete, Roeyers and De Clercq, 2003; Verschaffel, DeCorte, Lasure, Van-Vaerenburgh, Bogaerts, & Ratinckxx 1999) and have generally produced good results.

It is not always absolutely clear which aspects of such programmes have been successful. 'Metacognitive training' can mean somewhat different things in different studies. Some studies may emphasize a form of reflection that is really an aspect of Piagetian formal operations and thus comes within the previous section; some emphasize the ability to discuss and compare arithmetical strategies; others may emphasize a planning ability more akin to aspects of working memory; still others may emphasize awareness of one's own knowledge state, including 'knowing when one doesn't know'. More research is needed on exactly which aspects of meta-cognition are important here.

Individualized remediation in arithmetic

We now turn from group-based techniques of helping children with arithmetical difficulties to more individualized component-based techniques that take into account individual children's strengths and weaknesses in specific components of arithmetic.

Some of the history of individualized remedial work

Of course, a great deal has altered over the years in mathematics education and remediation; but it is striking how many of the most modern practices have surprisingly early origins. Some forms of individualized, component-based techniques of assessing and remediating mathematical difficulties have been in existence at least since the 1920s (Buswell & John, 1926; Brownell, 1929; Greene & Buswell, 1930; Tilton, 1947; Williams & Whitaker, 1937). By the same token, they have never been used very extensively; and there are many books, both old and new, about mathematical development and mathematics education that do not even refer to such techniques or to the theories behind them.

Weaver (1954) was a strong advocate of differentiated instruction and remediation in arithmetic. He put forward several important points that have since been strongly supported by the evidence, centrally that 'arithmetic competence is not a unitary thing but a composite of several types of quantitative ability: e.g. computational ability, problem-solving ability, etc.'; that '(t)hese abilities overlap to varying degrees, but most are sufficiently independent to warrant separate evaluations'; and that 'children exhibit considerable variation in their profiles or patterns of ability in the various patterns of arithmetic instruction' (pp. 300–301). He argued (pp. 302–303) that any 'effective program of differentiated instruction in arithmetic must include provision for comprehensive evaluation, periodic diagnosis, and appropriate remedial work' and that '(e)xcept for extreme cases of disability, which demand the aid of clinicians and special services, remedial teaching is basically *good* teaching, differentiated to meet specific instructional needs'.

For a long time, some researchers and educators have emphasized the importance of investigating the strategies that individual children use in arithmetic: especially those faulty arithmetical procedures that lead to errors (Buswell & John, 1926; Brownell, 1929; VanLehn, 1990). Thus, some children might add without carrying (e.g. 23 + 17 = 310); others might add all the digits without any reference to whether they are tens or units (e.g. 23 + 17 = 13); others, when adding a single-digit number to a two-digit number, might add it to both the tens and the units (e.g. 34 + 5 = 89).

Many papers on mathematical difficulties have included lists of such faulty procedures. In early studies (Greene & Buswell, 1930; Tilton, 1947; Williams & Whitaker, 1937), such flaws tend to be described as 'bad habits'. In some more recent studies (Brown & Burton, 1978; VanLehn, 1990), they are described as 'bugs', by analogy with malfunctioning computer programs.

Efforts are made to diagnose such incorrect strategies, so that they can be corrected. In the words of Tilton (1947, pp. 84–85):

Many errors are systematic. In other words, not as many errors are accidental and attributable to carelessness as teachers are inclined to think ... If the youngsters who have such incorrect rules are to be helped, the teacher should know the child's rule, because the child's need is just as much to unlearn his incorrect rule as it is to learn the correct rule. To work in ignorance of his rules is to give him a feeling of confusion.

Brown and Burton (1978) devised a computer program, BUGGY, to diagnose a wide variety of incorrect rules and strategies.

If componential theories of arithmetical ability and their applications to differentiated instruction and remediation in arithmetic were already being advocated when our contemporary schoolchildren's great-grandparents were at school, why have they had comparatively little impact on theory and practice? Part of the reason is practical: in under-resourced classrooms, it is difficult to provide individualized instruction. Until the 1960s, primary class sizes of 40 or more were common in Britain. At the beginning of the 21st century, the average number of children per class in British primary schools is just over 26 (DfES, 2005).

If differentiated instruction is used at all under overcrowded conditions, it tends to take the form of grouping children according to their perceived overall ability, either in all academic areas or, at best, in specific school subjects (here mathematics). Therefore, in some quarters, differentiated instruction may be viewed negatively, due to associations with educational methods that separate those labelled as 'less able' from those labelled as 'able'; and involve lower expectations and sometimes worse teaching of the former group (see section on 'How schools have coped with individual differences in arithmetic'). In fact, the true aim of differentiated instruction is to identify strengths and weaknesses within the same domain in the same individual and to use the strengths to overcome or compensate for the weaknesses. Such an aim is quite incompatible with labelling individuals as globally 'bad' at a subject and with regarding their weaknesses as purely innate and not susceptible to intervention. Nevertheless, some people confuse the appropriate use of differentiated instruction with its misuse.

Another reason for the limited use of such intervention techniques is that there has been relatively little communication of findings: one of the problems that have bedevilled the whole area of mathematical development. Many an interesting study has remained in near obscurity, or has only reached a particular category of individuals. Communications between teachers, researchers in education, researchers in psychology and policymakers have been limited, as often have been communications between researchers within the same discipline in different countries and at different times.

Potential problems with individualized instruction and remediation: Past and present

What are the potential problems that can arise with individualized instruction and remediation? Apart from the practical problems arising from inadequate resources, there can be problems with the methods that are used. In particular, there may be gaps in the selection of arithmetical components for remediation. Indeed, in our present state of knowledge there must be, since we do not yet have a full understanding of the different components of arithmetic; the relationships between them; and the nature and causes of individual differences in them. Nevertheless, there has been sufficient knowledge in the area for quite some time to permit successful work in the area.

Moreover, appropriate individualized instruction depends on appropriate selection of the components of arithmetic to be used in assessment and intervention. This is still an issue for debate and one that requires considerable further research. One of the main potential problems, which was more common in the past than nowadays, is to assume that the components to be addressed must necessarily correspond to specific arithmetical operations: e.g. treating 'addition', 'subtraction', 'multiplication', 'division' etc. as separate components. It is, of course, quite possible for children to have specific problems with a particular arithmetical operation. Indeed, as we have seen, it is possible for a particular arithmetical operation to be selectively impaired in adult patients following brain damage. Nevertheless, it is an oversimplification to assume that these operations are likely to be the primary components of arithmetical processing. Current classifications tend to place greater emphasis on the type of cognitive process: e.g. the broad distinctions between factual knowledge ('knowing that'), procedural knowledge ('knowing how'), conceptual knowledge ('knowing what it all means') and in some theories utilizational knowledge ('knowing when to apply it') (see, for example, Greeno, Riley, & Gelman, 1984). A potential danger of overemphasizing the different operations as separate components is that it may encourage children, and perhaps adults, to ignore the relationships between the different operations.

Another potential problem – again more common in the past albeit still a danger nowadays – is looking at children's difficulties *only* in terms of *procedural* errors. It is, of course, important to investigate the strategies that individual children use in arithmetic, including those faulty arithmetical procedures that lead to errors. Nonetheless, diagnosing the incorrect strategies is not always the final step. There may be a conceptual reason why the incorrect strategy is acquired and maintained or there may be unperceived conceptual strengths, which need to be noted and built on (Ginsburg, 1977; Tilton, 1947).

Such diagnostic work is vital. Children do indeed frequently acquire incorrect strategies, which can become entrenched, especially if the child is given too much of the wrong sort of arithmetical practice. Nonetheless, diagnosing the incorrect strategies is not always the final step. There may be a *conceptual reason* why the incorrect strategy is acquired and maintained. In the case of the faulty subtraction strategies described earlier, their acquisition could result from an assumption that larger numbers cannot be subtracted from smaller numbers, combined with an inadequate under-standing of place value that makes it difficult for children to understand the nature and purpose of borrowing. As Tilton (1947, p. 85) goes on to remark:

> Many of the errors made by these . . . children seemed to be due to an insufficient understanding of the meaning of numbers. It seems as if these children had been asked to learn the rules for the manipulation of numbers in addition, subtraction and multiplication without having learned the meaning of the symbols that they have been asked to manipulate.

More generally, almost any assessment or intervention project will involve some degree of oversimplification. Ginsburg (1972) pointed out that:

> [C]hildren's knowledge of mathematics is extraordinarily complex and often much different from what we had supposed it to be . . . In the case of every child we have interviewed or observed, there have emerged startling contradictions, unsuspected strengths or weaknesses, and fascinating complexities.

As a result: '[E]fforts at individualized instruction do not work as well as they could because they hold faulty conceptions of the child's knowledge and because they employ inadequate techniques for measuring it.'

Assessments

Effective interventions imply some form of assessment, whether formal or informal, to (a) indicate the strengths, weaknesses and educational needs of an individual or group; and (b) to evaluate the effectiveness of the inter-vention in improving performance.

Assessments may or may not be 'tests' in the conventional sense. Ollerton and Watson (2001, p. 87) list 23 methods used to assess pupils. These range from traditional written tests and multiple-choice tests through marking written work and extended projects to 'hearing a response which is unexpected and reveals other knowledge'.

There are a variety of standardized tests used for assessing children's arithmetic. Many test batteries for measuring abilities (e.g. the British Abilities Scales and their American counterpart, the Differentiated Apti-tude Tests) include tests both of calculation efficiency and of mathematical reasoning, the latter usually taking the form either of number pattern recognition or word problem solving. IQ scales, such as the Wechsler

Intelligence Scale for Children and the Wechsler Adult Intelligence Scale, include arithmetic subtests that tend to emphasize word problem solving. Some tests, used in school contexts, place greater emphasis on whether children have mastered particular aspects of the arithmetic curriculum. Others are devised for the specific purpose of assessing particular mathematical components, which are to be dealt with, or have been dealt with, in an intervention programme. Some researchers over the years have argued that the exclusive use of standardized tests may result in missing crucial aspects of an individual's strategies and difficulties and have emphasized the importance of individual interviews and case study methods (Brownell & Watson, 1936; Ginsburg, 1977, 1997).

Butterworth (2002) has devised a computerized screening test of basic numerical skills: incorporating the recognition of small numerosities; estimation of somewhat larger numerosities; and comparisons of number size. These are intended to identify severe arithmetical difficulties (dyscalculia) rather than to assess individual differences in the general population.

There are advantages and disadvantages to the use of any type of assessment. Traditional tests may (but need not) lead to an emphasis on comparing pupils or schools rather than on identifying the educational needs of individual pupils. They may thus lead to anxiety in both teachers and pupils and encourage or pressurize teachers to teach 'to the test' rather than to teach for knowledge and understanding. They may be relatively unsuitable for people who have not had extensive experience of being tested; and in particular for people who have not had recent experience of schooling: thus they may be much less suitable for adults than for children. Observational and interview-based techniques involve fewer such problems, are potentially more flexible and may provide richer and more detailed information about the strategies that a child is using at a given time. However, they usually require more time and resources to be carried out properly and are more potentially vulnerable to the conscious or unconscious biases of the person who is carrying out the assessment.

Computer programs for individual instruction

With the increasing development and availability of computer technology, a number of computer programs have been developed for individualized instruction and remedial work (Errera, Patkin, & Milgrom, 2001; Lepper & Gurtner, 1989). Computerized individualized instruction systems have the same potential advantages (adaptability to individual patterns of learning; lack of social pressure) and disadvantages (lack of social interaction and communication; often exclusive emphasis on the response rather than on the cognitive process of reaching it) as other individualized self-teaching systems. In addition, they have the important advantage that computers are motivating to many children; and that, with increasing availability of home computers and computer games, they may be used outside as well as within the school context.

Computer programs in the past tended to take a simplistic approach to children's errors and to reward correct answers and reject incorrect answers without scope for analyzing how the errors occurred (Hativa, 1988). The more sophisticated forms of programming that are available today make it much more possible to diagnose and interpret misconceptions; although, as with any test, they may not pick up a particular individual's interpretations and misinterpretations, especially if these are somewhat untypical of the population as a whole.

Individualized intervention programmes with young children: Current work

Two independently developed, individualized intervention programmes, which address numeracy in young children and take componential approaches based on cognitive theories of arithmetic, are the Mathematics Recovery programme (Wright, Martland, & Stafford, 2000; Wright, Martland, Stafford, & Stanger, 2002) and the Numeracy Recovery programme (Dowker, 2001). There are some important differences between the two programmes. Notably, the Mathematics Recovery programme is much more intensive than the Numeracy Recovery programme; and the Mathematics Recovery programme places more emphasis on methods of counting and number representation and the Numeracy Recovery programme on estimation and derived fact strategy use. From a more theoretical point of view, the Mathematics Recovery programme places greater emphasis on broad developmental stages, while the Numeracy Recovery programme treats mathematical development to a greater extent as involving potentially independent, separately developing skills and processes. Despite these distinctive features, the two programmes have other important common features besides being individualized and componential. Both programmes are targeted at the often neglected early primary school age group (6- to 7-year-olds); both deal mainly with number and arithmetic rather than other aspects of mathematics; and both place a greater emphasis than most programmes on collaboration between researchers and teachers.

Mathematics Recovery

The Mathematics Recovery programme was designed in Australia by Wright and his colleagues (Wright et al., 2000, 2002). In this programme, teachers provide intensive individualized intervention to low-attaining 6- and 7-year-olds. Children in the programme undergo 30 minutes of individualized instruction per day over a period of 12 to 14 weeks.

The choice of topics within the programme is based on the Learning Framework in Number, devised by the researchers. This divides the learning of arithmetic into five broad stages: emergent (some simple counting, but few numerical skills); perceptual (can count objects and sometimes add small sets of objects that are present); figurative (can count well and use 'counting-all' strategies to add); counting-on (can add by 'counting-on-from-larger' strategy and subtract by counting down; can read numerals up to 100 but have little understanding of place value); and facile (know some number facts; are able to use some derived fact strategies; can multiply and divide by strategies based on repeated addition; may have difficulty with carrying and borrowing).

Children are assessed, before and after intervention, in a number of key topics. They undergo interventions based on their initial performance in each of the key topics. The key topics that are selected vary with the child's overall stage. For example, the key topics at the emergent stage are (1) number word sequences from 1 to 20; (2) numerals from 1 to 10; (3) counting visible items (objects); (4) spatial patterns (e.g. counting and recognizing dots arranged in domino patterns and in random arrays); (5) finger patterns (recognizing and demonstrating quantities up to 5 shown by number of fingers); and (6) temporal patterns (counting sounds or movements that take place in a sequence). The key topics at the next, perceptual, stage are: (1) number word sequences from 1 to 30; (2) numerals from 1 to 20; (3) figurative counting (counting on and counting back, where some objects are visible but others are screened); (4) spatial patterns (more sophisticated use of domino patterns; grouping sets of dots into 'lots of 2'; 'lots of 4', etc.); (5) finger patterns (recognizing, demonstrating and manipulating patterns up to 10 shown by numbers of fingers); and (6) equal groups and sharing (identifying equal groups and partitioning sets into equal groups). The key topics at later stages place greater emphasis on arithmetic and less on counting. Despite the overall division into stages, the programme acknowledges and adapts to the fact that some children can be at a later stage for some topics than for others.

There are many activities that are used for different topics and stages within the Mathematics Recovery programme. For example, activities dealing with temporal patterns at the emergent stage include children counting the number of chopping movements made with the adult's hands; makes with his/her hands; producing a requested number of chopping movements with their own hands; counting the number of times they hear the adult clap; and clapping their own hands a requested number of times. Activities dealing with number word sequences in fives at the counting-on stage include children being presented with sets of five-dot cards; counting the dots as each new card is presented; counting to 30 in fives without counting the dots; counting to 30 in fives without the cards; counting to 50 in fives without the cards; and counting backward in fives from 30, first with and then without the cards.

Children in the programme improved very significantly on the topics that form the focus of the problem: often reaching age-appropriate levels in these topics. The teachers who worked on the programme found the experience very useful; felt that it helped them to gain a better understanding of children's mathematical development; and used ideas and techniques from the programme in their subsequent classroom teaching.

Numeracy Recovery

The Numeracy Recovery programme (Dowker, 2001), piloted with 6- and 7-year-olds (mostly Year 2) in some primary schools in Oxford, is funded by the Esmee Fairbairn Charitable Trust. The scheme involves working with children who have been identified by their teachers as having problems with arithmetic. One hundred and seventy five children (about 15% of the children in the relevant classes) have so far begun or undergone intervention.

These children are assessed on nine components of early numeracy, which are now summarized and described. The children then receive weekly individual intervention (half an hour a week) in the particular components with which they have been found to have difficulty. The interventions are carried out by the classroom teachers, using techniques proposed by Dowker (2001).

The teachers are released (each teacher for half a day weekly) for the intervention, by the employment of supply teachers for classroom teaching. Each child typically remains in the programme for 30 weeks, although the time is sometimes shorter or longer, depending on teachers' assessments of the child's continuing need for intervention. New children join the project periodically.

The interventions are based on an analysis of the particular subskills that children bring to arithmetical tasks, with remediation of the specific areas where children show problems. The components addressed here are not to be regarded as an all-inclusive list of components of arithmetic, either from a mathematical or educational point of view. Rather, the components were selected because earlier research studies and discussions with teachers have indicated them to be important in early arithmetical development and because research has shown them to vary considerably between individual children in the early school years.

The distinctive characteristics of the intervention scheme are as follows:

1   It is based on the componential view of arithmetical ability, which has been emphasized throughout this book. Thus, arithmetic is seen not as a unitary ability, but as composed of multiple components, themselves divisible into many subcomponents. Each of these components shows continuous variation within the population from extreme talent to extreme deficit.

2   The scheme involves close collaboration between the researcher and the classroom teachers. The teachers have been involved at all levels: in preliminary discussions with the researcher to help to establish the areas with which children most frequently experience difficulty and which are therefore important to address in an intervention programme; in selecting the children most likely to benefit from intervention; and in actually carrying out the intervention work. This collaboration has a number of important benefits:

— The teachers have assisted the researcher in making an informed selection of the components which most frequently create problems for children in the mathematics classroom.

— The intervention is carried out in the context in which the children are receiving the majority of their mathematics instruction, which increases continuity between the children's learning in intervention sessions and in the classroom. This may make them more likely to transfer their learning from the intervention setting to their everyday schoolwork.

— The teachers can transfer the intervention techniques and the understanding that the individualized work gives them of children's individual strengths and deficits to classroom work with the same children and sometimes other children.

— The children's arithmetical strengths and weaknesses are observed from several perspectives: standardized test performance; performance on the different components during the individualized assessments; their performance during the intervention sessions; and their performance in the classroom situation. This combination of assessment methods helps to overcome the disadvantages of any single type of assessment, and produces a more rounded picture of the children's patterns of abilities and deficits.

3   Although the project is individualized, it is relatively non-intensive. Children in the programme receive about half an hour of intervention per week. While some children would undoubtedly benefit from more intensive intervention programmes if these were practically possible, a significant number of children need just a relatively small amount of individualized and targeted attention in conjunction with more group-based activities. For such children, extremely intensive programmes might actually take too much time away from class work that would benefit them. Thus, the programme is aimed at the lower 15 or 20% of attainers in arithmetic, rather than specifically at the much smaller number of children who have severe arithmetical difficulties.

COMPONENTS THAT ARE THE FOCUS OF THE NUMERACY RECOVERY PROJECT

The components that are the focus of the project include (1) procedures and (2) principles related to basic counting; (3) use of written arithmetical symbolism; (4) use of place value in arithmetic; (5) understanding and solution of word problems; (6) translation between concrete, verbal and numerical formats; (7) use of derived fact strategies for calculation; (8) arithmetical estimation; and (9) memory for number facts.

Remediation for these components principally involves techniques devised by the author, supplemented by exercises and games taken from published materials (e.g. Baker & Petty, 1998; Burgess, 1995a, 1995b; Hopkins, 1997a, 1997b; Long, 1996; Straker, 1996). Techniques devised and used by the teachers themselves also play a major role in the project.

The components and the main intervention techniques will now be summarized.

1   *Counting procedures.* Children are asked to count sets of 10 and 20 objects; and are also asked to count verbally as high as they can.

    Intervention. Children are given practice in counting sets of objects, ranging in number from 5 to 25.

2   *Counting-related principles and their application.* (Originally, components (1) and (2) were grouped together on the assumption that very few children as old as 6 or 7 would have difficulty with counting. A higher proportion than expected had such difficulties; so that different components of counting – are here considered separately.)

    The order irrelevance principle (that counting the same set of items in different orders will result in the same number) is usually the latest of the main counting principles to be acquired (see Chapter 3). Evidence suggests that understanding the order irrelevance principle is closely related to the ability to predict the result of adding or subtracting an item from a set.

    The children are assessed on: the *order irrelevance principle*. The children watch an adult count a set of objects, and are then asked to predict the result of further counts in the reverse order; after the addition of an object; and after the subtraction of an object; *repeated addition by 1*. Children are shown a set of five items and then asked repeatedly how many there will be 'if we put one more there'. This is repeated up to 15 items; *repeated subtraction by 1*. Children are shown a set of 10 items, and then shown one item being subtracted, and asked repeatedly how many there will be 'if we take one away'. This is repeated down to zero items.

    Intervention. For the order irrelevance principle, children practise counting and answering cardinality and order irrelevance questions about very small numbers of counters (up to five); and are then given further practice with increasingly large sets.

    For repeated addition by 1 and repeated subtraction by 1, children are given practice in observing and predicting the results of such repeated additions and subtractions with counters (up to 20).

They are then given verbal 'number after' and 'number before' problems: 'What is the number before 8?', 'What is the number after 14?', etc.

3   *Written symbolism for numbers.* There is much evidence that children often experience difficulties with written arithmetical symbolism of all sorts and, in particular, with representing quantities as numerals (Fuson, 1992; Ginsburg, 1989). With regard to this component, children are asked to read aloud a set of single-digit and two-digit numbers. A similar set of numbers is dictated to them for writing.

Intervention. Children practise reading and writing numbers. Children with difficulties in reading or writing two-digit numbers (tens and units) are given practice in sorting objects into groups of ten, and recording them as '20', '30', etc. They are then given such sorting and recording tasks where there are extra units as well as the groups of ten.

4   *Understanding the role of place value in number operations and arithmetic.* This involves the ability to add tens to units ($20 + 3 = 23$); the ability to add 10s to 10s ($20 + 30 = 50$); and the ability to combine the two into one operation ($20 + 33 = 53$). A related task involves pointing to the larger number in pairs of two-digit numbers that vary either just with regard to the units (e.g. 23 versus 26); just with regard to the 10s (e.g. 41 versus 51); or where both tens and units vary in conflicting directions (e.g. 27 versus 31; 52 versus 48).

Intervention. Children are shown the addition of tens to units and the addition of tens to tens in several different forms: written numerals; number line or number block; hands and fingers in pictures; 10-pence pieces and pennies; any apparatus (e.g. Multilink or Unifix) with which the child is familiar. The fact that these give the same answers is emphasized.

Children whose difficulties are more specific to the use of place value in arithmetic may be given practice with arithmetical patterns such as: '20 + 10; 20 + 11; 20 + 12', etc.; being encouraged to use apparatus when necessary.

5   *Word problem solving.* This component involves comprehending addition and subtraction story problems of various semantic types (DeCorte & Verschaffel, 1987); selecting the appropriate operations; and solving the problems (see Chapter 4).

Intervention. Children are given addition and subtraction word problems, which are discussed with them: 'What are the numbers that we have to work with?' 'What do we have to do with the numbers?' 'Do you think that we have to do an adding sum or a taking-away sum?' 'Do you think that John has more sweets or fewer sweets than he used to have?', etc. They are encouraged to use counters to represent the operations in the word problems, as well as writing the sums numerically.

6   *Translation between arithmetical problems presented in concrete, verbal and numerical formats.* As discussed in Chapter 5, translation between concrete, verbal and numerical formats is a crucial aspect of children's arithmetical development.

The intervention programme includes tasks of translating in all possible directions between numerical (written sums); concrete (operations with counters); and verbal (word problem) formats for both addition and subtraction.

For example, in translating from verbal to numerical, children are presented with word problems (e.g. 'Katie had five apples; she ate two, so now she has three left') and are asked to 'write down the sum that goes with the story'.

Intervention. Children are shown the same problems in different forms and shown that they give the same results. They are also encouraged to represent word problems and concrete problems by numerical sums and to represent numerical problems and word problems by concrete objects.

7   *Derived fact strategies in addition and subtraction.* As discussed in Chapter 5, one crucial aspect of arithmetical reasoning is the ability to derive and predict unknown arithmetical facts from known facts, for example by using arithmetical principles such as commutativity, associativity, the addition/subtraction inverse principle, etc.

Children are given the Addition and Subtraction Principles Test developed by Dowker (1995, 1998; Chapter 5 of this book). In this test, they are given the answer to a problem and then asked them to solve another problem that could be solved quickly by the appropriate use of an arithmetical principle (e.g. they may be shown the sum '23 + 44 = 67' and then asked to do the sum 23 + 45, or 44 + 23). Problems preceded by answers to numerically unrelated problems are given as controls.

The children are asked whether 'the top sum' helps them to do 'the bottom sum', and why. The actual addition and subtraction problems involved vary in difficulty, ranging from those which the child can readily calculate mentally, through those just beyond the child's calculation capacity, to those very much too difficult for the child to solve. The particular derived fact strategies that are the main focus of this project are those involving commutativity (e.g. if 8 + 6 = 14, then 6 + 8 = 14); the associativity-based N + 1 principle (if 9 + 4 = 14, then 9 + 5 = 14 + 1 = 15) and the N − 1 principle (e.g. if 9 + 4 = 13, then 9 + 3 = 13 − 1 = 12).

Intervention. Children are presented with pairs of arithmetic problems. The 'derived fact strategy' techniques are pointed out and explained to them; and they are invited to solve similar problem.

If they fail to do so, the strategies are demonstrated to them for single-digit addition and subtraction problems, with the help of manipulable objects and of a number line; and they are again invited to carry out other derived fact strategy problems.

8   *Arithmetical estimation.* The ability to estimate an approximate answer to an arithmetic problem, and to evaluate the reasonableness of an arithmetical estimate, are discussed in Chapter 6.

In assessing and remediating this component, children are given a task devised by the author (Dowker, 1997). They are presented with a series of problems of varying degrees of difficulty and with estimates made for these problems by imaginary characters (Tom and Mary). The children are asked to evaluate 'Tom and Mary's' estimates on a five-point scale from 'Very good' to 'Very silly'; and to suggest 'good guesses' for these problems themselves. Once again, the actual addition and subtraction problems involved vary in difficulty, ranging where possible from those which the child can readily calculate mentally, through those just beyond the child's calculation capacity, to those very much too difficult for the child to solve.

Intervention. Children are shown other arithmetical estimates by 'Tom and Mary' and asked to evaluate them. They are encouraged to give reasons for their evaluations.

9   *Number fact retrieval.* Number fact retrieval is discussed in Chapter 7. In this programme, this skill is principally assessed through Russell and Ginsburg's (1984) Number Facts Test.

Intervention. Children are presented with some of the basic addition and subtraction facts (e.g. $3 + 3 = 6$; $6 + 6 = 12$). They are presented with the same sums repeatedly in the same session and in successive sessions. They also play 'number games' (e.g. some from Straker, 1996) that reinforce number fact knowledge.

SOME RESULTS FROM THE NUMERACY RECOVERY PROJECT

The children in the project, together with some of their classmates and children from other schools, are given three standardized arithmetic tests: the British Abilities Scales Basic Number Skills subtest (1995 revision), the WOND Numerical Operations test and the WISC arithmetic subtest. The first two place greatest emphasis on computation abilities and the last on arithmetical reasoning. The children are retested at intervals of approximately 6 months.

The initial scores on standardized tests and retest scores after 6 months of the first 146 children to take part in the project have now been analyzed. Not all of the data from 'control' children are yet available, but the first 85 'control' children to be retested showed no significant improvement in standard (i.e. age-corrected) scores on any of the tests. In any case, the tests are standardized, so it is possible to estimate the extent to which children are or are not improving relative to others of their age in the general population.

The children in the intervention group have so far shown very significant improvements. (Average standard scores are 100 for the BAS Basic Number Skills subtest and the WOND Numerical Operations subtest and 10 for the WISC arithmetic subtest.) The median standard scores on the BAS Basic Number Skills subtest were 96 initially and 100 after approximately 6 months. The median standard scores on the WOND Numerical Operations test were 91 initially and 94 after 6 months. The median standard scores on the WISC arithmetic subtest were 7 initially and 8 after 6 months (the means were 6.8 initially and 8.45 after 6 months). Wilcoxon statistical tests showed that all these improvements were highly significant. One hundred and one of the 146 children have been retested over periods of at least a year and have been maintaining their improvement.

Comments by teachers include:

> The children are responding very well to the materials and to the extra support . . . They are working through activities linked to basic number skills to establish and reinforce early concepts. Feedback from staff, children and parents has been very positive.

> [The project] has given us valuable information about pupils' learning needs in a core subject, and has provided us with the funding to support the most needy children with individual tuition . . . As a consequence, we have seen the targeted pupils improve considerably in competence and confidence.

> Working with children individually gives greater opportunity for analysing their thinking through individual questioning . . . There is more time and opportunity for using apparatus and asking children to demonstrate what they are doing. These children are often very reluctant to verbalize what they are thinking and in a whole class or even small group situation, there is not the time to wait for or expect their replies. By giving the children 'thinking time', their confidence and willingness to 'have a go' develops as they offer explanations . . . The children seem to enjoy coming to the sessions and it has been possible to raise their self-esteem in mathematics in most cases.

Thus, the study strongly supports the view that children's arithmetical difficulties are highly susceptible to intervention. It is not the case that a large number of children are simply 'bad at maths'. It is particularly notable that strong improvements occurred in the WISC arithmetic subtest: a test sometimes regarded as a measure of 'general intelligence' rather than educational achievement.

Moreover, individualized work with children who are falling behind in arithmetic has a significant impact on their performance. The amount of time given to such individualized work does not, in many cases, need to be very large to be effective: these children received approximately half an hour a week and showed considerable benefits.

Further research is planned to evaluate the project more rigorously including a comparison with a larger number of matched 'controls'. Moreover, future studies will investigate changes with time in performance on the different components, not only by children who have arithmetical difficulties, and may undergo intervention, but also by higher achievers. The aim is to integrate the implementation and evaluation of the intervention scheme with the investigation of individual differences in and relationships between the selected components of arithmetic. Thus, the intervention project, which was inspired by my earlier research and conclusions about the components of arithmetic, will now also serve as a training study to test theories about these components.

More broadly, it appears that individualized, component-based approaches to intervention can be highly effective. Further research is, of course, necessary to show whether and to what extent such interventions are more effective in improving children's arithmetic than other interventions that provide children with individual attention: e.g. interventions in literacy or interventions in arithmetic that are conducted on a one-to-one basis but not targeted toward individual strengths and weaknesses. It is also desirable to investigate whether different approaches to such intervention (e.g. age when intervention starts; degree of intensiveness) may be differentially appropriate to different groups of children. It would also be desirable to investigate the potential for similar types of intervention in areas of mathematics other than numeracy: e.g. geometry and measurement.

Interventions with adults

Most intervention programmes have been with children or adolescents. Since numeracy difficulties have lifelong implications, it is important that more work be carried out on diagnosis and intervention for such difficulties in adults. Numeracy is increasingly included in 'basic skills' programmes for adults; although most such programmes do not differentiate between adults who have not learned such skills due to lack of educational opportunity and those who have specific difficulties in arithmetic.

Some intervention programmes have been devised for people who have become dyscalculic as a result of brain damage in adulthood. As Girelli and Seron (2001) point out, most such programmes have involved practice either in the transcoding (reading and writing) of numerals. It would be highly desirable for more flexible and varied programmes to be devised, since acquired (like developmental) arithmetical impairments are so very varied in form.

Could interventions be useful for children without arithmetical difficulties?

This chapter has focused on intervention projects with children who have some degree of difficulty in arithmetic. Could the same principles – especially those of individualized component-based assessment and teaching – be applicable to normally achieving and arithmetically gifted children? After all, a central theme of this book is that *all* children can show uneven development of different components, with selective strengths and weaknesses, and that children with arithmetical difficulties represent the lower end of a continuum – or several continua – of performance, rather than forming a sharply demarcated group. Of course, children with arithmetical difficulties are likely to need to take priority over others when resources are relatively limited; but it is likely that *all* children could benefit from at least occasional individualized diagnostic assessment and intervention.

A few studies have suggested that giving unselected children individual or small-group sessions of training in specific components of arithmetic such as counting principles and procedures, comparison of quantities, understanding commutativity and arithmetical estimation can lead to significant improvement in arithmetic as a whole (Kaufmann, Handl, & Thony, 2003).

Some mainstream teaching techniques have involved individualized assessment and instruction in selected components of arithmetic. An example is the individually programmed instruction scheme developed in Canada in the late 1960s (Maguire, 1971). Elementary school children were administered pretests in different components of the arithmetic curriculum: addition, subtraction, multiplication, division, fractions, geometry, etc. They were assigned to a particular level on each component and were given worksheets appropriate to their level. The scheme allowed for the possibility that children might be at different levels on different components; e.g. at a high level on subtraction but a lower level on multiplication. After completing the worksheets for each component, the children were given a post-test and if successful, moved on to the next level.

The programme had the disadvantage that the components were selected purely according to their use as topics in the curriculum, rather than representing different types of cognitive process. Also, the programme simply assessed performance on the basis of number of errors made and there was no provision in the programme for analyzing what *type* of errors were made or *why* they were made. And in fact the programme was less successful than some other programmes: the pupils involved in the programme liked mathematics better than control children did, but did not perform much better at it (Maguire, 1971).

It is increasingly recognized that *children with special talents in arithmetic* may need special provision (Dowker & Dowker, 1979; Kolshy, 2001). So far, where there has been such provision, it has typically involved giving more able children more advanced work across the board than their peers, or, perhaps more interestingly, organizing clubs, group activities and masterclasses for them. It is less common for provision for arithmetically talented children to involve assessing their individual strengths and weaknesses and tailoring instruction to these. Often it is assumed that such children have a uniform talent in mathematics and would not need such individualized assessment; yet, in fact, mathematically talented children and adults often do show specific strengths and relative weaknesses in particular aspects of mathematics (see Chapters 1 and 2).

Although flexible response to individual strengths and weaknesses is particularly important when dealing with children who have significant mathematical difficulties – or exceptional mathematical talent – it would indeed seem desirable for *all* children. Not all children need intervention; but all could at times benefit from individual consideration. We may close with the words of Emma, seemingly a classic example of the type of person who could be expected to 'get by' without much individual attention or adaptations to specific needs. She would never be regarded as having even mild mathematical difficulties. She is a 20-year-old Oxbridge student, who did well in school examinations in mathematics and science and is now coping well with a course with a significant numerical component. When she discovered that I carry out research on mathematical development, she remarked:

> I hate maths. I'm all right at maths. I did well in GCSE Maths, and got a good mark in [a mathematics-related component of my Oxbridge University course]. But it makes me nervous. I recognize myself in your descriptions of 'mathematics anxiety'. It's the only subject that I can remember crying about. My mother would ask me why I was crying, and I would say, 'Because I can't do this maths problem.' [Did you always dislike maths, or only when you got to secondary school?] Only at secondary school. I was at a small primary school, and the classes were very small, and I could always ask when I didn't understand something. At secondary school, the classes were much bigger, and that was when SATS [Standardized Assessment Tests] had just been introduced, so the teachers were very busy preparing us for them, and they always had to get on. If you asked a question, they would say, 'Come and ask me later on; I haven't got time now.' Well, in the break, you don't really want to go and talk to your maths teacher! So I wouldn't get to understand these things . . . It was a confidence thing, too.

If even the Emmas of the world are suffering from the lack of individualized mathematics education, then so are most children. In an ideal world, smaller classes and better resources would make it possible for all children to receive the individual attention they need. Until and unless this is achieved, it remains important to target and provide interventions for those in particular need and to ensure that schools and society at least recognize the existence of individual patterns of strengths and weaknesses in arithmetic.

Conclusions

The research reviewed in this book supports the points outlined in the Introduction.

In particular, arithmetical ability is not unitary, but is made up of many different components. Each of these components varies continuously in the population from severe deficits to high levels of talent. The components correlate with one another, but individuals can show strong discrepancies, in either direction, between almost any two components. It is misleading, and usually counterproductive, to label individuals as globally 'good' or 'bad' at arithmetic.

Individual differences in arithmetic and in its components are very great and are caused by many different, interacting factors. Some factors are intrinsic to the individual; some factors involve the home, school or cultural environment. In practice, 'nature' and 'nurture' interact so much that it is almost impossible to separate one from the other.

Many children have difficulties with some or most aspects of arithmetic. It is hard to estimate the proportion that has difficulties, since this depends on the criteria that are used. Moreover, as arithmetical thinking involves such a wide variety of components, there are many forms and causes of arithmetical difficulty, which may assume different degrees of importance in different tasks and situations. It is likely that at least 15 to 20% of the population have difficulties with certain aspects of arithmetic, which are sufficient to cause significant practical and educational problems for the individual.

Arithmetical difficulties can be ameliorated considerably by intervention, especially intervention based on the fact that arithmetic is made up of numerous subcomponents and takes account of the specific strengths and weaknesses of individuals. Several studies have suggested that individualized work with children who are falling behind in arithmetic has a significant impact on their performance. The amount of time given to such individualized work does not, in many cases, need to be very large to be effective.

At the other end of the scale, some individuals show marked talent in arithmetic and interest in number. Such arithmetical talent takes various forms, is often, but by no means always, associated with high 'general intelligence'.

One important feature of arithmetical talent – and to a somewhat lesser extent, of *all* arithmetical thinking – is marked variability in strategy use. High levels of mathematical ability are associated not so much with an ability to home in on one or two 'best strategies', but with access to and a willingness and ability to use a very wide variety of strategies. Indeed, people in general use a wider variety of strategies for arithmetic problems than would be suggested by very simple theories of arithmetical thinking and performance. It may be that both novices and experts use a particularly wide variety of strategies, while people at an intermediate level of knowledge and understanding are more likely to rely on a few well-learned strategies.

There is marked convergence between the results of research in psychology, education and neuroscience. All support the componential nature of arithmetic and the importance of investigating individual patterns of strengths and weaknesses in these components. For example, psychological and educational studies of both children and adults converge in suggesting that exact calculation and arithmetical estimation correlate with each other, but that there are often marked discrepancies between these two forms of arithmetic. Neuropsychological studies of patients and brain-imaging studies of typical adults support these findings, by suggesting that exact calculation and arithmetic use somewhat different networks in the brain.

Up to now, research in different disciplines has tended to proceed independently. In the future, we may hope that research on arithmetic within psychology, neuroscience and education will become increasingly integrated, with increasing communication between researchers in different disciplines, teachers and policymakers. This will permit a greater understanding of individual differences in arithmetic; of their relationships to experience and to the brain; and of the implications for education in general and for helping those with unusual difficulties *or* talents within arithmetic.

Teaching numbers

by Gary Soto

The moon is one.
The early stars a few more . . .
The sycamore is lean
With sparrows, four perhaps,
Three hunched like hoods
And one by itself,
Wiping a beak
In the rag of its shoulder.

From where we sit
We could count to a thousand
By pointing at oranges
On trees, bright lanterns
Against the dusk, globes
Of water that won't come down.

Follow me with this, then:
A stray on two legs
At a trash can, one kite in a tree,
And a couple with four hands,
Three in pockets and one scratching
An ear busy with sound:
Door, cat, trembling leaf.

(The world understands numbers –
At birth you're not much
And when lowered into the earth
You're even less, a broken
Toy of 108 bones and 23 teeth
That won't stop laughing.)

But no talk of this
For the dog is happy with an eggshell
And oranges are doing wonders
At this hour in the trees
And there is popcorn to pick
From my small bowl of hands.

Let's start again
With numbers that will help.

The moon is one,
The early stars a few more.

References

Abed, A.S. & Alkhateeb, H.M. (2000). Mathematics anxiety among eighth-grade students of the United Arab Emirates. *Psychological Reports, 86,* 835–847.

Ackerman, P.T., Anhalt, J.M., & Dykman, R.A. (1986). Arithmetic automatization failure in children with attention and reading disorders: Associations and sequela. *Journal of Learning Disabilities, 19,* 222–232.

Adams, J. & Hitch, G. (1998). Mental arithmetic and working memory. In C. Donlan (Ed.), *The development of mathematical skills* (pp. 153–173). Hove, UK: Psychology Press.

Adetula, L.O. (1996). Effects of counting and thinking strategies in teaching addition and subtraction problems. *Educational Research, 38,* 183–198.

Adey, P. & Shayer, M. (1994). *Really raising standards.* London: Routledge.

Adhami, M., Johnson, D., & Shayer, M. (1998). *Thinking maths: Accelerated learning in mathematics.* Oxford: Heinemann.

Ahlberg, A. & Csocsan, E. (1999). How children who are blind experience numbers. *Journal of Visual Impairment and Blindness, 93,* 549–560.

Aiken, L.R. (1972). Biodata correlates of attitude toward mathematics in three age and two sex groups. *School Science and Mathematics, 72,* 5, 386–395.

Aiken, L.R. & Dreger, R.M. (1961). The effect of attitudes on performance in mathematics. *Journal of Educational Psychology, 52,* 19–24.

Ainley, J. (1990). Playing games and learning mathematics. In L. Steffe & T. Wood (Eds.), *Transforming children's mathematics education* (pp. 84–91). Hillsdale, NJ: Lawrence Erlbaum Associates Inc.

Ainley, J. (2000). Constructing mathematical activity in primary classrooms. In C. Tikly & A. Wolf (Eds.), *The maths we need now: Demands, deficits and remedies* (pp. 138–153). London: University of London, Institute of Education (Bedford Way Papers).

Ainsworth, S., Wood, D., & O'Malley, C. (1998). There is more than one way to solve a problem: Evaluating a learning environment that supports the development of children's multiplication skills. *Learning and Instruction, 8,* 141–157.

Alibali, M. & DiRusso, A. (1999). The function of gesture in learning to count: More than keeping track. *Cognitive Development, 14,* 37–56.

Allardice, B. (1977). The development of written representations for some mathematics concepts. *Journal of Mathematical Behaviour, 1,* 135–148.

Allardice, B.S. & Ginsburg, H.P. (1983). Children's psychological difficulties in mathematics. In H.P. Ginsburg (Ed.), *The development of mathematical thinking* (pp. 319–351). New York: Academic Press.

Alpert, A. (1928). The solving of problem situations by preschool children. *Teachers College Contributions to Education*, No. 23.

Ambrose, R., Baek, J.M., & Carpenter, T.P. (2003). Children's invention of multi-digit multiplication and division problems. In A. Baroody & A. Dowker (Eds.), *The development of arithmetical concepts and skills* (pp. 305–336). Mahwah, NJ: Lawrence Erlbaum Associates, Inc.

Andrade, J. (Ed.) (2001). *Working memory in perspective*. Hove, UK: Psychology Press.

Anghileri, J. (1997). Uses of counting in multiplication and division. In I. Thompson (Ed.), *Teaching and learning early number* (pp. 41–51). Buckingham: Open University Press.

Anghileri, J. (Ed.) (1995). *Children's mathematics in the primary years: Perspectives on children's learning*. London: Cassell.

Ansari, D. & Karmiloff-Smith, A. (2002). Atypical trajectories of number develop-ment: A neuroconstructivist perspective. *Trends in Cognitive Sciences*, *6*, 511–516.

Antell, S. & Keating, L. (1983). Perception of numerical invariance in neonates. *Child Development*, *54*, 695–701.

Anttonen, R.G. (1969). A longitudinal study in mathematics attitude. *Journal of Educational Research*, *62*, 467–471.

Aram, D. & Ekelman, B. (1988). Scholastic aptitude and achievement among children with unilateral brain lesions. *Neuropsychologia*, *14*, 903–916.

Arnold, D.H., Fisher, P., Doctoroff, G., & Dobbs, J. (2002). Accelerating math development in Head Start classrooms. *Journal of Educational Psychology*, *94*, 762–770.

Ashcraft, M.H. & Christ, K.S. (1995). The frequency of arithmetic facts in ele-mentary texts: Addition and multiplication in grades 1 to 6. *Journal for Research in Mathematics Education*, *26*, 396–421.

Ashcraft, M.H. & Faust, M.W. (1994). Mathematics anxiety and mental arithmetic performance: An exploratory investigation. *Cognition and Emotion*, *8*, 97–125.

Ashcraft, M.H. & Fierman, B.A. (1982). Mental addition in third, fourth and sixth graders. *Journal of Experimental Child Psychology*, *33*, 216–234.

Ashcraft, M.H. & Kirk, E.P. (2001). The relationships between working memory, math anxiety and performance. *Journal of Experimental Psychology: General*, *130*, 224–237.

Ashcraft, M., Yamashita, T., & Aram, D. (1992). Mathematics performance in left and right brain-lesioned children and adolescents. *Brain and Cognition*, *19*, 208–252.

Ashcraft, M.H., Kirk, E.P., & Hopko, D. (1998). On the cognitive consequences of mathematics anxiety. In C. Donlan (Ed.), *The development of mathematical skills* (pp. 175–196). Hove, UK: Lawrence Erlbaum Associates, Ltd.

Askew, M. & Brown, M. (1997). *The teaching and assessment of number at Key Stages 1 to 3*. London: SCAA.

Askew, M. & Brown, M. (Eds.) (2001). *Teaching and learning primary numeracy: Policy, practice and effectiveness*. NOTTS: British Educational Research Association.

Askew, M., Bibby, M., & Brown, M. (2001). *Raising attainment in primary number sense: From counting to strategy*. London: Beam Education.

Atkinson, S. (1992). The power of the child's own intuitive methods. In S. Atkinson

(Ed.), *Mathematics with reason: The emergent approach to primary maths* (pp. 43–53). London: Hodder & Stoughton.

Attisha, M. & Yazdani, M. (1984). An expert system for diagnosing children's multiplication errors. *Instructional Science, 13*, 79–82.

Backhouse, J., Haggarty, L., Pirie, S., & Stratton, J. (1992). *Improving the learning of mathematics*. London: Cassell.

Baddeley, A. (1986). *Working memory*. Oxford: Oxford University Press.

Baddeley, A.D. & Hitch, G.J. (1974). Working memory. In G.H. Bower (Ed.), *The psychology of learning and motivation* (pp. 47–90). New York: Academic Press.

Baker, A. & Petty, K. (1998). *Little Rabbit's first number book*. New York: Kingfisher.

Banks, C. (1998). *Young children's use of derived fact strategies for numerical and concrete problems*. Undergraduate project, University of Oxford.

Barouillet, P., Fayol, M., & Lathuliere, E. (1997). Selecting between competitors in multiplication tasks: An explanation of the errors produced by adolescents with learning difficulties. *International Journal of Behavioural Development, 21*, 253–275.

Baroody, A.J. (1984). More precisely defining and measuring the order-irrelevance principle. *Journal of Experimental Child Psychology, 38*, 33–41.

Baroody, A.J. (1987). *Children's mathematical thinking: A developmental framework for preschool, primary and special education teachers*. New York: Teachers' College Press.

Baroody, A. (1988). Mental addition development of children classified as mentally handicapped. *Educational Studies in Mathematics, 19*, 369–388.

Baroody, A.J. (1989). Kindergartners' mental addition with single-digit combinations. *Journal for Research in Mathematics Education, 20*, 159–172.

Baroody, A.J. (1992a). The development of kindergartners' mental addition strategies. *Learning and Individual Differences, 4*, 215–235.

Baroody, A.J. (1992b). The development of preschoolers' counting skills and principles. In J. Bideaud (Ed.), *Pathways to number: Children's developing numerical abilities*. Hillsdale, NJ: Lawrence Erlbaum Associates, Inc.

Baroody, A.J. (1993). The relationship between the order-irrelevance principle and counting skill. *Journal for Research in Mathematics Education, 24*, 415–427.

Baroody, A.J. with Coslick, R.T. (1998). *Fostering children's mathematical power: An investigative approach to K-8 mathematics instruction*. Mahwah, NJ: Lawrence Erlbaum Associates, Inc.

Baroody, A.J. & Gannon, K.E. (1984). The development of the commutativity principle and economical addition strategies. *Cognition and Instruction, 1*, 321–339.

Baroody, A.J. & Gatzke, M.R. (1991). The estimation of set size by potentially gifted kindergarten-age children. *Journal for Research in Mathematics Education, 22*, 59–68.

Baroody, A.J. & Ginsburg, H.P. (1986). The relationship between initial meaningful and mechanical knowledge of arithmetic. In J. Hiebert (Ed.), *Conceptual and procedural knowledge of mathematics: The case of mathematics* (pp. 75–112). Hillsdale, NJ: Lawrence Erlbaum Associates, Inc.

Baroody, A.J. & Snyder, P. (1983). A cognitive analysis of basic arithmetic abilities of TMR children. *Education and Training of the Mentally Retarded, 18*, 253–259.

Baroody, A.J., Berent, R., & Packman, D. (1982). The use of mathematical structure by inner city children. *Focus on Learning Problems in Mathematics*, *4*, 5–13.

Baroody, A.J., Ginsburg, H.P., & Waxman, B. (1983). Children's use of mathematical structure. *Journal for Research in Mathematics Education*, *14*, 156–168.

Basic Skills Agency (1997). *International Numeracy Survey*. London: Basic Skills Agency.

Bath, J.B., Chinn, S.J., & Knox, D.E. (1986). *Test of cognitive style in mathematics: Manual*. East Aurora, NY: Slosson.

Bearden, C.E., Woodin, M.F., Wang, P.P., Moss, E., McDonald-McGinn, D., Zackai, E., Emmanuel, B., & Cannon, T.D. (2001). The neurocognitive phenotype of the 22q11.2 deletion syndrome: Selective deficit in visual-spatial memory. *Journal of Clinical and Experimental Neuropsychology*, *18*, 447–464.

Bebout, H.C. (1990). Children's symbolic representation of addition and subtraction word problems. *Journal for Research in Mathematics Education*, *21*, 123–131.

Beentjes, J.W.J. & Jonker, V.H. (1987). Inconsistency in addition and subtraction strategies. *Journal of Experimental Education*, *56*, 4–7.

Beishuizen, M. (1993). Mental strategies and materials or models for addition up to 100 in Dutch second grades. *Journal for Research in Mathematics Education*, *24*, 294–323.

Beishuizen, M. (1997). Mental arithmetic: Mental recall or mental strategies? *Mathematics Teaching*, *160*, 16–19.

Beishuizen, M. (2001). Different approaches to mastering mental calculation strategies. In J. Anghileri (Ed.), *Principles and practices in arithmetic teaching* (pp. 119–130). Buckingham: Open University Press.

Beishuizen, M. & Anghileri, J. (1998). Which mental strategies in the early number curriculum? A comparison of British ideas and Dutch views. *British Educational Research Journal*, *24*, 519–538.

Beishuizen, M., Van Putten, C.M., & Van Mulken, F. (1997). Mental arithmetic and strategy use with indirect number problems up to one hundred. *Learning and Instruction*, *7*, 87–106.

Benbow, C.P. (1988). Sex differences in mathematical reasoning ability in intellectually talented preadolescents: Their nature, effects and possible causes. *Behavioural and Brain Sciences*, *11*, 169–232.

Benbow, C.P. (1992). Academic achievement in mathematics and science between the ages of 13 and 23: Are there differences among students in the top one per cent of mathematical ability? *Journal of Educational Psychology*, *84*, 51–61.

Benedict, R., Shapiro, A., Duffner, P., & Jaeger, J. (1998). Acquired oral reading vocabulary following the onset of amnesia in childhood. *Journal of the International Neuropsychological Society*, *4*, 179–189.

Benezet, L.P. (1935). The teaching of arithmetic: The story of an experiment. *Journal of the National Education Association*, *24*, 241–244, 301–303.

Bergeron, J. & Herscovits, N. (1987). Unit fractions of a continuous whole. In J. Bergeron, N. Herscovits, & C. Kieran (Eds.), *Proceedings of the Eleventh International Conference on the Psychology of Mathematics Education*, (Vol. 2, pp. 357–365), Montreal: PME.

Betz, N.E. (1978). Prevalence, distribution and correlates of maths anxiety in college students. *Journal of Counseling Psychology*, *25*, 441–448.

Biddle, B.J. (2001). *Social class, poverty and education*. London: Routledge.

Bialystok, E. & Codd, T. (1997). Cardinal limits: Evidence from language awareness and bilingualism for development of number concepts. *Cognitive Development, 12*, 85–106.

Bierhoff, H. (1996). *Laying the foundations of numeracy: A comparison of primary school textbooks in Britain, Germany and Switzerland*. London: National Institute of Economic and Social Research.

Binet, A. (1894). *Psychologie des grands calculateurs et joueurs d'échecs*. Paris: Hachette.

Binet, A. (1969). The perception of lengths and numbers in some small children. In R.H. Pollack and M.W. Brenner (Eds.), *The experimental psychology of Alfred Binet* (pp. 79–92). New York: Springer.

Bird, M. (1992). A simple starting point. In S. Atkinson (Ed.), *Mathematics with reason: The emergent approach to primary maths* (pp. 123–127). London: Hodder & Stoughton.

Bisanz, J. & Lefevre, J.A. (1990). Strategic and non-strategic processing in the development of mathematical cognition. In D.F. Bjorklund (Ed.), *Children's strategies: Contemporary views of cognitive development* (pp. 213–244). Hillsdale, NJ: Lawrence Erlbaum Associates, Inc.

Bishop, D. (1997). *Uncommon understanding: Development and disorders of language comprehension in children*. Hove, UK: Psychology Press.

Bishop, D.V.M. (2001). Genetic and environmental risks for specific language impairment in children. *Philosophical Transactions of the Royal Society of London, Series B, 356*, 369–380.

Blatchford, P. (1992). Children's attitude to work at 11 years. *Educational Studies, 18*, 107–118.

Blatchford, P. (1996). Pupils' views on school work and school from 7 to 16 years. *Research Papers in Education, 11*, 3, 263–288.

Boaler, J. (1997). *Experiencing school mathematics: Teaching styles, sex and school*. Buckingham: Open University Press.

Boulton-Lewis, G.M. (1993). Young children's representations and strategies for subtraction. *British Journal of Educational Psychology, 63*, 441–456.

Boulton-Lewis, G.M. & Tait, K. (1994). Young children's representations and strategies for addition. *British Journal of Educational Psychology, 64*, 231–242.

Brainerd, C.J. (1973). Mathematical and behavioural foundations of number. *Journal of Genetic Psychology, 88*, 221–281.

Brainerd, C.J. (1979). *The origins of the number concept*. New York: Praeger.

Brannon, E.M. & Van de Walle, G.A. (2001). The development of ordinal numerical competence in young children. *Cognitive Psychology, 43*, 53–81.

Brenner, M.E., Herman, H., Ho, H.Z., & Zimmer, T.M. (1999). Cross-national comparisons of representational competence. *Journal for Research in Mathematics Education, 30*, 541–557.

Briars, D.J. & Siegler, R.S. (1984). A featural analysis of children's counting knowledge. *Developmental Psychology, 20*, 607–618.

Briggs, M. & Crook, J. (1991). Bags and baggage. In E. Love & D. Pimm (Eds.), *Teaching and learning mathematics*. London: Hodder & Stoughton.

Brissiaud, R. (1992). A tool for number construction: Finger symbol sets. In J. Bideaud, C. Meljac, & J.P. Fischer (Eds.), *Pathways to number: Children's developing numerical abilities* (pp. 41–65). Hillsdale, NJ: Lawrence Erlbaum Associates, Inc.

Brolin H. & Bjork, L.E. (1992). Introducing calculators in Swedish schools. In J. Fey

& C. Hirsch (Eds.), *Calculators in mathematics education* (pp. 226–232). Reston, VA: National Council of Teachers of Mathematics.

Brooker, L. (2002). *Starting school: Young children learning cultures*. Buckingham: Open University Press.

Brown, A. (1987). Metacognition, executive control, self-regulation and other more mysterious mechanisms. In F.E. Weinert & R.H. Kluwe (Eds.), *Metacognition, motivation and understanding*. Hillsdale, NJ: Lawrence Erlbaum Associates, Inc.

Brown, M. (1981). Place value and decimals. In K. Hart & CSMS (Eds.), *Children's understanding of mathematics 11 to 16* (pp. 48–65). London: John Murray.

Brown, M. (2001). Influences on the teaching of number in England. In J. Anghileri (Ed.), *Principles and practices in arithmetic teaching* (pp. 35–48). Buckingham: Open University Press.

Brown, J.S. & Burton, R.B. (1978). Diagnostic models for procedural bugs in basic mathematical skills. *Cognitive Science, 2*, 155–192.

Brown, M., Askew, M., Rhodes, V., Denvir, H., Wiliam, D., Ranson, E., & Millett, A. (2002, April). *Progression and regression in numeracy learning: Some results from survey and case study data from the Leverhulme Numeracy Research Programme*. Paper presented at the American Educational Research Association, Chicago.

Brown, R.S. & VanLehn, K. (1980). Repair theory: A generative theory of bugs in procedural skills. *Cognitive Science, 4*, 379–426.

Brownell, W.A. (1929). Remedial cases in arithmetic. *Peabody Journal of Education, 7*, 100–107.

Brownell, W. (1938). Two kinds of learning in arithmetic. *Journal of Educational Research, 31*, 656–664.

Brownell, W.A. & Watson, B. (1936). The comparative worth of two diagnostic techniques in arithmetic. *Journal of Educational Research, 29*, 664–676.

Brush, L. (1978). Preschool children's knowledge of addition and subtraction. *Journal for Research in Mathematics Education, 9*, 44–54.

Bruner, J.S. (1973). *Beyond the information given*. London: Allen & Unwin.

Bryant, D.P., Bryant, B.R., & Hammill, D.D. (2000). Characteristic behaviours of students with learning disabilities who have teacher-defined math weaknesses. *Journal of Learning Disabilities, 33*, 168–179.

Bryant, P.E. (1974). *Perception and understanding in young children: An experimental approach*. London: Methuen.

Bryant, P.E. (1985). The distinction between knowing when to do a sum and knowing how to do it. *Educational Psychology, 5*, 207–215.

Bryant, P.E. (1992). Arithmetic in the cradle. *Nature, 358*, 712–713.

Bryant, P.E. & Kopytinska, H. (1976). Spontaneous measurement by young children. *Nature, 260*, 773–774.

Bryant, P.E. & Trabasso, T. (1971). Transitive inferences and memory in young children. *Nature, 232*, 456–458.

Bryant, P.E., Christie, C., & Rendu, A. (1999). Children's understanding of the relation between addition and understanding: inversion, identity and decomposition. *Journal of Experimental Child Psychology, 74*, 194–212.

Bull, R. & Johnston, R.S. (1997). Children's arithmetical difficulties: Contributions from processing speed, item identification and short-term memory. *Journal of Experimental Child Psychology, 65*, 1–24.

Bull, R. & Scherif, G. (2001). Executive functioning as a predictor of children's mathematics ability: Inhibition, switching, and working memory. *Developmental Neuropsychology, 19*, 273–293.

Bull, R., Johnston, R.S., & Roy, J.A. (1999). Exploring the roles of the visual-spatial sketch pad and central executive in children's arithmetical skills: Views from cognition and developmental neuropsychology. *Developmental Neuropsychology, 15*, 421–442.

Bullock, M. & Gelman, R. (1977). Numerical relationships in young children: The ordering principle. *Child Development, 48*, 427–434.

Burgess, L. (1995a). *Counting: Key skills in maths for ages 5 to 7*. Oxford: Heinemann.

Burgess, L. (1995b). *Pattern: Key skills in maths for ages 5 to 7*. Oxford: Heinemann.

Buswell, G.T. & John, L. (1926). Diagnostic studies in arithmetic. *Supplementary Educational Monographs, 30*. Chicago: University of Chicago Press.

Butterworth, B. (1999). *The mathematical brain*. London: Macmillan.

Butterworth, B. (2001). What makes a prodigy? *Nature Neuroscience, 4*, 11–12.

Butterworth, B. (2002, September). *Screening for dyscalculia: A new approach*. Paper presented at the Conference on Mathematical Difficulties: Psychology, Neuroscience and Interventions, Oxford.

Butterworth, G. & Bryant, P.E. (1990). *Causes of development: Interdisciplinary mechanisms*. Hove, UK: Lawrence Erlbaum Associates Ltd.

Butterworth, B., Cipolotti, L., & Warrington, E.K. (1996). Short-term memory impairment and arithmetical ability. *Quarterly Journal of Experimental Psychology, 49A*, 251–262.

Butterworth, B., Grana, A., Piazza, M., Girelli, L., Price, C., & Skuse, D. (1999). Language and the origins of number skills: Karyotypic differences in Turner's syndrome. *Brain and Language, 69*, 486–488.

Buxton, L. (1981). *Do you panic about maths? Coping with maths anxiety*. London: Heinemann.

Buys, K. (2001). Progressive mathematization: Sketch of a learning strand. In J. Anghileri (Ed.), *Principles and practices in arithmetic teaching* (pp. 107–118). Buckingham: Open University Press.

Bynner, J. & Parsons, S. (2000). The impact of poor numeracy on employment and career progression. In C. Tikly & A. Wolf (Eds.), *The maths we need now* (pp. 26–51). London: University of London Institute of Education (Bedford Way Papers).

Bzufka, M.W., Hein, J., & Neumarker, K.J. (2000). Neuropsychological differentiation of subnormal arithmetic abilities in children. *European Child and Adolescent Psychiatry, 9*, 65–76.

Cacciatori, E., Grana, A., Girelli, L., & Semenza, C. (2000). The status of zero in the semantic system: A neuropsychological study. *Brain and Language, 74*, 414–417.

Cain-Caston, M. (1993). Parent and student attitudes toward mathematics as they relate to third grade mathematics achievement. *Journal of Instructional Psychology, 20*, 2, 96–101.

Calkins, M. (1892). A statistical study of pseudo-chromesthesia and mental forms. *American Journal of Psychology, 5*, 439–464.

Camos, V., Fayol, M., Lacert, P., Bardi, A., & Lacquiere, C. (1998). Counting in dysphasic and dyspraxic children. *A.N.A.E., 10*, 86–91.

Campbell, J. (1987). The role of associative interference in learning and retrieving arithmetic facts. In D. Rogers & J.A Sloboda (Eds.), *Cognitive processes in mathematics* (pp. 107–122). Oxford: Clarendon Press.

Campbell, J. (1994). Numerical cognition: Evidence for hyperspecific, interactive operations. *Cahiers de Psychologie Cognitive, 13,* 297–320.

Campbell, J. & Xue, Q. (2001). Cognitive arithmetic across cultures. *Journal of Experimental Psychology: General, 130,* 299–315.

Canisia, M. (1962). Mathematical ability as related to reasoning and use of symbols. *Educational and Psychological Measurement, 22,* 105–127.

Canobi, K.H., Reeve, R.A., & Pattison, P.E. (1998). The role of conceptual understanding in children's addition problem solving. *Developmental Psychology, 34,* 882–891.

Caramazza, A. & McCloskey, M. (1987). Dissociations of calculation processes. In G. Deloche & X. Seron (Eds.), *Mathematical disabilities: A cognitive neuropsychological perspective* (pp. 221–234). Hillsdale, NJ: Lawrence Erlbaum Associates, Inc..

Cardelle-Elawar, M. (1992). Effects of teaching metacognitive skills with low mathematics ability. *Teaching and Teacher Education, 8,* 109–121.

Carpenter, T.P. (1980). *Heuristic strategies used to solve addition and subtraction problems.* Paper presented at the 4th Annual Meeting of the International Group for the Psychology of Mathematics Education, Berkeley, CA.

Carpenter, T.P. (1985). Learning to add and subtract: An exercise in problem solving. In E. Silver (Ed.), *Teaching and learning mathematical problem solving: Multiple research perspectives* (pp. 17–40). Hillsdale, NJ: Lawrence Erlbaum Associates, Inc.

Carpenter, T.P. & Moser, J. (1982). The development of addition and subtraction problem solving skills. In T.P. Carpenter, J. Moser, & T. Romberg (Eds.), *Addition and subtraction: A cognitive perspective* (pp. 9–24). Hillsdale, NJ: Lawrence Erlbaum Associates, Inc.

Carpenter, T.P. & Moser, J.M. (1984). The acquisition of addition and subtraction concepts in grades one to three. *Journal for Research in Mathematics Education, 13,* 179–202.

Carpenter, T.P., Hiebert, J., & Moser, J.M. (1981). Problem structure and first-grade children's initial solution processes for simple addition and subtraction problems. *Journal for Research in Mathematics Education, 18,* 83–97.

Carpenter, T.P., Moser, J.M., & Bebout, H.C. (1988). Representation of addition and subtraction word problems. *Journal for Research in Mathematics Education, 19,* 345–357.

Carpenter, T.P., Ansell, E., Franke, M.L., Fennema, E., & Weisbeck, L. (1993). Models of problem solving: A study of kindergarten children's problem solving processes. *Journal for Research in Mathematics Education, 24,* 428–441.

Carpenter, T.P., Franke, M.L., Jacobs, V.R., Fennema, E., & Empson, S.B. (1998). A longitudinal study of invention and understanding in children's multidigit addition and subtraction. *Journal for Research in Mathematics Education, 29,* 3–20.

Carr, M. & Davis, H. (2001). Gender differences in arithmetic strategy use: A function of skill and preference. *Contemporary Educational Psychology, 26,* 330–347.

Carr, M. & Jessup, D.L. (1995). Cognitive and metacognitive predictors of mathematics strategy use. *Learning and Individual Differences, 7,* 235–247.

Carr, M. & Jessup, D.L. (1997). Gender differences in first grade mathematics strategy use: Social and metacognitive influences. *Journal of Educational Psychology, 89*, 318–328.

Carr, M., Alexander, J., & Folds-Bennett, T. (1994). Metacognition and mathematics strategy use. *Applied Cognitive Psychology, 8*, 583–595.

Carraher, T.N., Carraher, D.W., & Schliemann, A.D. (1985). Mathematics in the streets and in the schools. *British Journal of Developmental Psychology, 3*, 21–29.

Cartwright, M.L. (1955). *The mathematical mind.* The James Bryce Memorial Lecture, Somerville College, Oxford.

Casas, A.M. & Garcia Castellar, R. (2004). Mathematics education and learning disabilities in Spain. *Journal of Learning Disabilities, 37*, 62–73.

Case, R. (1998). *A psychological model of number sense and its development.* Paper presented at the Annual Meeting of the American Educational Research Association, San Diego, CA.

Case, R. & Griffin, S. (1990). Child cognitive development: The role of central conceptual structures in the development of scientific and social thought. In C.A. Hauert (Ed.), *Developmental psychology: Cognitive, perceptuo-motor and psychological perspectives.* North Holland: Elsevier.

Case, R. & Sowder, J.T. (1990). The development of computational estimation: A neo-Piagetian analysis. *Cognition and Instruction, 7*, 79–104.

Case, R., Kurland, M., & Goldberg, J. (1982). Operational efficiency and the growth of short-term memory span. *Journal of Experimental Child Psychology, 33*, 386–404.

Casey, M.B., Pezaris, E., & Nuttall, R.L. (1992). Spatial ability as a predictor of mathematical achievement: The importance of sex and handedness patterns. *Neuropsychologia, 30*, 35–45.

Casey, M.B., Nuttall, R.L., & Benbow, C.P. (1995). The importance of spatial ability on gender differences in mathematics college test scores across diverse samples. *Developmental Psychology, 31*, 697–705.

Castro-Caldas, A., Petersson, K., Reis, A., Stone-Elander, S., & Ingvar, M. (1998). The illiterate brain: Learning to read and write during childhood influences the functional organization of the adult brain. *Brain, 121*, 1053–1063.

Chang, L. (1985). Who are the mathematically gifted elementary school students? *Roeper Review, 8*, 76–79.

Cheng, P.W. (1985). Restructuring versus automaticity: Alternative accounts of skill acquisition. *Psychological Review, 92*, 414–423.

Chinn, S.J. & Ashcroft, J.R. (1998). *Mathematics for dyslexics: A teaching handbook* (2nd ed.). London: Whurr.

Chipman, S., Krantz, D., & Silver, R. (1992). Mathematics anxiety and science careers among able college women. *Psychological Science, 3*, 292–295.

Chochon, F., Cohen, L., Van de Moortele, P., & Dehaene, S. (1999). Differential contributions of the left and right inferior parietal lobules to number processing. *Journal of Cognitive Neuroscience, 11*, 617–630.

Chukovsky, K. (1983). *Ot dvukh do pyati* (p. 150). Minsk: Narodnaya Asveta.

Cipolotti, L. & Butterworth, B. (1995). Toward a multiroute model of number processing: Impaired number transcoding with preserved calculation skills. *Journal of Experimental Psychology: General, 124*, 375–390.

Cipolotti, L. & Delacycostello, A. (1995). Selective impairment for simple division. *Cortex, 31*, 433–449.

Cipolotti, L., Butterworth, B., & Denes, G. (1991). A specific deficit for numbers in a case of dense acalculia. *Brain, 114,* 2619–2637.

Cipolotti, L., Butterworth, B., & Warrington, E.K. (1994). From one thousand nine hundred and forty-five to 1000, 945. *Neuropsychologia, 32,* 503–509.

Clarke, S. (1992). Do they really know how to do it? In S. Atkinson (Ed.), *Mathematics with reason: The emergent approach to primary maths* (pp. 84–90). London: Hodder & Stoughton.

Clay, M. (1985). *The early detection of reading difficulties: A diagnostic survey with recovery procedures* (3rd ed.). Auckland, NZ: Heinemann.

Clayton, J. (1988, May). Estimation in schools. *Proceedings of the Weekend Conference of the British Society for Research into Learning Mathematics, Warwick* (pp. 9–10).

Clearfield, M.W. & Mix, K.S. (1999). Number versus contour length in infants' discrimination of small visual sets. *Psychological Science, 10,* 408–411.

Cobb, P., Yackel, E., & Wood, T. (1991). Curriculum and teacher development: Psychological and anthropological perspectives. In E. Fennema, T.P. Carpenter, & S.J. Lamon (Eds.), *Integrating research on teaching and learning mathematics* (pp. 83–120). Albany, NY: State University of New York Press.

Cockcroft, W.H. (1982). *Mathematics counts.* London: HMSO.

Cohen, L. & Dehaene, S. (1994). Amnesia for arithmetic facts: A single case study. *Brain and Language, 19,* 214–232.

Cohen, L.B. & Marks, K.S. (2002). How infants process addition and subtraction events. *Developmental Science, 5,* 186–201.

Cohen, L., Dehaene, S., Chochon, F., Lehricy, S., & Naccache, L. (2000). Language and calculation within the parietal lobe: A combined cognitive, anatomical and fMRI study. *Neuropsychologia, 38,* 1426–1440.

Cole, M., Gay, J., & Glick, J. (1968). Some experimental studies of Kpelle quantitative behaviour. *Psychonomic Monograph 2,* (10, Whole No. 26).

Collar, D.J. (1920). A statistical survey of arithmetical ability. *British Journal of Psychology, 11,* 123–158.

Connor, J.A. & Serbin, L.A. (1985). Visual-spatial skill: Is it important for mathematics? Can it be taught? In S. Chapman, L. Bush, & A. Wilson, *Women and mathematics: Balancing the equation.* New York: Lawrence Erlbaum Associates, Inc.

Cooper, R. (1984). Early number development: Discovering number space with addition and subtraction. In C. Sophian (Ed.), *Origin of cognitive skills* (pp. 157–192). Hillsdale, NJ: Lawrence Erlbaum Associates, Inc.

Cornoldi, C. & Lucangeli, D. (2004). Arithmetic education and learning disabilities in Italy. *Journal of Learning Disabilities, 37,* 42–49.

Court, S.R.A. (1920). Numbers, time and space in the first five years of a child's life. *Pedagogical Seminary, 27,* 71–89.

Cowan, R. (1979). A reappraisal of the relation between performances of quantitative identity and quantitative equivalence conservation tasks. *Journal of Experimental Child Psychology, 28,* 68–80.

Cowan, R. (1987). Assessing children's understanding of one-to-one correspondence. *British Journal of Developmental Psychology, 5,* 149–153.

Cowan, R. & Biddle, S. (1989). Children's understanding of one-to-one correspondence in the context of sharing. *Educational Psychology, 9,* 133–140.

Cowan, R. & Renton, M. (1996). Do they know what they are doing? Children's use of economical addition strategies and knowledge of commutativity. *Educational Psychology, 16*, 407–420.

Cowan, R., Dowker, A., Christakis, A., & Bailey, S. (1996). Even more precisely assessing children's understanding of the order irrelevance principle. *Journal of Experimental Child Psychology, 62*, 84–101.

Cowan, R., O'Connor, N., & Samella, K. (2003). The skills and methods of calendrical savants. *Intelligence, 31*, 51–65.

Crites, T. (1992). Skilled and less skilled estimators' strategies for estimating discrete quantities. *The Elementary School Journal, 92*, 601–619.

Cumming, J.J. & Elkins, J. (1999). Lack of automaticity in the basic addition facts as a characteristic of arithmetic learning problems and instructional needs. *Mathematical Cognition, 5*, 149–180.

Dagenbach, D. & McCloskey, M. (1992). The organisation of arithmetical facts in memory: Evidence from a brain-damaged patient. *Brain and Cognition, 20*, 343–366.

Daley, K.E. & Lefevre, J.A. (1997). *Adults' subtraction: A comparison of self-report and no self-report conditions*. Paper presented at the Annual Meeting of the Canadian Society for Brain, Behavior and Cognitive Sciences, Winnipeg, Manitoba.

Daneman, M. & Carpenter, P.A. (1980). Individual differences in working memory and reading. *Journal of Verbal Learning and Verbal Behaviour, 19*, 450–466.

Dark, V.J. & Benbow, C.P. (1990). Enhanced problem translation and short-term memory: components of mathematical talent. *Journal of Educational Psychology, 82*, 420–429.

Davenport, P. & Howe, C. (1999). Conceptual gain and successful problem-solving in primary school mathematics. *Educational Studies, 25*, 55–78.

Davie, R., Butler, N., & Goldstein, H. (1972). *From birth to seven*. London: Longman.

Davies, G.R. (1914). Elements of arithmetical ability. *Journal of Educational Psychology, 5*, 131–140.

DeAbreu, G. (1994). *The relationship between home and school mathematics in a farming community in rural Brazil*. Unpublished PhD thesis, University of Cambridge.

DeCorte, E. & Verschaffel, L. (1987). The effect of semantic structure on first graders' strategies for solving addition and subtraction word problems. *Journal for Research in Mathematics Education, 18*, 363–381.

DeCorte, E., Verschaffel, L., Janssens, V., & Joillet, L. (1984). *Teaching word problems in the first grade: A confrontation of educational practice with the results of recent research*. Paper presented at the 5th International Conference on Mathematics Education, Adelaide, Australia.

Defays, D. (1995). Numbo: A study in cognition and recognition. In D. Hofstadter, *Fluid concepts and creative analogies* (pp. 130–154). New York: Basic Books.

Dehaene, S. (1992). Varieties of numerical abilities. *Cognition, 44*, 1–42.

Dehaene, S. (1997). *The number sense*. London: Macmillan.

Dehaene, S. & Akhavein, R. (1995). Attention, automaticity and levels of representation in number processing. *Journal of Experimental Psychology: Learning, Memory and Cognition, 21*, 314–326.

Dehaene, S. & Cohen, L. (1991). Two mental calculation systems: A case study of severe acalculia with preserved approximation. *Neuropsychologia, 29*, 1045–1074.

Dehaene, S. & Cohen, L. (1995). Toward an anatomical and functional model of number processing. *Mathematical Cognition, 1*, 83–120.

Dehaene, S. & Cohen, L. (1997). Cerebral pathways for calculation: Double dissociation between rote verbal and quantitative knowledge of arithmetic. *Cortex, 33*, 219–250.

Dehaene, S. & Cohen, L. (1998). Levels of representation in number processing. In H. Whitaker & B. Stemmer (Eds.), *Handbook of Neurolinguistics* (pp. 331–341). New York: Academic Press.

Dehaene, S., Bossini, S., & Giraux, F. (1993). The mental representation of parity and numerical magnitude. *Journal of Experimental Psychology: General, 122*, 371–396.

Dehaene, S., Tzourio, N., Frank, V., Raynaud, L., Cohen, L., Mehler, J., & Mazoyer, B. (1996). Cerebral activations during number multiplication and comparison: A PET study. *Neuropsychologia, 34*, 1097–1116.

Dehaene, S., Spelke, E., Pinel, P., Stanescu, R., & Tsivkin, S. (1999). Sources of mathematical thinking: Behavioural and brain-imaging evidence. *Science, 5416*, 970–974.

Delazer, M. (2003). Neuropsychological findings on conceptual knowledge of arithmetic. In A. Baroody & A. Dowker (Eds.), *The development of arithmetical concepts and skills*. Mahwah, NJ: Lawrence Erlbaum Associates, Inc.

Delazer, M. & Bartha, L. (2001). Transcoding and calculation in aphasia. *Aphasiology, 15*, 649–679.

Delazer, M. & Benke, T. (1997). Arithmetic facts without meaning. *Cortex, 33*, 697–710.

Delazer, M. & Butterworth, B. (1997). A dissociation of number meanings. *Cognitive Neuropsychology, 14*, 613–636.

Delazer, M., Ewen, P., & Benke, T. (1997). Priming arithmetic facts in amnesic patients. *Neuropsychologica, 35*, 623–634.

Delazer, M., Girelli, L., Semenza, C., & Denes, G. (1999). Numerical skills and aphasia. *Journal of the International Neuropsychological Society, 5*, 213–221.

Delgado, A.R. & Prieto, G. (2004). Cognitive mediators and sex-related differences in mathematics. *Intelligence, 32*, 25–32.

Dellatolas, G., Von Aster, M., Willadino-Braga, L., Meier, M., & Deloche, G. (2000). Number processing and mental calculation in school children aged 7 to 10 years: A transcultural comparison. *European Child and Adolescent Psychiatry, 9* (Supplement 2), 102–110.

Deloche, G. & Seron, X. (1987). Numeral transcoding: A general production model. In G. Deloche & X. Seron (Eds.), *Mathematical disabilities: A cognitive neuropsychological model*. Hillsdale, NJ: Lawrence Erlbaum Associates, Inc.

Deloche, G., Seron, X., Larroque, C., Magnien, C., Metz-Lutz, M., Riva, I., Scils, J., Dordain, M., Ferrand, I., Baeta, E., Basso, A., Claros Salinas, D., Gaillard, E., Goldenberg, G., Howard, D., Mazzucchi, A., Tzavaras, A., Vendrell, J., Bergego, C., & Pradat-Diehl, P. (1994). Calculation and number processing: assessment battery: Role of demographic factors. *Journal of Clinical and Experimental Neuropsychology, 16*, 195–208.

Deloche, G., Souza, L., Willadino-Braga, L., & Dellatolas, G. (1999). Assessment of calculation and number processing by adults: Cognitive and neuropsychological issues. *Perceptual and Motor Skills, 89*, 707–738.

Deluka, J.W., Deldotto, J.E., & Rourke, B.P. (1987). Subtypes of arithmetic disabled children: A neuropsychological taxonomic approach. *Journal of Clinical and Experimental Neuropsychology, 9*, 26.

Demby, A. (1993). L'usage de la compensation additionnaire-soustraire et multiplier-diviser par les élèves de onze ans. *Educational Studies in Mathematics, 24*, 239–249.

Denvir, B. & Brown, M. (1986). Understanding of concepts in low attaining 7–9 year olds: Part 1: Description of descriptive framework and diagnostic instrument. *Educational Studies in Mathematics, 17*, 15–36.

Department for Education and Skills (2005). *Supporting children with gaps in their mathematical understanding*. London: DfES.

Department of Education and Science and the Welsh Office (1989). *Mathematics in the National Curriculum: Non-statutory guidelines*. London: HMSO.

Desforges, A. & Desforges, C. (1980). Number-based strategies of sharing in young children. *Educational Studies, 6*, 97–109.

Desoete, A., Roeyers, H., & De Clercq, A. (2003). Can offline metacognition enhance mathematical problem solving? *Journal of Educational Psychology, 95*, 188–200.

Desoete, A., Roeyers, H., & De Clercq, A. (2004). Children with mathematics learning disabilities in Belgium. *Journal of Learning Disabilities, 37*, 32–41.

DfEE (1999). *The National Numeracy Strategy: Framework for teaching mathematics, reception to year 6*. London: Department for Education and Employment.

Donlan, C. (1998). Number without language? Studies of children with specific language impairments. In C. Donlan (Ed.), *The development of mathematical skills* (pp. 255–274). Hove, UK: Psychology Press.

Donlan, C. (2003). Early numeracy skills in children with specific language impairment: Number system knowledge and arithmetical strategies. In A. Baroody & A. Dowker (Eds.), *The development of arithmetical concepts and skills* (pp. 337–358). Mahwah, NJ: Lawrence Erlbaum Associates, Inc.

Donlan, C. & Gourlay, S. (1999). The importance of non-verbal skills in the acquisition of place value knowledge: Evidence from normally developing and language-impaired children. *British Journal of Developmental Psychology, 17*, 1–19.

Dowker, A.D. (1989a, October). *Computational estimation by young children*. Paper presented at British Society for Research into Learning Mathematics Conference, Brighton.

Dowker, A.D. (1989b). Rhyme and alliteration in poems elicited from young children. *Journal of Child Language, 16*, 181–202.

Dowker, A.D. (1990, October). Computational estimation by young children. *Proceedings of the Day Conference of the British Society for Research into Learning Mathematics* (pp. 4–7).

Dowker, A.D. (1991). Modified repetition in poems elicited from young children. *Journal of Child Language, 18*, 625–639.

Dowker, A.D. (1992). Computational estimation strategies of professional mathematicians. *Journal for Research in Mathematics Education, 23*, 45–55.

Dowker, A.D. (1994, December). *Adults with mild specific calculation difficulties*. Paper presented at the British Psychological Society London Conference.

Dowker, A.D. (1995). Children with specific calculation difficulties. *Links, 2*, 7–12.

Dowker, A.D. (1996). How important is spatial ability to arithmetic? *Brain and Behavioural Sciences, 19*, 251.

Dowker, A.D. (1997). Young children's addition estimates. *Mathematical Cognition*, *3*, 141–154.

Dowker, A. (1998). Individual differences in arithmetical development. In C. Donlan (Ed.), *The development of mathematical skills* (pp. 275–302). London: Taylor & Francis.

Dowker, A.D. (2001). Numeracy recovery: A pilot scheme for early intervention with young children with numeracy difficulties. *Support for Learning*, *16*, 6–10.

Dowker, A.D. (2003a). Young children's estimates for addition: The zone of partial knowledge and understanding. In A. Baroody & A. Dowker (Eds.), *The development of arithmetical concepts and skills* (pp. 243–266). Mahwah, NJ: Lawrence Erlbaum Associates, Inc.

Dowker, A. (2003b). Interventions in numeracy: Individualized approaches. In I. Thompson (Ed.), *Enhancing primary school mathematics teaching and learning* (pp. 127–135). Milton Keynes: Open University Press.

Dowker, A. (2003c). Brain-based research: Implications for mathematics education. In I. Thompson (Ed.), *Enhancing primary school mathematics teaching and learning* (pp. 191–198). Milton Keynes: Open University Press.

Dowker, C.H. & Dowker, Y.N. (1979). Helping gifted children with mathematics. *Journal of the Gifted Child*, *1*, 52–66.

Dowker, A. & Lloyd, D. (in press). Linguistic influences on numeracy: The case of Welsh. In G. Roberts (Ed.), *Education Transactions B*.

Dowker, A., Heal, H., Phillips, C., & Wilson, A. (1994, September). *Developmental psychologists in the reception class: Children's ideas about age differences in abilities*. Paper presented at the British Psychological Society Developmental Section Conference.

Dowker, A., Cameron, N., & Grech, M. (1995, April). *Children's ideas about the nature and sources of age and individual differences in abilities*. Paper presented at Piaget-Vygotsky Centennial Conference.

Dowker, A.D., Cameron, N., & Grech, M. (1996a, April). *Children's ideas about the nature and sources of age and individual differences in abilities*. Paper presented at Piaget-Vygotsky Centennial Conference.

Dowker, A.D., Huke, K., & Morris, E. (1999, September). *Does calculator use inhibit mathematical reasoning?* Paper delivered at the Symposium on Mathematical Cognition, Learning and Development, British Psychological Society Developmental Section Conference.

Dowker, A.D., Flood, A., Griffiths, H., Harriss, L., & Hook, L. (1996b). Estimation strategies of four groups. *Mathematical Cognition*, *2*, 113–135.

Dowker, A.D., Dye, L., & Lowe, M. (2000, June). *Children's ideas about age differences: Is drawing different from other domains?* Paper presented at Jean Piaget Society Annual Conference.

Dowker, A., Gent, M., & Tate, L. (2001, July). *Is arithmetic a foreign language? Young children's translations between arithmetical problems in numerical, concrete and word problem formats*. Paper presented at the European Congress of Psychology, London.

Durkin, K. & Shire, B. (1988). Lexical ambiguity in mathematical contexts. In K. Durkin & B. Shire (Eds.), *Language in mathematical education: Research and practice* (pp. 71–84). Milton Keynes: Open University Press.

Durkin, K. & Shire, B. (1991). Lexical ambiguity in mathematical contexts. In

K. Durkin & B. Shire (Eds.), *Language in mathematical education: Research and practice* (pp. 71–84). Buckingham: Open University Press.

Durkin, K., Crowther, R.D., & Shire, B. (1986). Children's processing of polysemous vocabulary in school. In K. Durkin (Ed.), *Language development in the school years*. London: Croom Helm.

Duverne, S., Lemaire, P., & Michel, B.F. (2003). Alzheimer's disease disrupts fact retrieval processes but not arithmetical strategies. *Brain and Cognition, 52*, 302–318.

Edgeworth, M. & Edgeworth, R.L. (1798). *Practical education*. London: J. Johnson.

Ehlers, S., Nyden, A., Gillberg, C., Dahlgren-Sandberg, A., Dahlgren, S.O., Hjelmquist, E., & Oden, A. (1997). Asperger syndrome, autism and attention disorders: A comparative study of the cognitive profiles of 120 children. *Journal of Child Psychology and Psychiatry, 38*, 207–217.

Elkind, D. (1966). Conservation across illusory transformations in young children. *Acta Psychologica, 25*, 389–400.

Elkind, D. (1967). Piaget's conservation problems. *Child Development, 38*, 15–27.

Ellerton, N.F. (1986). Children's made-up mathematics problems: A new perspective on talented mathematicians. *Educational Studies in Mathematics, 17*, 261–271.

Ellis, N.C. (1992). Linguistic relativity revisited: The bilingual word length effect in working memory during counting, remembering numbers and mental calculation. In R.J. Harris (Ed.), *Cognitive processing in bilinguals*. Amsterdam: Elsevier Science.

Ellis, N.C. & Hennelly, R.A. (1980). A bilingual word length effect: Implications for intelligence testing and the relative ease of mental calculation in Welsh and English. *British Journal of Psychology, 71*, 43–52.

Elman, J., Bates, E.A., Johnson, M.H., Karmiloff-Smith, A., Parisi, D., & Plunkett, K. (1996). *Re-thinking innateness: A connectionist perspective on development*. Cambridge, MA: MIT Press.

El-Naggar, O. (1996). *Specific learning difficulities in mathematics: A classroom approach*. London: NASEN.

English, L. (1998). Children's problem posing within formal and informal contexts. *Journal for Research in Mathematics Education, 29*, 83–101.

Erlwanger, S. (1973). Benny's conceptions of rules and answers in IPI mathematics. *Journal of Mathematical Behaviour, 1*, 7–26.

Ernest, P. (1986). Games: A rationale for their use in the teaching of mathematics in school. *Mathematics in School, 15*, 2–5.

Errera, A., Patkin, D., & Milgrom, T. (2001). A didactics-driven intelligent tutoring system. In M. van den Heuvel-Panhuizen (Ed.), *Proceedings of the 25th Conference of the International Group of the Psychology of Mathematics Education* (pp. 401–408). Utrecht: Freudenthal Institute.

Estes, B. & Combs, A. (1966). Perception of quantity. *Journal of Genetic Psychology, 108*, 333–336.

Evans, J. (2000). *Adults' mathematical thinking and emotions: A study of numerate practices*. London: Routledge.

Ewers-Rogers, J. (2002). *Very young children's understanding and use of numbers and number symbols*. Unpublished PhD thesis, University of London, Institute of Education.

Fayol, M., Barouillet, P., & Marinthe, C. (1998). Predicting arithmetical achievement from neuropsychological performance: A longitudinal study. *Cognition, 68*, 63–70.

Fazio, B. (1994). The counting abilities of children with specific language impairments: A comparison of oral and gestural tasks. *Journal of Speech and Hearing Research, 37*, 358–368.

Fazio, B. (1996). Mathematical abilities of children with specific language impairments: A follow-up study. *Journal of Speech and Hearing Research, 39*, 839–849.

Fazio, B. (1999). Arithmetic calculation, short-term memory and language performance in children with specific language impairment: A 5-year follow-up. *Journal of Speech, Language and Hearing Research, 42*, 420–431.

Fei, H.F. (2000). Why they fall behind in math: A study of underlying cognitive factors of second-grade high-math achievers and low-math achievers in Taiwan. *Dissertation Abstracts International, 60*, 4356.

Feigenson, L., Carey, S., & Spelke, E. (2002). Infant's discrimination of number versus continuous extent. *Cognitive Psychology, 44*, 33–66.

Fennema, E. (1989). The study of affect and mathematics: A proposed generic model for research. In D.B. McLeod & V.M. Adams (Eds.), *Affect and mathematical problem solving: A new perspective* (pp. 205–219). New York: Springer-Verlag.

Fennema, E. & Peterson, P. (1985). Autonomous learning behaviour: A possible explanation of gender-related differences in mathematics. In L.C. Wilkinson & C. Marrett (Eds.), *Gender influences in classroom interaction* (pp. 17–35). Orlando, FL: Academic Press.

Fennema, E. & Sherman, J.A. (1976). The Fennema-Sherman Mathematics Attitude Scales: Instruments designed to measure attitudes to the learning of mathematics by females and males. *Journal for Research in Mathematics Education, 7*, 324–326.

Fischbein, E. & Schnarch, D. (1997). The evolution with age of probabilistic, intuitively based misconceptions. *Journal for Research in Mathematics Education, 28*, 96–105.

Fischer, J.P. (1981). Développement et fonctions du comptage chez l'enfant de 3 à 6 ans. *Recherches en Didactique des Mathematiques, 2*, 277–302.

FitzGibbon, C.T. (1981). *Time use and peer tutoring in urban secondary schools: Report for the SSRC.* Newcastle upon Tyne: University of Newcastle, School of Education.

Flansburg, S. (1993). *Math magic.* New York: Morrow.

Flavell, J. (1979). Metacognition and cognitive monitoring: A new area of cognitive-developmental research. *American Psychologist, 34*, 906–911.

Flegg, G. (Ed.) (1989). *Numbers through the ages.* London: Macmillan.

Fleischner, J.E., Garnett, K., & Shepherd, M.J. (1982). Proficiency in arithmetic basic fact computation of learning disabled and nondisabled children. *Focus on Learning Problems in Mathematics, 4*, 47–56.

Fletcher, K., Huffman, L., Bray, N., & Grupe, L. (1998). The use of the microgenetic method with children with disabilities: Discovering competence. *Early Education and Development, 9*, 357–373.

Fluck, M. & Henderson, L. (1996). Counting and cardinality in English nursery pupils. *British Journal of Educational Psychology, 66*, 501–517.

Forrester, M.A. & Pike, C.D. (1998). Learning to estimate in the mathematics classroom: A conversation-analytic approach. *Journal for Research in Mathematics Education, 29*, 334–356.

Forrester, M.A., Latham, J., & Shire, B. (1990). Exploring estimation in young primary school children. *Educational Psychology, 10*, 283–300.

Fox, L.S. (1995). Effect of practice of basic addition facts on third graders' arithmetic performance. *Dissertation Abstracts International, Section B: The Sciences and Engineering, 55*, 5586.

Foxman, D. & Beishuizen, M. (1999). Untaught mental calculation methods used by 11-year-olds: Some evidence from the APU survey in 1987. *Mathematics in School*, November.

Freeman, N., Antonucci, C., & Lewis, C. (2000). Early representation of the cardinality principle: Early conception of error in a counterfactual test. *Cognition, 74*, 71–89.

Friedman, L. (1995). The space factor in mathematics: Gender differences. *Review of Educational Research, 5*, 22–50.

Frith, U. (1986). A developmental framework for developmental dyslexia. *Annals of Dyslexia, 36*, 69–81.

Frydman, O. & Bryant, P. (1988). Sharing and the understanding of number equivalence by young children. *Cognitive Development, 3*, 323–339.

Furst, A.J. & Hitch, G.J. (2000). Separate roles for executive and phonological components of working memory in mental arithmetic. *Memory and Cognition, 28*, 774–782.

Fuson, K.C. (1982). An analysis of the counting-on procedure in addition. In T.P. Carpenter, J.M. Moser, & T.A. Romberg (Eds.), *Addition and subtraction: A cognitive perspective* (pp. 67–81). Hillsdale, NJ: Lawrence Erlbaum Associates, Inc.

Fuson, K. (1986). Roles of representation and verbalization in the teaching of multi-digit addition and subtraction. *European Journal of the Psychology of Education, 1*, 35–56.

Fuson, K. (1988). *Children's counting and concepts of number*. New York: Springer-Verlag.

Fuson, K.C. (1990). Issues in place-value and multi-digit addition and subtraction learning and teaching. *Journal for Research in Mathematics Education, 21*, 273–280.

Fuson, K. (1992). Research on whole number addition and subtraction. In D.A. Grouws (Ed.), *Handbook of research on mathematics teaching and learning* (pp. 243–275). New York: Macmillan.

Fuson, K. & Burghardt, B. (2003). Multidigit addition and subtraction methods invented in small groups and teacher support of problem solving and reflection. In A. Baroody & A. Dowker (Eds.), *The development of arithmetical concepts and skills* (pp. 267–304). Mahwah, NJ: Lawrence Erlbaum Associates, Inc.

Fuson, K. & Kwon, Y. (1992). Korean children's understanding of multi-digit addition and subtraction. *Child Development, 63*, 491–506.

Fuson, K.C. & Smith, S.T. (1997). Supporting multiple 2-digit conceptual structures and calculation methods in the classroom. In M. Beishuizen, K.P.E. Gravemeijer, & E.C.D. Van Lieshout (Eds.), *The role of contexts and models in the development of mathematical strategies and procedures* (pp. 163–198). Utrecht, The Netherlands: Freudenthal Institute.

Fuson, K., Fraivillig, J., & Burghardt, B. (1992). Relationships children construct among number words, multiunit base ten blocks and written multidigit addition. In J. Campbell (Ed.), *The nature and origins of mathematical skills* (pp. 39–112). North Holland: Elsevier Science.

Fuson, K., Wearne, D., Hiebert, J., Human, P., Murray, H., Olivier, A., Carpenter, T.P., & Fennema, E. (1997). Children's conceptual structures for multidigit numbers and methods of multidigit addition and subtraction. *Journal for Research in Mathematics Education, 28*, 130–162.

Gagne, R.M., Major, J.R., Garstens, H.L., & Paradise, N.E. (1962). Factors in acquiring knowledge of a mathematical task. *Psychological Monographs, 76*, 526.

Gaillard, F. (2000). Une analyse neurocognitive du nombre/ A neurocognitive analysis of number. *Revistsal Latiana de Pensamiento y Lenguaje, 8*, 13–32.

Galton, F. (1880). Visualized numerals. *Nature, 21*, 252–256.

Gardner, H. (1983). *Frames of mind.* London: Heinemann.

Garnett, K. (1992). Developing fluency with basic number facts: Intervention for students with learning disabilities. *Learning Disabilities Research and Practice, 7*, 210–216.

Garnett, K. & Fleischner, J.E. (1983). Automatization and basic fact performance of normal and learning disabled children. *Learning Disabilities Quarterly, 16*, 223–230.

Gathercole, S.E. & Pickering, S. (2000). Working memory deficits in children with low achievements in the national curriculum at 7 years of age. *British Journal of Educational Psychology, 70*, 177–194.

Geary, D.C. (1990). A componential analysis of an early learning deficit in mathematics. *Journal of Experimental Child Psychology, 49*, 363–383.

Geary, D.C. (1993). Mathematical disabilities: Cognitive, neuropsychological and genetic components. *Psychological Bulletin, 114*, 345–362.

Geary, D. (1996). Sexual selection and sex differences in mathematical abilities. *Behavioral and Brain Sciences, 19*, pp. 212 et seq.

Geary, D.C. & Brown, S.C. (1991a). Cognitive addition: Strategy choice and speed-of-processing differences in gifted, normal and mathematically disabled children. *Developmental Psychology, 27*, 398–406.

Geary, D.C. & Brown, S.C. (1991b). Strategy choices and speed-of-processing differences in gifted, normal and mathematically disabled children. *Developmental Psychology, 27*, 787–797.

Geary, D.C. & Hoard, M.K. (2001). Numerical and arithmetical deficits in learning-disabled children: Relation to dyscalculia and dyslexia. *Aphasiology, 15*, 635–647.

Geary, D.C. & Widaman, K.F. (1987). Individual differences in cognitive arithmetic. *Journal of Experimental Psychology: General, 116*, 154–171.

Geary, D.C. & Widaman, K.F. (1992). Numerical cognition: On the convergence of componential and psychometric models. *Intelligence, 16*, 47–80.

Geary, D.C., Widaman, K.F., Little, T.D., & Cormier, P. (1987). Cognitive addition: Comparison of learning disabled and academically normal elementary school children. *Cognitive Development, 2*, 249–269.

Geary, D.C, Brown, S.C., & Samaranayake, V.A. (1991). Cognitive addition: A short longitudinal study of strategy choice and speed-of-processing differences in normal and mathematically disabled children. *Developmental Psychology, 27*, 398–406.

Geary, D., Bow-Thomas, C., & Yao, Y. (1992). Counting knowledge and skill in cognitive addition: A comparison of normal and mathematically disabled children. *Developmental Psychology*, *27*, 787–797.

Geary, D.C., Hoard, M.K., & Hamson, C.O. (1999a). Numerical and arithmetical cognition: Patterns of functions and deficits in children at risk for a learning disability. *Journal of Experimental Child Psychology*, *74*, 213–239.

Geary, D.C., Liu, F., Chen, G.P., Saults, S.J., & Hoard, M.K. (1999b). Contributions of computational fluency to cross-national differences in arithmetical reasoning abilities. *Journal of Educational Psychology*, *91*, 716–719.

Geary, D.C., Hamson, C.O., & Hoard, M.K. (2000). Numerical and arithmetical cognition: A longitudinal study of process and concept deficits in children with learning disability. *Journal of Experimental Child Psychology*, *77*, 236–263.

Gelman, R. (1980). What young children know about numbers. *Educational Psychologist*, *15*, 54–68.

Gelman, R. (1982). Accessing one-to-one correspondence: Still another paper about conservation. *British Journal of Psychology*, *73*, 209–220.

Gelman, R. (1997). Constructing and using conceptual competence. *Cognitive Development*, *12*, 305–313.

Gelman, R. & Gallistel, C.R. (1978). *The child's understanding of number*. Cambridge, MA: Harvard University Press.

Gelman, R. & Meck, E. (1983). Preschoolers' counting: Principles before skill. *Cognition*, *13*, 343–359.

Gelman, R., Meck, E., & Merkin, S. (1986). Young children's numerical competence. *Cognitive Development*, *1*, 1–29.

Genkin, A.A. (1960, Summer). *A psychoneurological approach to the study of incapacity in mathematics*. Paper presented at the Conference on the Problem of Abilities, University of Leningrad.

Gersten, R., & Chard, D. (1999). Number sense: Rethinking arithmetic instruction for students with mathematical disabilities. *Journal of Special Education*, *44*, 18–21.

Gierl, M.J. & Bisanz, J. (1995). Anxieties and attitudes related to mathematics in grades 3 and 6. *Journal of Experimental Education*, *63*, 2, 139–158.

Gifford, S. (1997). 'When should they start doing sums?' A critical consideration of the 'emergent mathematics' approach. In I. Thompson (Ed.), *Teaching and learning early number* (pp. 75–88). Milton Keynes: Open University Press.

Gilles, P.-Y, Masse, C., & Lemaire, P. (2001). Individual differences in arithmetic strategy use. *Année Psychologique*, *101*, 9–32.

Ginsburg, H.P. (1972). Children's knowledge and individualized instruction. *Educational Technology*, 8–12.

Ginsburg, H.P. (1977). *Children's arithmetic: How they learn it and how you teach it*. New York: Teachers' College Press.

Ginsburg, H.P. (1989). *Children's arithmetic* (2nd ed.). Austin, TX: Pro-Ed.

Ginsburg, H.P. (1997). *Entering the child's mind: The clinical interview in psychological research and practice*. New York: Cambridge University Press.

Ginsburg, H.P. & Asmussen, K. (1988). Hot mathematics. *New Directions for Child Development*, *41*, 89–111.

Ginsburg, H.P. & Russell, R.L. (1981). Social class and racial influences on early mathematical thinking. *Monographs of the Society for Research in Child Development*, *46* (Serial No. 193).

Ginsburg, H.P., Choi, Y.E., Lopez, L.S., Netley, R., & Chao-Yuan, C. (1997).

Happy birthday to you: Early mathematical thinking of Asian, South American and US children. In T. Nunes & P.E. Bryant (Eds.), *Learning and teaching mathematics: An international perspective* (pp. 163–207). Hove, UK: Psychology Press.

Ginsburg, H.P., Balfanz, R., & Greenes, C. (1999). Challenging mathematics for young children' in A. Costa (Ed.), *Teaching for intelligence, II: A collection of articles*. Arlington Heights, IL: Skylight.

Girelli, L. & Delazer, M. (1996). Subtraction bugs in an acalculic patient. *Cortex*, *32*, 547–555.

Girelli, L. & Seron, X. (2001). Rehabilitation of number processing and calculation skills. *Aphasiology*, *15*, 695–712.

Goldin, G.A. (1982). Mathematical language and problem-solving. In R. Skemp (Ed.), Understanding the symbolism of mathematics. *Visible Language*, *16* (Special Issue), 221–238.

Goldin, G.A. (1987). Cognitive representational systems for mathematical problem solving. In C. Janvier (Ed.), *Problems of representation in the teaching and learning of mathematics* (pp. 125–145). Hillsdale, NJ: Lawrence Erlbaum Associates, Inc.

Goldin, G.A. & Kaput, J. (1996). A joint perspective on the idea of representation in learning and doing mathematics. In L.P. Steffe, P. Nesher, P. Cobb, G.A. Goldin, & J. Greer (Eds.), *Theories of mathematical learning* (pp. 397–430). Hillsdale, NJ: Lawrence Erlbaum Associates, Inc.

Goldin-Meadow, S., Alibali, M., & Church, R. (1993). Transitions in concept acquisition: Using the hand to read the mind. *Psychological Review*, *100*, 279–297.

Goldin-Meadow, S., Nusbaum, H., Kelly, S.D., & Wagner, S. (2001). Explaining math: Gesturing lightens the load. *Psychological Science*, *12*, 516–522.

Goldman, J. (1965). *Brave new school*. London: Hodder & Stoughton.

Gonzalez, J.E.J. & Espinel, A.I.G. (1999). Is IQ-achievement discrepancy relevant in the definition of arithmetic-learning difficulties? *Learning Disability Quarterly*, 291–301.

Gopnik, M. (1992). When language is a problem. In R. Campbell (Ed.), *Mental lives: Case studies in cognition* (pp. 61–83). Oxford: Blackwell.

Gottesman, M. (1973). Conservation development in blind children. *Child Development*, *44*, 824–827.

Grafman, J., Kampen, D., Rosenberg, J., Salazar, A., & Boller, F. (1989). Calculation abilities in a patient with a virtual left hemispherectomy. *Behavioral Neurology*, *2*, 183–194.

Graham, D.J. & Campbell, J.I. (1992). Network interference and number-fact retrieval: Evidence from children's alphaplication. *Canadian Journal of Psychology*, *46*, 65–91.

Grauberg, E. (1998). *Elementary mathematics and language difficulties*. London: Whurr.

Gray, C. & Mulhern, G. (1995). Does children's memory for addition facts predict general mathematical ability? *Perceptual and Motor Skills*, *81*, 163–167.

Gray, E. (1991). An analysis of diverging approaches to simple arithmetic: Preference and its consequences. *Educational Studies in Mathematics*, *22*, 551–574.

Gray, E. (1997). Compressing the counting process: Developing a flexible interpretation of symbols. In I. Thompson (Ed.), *Teaching and learning early number* (pp. 63–72). Buckingham: Open University Press.

Gray, E. & Tall, D. (1994). Duality, ambiguity and flexibility: A proceptual view of simple arithmetic. *Journal for Research in Mathematics Education, 25,* 115–144.

Gréco, P. (1962). Quantité et quotité: Nouvelles recherches sur la correspondance terme-à-terme et la conservation des ensembles. In P. Gréco & A. Morf (Eds.), *Structures numériques élémentaires. Études d'épistémologie génétique* (Vol. 13, pp. 1–70). Paris: PUF.

Greeno, T., Riley, M., & Gelman, R. (1984). Young children's counting and understanding of principles. *Cognitive Psychology, 16,* 94–143.

Greene, C.E. & Buswell, G.T. (1930). Testing, diagnosis and remedial work in arithmetic. *Yearbook of the National Society for the Study of Education, 1930, Part 1,* 269–319.

Greer, B. (1987). Understanding of arithmetical operations as models of situations. In J. Sloboda & D. Rogers (Eds.), *Cognitive processes in mathematics* (pp. 60–80). Oxford: Oxford University Press.

Greer, B. (1996). Theories of mathematics education: The role of cognitive analyses. In L. Steffe, P. Nesher, P. Cobb, G. Goldin, & B. Greer (Eds.), *Theories of mathematical learning* (pp. 179–217). Mahwah, NJ: Lawrence Erlbaum Associates, Inc.

Gregory, A., Snell, J., & Dowker, J. (1999, September). *Young children's attitudes to mathematics: A cross-cultural study.* Paper presented at the Conference on Language, Reasoning and Early Mathematical Development, University College London.

Greiffenstein, M.F. & Baker, J.W. (2002). Neuropsychological and psychosocial correlates of adult arithmetic deficiency. *Neuropsychology, 16,* 451–458.

Griffin, S., Case, R., & Sandieson, R. (1992). Synchrony and asynchrony in the development of elementary mathematical knowledge: Toward a representational theory of children's intellectual growth. In R. Case (Ed.), *The mind's staircase: Exploring the central underpinnings of children's theory and knowledge.* Hillsdale, NJ: Lawrence Erlbaum Associates, Inc.

Griffin, S., Case, R., & Siegler, R (1994). Rightstart: Providing the central conceptual prerequisites for first formal learning of arithmetic to students at risk for school failure. In K. McGilly (Ed.), *Classroom learning: Integrating cognitive theory and classroom practice.* Boston: MIT Press.

Groen, G.J. & Parkman, J.M. (1972). A chronometric analysis of simple addition. *Psychological Review, 79,* 329–343.

Grossman, A.S. (1983). Decimal notation: An important research finding. *Arithmetic Teacher, 30,* 32–33.

Gross-Tsur, V., Manor, O., & Shalev, R. (1996). Developmental dyscalculia: prevalence and democratic features. *Developmental Medicine and Child Neurology, 38,* 25–33.

Gruber, O., Indefrey, P., Steinmetz, H., & Kleinschmidt, A. (2001). Dissociating neural correlates of cognitive components in mental calculation. *Cerebral Cortex, 11,* 350–369.

Gupta, K. (1932). A few hints on the teaching of mathematics. *Indian Journal of Psychology, 7,* 75–86.

Hadamard, J. (1945). *The psychology of invention in the mathematical field.* Princeton, NJ: Princeton University Press.

Haier, R.J. (2001). PET studies of learning and individual differences. In J. McClelland & R. Siegler (Eds.), *Mechanisms of cognitive development* (pp. 123–148). Mahwah, NJ: Lawrence Erlbaum Associates, Inc.

Hanich, L.B., Jordan, N.C., Kaplan, D., & Dick, J. (2001). Performance across different areas of mathematical cognition in children with learning difficulties. *Journal of Educational Psychology*, *93*, 615–626.

Harlen, W. & Malcolm, H. (1999). *Setting and streaming: A research review* (Rev. ed.). Edinburgh: Scottish Council for Research in Education.

Hart, K. (1981). The hierarchies. In K. Hart & CSMS Maths Team (Eds.), *Children's understanding of mathematics 11–16* (pp. 187–207). London: John Murray.

Hart, K. (1989). There is little connection. In P. Ernest (Ed.), *Mathematics teaching: The state of the art* (pp. 138–142). London: Falmer.

Hartje, W. (1987). The effect of spatial disorders on arithmetical skills. In G. Deloche & X. Seron (Eds.), *Mathematical disabilities: A cognitive neuropsychological perspective* (pp. 121–136). Hillsdale, NJ: Lawrence Erlbaum Associates, Inc.

Hartnett, P. & Gelman, R. (1998). Early understandings of numbers: Paths or barriers to the construction of new understandings. *Learning and Instruction, 8*, 341–374.

Hatano, G. (1988). Social and motivational bases for mathematical understanding. In G.B. Saxe & M. Gearhart (Eds.), *Children's mathematics*. Hillsdale, NJ: Lawrence Erlbaum Associates, Inc.

Hatano, G., Miyake, Y., & Binks, M.G. (1977). Performance of expert abacus operators. *Cognition, 5*, 47–55.

Hativa, N. (1988). Sigal's ineffective computer-based practice of arithmetic: A case study. *Journal for Research in Mathematics Education, 19*, 195–214.

Haylock, D. (2001). *Mathematics explained for primary teachers* (2nd ed.). London: Paul Chapman.

Heath, S.B. (1983). *Ways with words: Language, life and work in communities and classrooms*. Cambridge: Cambridge University Press.

Heavey, L (2003). Arithmetical savants. In A. Baroody & A. Dowker (Eds.), *The development of arithmetical concepts and skills* (pp. 409–434). Mahwah, NJ: Lawrence Erlbaum Associates, Inc.

Hecht, S. (1998). Toward an information processing account of individual differences in fraction skills. *Journal of Educational Psychology, 15*, 545–589.

Hecht, S.A. (2002). Counting on working memory in simple arithmetic when counting is used for problem solving. *Memory and Cognition, 30*, 447–455.

Hembree, R, (1990). The nature, effects and relief of mathematics anxiety. *Journal for Research in Mathematics Education, 21*, 33–46.

Hembree, R. & Dessart, D.J. (1992). Research on calculators in mathematics education. In J. Fey & C. Hirsch (Eds.), *Calculators in mathematics education* (pp. 23–32). Reston, VA: National Council of Teachers of Mathematics.

Henry, L. & Maclean, M. (2003). Relationships between working memory, expressive vocabulary and arithmetical reasoning in children with and without intellectual disabilities. *Educational and Child Psychology, 20*, 3, 51–64.

Hermelin, B. (2001). *Bright splinters of the mind: A personal story of research with autistic savants*. London: Jessica Kingsley.

Hermelin, B. & O'Connor, N. (1986). Spatial representations in mathematically and in artistically gifted children. *British Journal of Educational Psychology, 56,* 150–157.

Hermelin, B. & O'Connor, N. (1991). Factors and primes: A specific numerical ability. *Psychological Medicine, 20,* 163–169.

Herndon, J. (1971). *How to survive in your native land.* New York: Simon and Schuster.

Hickok, G., Bellugi, U., & Klima, E. (1998). The neural organization of language: Evidence from sign language aphasia. *Trends in Cognitive Sciences, 4,* 129–136.

Hiebert, J. & Carpenter, T.P. (1982). Piagetian tasks as readiness measures in mathematics instruction: A critical review. *Educational Studies in Mathematics, 13,* 329–345.

Hiebert, J. & Lefevre, P. (1986). Conceptual and procedural knowledge in mathematics: An introductory analysis. In J. Hiebert (Ed.), *Conceptual and procedural knowledge: The case of mathematics* (pp. 1–7). Hillsdale, NJ: Lawrence Erlbaum Associates, Inc.

Hiebert, J. & Wearne, D. (1992). Links between teaching and learning place value with understanding in first grade. *Journal for Research in Mathematics Education, 23,* 98–122.

Hiebert, J., Carpenter, T.P., & Moser, J.M. (1982). Cognitive development and children's solutions to verbal arithmetic problems. *Journal for Research in Mathematics Education, 13,* 83–98.

Hitch, G. (1978). The role of short-term working memory in arithmetic. *Cognitive Psychology, 10,* 302–310.

Hitch, G. & McAuley, E. (1991). Working memory in children with specific arithmetical learning difficulties. *British Journal of Psychology, 82,* 375–386.

Hittmair-Delazer, M., Semenza, L., & Denes, G. (1994). Concepts and facts in calculation. *Brain, 117,* 715–728.

Hittmair-Delazer, M., Sailer, V., & Berke, T. (1995). Impaired arithmetical facts but intact conceptual knowledge: A single case study of dyscalculia. *Cortex, 31,* 139–147.

Ho, H., Senturk, D., Lam, A.G., Zimmer, J.M., Hong, S., Okamoto, Y., Chiu, S., Nakazawa, Y., & Peng, C. (2000). The affective and cognitive dimensions of math anxiety: A cross-national study. *Journal for Research in Mathematics Education, 31,* 362–379.

Hoard, M., Geary, D., & Hamson, C. (1999). Numerical and arithmetical cognition: Performance of low and average IQ children. *Mathematical Cognition, 5,* 65–91.

Hoffer, T.B. (1992). Middle school ability grouping and student achievement in science and mathematics. *Educational Evaluation and Policy Analysis, 14,* 205–227.

Hofstadter, D. (1982). Metamagical themas: Number numbness, or why innumeracy may be just as dangerous as illiteracy. *Scientific American, 246,* 16–23.

Hollamby, L. (1962). *Young children living and learning.* London: Longman.

Holt, J. (1965). *How children fail.* Harmondsworth: Penguin.

Holt, J. (1966). *How children fail.* New York: Pitman.

Hone, K. (1990). *Young children's representations of word problems.* Unpublished undergraduate research project, University of Oxford.

Hook, L. (1992). *Estimation strategies of psychology students.* Unpublished undergraduate research project, University of Oxford.

Hooper, F. (1969). Piaget's conservation tasks: The logical and developmental priority of identity conservation. *Journal of Experimental Child Psychology*, *8*, 234–249.

Hope. J.A. (1987). A case study of a highly skilled mental calculator. *Journal for Research in Mathematics Education*, *18*, 331–342.

Hope, J.A. & Sherrill, J.M. (1987). Characteristics of unskilled and skilled mental calculators. *Journal for Research in Mathematics Education*, *18*, 98–111.

Hopkins, L. (1997a). *Platform Maths 1*. Bath: Leopard Learning.

Hopkins, L. (1997b). *Platform Maths 2*, Bath: Leopard Learning.

Hough, M.S. (1990). Narrative comprehension in adults with right and left hemisphere damage. *Brain and Language*, *38*, 253–275.

Houssart, J. (2001). Counting difficulties at Key Stage 2. *Support for Learning*, *16*, 11–16.

Howe, M.J. (1990). *The origins of exceptional abilities*. Oxford: Blackwell.

Hughes, M. (1986). *Children and number*. Oxford: Blackwell.

Hughes, M., Desforges, C., & Mitchell, C. (2000). *Numeracy and beyond: Applying mathematics in the primary school*. Milton Keynes: Open University Press.

Hunter, I. (1962). An exceptional talent for calculative thinking. *British Journal of Psychology*, *53*, 243–258.

Huntley-Fenner, G. & Cannon, E. (2000). Preschoolers' magnitude comparisons are mediated by a preverbal analog magnitude mechanism. *Psychological Science*, *11*, 147–152.

Hutton, L.A. & Levitt, E. (1987). An academic approach to the remediation of mathematics anxiety. In H. Van de Ploeg, M. Henk, & R. Schwarzer (Eds.), *Advances in test anxiety research* (Vol. 5, pp. 207–211). Berwyn, PA: Swets North America.

Hyde, J.S., Fennema, E., & Lamon, S.J. (1990a). Gender differences in mathematics performance: A meta-analysis. *Psychological Bulletin*, *107*, 139–155.

Hyde, J.S., Fennema, E., Ryan, M., Frost, L.A., & Hopp, C. (1990b). Gender comparisons of mathematics attitudes and affect: A meta-analysis. *Psychology of Womenly Quarterly*, 14, 299–324.

Ilg, F. & Ames, L.B. (1951). Developmental trends in arithmetic. *Journal of Genetic Psychology*, *79*, 3–28.

Ireson, J. & Hallam, S. (2001). *Ability grouping in education*. London: Chapman.

Isaacs, E.B., Edmonds, C.J., Lucas, A., & Gadian, D.G. (2001). Calculation difficulties of children with very low birthweight: A neural correlate. *Brain*, *124*, 1701–1707.

Ishida, J. & Koyasu, M. (1988). The effect of problem structure upon choosing operations and making up stories in word arithmetic problems. *Science Education*, *12*, 14–21.

Ittyerah, M. & Samarapungavan, A. (1989). The performance of congenitally blind children in cognitive developmental tasks. *British Journal of Developmental Psychology*, *7*, 129–139.

Iverson, J.M. & Goldin-Meadow, S. (1997). What's communication got to do with it? Gesture in children blind from birth. *Developmental Psychology*, *33*, 453–467.

Jackson, M. & Warrington, E.K. (1986). Arithmetic skills in patients with unilateral lesions. *Cortex*, *22*, 611–620.

Jarvis, H.L. & Gathercole, S.E. (2003). Verbal and non-verbal working memory and achievements on National Curriculum tests at 11 and 14 years of age. *Educational and Child Psychology*, *20*, 3, 123–139.

Jimenez, J.E. & Garcia, A.I. (2002). Strategy choice in solving problems: Are there differences between students with learning difficulties, G-V performance, and typical achievement students? *Learning Disability Quarterly, 25*, 113–122.

Johnson, D.C. (1979). Teaching estimation and reasonableness of results. *Arithmetic Teacher, 27*, 34–35.

Johnson, M.H. (2000). Functional brain development in infants: Elements of an interactive specialization framework. *Child Development, 71*, 75–81.

Jones, K. & Wakefield, P. (1999). How many all together? Peer support in mathematics at Key Stages 1 and 2. *Support for Learning, 13*, 65–69.

Jordan, N.C. & Hanich, L.B. (2000). Mathematical thinking in second grade children with different forms of LD. *Journal of Learning Disabilities, 33*, 567–578.

Jordan, N.C. & Montani, T.O. (1997). Cognitive arithmetic and problem solving: A comparison of children with specific and general mathematics difficulties. *Journal of Learning Disabilities, 30*, 624–634.

Jordan, N., Huttenlocher, J., & Levine, S.C. (1992). Differential calculation abilities in young children from middle and low income families. *Developmental Psychology, 28*, 644–653.

Jordan, N., Huttenlocher, J., & Levine, S.C. (1994a). Assessing early arithmetic abilities: Effects of verbal and nonverbal response types on the calculation performance of middle and low income children. *Learning and Individual Differences, 6*, 413–442.

Jordan, N.C., Levine, S.C., & Huttenlocher, J. (1994b). Development of calculation abilities in middle and low income children after formal instruction in school. *Journal of Applied Developmental Psychology, 15*, 223–240.

Jordan, N.C., Hanich, L., & Uberti, H.Z. (2003). Mathematical thinking and learning difficulties. In A. Baroody & A. Dowker (Eds.), *The development of arithmetical concepts and skills* (pp. 359–383). Mahwah, NJ: Lawrence Erlbaum Associates, Inc.

Judd, C.H. (1927). Psychological analysis of the fundamentals of arithmetic. *Supplementary Educational Monographs, 31*, 121.

Judd, T.P. & Bilsky, L.H. (1989). Comprehension and memory in the solution of verbal arithmetic problems by mentally retarded and nonretarded individuals. *Journal of Educational Psychology, 81*, 541–546.

Kamii, C. (1985). *Young children reinvent arithmetic: Implications of Piaget's theory.* New York: Teachers' College Press.

Karmiloff-Smith, A. (1991). Beyond modularity: Innate constraints and developmental theory. In S. Carey & R. Gelman (Eds.), *The epigenesis of mind: Essays on biology and cognition.* Hillsdale, NJ: Lawrence Erlbaum Associates, Inc.

Karmiloff-Smith, A. (1998). Is atypical development necessarily a window on the normal mind/brain?: The case of Williams syndrome. *Developmental Science, 1*, 273–277.

Kaufman, A.S. (1994). *Intelligent testing with the WISC-III.* New York: John Wiley & Sons.

Kaufmann, L., Handl, P., & Thony, B. (2003). Evaluation of a numeracy intervention program focusing on basic numerical knowledge and conceptual knowledge: A pilot study. *Journal of Learning Disabilities, 36*, 564–573.

Kaufmann, L., Montanes, P., Jacquier, M., Matallana, D., Eibl, G., & Delazer, M. (2002). About the relationship between basic numerical processing and arithmetic in early Alzheimer's disease: A follow-up study. *Brain and Cognition, 48*, 398–405.

Kaufmann, L., Pohl, R., Semenza, C., & Delazer, M. (2003). About the effectiveness of a specific numeracy program in kindergarten children: A pilot study. *Journal of Learning Disabilities*.

Kay, J. & Yeo, D. (2003). *Dyslexia and maths*. London: Fulton.

Kaye, D., Post, T., Hall, V., & Dineen, J. (1986). Emergence of information-retrieval strategies in numerical cognition: A developmental study. *Cognition and Instruction*, *3*, 127–150.

Kazui, H., Kitagaki, H., & Mori, E. (2000). Cortical activation during retrieval of arithmetical facts and actual calculation: A functional magnetic resonance imaging study. *Psychiatry and Clinical Neurosciences*, *54*, 479–485.

Kearins, J. (1988). Number experience and performance in Australian Aboriginal and Western children. In K. Durkin & B. Shire (Eds.), *Language in mathematical education: Research and practice* (pp. 247–255). Milton Keynes: Open University Press.

Kearins, J. (1991). Number experience and performance in Australian Aboriginal and Western children. In K. Durkin & B. Shire (Eds.), *Language in mathematical education: Research and practice* (pp. 247–255). Buckingham: Open University Press.

Keeler, M.L. & Swanson, H.L. (2001). Does strategy knowledge influence working memory in children with mathematical disabilities? *Journal of Learning Disabilities*, *34*, 418–434.

Kennedy, W.A., Willcutt, H., & Smith, A. (1963). Wechsler profiles of mathematically gifted adolescents. *Psychological Reports*, *12*, 259–262.

Keogh, B.K., Major, S.M., Reid, H.P., Gandara, P., & Omari, H. (1978). Marker variables: A search of comparability and generalizability in the field of learning disabilities. *Learning Disabilities Quarterly*, *1*, 5–11.

Keogh, B.K., Major, S.M., Omari, H., Gandara, P., & Reid, H.P. (1980). Proposal for markers in learning disabilities research. *Journal of Abnormal Child Psychology*, *8*, 21–31.

Kerkman, D. & Siegler, R.S. (1993). Individual differences in adaptive flexibility in lower income children's strategy choices. *Learning and Individual Differences*, *5*, 113–136.

Kerkman, D. & Siegler, R.S. (1997). Measuring individual differences in children's addition strategy choices. *Learning and Individual Differences*, *9*, 1–18.

Kiefer, M., Abel, A., & Weisbrod, A. (2002). Arithmetic fact retrieval and working memory in schizophrenia. *Schizophrenia Research*, *53*, 219–227.

Kiessling, L., Denckla, M., & Carlton, M. (1983). Evidence of differential hemispheric function in children with hemiplegic cerebral palsy. *Developmental Medicine and Child Neurology*, *25*, 727–734.

Kilpatrick, J., Swafford, J., & Findell, B. (Eds.) (2002). *Adding it up: Helping children learn mathematics*. Washington, DC: National Academies Press.

Kinoshita, Y. (1989). Developmental changes in understanding the limitations of majority decisions. *British Journal of Developmental Psychology*, *7*, 97–112.

Kintsch, W. & Greeno, J. (1985). Understanding and solving word arithmetic problems. *Psychological Review*, *92*, 109–129.

Kirkby, D. (1992). *Games in the teaching of mathematics*. Cambridge: Cambridge University Press.

Kirkpatrick, E.A. (1908). *Fundamentals of child study*. New York: Macmillan.

Klein, J.S. & Bisanz, J. (2000). Preschoolers doing arithmetic: The concepts are willing but the working memory is weak. *Canadian Journal of Experimental Psychology*, *54*, 105–116.

Knopnik, V.S., Alarcon, M., & DeFries, J.C. (1997). Comorbidity of mathematics and reading deficits; Evidence for a genetic etiology. *Behavior Genetics*, *27*, 447–453.

Kobayashi, T., Hiraki, K., Mugitani, R., & Hasegawa, T. (2004). Baby arithmetic: One object plus one tone. *Cognition*, *91*, 23–34.

Koloto, A. (1995). *Estimation in Tongan schools*. Unpublished PhD thesis, University of Waikato, New Zealand.

Kolshy, V. (2001). *Teaching mathematics to able children*. London: David Fulton.

Kolubya, M.M. & Glencross, M.J. (1997). Mathematics and attitudes of senior secondary school students in Transkei, South Africa. *Psychological Reports*, *80*, 915–919.

Kosc, L. (1974). Developmental dyscalculia. *Journal of Learning Disabilities*, *7*, 165–171.

Kroesbergen, E. & Van Luit, J. (2003). Mathematics interventions for children with special educational needs: A meta-analysis. *Remedial and Special Education*, *24*, 97–114.

Krutetskii, V.A. (1968). *The psychology of mathematical abilities in schoolchildren* (J. Teller trans., J. Kilpatrick & I. Wirzsup (Eds.), 1976). Chicago: University of Chicago Press.

Krutetskii, V.A. (1976). *The psychology of mathematical abilities in schoolchildren*. London: University of Chicago Press.

Kurdek, L.A. & Sinclair, R.J. (2001). Predicting reading and mathematics achievement in fourth-grade children from kindergarten readiness scores. *Journal of Educational Psychology*, *93*, 451–455.

Kyttala, M., Aunio, P., Lehto, J.E., Van Luit, J., & Hautamaki, J. (2003). Visuo-spatial working memory and early numeracy. *Educational and Child Psychology*, *20*, 3, 65–76.

Lancy, D. (1983). *Cross-cultural studies in cognition and mathematics*. New York: Academic Press.

Lankford, F.G. (1974). What can a teacher learn about a pupil's thinking through oral interviews? *Arithmetic Teacher*, *21*, 26–32.

Lane, S. (1993). *Arithmetical strategies in blind children*. Unpublished undergraduate project, Oxford University.

Lave, J. (1988). *Cognition in action*. Cambridge: Cambridge University Press.

Lave, J., Murtagh, M., & de la Rocha, O. (1984). The dialectic of arithmetic in grocery shopping. In B. Rogoff & J. Lave (Eds.), *Everyday cognition: Its development in social context*. Cambridge, MA: Harvard University Press.

Lawler, R.W. (1985). *Computer experience and cognitive development: A child's learning in a computer culture*. New York: John Wiley & Sons.

Lee, K.M. & Kang, S.Y. (2002). Arithmetic operation and working memory: Differential suppression in dual tasks. *Cognition*, *83*, 63–68.

Lefevre, J.A. & Kulak, A.G. (1994). Individual differences in the obligatory activation of addition facts. *Memory and Cognition*, *22*, 188–200.

Lefevre, J.A., Kulak, A.G., & Heymans, S.L. (1992). Factors influencing selection of university majors varying in mathematical content. *Canadian Journal of Psychology*, *24*, 276–289.

Lefevre, J.A., Greenham, S.L., & Waheed, N. (1993). The development of procedural and conceptual knowledge in computational estimation. *Cognition and Instruction, 11*, 95–132.

Lefevre, J.A., Bisanz, J., Daley, K.E., Buffone, L., Greenham, S.L., & Sadesky, G.S. (1996a). Multiple routes to solution of single-digit multiplication problems. *Journal of Experimental Psychology: General, 123*, 284–306.

Lefevre, J.A., Sadesky, G.S., & Bisanz, J. (1996b). Selection of procedures in mental addition: Re-assessing the problem-size effect in adults. *Journal of Experimental Psychology: Learning, Memory and Cognition, 22*, 216–230.

Lefevre, J.A., Smith-Chant, B., Hiscock, K., Daley, K., & Morris, J. (2003). Young adults' strategies in simple arithmetic: Implications for the development of mathematical representation. In A. Baroody & A. Dowker (Eds.), *The development of arithmetical concepts and skills* (pp. 203–228). Mahweh, NJ: Lawrence Erlbaum Associates, Inc.

Lehmann, W. & Juling, I. (2002). Spatial reasoning and mathematical abilities: Independent constructs or two sides of the same coin? *Psychologie in Erziehung und Unterricht, 49*, 31–43.

Lehr, M. (1953). Foreword. In C. Stern, *Children discover arithmetic: An introduction to structural arithmetic*. London: Harrup & Co.

Lemaire, P. & Fayol, M. (1995). When plausibility judgements supersede fact retrieval: The example of the odd-even effect on product verification. *Memory and Cognition, 23*, 34–48.

Lemaire, P., Barrett, S.E., Fayol, M., & Abdi, H. (1994). Automatic activation of addition and multiplication facts in elementary school children. *Journal of Experimental Child Psychology, 57*, 224–258.

Lemaire, P., Lecacheur, M., & Farioli, F. (2000). Children's strategy use in computational estimation. *Canadian Journal of Psychology, 54*, 141–148.

Lemoyne, G. & Favreau, M. (1981). Piaget's concept of number development: Its relation to mathematics learning. *Journal for Research in Mathematics Education, 12*, 179–190.

Lepper, M.R. & Gurtner, J.L. (1989). Children and computers: Approaching the twenty-first century. *American Psychologist, 44*, 170–178.

Leslie, A.M. (2000). 'Theory of mind' as a mechanism of selective attention. In M.S. Gazzaniga (Ed.), *The new cognitive neurosciences* (pp. 1235–1248). Cambridge, MA: MIT Press.

Lester, F.K. (1984). Preparing teachers to teach rational numbers. *Arithmetic Teacher, 31*, 54–56.

Levin, H.H., Glass, G.V., & Meister, G.R. (1984). *Cost effectiveness of four educational interventions: Project report No. 84A11*. Stanford: Stanford University Institute for Research on Educational Finance and Governance.

Levine, D.R. (1982). Strategy use and estimation of college students. *Journal for Research in Mathematics Education, 13*, 350–359.

Levine, M.D., Lindsay, R.L., & Reed, M.S. (1992). The wrath of math: Deficiencies of mathematical mastery in the school child. *Pediatric Clinics of North America, 39*, 526–536.

Levitin, D.J. & Bellugi, I. (1998). Musical abilities in individuals with Williams syndrome. *Music Perception, 15*, 357–389.

Levitt, E.E. & Hutton, L.A. (1983). Correlates and possible causes of mathematics anxiety. In C.D. Spielberger & H. Butcher (Eds.), *Advances in personality assessment* (Vol. 3, pp. 129–140). Hillsdale, NJ: Lawrence Erlbaum Associates, Inc.

Lewis, C. (1981). Skill in algebra. In J.R. Anderson (Ed.), *Cognitive skills and their acquisition*. Hillsdale, NJ: Lawrence Erlbaum Associates, Inc.

Lewis, C., Hitch, G.J., & Walker, P. (1994). The prevalence of specific arithmetical difficulties in 9- to 10-year-old boys and girls. *Journal of Child Psychology and Psychiatry, 35*, 283–292.

Lindsay, R.L. (2001). Attentional function as measured by a continuous performance task in children with dyscalculia. *Journal of Developmental and Behavioural Pediatrics, 22*, 287–292.

Lindvall, C.M. & Ibarra, C.G. (1982). Incorrect procedures used by primary grade pupils in solving open addition and subtraction problems. *Journal for Research in Mathematics Education, 11*, 50–62.

Locke, J. (1690). *An essay concerning human understanding*. London.

Long, L (1996). *Domino 1,2,3: A counting book*. London: Franklin Watts.

Lou, Y., Abrami, P.C., Spence, J.C., Poulsen, C., Chambers, B., & D'Appolinia, S. (1996). Within-class grouping: A meta-analysis. *Review of Educational Research, 66*, 423–458.

Lubinski, D. & Humphreys, L.G. (1991). A broadly based analysis of mathematical giftedness. *Intelligence, 14*, 327–355.

Lucangeli, D., Coi, G., & Bosco, P. (1997). Metacognitive awareness in good and poor math problem solvers. *Learning Disabilities Research and Practice, 12*, 209–212.

Lucangeli, D., Cornoldi, C., & Tellarini, M. (1998). Metacognition and learning difficulties in mathematics. In T. Scruggs & M. Mastropieri (Eds.), *Advances in learning and behavioural disabilities* (Vol. 12, pp. 219–244). Stamford, CT: JAI Press.

Luchelli, F. & Derenzi, E. (1993). Primary dyscalculia after a medial frontal lesion of the left hemisphere. *Journal of Neurology, Neurosurgery and Psychiatry, 56*, 304–307.

Lummis, M. & Stevenson, H.W. (1990). Gender differences in beliefs and achievement: A cross-cultural study. *Developmental Psychology, 26*, 254–263.

Lynn, R. & Gault, A. (1986). The relation of musical ability to general intelligence and the major primaries. *Research in Education, 36*, 59–64.

Ma, L. (1998). *Knowing and teaching elementary mathematics: Teachers' understanding of mathematics in China and the United States*. Mahwah, NJ: Lawrence Erlbaum Associates, Inc.

Ma, X. (1999). A meta-analysis of the relationship between anxiety toward mathematics and achievement in mathematics. *Journal for Research in Mathematics, 30*, 520–540.

Ma, X. & Kishor, N. (1997). Assessing the relationship between attitude toward mathematics and achievement in mathematics: A meta-analysis. *Journal for Research in Mathematics Education, 28*, 26–47.

Macaruso, P. & Sokol, S.M. (1998). Cognitive neuropsychology and developmental dyscalculia. In C. Donlan (Ed.), *The development of mathematical skills* (pp. 201–225). Hove, UK: Psychology Press.

MacCuish, N. (1986). Children's conceptions of multiplication. *Proceedings of the 10th International Conference on the Psychology of Mathematics Education* (pp. 49–54). London: PME 10.

Mackintosh, N.J. (1998). *IQ and human intelligence*. London: Oxford University Press.

Maclean, M. & Whitburn, J. (1996, August). *Number name systems and children's early number knowledge: A comparison of Welsh and English speakers*. Paper presented at the XVIth Biennial ISSBD Conference, Quebec City.

Madell, R. (1982). Children's natural processes. *Arithmetic Teacher, 32*, 20–22.

Maguire, T. (1971). Evaluation of the IPI project. *Alberta Journal of Educational Research, 17*, 255–273.

Mandler, G. & Szebo, B.J. (1982). Subitizing: An analysis of its component processes. *Journal of Experimental Psychology: General, 111*, 1–22.

Maqsud, M. (1998). Effects of metacognitive instruction on mathematics achievement and attitude toward mathematics of low mathematics achievers. *Educational Research, 40*, 237–243.

Markowits, Z. & Sowder, J. (1994). Developing number sense: An intervention in Grade 7. *Journal for Research in Mathematics Education, 25*, 4–29.

Marshall, R.M., Schafer, V.A., O'Donnell, L., & Elliott, J. (2000). Developmental cognitive neuropsychology of number processing and calculation: Varieties of developmental dyscalculia. *European Child and Adolescent Psychiatry, 9*, 41–57.

Martins, I.P., Parreira, J., Albuquerque, L., & Ferro, J.M. (1999a). Capacités de calcul chez des enfants scolarises avec des lésions cérébrales acquises. *A.N.A.E., 51*, 6–12.

Martins, I.P., Ferreira, J., & Borges, L. (1999b). Acquired procedural dyscalculia associated to a left parietal lesion in a child. *Child Neuropsychology, 5*, 265–273.

Marzocchi, G.M., Lucangeli, D., DeMeo, T., Fini, F., & Cornoldi, C. (2002). The disturbing effect of irrelevant information on arithmetic problem solving in inattentive children. *Developmental Neuropsychology, 21*, 73–92.

May, C.D. (2000). Neuropsychological predictors of arithmetic ability in children. *Dissertation Abstracts International, 61*, 1644.

Maybery, M.Y. & Do, N. (2003). Relationships between facets of working memory and performance on a curriculum-based mathematics test in children. *Educational and Child Psychology, 20*, 3, 77–92.

Mazzocco, M. (1998). Approaches to describing mathematics difficulties in girls with Turner syndrome. *Pediatrics, 102*, 492–496.

Mazzocco, M. (2001). Math learning disability and math LD subtypes: Evidence from studies of Turner syndrome, Fragile X syndrome, and neurofibromatosis type 1. *Journal of Learning Disabilities, 34*, 520–533.

Mazzocco, M. (in press). Math learning disability and math LD subtypes: Evidence from studies of Turner syndrome, fragile X syndrome and neurofibromatosis type 1. *Journal of Learning Disabilities*.

Mazzocco, M. & Myers, G.F. (2003). Complexities in identifying and defining mathematics learning disability in the primary school years. *Annals of Dyslexia, 53*, 218–253.

McCloskey, M. (1992). Cognitive mechanisms in numerical processing: Evidence from acquired dyscalculia. *Cognition, 44*, 107–157.

McCloskey, M., Caramazza, A., & Basili, A. (1985). Cognitive mechanisms in number processing and calculation: Evidence from dyscalculia. *Brain and Cognition, 4*, 171–196.

McCloskey, M., Aliminosa, D., & Sokol, S. (1991). Facts, rules and procedures in normal calculation: Evidence from multiple single-patient studies of impaired arithmetic fact retrieval. *Brain and Cognition, 17,* 154–203.

McEvoy, J. & O'Moore, A.M. (1991). Number conservation: A fair assessment of numerical understanding? *Irish Journal of Psychology, 12,* 325–337.

McGarrigle, J. & Donaldson, M. (1974). Conservation accidents. *Cognition, 3,* 341–350.

McIntosh, A. (1977). When will they ever learn? *Forum, 3.* (Reprinted in A. Floyd (Ed.) (1985) *Developing mathematical thinking* (pp. 6–11). Milton Keynes: Open University Press.

McKenzie, B., Bull, R., & Gray, C. (2003). The effects of phonological and visual-spatial interference on children's arithmetical performance. *Educational and Child Psychology, 20,* 3, 93–107.

McLean, J.F. & Hitch, G.J. (1999). Working memory impairments in children with specific arithmetic learning difficulties. *Journal of Experimental Child Psychology, 74,* 240–260.

McLeod, D.B. (1991). Research on learning and instruction in arithmetic: The role of affect. In E. Fennema, T.P. Carpenter, & S.J. Lamon (Eds.), *Integrating research on teaching and learning mathematics* (pp. 55–82). Albany, NY: State University of New York Press.

McLeod, D. (1992). Research on affect in mathematics: A reconceptualization. In D.A. Grouws (Ed.), *Handbook of research on mathematics teaching and learning* (pp. 575–596). New York: Macmillan.

McNeil, J.E. & Warrington, E.K. (1993). A modality-specific case of dyscalculia. *Journal of Clinical and Experimental Psychology, 15,* 415.

McNeil, J.E. & Warrington E.K. (1994). A dissociation between addition and subtraction with written calculation. *Neuropsychologia, 32,* 717–728.

Menninger, K. (1969). *Number words and number symbols: A cultural history of numbers.* Cambridge, MA: MIT Press.

Menon, V., Rivera, S.M., White, C.D., Eliez, S., Glover, G.H., & Reiss, A.L. (2000). Functional optimization of arithmetic processing in perfect performers. *Cognitive Brain Research, 9,* 343–345.

Merttens, R. (1996). Introduction: Primary maths in crisis – what is to be done? In R. Merttens (Ed.), *Teaching numeracy: Maths in the primary classroom.* Leamington Spa: Scholastic.

Merttens, R. & Brown, T. (1996). Number operations and procedures. In R. Merttens (Ed.), *Teaching numeracy: Mathematics in the primary classroom* (pp. 77–98). Leamington Spa: Scholastic.

Mevarech, Z.R. (1995). Metacognition, general ability and mathematical under-standing. *Early Education and Development,* 155–168.

Miles, T.R. (1990). *Dyslexia: The pattern of difficulties* (2nd ed.). London: Whurr.

Miles, T.R. (1993). *Dyslexia: The pattern of difficulties* (3rd ed.). London: Whurr.

Miles, T.R. & Miles, E. (Eds.) (1992). *Dyslexia and mathematics.* London: Routledge.

Miles, T.R., Haslum, M.N., & Wheeler, T.J. (2001). The mathematical abilities of dyslexic 10-year-olds. *Annals of Dyslexia, 51,* 299–321.

Miller, K. (1984). Child as the measurer of all things: Measurement problems and the development of quantitative concepts. In C. Sophian (Ed.), *Origins of cognitive skills.* Hillsdale, NJ: Lawrence Erlbaum Associates, Inc.

Miller, K.F., Smith, C.M., Zhu, J., & Zhang, H. (1995). Preschool origins of cross-national differences in mathematical competence: The role of number-naming systems. *Psychological Science, 6,* 56–60.

Miller, L.K. (1989). *Musical savants.* Mahwah, NJ: Lawrence Erlbaum Associates, Inc.

Miller, S.P. & Mercer, C.D. (1997). Educational aspects of mathematical disabilities. *Journal of Learning Disabilities, 30,* 47–56.

Miura, I. & Okamoto, Y. (2003). Language supports for mathematics understanding and performance. In A. Baroody & A. Dowker (Eds.), *The development of arithmetical concepts and skills* (pp. 229–242). Mahwah, NJ: Lawrence Erlbaum Associates, Inc.

Miura, I., Kim, C., Chang, C.M., & Okamoto, Y. (1988). Effects of language characteristics on children's cognitive representations of number: Cross-cultural comparisons. *Child Development, 59,* 1445–1450.

Miura, I., Okamoto, Y., Kim, C., Steere, M., & Fayol, M. (1993). First graders' cognitive representation of number and understanding of place value: Cross-cultural comparisons – France, Japan, Korea, Sweden and the United States. *Journal of Educational Psychology, 85,* 24–30.

Mix, K. (1999). Similarity and numerical equivalence: Appearances count. *Cognitive Development, 14,* 269–297.

Mix, K.S., Huttenlocher, J., & Levine, S.C. (2002). *Quantitative development in infancy and early childhood.* Oxford: Oxford University Press.

Montague, M. & Bos, C.S. (1990). Cognitive and metacognitive characteristics of eighth-grade students' mathematical problem-solving. *Learning and Individual Differences, 2,* 371–388.

Montague, M., Woodward, J., & Bryant, D.P. (Eds.) (2004). *Journal of Learning Disabilities, 37,* 1: Special issue: *International Perspectives on Mathematics and Learning Disabilities.*

Mortimore, P. (1988). *School matters: The junior years.* Wells: Open Books.

Morton, J. & Frith, U. (1995). Causal modelling: A structural approach to developmental psychopathology. In D. Cichetti & D. Cohen (Eds.), *Developmental psychopathology* (*Vol. 1: Theory and methods,* pp. 357–390). New York: John Wiley & Sons.

Moyer, J., Sowder, L., & Threadgill-Sowder, J. (1984). Story problem formats: Verbal versus telegraphic. *Journal for Research in Mathematics Education, 15,* 64–68.

Munn, P. (1997). Children's beliefs about counting. In I. Thompson (Ed.), *Teaching and learning early number* (pp. 9–19). Buckingham: Open University Press.

Munn, P. (1998). Symbolic function in pre-schoolers. In C. Donlan (Ed.), *The development of mathematical skills* (pp. 44–71). Hove, UK: Psychology Press.

Murray, J. (1941). Types of errors in the basic number facts. In Scottish Council for Research in Education (Ed.), *Studies in arithmetic* (Vol. 2, pp. 103–133). London: University of London Press.

Naglieri, J.A. & Johnson, D. (2000). Effectiveness of a cognitive strategy intervention in improving arithmetic computation based on the PASS theory. *Journal of Learning Disabilities, 33,* 591–597.

National Centre for Literacy and Numeracy (1997). *Summary of objectives.* Reading: NCLN.

Nesher, P. (1982). Levels of description in the analysis of addition and subtraction. In T.P. Carpenter, J. Moser, & T. Romberg (Eds.), *Addition and subtraction: A cognitive perspective* (pp. 35–38). Hillsdale, NJ: Lawrence Erlbaum Associates, Inc.

Nesher, P. & Katriel, T. (1977). A semantic analysis of addition and subtraction word problems in arithmetic. *Educational Studies in Mathematics, 8,* 251–269.

Nesher, P. & Teubal, E. (1974). Verbal cues as an interfering factor in problem solving. *Educational Studies in Mathematics, 6,* 141–151.

Neumarker, K.J. (2000). Mathematics and the brain: Uncharted territory? *European Child and Adolescent Psychiatry, 9,* 2–10.

Newcombe, N.S. (2002). The nativist-empiricist controversy in the context of recent research on spatial and quantitative development. *Psychological Science, 13,* 395–401.

Newport, E.L. (1990). Maturational constraints on language learning. *Cognitive Science, 14,* 11–28.

Newson, J. & Newson, E. (1968). *Four years old in an urban community.* Oxford: Oxford University Press.

Newson, J. & Newson, E. (1977). *Perspectives on school at seven years old.* London: Allen & Unwin.

Nietfield, J. & Schraw, G. (2002). The effect of knowledge and strategy training on monitoring accuracy. *Journal of Educational Research, 95,* 131–142.

Nunes, T. & Bryant, P.E. (1996). *Children doing mathematics.* Oxford: Blackwell.

Nunes, T. & Moreno, C. (1998). Is hearing impairment a cause of difficulties in learning mathematics? In C. Donlan (Ed.), *The development of mathematical skills* (pp. 227–254). Hove, UK: Psychology Press.

Nunes, T., Schliemann, A.D., & Carraher, D.W. (1993). *Street mathematics and school mathematics.* Cambridge: Cambridge University Press.

Nyangeni, N.P. & Glencross, M.J. (1997). Sex differences in mathematics achievement and attitude toward mathematics. *Psychological Reports, 80,* 603–608.

O'Boyle, M. (2000). A new millennium in cognitive neuropsychology research: The era of individual differences? *Brain and Cognition, 42,* 135–138.

O'Boyle, M., Gill, H.S., Benbow, C.P., & Alexander, J.E. (1994). Concurrent tapping in mathematically gifted males: Evidence for enhanced right hemisphere involvement during linguistic processing. *Cortex, 30,* 519–526.

O'Connor, N., Cowan, R., & Samella, K. (2000). Calendrical calculation and intelligence. *Intelligence, 28,* 31–48.

O'Connor, N. & Hermelin, B. (1984). Idiot-savant calculators: Maths or memory? *Psychological Medicine, 16,* 885–893.

Ogden, J. (1996). Kate's story: A whole life with half a brain. In J. Ogden (Ed.), *Fractured minds: A case-study approach to cognitive neuropsychology* (pp. 252–264). Oxford: Oxford University Press.

Ollerton, M. & Watson, A. (2001). *Inclusive mathematics 11–18.* London: Continuum.

Onwuegbuzie, A.J. (2000). Statistics anxiety and the role of self-perceptions. *Journal of Educational Research, 93,* 323–330.

Opie, I. & Opie, P. (1969). *Children's games in street and playground.* London: Allen Lane.

Orr, E.W. (1989). *Twice as less: Black English and the performance of black students in mathematics and science.* New York: Norton.

Orton, A. & Frobisher, L. (1996). *Insights into teaching mathematics.* London: Cassell.

Ostad, S.A. (1997). Developmental differences in addition strategies: A comparison of mathematically disabled and mathematically normal children. *British Journal of Educational Psychology, 67,* 345–357.

Ostad, S. (1998). Developmental differences in solving simple arithmetic problems and simple number fact problems: A comparison of mathematically normal and mathematically disabled children. *Mathematical Cognition, 4,* 1–19.

Palincsar, A.S. & Brown, D.A. (1987). Enhancing instructional time through attention to metacognition. *Journal of Learning Disabilities, 20,* 66–75.

Parkin, A. (1993). *Memory: Phenomena, experiment and theory.* Oxford: Blackwell.

Passolunghi, M.C. & Siegel, L.S. (2001). Short-term memory, working memory and inhibitory control in children with difficulties in arithmetic problem-solving. *Journal of Experimental Child Psychology, 80,* 44–57.

Paterson, S., Brown, J., Gsoedl, M.K., Johnson, M.H., & Karmiloff-Smith, A. (1999). Cognitive modularity and genetic disorders. *Science, 286,* 2355–2358.

Paulesu, E., Frith, U., Snowling, M., Gallagher, A., Morton. J., Frackowiak, R., & Frith, C.D. (1996). Is developmental dyslexia a disconnection syndrome?: Evidence from PET scanning. *Brain, 119,* 143–157.

Paulesu, E., McCrory, E., Fazio, F., Menoncello, L., Brunswick, N., Cappa, S.M., Cotelli, M., Cossu, G., Corte, F., Corusso, N., Pesenti, S., Gallagher, A., Pesumi, D., Price, C., Frith, C.D., & Frith, U. (2000). A cultural effect on brain function. *Nature Neuroscience, 3,* 91–96.

Paull, D.R. (1971). *The ability to estimate in mathematics.* Unpublished doctoral dissertation, Columbia University.

Peak, D. & Dowker, A. (1995, September). *Numerosity estimation by young children.* Paper presented at the International Conference on Mathematics and Language, London.

Pears, R. & Bryant, P.E. (1990). Transitive inferences by young children about spatial position. *British Journal of Psychology, 81,* 497–510.

Pellegrino, J.W. & Goldman, S.R. (1987). Information processing and elementary mathematics. *Journal of Learning Disabilities, 20,* 23–32.

Penner-Wilger, M., Leth-Steenson, C., & LeFevre, J.A. (2002). Decomposing the problem-size effect: A comparison of response-time distributions across cultures. *Memory and Cognition, 30,* 1160–1167.

Pennington, B.F. (1990). The genetics of dyslexia. *Journal of Child Psychology and Psychiatry, 31,* 193–201.

Pennington, B.F. (1995). Genetics of learning disabilities. *Journal of Child Neurology, 10* (Supplement 1), 69–77.

Pennington, B.F., Wallach, L., & Wallach, M. (1980). Nonconservers' use and understanding of number and arithmetic. *Genetic Psychology Monographs, 10,* 231–243.

Pesenti, M., Seron, X., & VanDerLinden, M. (1994). Selective impairment as evidence for mental organization of arithmetic facts: BB, a case of preserved subtraction? *Cortex, 30,* 661–671.

Pesenti, M., Seron, X, Samson, D., & Duroux, B. (1999). Basic and exceptional calculation abilities in a calculating prodigy: A case study. *Mathematical Cognition, 5,* 97–148.

Pesenti, M., Deporter, N., & Seron, X. (2000). Noncommutativity of the N + 0 arithmetical rule: A case of dissociated impairment. *Cortex, 36,* 445–454.

Pettito, A.L. & Ginsburg, H.P. (1982). Mental arithmetic in Africa and America:

Strategies, principles and explanations. *International Journal of Psychology*, *17*, 81–102.

Piaget, J. (1952). *The child's conception of number*. London: Routledge & Kegan Paul.

Piaget, J. (1968). Quantification, conservation and nativism. *Science*, *162*, 976–979.

Piaget. J. (1970). *Genetic epistemology* (E. Duckworth Trans.). NY: Columbia University Press.

Pimm, D. (1987). *Speaking mathematically: Communication in mathematics classrooms*. London: Routledge & Kegan Paul.

Pitta-Pantazi, D. & Gagatsis, A. (2001). Exploring a high achiever's and a low achiever's strategies and images in early number work. *Early Child Development and Care*, *166*, 63–79.

Plunkett, S. (1979). Decomposition and all that rot. *Mathematics in School*, *8*, 2–5.

Poeck, K. (1964). Phantoms following amputation in early childhood and in congenital absence of limbs. *Cortex*, *1*, 269–275.

Poincaré, H. (1908). L'invention mathématique. *Revue du Mois*, *6*.

Posner, J.K. (1982). The development of mathematical knowledge in two West African societies. *Child Development*, *53*, 200–208.

Posner, M.I. & McCandliss, B.D. (1999). Brain circuitry during reading. In P.A. McMullen & R.M. Klein (Eds.), *Converging methods for understanding reading and dyslexia* (pp. 305–337). Cambridge, MA: MIT Press.

Post, T.R., Harel, G., Behr, M.J., & Lesh, R. (1991). Intermediate teachers' knowledge of rational number concepts. In E. Fennema, T.P. Carpenter, & S.J. Lamon (Eds.), *Integrating research on teaching and learning mathematics* (pp. 177–198). Albany, NY: State University of New York Press.

Poustie, J. (2001). *Mathematics solutions: An introduction to dyscalculia, Parts A and B*. London: Next Generation UK.

Power, R. & Dal Martello, M.F. (1997). From 834 to eighty thirty four. *Mathematical Cognition*, *3*, 63–85.

Prabhakaran, V., Rypma, B., & Gabrieli, J. (2001). Neural substrates of mathematical reasoning: A functional magnetic resonance imaging study of neocortical activation during performance of the necessary arithmetical operations test. *Neuropsychology*, *15*, 115–127.

Pritchard, R.A., Miles, T.R., Chinn, S.J., & Taggart, A.T. (1989). Dyslexia and knowledge of number facts. *Links*, *14*, 17–20.

Proudfoot, M. (1992). Teaching maths without relying on a scheme. In S. Atkinson (Ed.), *Mathematics with reason: The emergent approach to primary maths* (pp. 130–132). London: Hodder & Stoughton.

Putt, I.J. (1995). Preservice teachers' ordering of decimal numbers: When more is smaller and less is larger! *Focus on Learning Problems in Mathematics*, *17*, 1–15.

Putnam, R.T., De Bettencourt, L., & Leinhardt, G. (1990). Understanding of derived fact strategies in addition and subtraction. *Cognition and Instruction*, *7*, 245–285.

Ramachandran, V.S. (2003). *The emerging mind. The Reith Lectures*. London: BBC.

Renton, M. (1992). *Primary school children's strategies for addition*. PhD thesis, University of London Institute of Education.

Resnick, L. (1982). Syntax and semantics in learning to subtract. In T. Carpenter, J. Moser, & T. Romberg (Eds.), *Addition and subtraction: A cognitive perspective* (pp. 136–155). Hillsdale, NJ: Lawrence Erlbaum Associates, Inc.

Resnick, L. (1983). A developmental theory of number understanding. In H.P. Ginsburg (Ed.), *The development of mathematical thinking*. London: Academic Press.

Reyna, V. & Brainerd, C.J. (1991). Fuzzy-trace theory and children's acquisition of mathematical and scientific concepts. *Learning and Individual Differences, 3*, 27–59.

Reys, R.E. (1984). Mental computation and estimation: Past, present and future. *Elementary School Journal, 84*, 547–557.

Reys, R.E., Rybolt, J.F., Bestgen, B.J., & Wyatt, J.W. (1982). Processes used by good computational estimators. *Journal for Research in Mathematics Education, 13*, 183–201.

Reys, R.E., Reys, B.J., Nohda, N., Ishida, J., Yoshikawa, S., & Shimizu, K. (1991). Computational estimation performance and strategies used by fifth- and eighth-grade Japanese students. *Journal for Research in Mathematics Education, 22*, 39–58.

Richardson, F.C. & Suinn, R.M. (1972). The Mathematics Anxiety Rating Scale. *Journal of Counseling Psychology, 19*, 551–554.

Rickard, T.C., Romero, S.G., Basso, G., Wharton, C., Flitman, S., & Grafman, J. (2000). The calculating brain: An fMRI study. *Neuropsychologia, 38*, 325–335.

Riding, R.J. & Watts, M. (1997). The effect of cognitive style on the preferred format of instructional material. *Educational Psychology, 17*, 179–193.

Riding, R.J., Grimley, M., Dahraei, H., & Banner, G. (2003). Cognitive style, working memory and learning behaviour and attainment in school subjects. *British Journal of Educational Psychology, 73*, 149–169.

Riley, M.S., Greeno, J.G., & Heller, J.I. (1983). Development of children's problem-solving ability in arithmetic. In H.P. Ginsburg (Ed.), *The development of mathematical thinking* (pp. 153–196). New York: Academic Press.

Rittle-Johnson, B. & Siegler, R. (1998). The relation between conceptual and procedural knowledge in learning mathematics: A review. In C. Donlan (Ed.), *The development of mathematical skills* (pp. 75–110). Hove, UK: Lawrence Erlbaum Associates, Inc.

Roberts, G. (2000). Bilingualism and number in Wales. *International Journal of Bilingual Education and Bilingualism, 3*, 44–56.

Roberts, R. (2001). *Peep voices: A five-year diary. Supporting early learning at home.* Oxford: PEEP.

Robinson, C.S., Menchetti, B.M., & Torgesen, J.K. (2002). Toward a two-factor theory of one type of mathematics disabilities. *Learning Disabilities Research and Practice, 17*, 81–89.

Roebuck, J. (2001). The relation of children's musical ability to other cognitive abilities. Undergraduate research project, University of Oxford.

Rohrbeck, C.A., Ginsburg-Block, M.D., Fantuzzo, J.W., & Miller, T.R. (2003). Peer-assisted learning interventions with elementary school students: A meta-analytic review. *Journal of Educational Psychology, 95*, 240–257.

Rose, S.A. & Blank, M. (1974). The potency of context in children's cognition: An illustration through conservation. *Child Development, 45*, 499–502.

Rossor, M., Warrington, E., & Cipolotti, L. (1995). The isolation of calculation skills. *Journal of Neurology, 242*, 78–81.

Rourke, B.P. (1993). Arithmetical disabilities specific and otherwise: A neuro-psychological perspective. *Journal of Learning Disabilities, 26*, 214–226.

Rourke, B.P. & Finlayson, M.A.J. (1978). Neuropsychological significance of variations in patterns of academic performance: Verbal and visual-spatial abilities. *Journal of Abnormal Child Psychology, 6,* 121–133.

Roussel, J.L., Fayol, M., & Barouillet, P. (2002). Procedural versus direct retrieval strategies in arithmetic: A comparison between additive and multiplicative problem-solving. *European Journal of Cognitive Psychology, 14,* 61–104.

Rowe, J.C. (2001). An experiment in the use of games in the teaching of mental arithmetic. *Philosophy of Mathematics Education, 14,* 1–23.

Royer, J.M., Tronsky, L.N., Chan, Y., Jackson, S.J., & Marchant. J. (1999). Math fact retrieval as the cognitive mechanism underlying gender differences in math test performance. *Contemporary Educational Psychology, 24,* 181–266.

Rubenstein, R.N. (1985). Computational estimation and related mathematical skills. *Journal for Research in Mathematics Education, 16,* 106–119.

Rubenstein, R. (1988). Computational estimation and related mathematical skills. *Journal for Research in Mathematics Education, 16,* 106–119.

Russell, R. & Ginsburg, H.P. (1984). Cognitive analysis of children's mathematical difficulties. *Cognition and Instruction, 1,* 217–244.

Ruthven, K. (1998). The use of mental, written and calculator strategies of numerical computation within a 'calculator aware' curriculum. *British Educational Research Journal, 24,* 21–42.

Sackur-Grisvard, C. & Leonard, F. (1985). Intermediate cognitive organization in the process of learning a mathematical concept: The order of positive decimal numbers. *Cognition and Instruction, 2,* 157–174.

Samuel, J. & Bryant, P.E. (1984). Asking only one question in the conservation experiment. *Journal of Child Psychology and Psychiatry, 25,* 315–318.

Santana, N.M. (2001). Acalculia in mild Alzheimer's disease. *Dissertation Abstracts International, Section B: The Sciences and Engineering, 61,* 5004.

Satake, E. & Amato, P. (1995). Mathematics anxiety and achievement among Japanese elementary school students. *Educational and Psychological Measurement, 55.*

Sauble, I. (1955). Development of ability to estimate and to compute mentally. *Arithmetic Teacher, 2,* 33–39.

Saxe, G. (1979). Developmental relations between notational counting and number conservation. *Child Development, 50,* 180–187.

Saxe, G.B. (1982). Developing forms of arithmetical thought among the Oksapmin of Papua New Guinea. *Developmental Psychology, 18,* 583–594.

Saxe, G.B. (1985). Effects of schooling on arithmetical understandings: Studies with Oksapmin children in Papua New Guinea. *Journal of Educational Psychology, 77,* 503–513.

Saxe, G.B. (1990). The interplay between children's learning in school and out-of-school contexts. In M. Gardner & J. Greeno (Eds.), *Toward a scientific practice of science education.* Hillsdale, NJ: Lawrence Erlbaum Associates, Inc.

Saxe, G. (1991). *Culture and cognitive development: Studies in mathematical understanding.* Hillsdale, NJ: Lawrence Erlbaum Associates, Inc.

Schliemann, A., Araujo, C., Cassunde, M.A., Macedo, S., & Niceas, L. (1998). Use of multiplicative commutativity by school children and street sellers. *Journal for Research in Mathematics Education, 29,* 422–435.

Schmidt, W., McKnight, C., Cogan, L., Jackwerth, P., & Houang, R. (1999). *Facing the consequences: Using TIMSS for a closer look at US mathematics and science education*. Dordrecht, The Netherlands: Kluwer.

Schnider, A., Bassetti, C., Gutbrod, K., & Ozoda, C. (1995). Very severe amnesia with acute onset after isolated hippocampal damage due to systematic lupus erythematosus. *Journal of Neurology, Neurosurgery and Psychiatry, 59*. 644–646.

Schoenfield, A.H. (1987). What's so important about metacognition? In A.H. Schoenfield (Ed.), *Cognitive science and mathematics education* (pp. 189–215). Hillsdale, NJ: Lawrence Erlbaum Associates, Inc.

Schoenfield, A.H. (1992). Learning to think mathematically: Problem solving, metacognition, and sense making in mathematics. In D.A. Grouws (Ed.), *Handbook of research on mathematics teaching and learning* (pp. 334–370). New York: Macmillan.

Seidenberg, A. (1959). *The diffusion of counting practices*. Berkeley, CA: University of California Press.

Semenza, C. (2002). Conceptual knowledge in arithmetic: The core of calculation skills. *Cortex, 38*, 285–288.

Semenza, C., Micelli, L., & Girelli, L. (1997). A deficit for arithmetical procedures: Lack of knowledge or lack of monitoring? *Cortex, 33*, 483–498.

Seo, K.H. & Ginsburg, H.P. (2003). 'You've got to carefully read the math sentence. . . .': Classroom context and children's interpretations of the equals sign. In A.J. Baroody & A. Dowker (Eds.), *The development of arithmetic concepts and skills* (pp. 161–188). Mahwah, NJ: Lawrence Erlbaum Associates, Inc.

Seron, X. & Noel, M. (1995). Transcoding numbers from the Arabic code to the verbal one or vice versa: How many routes? *Mathematical Cognition, 1*, 215–243.

Seron, X., Deloche, G., & Noel, M.P. (1992a). Number transcoding by children: Modelling Arabic numbers under dictation. In J. Bideaud, C. Meljac, & J.P. Fischer (Eds.), *Pathways to number: Children's developing numerical abilities* (pp. 245–264). Hillsdale, NJ: Lawrence Erlbaum Associates, Inc.

Seron, X., Pesenti, M., Noel, M.P., Deloche, J., & Cornet, J.A. (1992). Images of numbers, or 'When 98 is upper left and 6 sky blue'. *Cognition, 44*, 159–196.

Shalev, R.S., Weirtman, R., & Amir, N. (1988). Developmental dyscalculia. *Cortex, 24*, 555–561.

Shalev, R.S., Manor, O., Amir, N., & Gross-Tsur, V. (1993). The acquisition of arithmetic in normal children: Assessment by a cognitive model of dyscalculia. *Developmental Medicine and Child Neurology, 35*, 593–601.

Shalev, R.S., Gross-Tsur, V., & Manor, O. (1997). Neuropsychological aspects of developmental dyscalculia. *Mathematical Cognition, 3*, 105–120.

Shalev, R.S., Manor, O., Kerem, B., Ayali, M., Badichi, N., Friedlander, Y., & Gross-Tsur, V. (2001). Developmental dyscalculia is a familial learning disability. *Journal of Learning Disabilities, 34*, 59–65.

Shallice, T. & Evans, M.E. (1978). The involvement of the frontal lobes in cognitive estimation. *Cortex, 14*, 294–303.

Sheffield, L. (1994). *The development of gifted and talented mathematics students and the National Council of Teachers of Mathematics Standards*. Connecticut, OH: The National Research on the Gifted and Talented.

Sheffield, L. (1999). The development of mathematically promising students in the United States. *Mathematics in School, 28*, 3.

Shire, B. & Durkin, K. (1989). Junior children's responses to conflict between the spatial and numerical meanings of 'up' and 'down'. *Educational Psychology, 9,* 141–147.

Shuard, K. (1992). Calculator use in the primary grades in England and Wales. In J. Fey & C. Hirsch (Eds.), *Calculators in mathematics education* (pp. 33–45). Reston, VA: National Council of Teachers of Mathematics.

Siegel, A.W., Goldsmith, L.T., & Madson, C.R. (1982). Skill in estimation problems of extent and numerosity. *Journal for Research in Mathematics Education, 13,* 211–232.

Siegel, L.S. & Ryan, E.P. (1989). The development of working memory in normally achieving and subtypes of learning disabled children. *Child Development, 60,* 973–981.

Siegler, R.S. (1987). The perils of averaging data over strategies: the example of children's addition. *Journal of Experimental Psychology: General, 116,* 260–264.

Siegler, R.S. (1988). Individual differences in strategy choice: Good students, not-so-good students and perfectionists. *Child Development, 59,* 833–851.

Siegler, R.S. (1991). In young children's counting, procedures precede principles. *Educational Psychology Review, 3,* 127–135.

Siegler, R.S. (2001). Children's discoveries and brain-damaged patients' rediscoveries. In J.L. McClelland & R.S. Siegler (Eds.), *Mechanisms of cognitive development: Behavioural and neural perspectives* (pp. 33–63). Mahwah, NJ: Lawrence Erlbaum Associates, Inc.

Siegler, R.S. & Engle, R.A. (1994). Studying change in developmental and neuropsychological contexts. *Cahiers de Psychologie Cognitive/Current Psychology of Cognition, 13,* 321–349.

Siegler, R.S. & Jenkins, E. (1989). *How children discover new strategies.* Hillsdale, NJ: Lawrence Erlbaum Associates, Inc.

Siegler, R.S. & Robinson, M. (1982). The development of numerical understandings. In H. Reese & L. Lipsitt (Eds.), *Advances in child development and behaviour* (Vol. 16, pp. 241–312). New York: Academic Press.

Siegler, R.S. & Shrager, J. (1984). Strategy choices in addition and subtraction: How do children know what to do? In C. Sophian (Ed.), *Origins of cognitive skills* (pp. 229–293). Hillsdale, NJ: Lawrence Erlbaum Associates, Inc.

Siegler, R.S. & Stern, E. (1998). Conscious and unconscious strategy discoveries: A microgenetic analysis. *Journal of Experimental Psychology: General. 127,* 377–397.

Sikora, D.M., Haley, P., Edwards, J., & Butler, R.W. (2002). Tower of London test performance in children with poor arithmetic skills. *Developmental Neuropsychology, 21,* 243–254.

Silver, E.A. & Metzger, W.R. (1989). Aesthetic influences on expert mathematical problem solving. In D.B. McLeod & V.M. Adams (Eds.), *Affect and mathematical problem solving: A new perspective* (pp. 59–74). New York: Springer-Verlag.

Sinclair, A., Siegrist, F., & Sinclair, H. (1983). Young children's ideas about the written number system. In D. Rogers & J. Sloboda (Eds.), *The development of symbolic skills.* New York: Plenum Press.

Skemp, R. (1976). Relational and instrumental understanding. *Mathematics Teaching, 77,* 20–26.

Slater, I. (1990). *Children's estimating skills.* BEd dissertation, Wolverhampton Polytechnic.

Slife, B., Weiss, J., & Bell, T. (1985). Separability of metacognition and cognition: Problem solving in learning. *Journal of Educational Psychology*, 77, 437–445.

Sloboda, J.A., Hermelin, B., & O'Connor, N. (1985). An exceptional musical memory. *Music Perception*, 3, 155–169.

Smedslund, J. (1966). Microanalysis of concrete reasoning 1. The difficulty of some combinations of addition and subtraction of one unit. *Scandinavian Journal of Psychology*, 7, 145–156.

Smith, J.P. (1995). Competent reasoning with rational numbers. *Cognition and Instruction*, 13, 3–50.

Smith, S.B. (1983). *The great mental calculators*. New York: Columbia University Press.

Smith, S.B. (1988). Calculating prodigies. In L. Obler & D. Fein (Eds.), *The exceptional brain: Neuropsychology of talent and special abilities* (pp. 19–45). London: Guildford.

Sokol, S.M. & McCloskey, M. (1991). Cognitive mechanism in calculation. In P.A. Frensch & R.J. Sternberg (Eds.), *Complex problem-solving: Principles and mechanisms* (pp. 85–116). Hillsdale, NJ: Lawrence Erlbaum Associates, Inc.

Sokol, S.M., McCloskey, M., Cohen, N.J., & Aliminosa, D. (1991). Cognitive representations and processes in arithmetic: Inferences from the performance of brain-damaged patients. *Journal of Experimental Psychology: Learning, Memory, and Cognition*, 17, 355–376.

Song, M. & Ginsburg, H.P. (1988). The effect of the Korean number system on children's counting: A natural experiment in numerical bilingualism. *International Journal of Psychology*, 23, 275–302.

Sophian, C. (1988). Limitations on preschool children's knowledge about counting: Using counting to compare two sets. *Developmental Psychology*, 24, 634–640.

Sophian, C. (1995). Representation and reasoning in early numerical development: Counting, conservation and comparisons between sets. *Child Development*, 66, 559–577.

Sophian, C. (1997). Beyond competence: The significance of performance for conceptual development. *Cognitive Development*, 12, 281–303.

Sophian, C. & Vong, K.I. (1995). The parts and wholes of arithmetic story problems: Developing knowledge in the preschool years. *Cognition and Instruction*, 13, 469–477.

Sophian, C., Harley, H., & Martin, C.S.M. (1995). Relational and representational aspects of early number development. *Cognition and Instruction*, 13, 253–268.

Sowder, J.T. (1992). Estimation and related topics. In D.A. Grouws (Ed.), *Handbook of research on teaching and learning*. London: Macmillan.

Sowder, J.T. & Wheeler, M.M. (1987). *The development of computational estimation and number sense: Two exploratory studies*. Research Rep. San Diego, CA: San Diego State University Center for Research in Mathematics and Science Education.

Sowder, J.T. & Wheeler, M.M. (1989). The development of concepts and strategies use in computational estimation. *Journal for Research in Mathematics Education*, 20, 130–146.

Sowder, L. (1988). Children's solution of story problems. *Journal of Mathematical Behaviour*, 7, 227–238.

Sowell, E.J., Bergwall, L.K., Zeigler, A.J., & Cartwright, R.M. (1990). Identification and description of mathematically gifted students: A review of empirical research. *Gifted Child Quarterly, 34*, 147–154.

Stanescu-Cosson, R., Pinel, P., Van de Moortele, P.F., Le Bihan, D., Cohen, L., & Dehaene, S. (2000). Understanding dissociations in dyscalculia: A brain-imaging study of the impact of number size on the cerebral networks for exact and approximate calculation. *Brain, 123*, 2240–2255.

Stanley, J.C. & Benbow, C.P. (1983). SMPY's first decade: Ten years of posing problems and solving them. *Journal of Special Education, 17*, 11–25.

Starkey, P. (1992). The early development of numerical reasoning. *Cognition, 43*, 93–126.

Starkey, P. & Cooper, R. (1980). Perception of numbers by human infants. *Science, 210*, 1033–1035.

Starkey, P. & Cooper, R. (1995). The development of subitizing in young children. *British Journal of Developmental Psychology, 13*, 399–420.

Starkey, P. & Klein, A. (2000). Fostering parental support for children's mathematical development: An intervention with Head Start. *Early Education and Development, 11*, 659–680.

Starkey, P., Spelke, E., & Gelman, R. (1990). Numerical abstraction by human infants. *Cognition, 36*, 97–128.

Staszewski, J.J. (1988). Skilled memory and expert mental calculation. In M.T.H. Chi, R. Glaser, & M.J. Farr (Eds.), *The nature of expertise*. Hillsdale, NJ: Lawrence Erlbaum Associates, Inc.

Steel, S. & Funnell, E. (2001). Learning multiplication facts: A study of children taught by discovery methods in England. *Journal of Experimental Child Psychology, 79*, 37–55.

Steeves, K. (1983). Memory as a factor in the computational efficiency of dyslexic children with high abstract reasoning ability. *Annals of Dyslexia, 33*, 141–152.

Steffe, L., Thompson, P., & Richards, J. (1982). Children's counting in arithmetical problem solving. In T. Carpenter, J. Moser, & T. Romberg (Eds.), *Addition and subtraction: A cognitive perspective*. Hillsdale, NJ: Lawrence Erlbaum Associates, Inc.

Steinberg, R. (1985). Instruction in derived facts strategies in addition and subtraction. *Journal for Research in Mathematics Education, 16*, 337–335.

Stern, E. (1992). Spontaneous use of conceptual mathematical knowledge in elementary school children. *Contemporary Educational Psychology, 17*, 266–277.

Stevenson, H.W. & Stigler, J.W. (1992). *The learning gap: Why our schools are failing and what we can learn from Japanese and Chinese education*. New York: Summit.

Stevenson, H.W., Lee, S.Y., Chen, C., Stigler, J.W., Hsu, C.C., & Kitamura, S. (1990). Contexts of achievement: A study of American, Chinese and Japanese children. *Monographs of the Society for Research into Child Development, 55* (Serial No. 221).

Stevenson, H.W., Chen, C., & Lee, S.Y. (1993). Mathematics achievement of Chinese, Japanese and American children: Ten years later. *Science, 259*, 53–58.

Stevenson, H.W., Hofer, B.K., & Randel, B. (2000). Mathematics achievement and attitudes about mathematics in China and the West. *Journal of Psychology in Chinese Societies, 1*, 1–16.

Stetic, W. (1999). Word problem solving as a function of problem type, situational context and drawing. *Studia Psychologica, 41*, 49–62.

Stigler, J. (1984). 'Mental abacus': The effect of abacus training on Chinese children's mental calculation. *Cognitive Psychology*, *16*, 145–176.

Stigler, J. & Perry, M. (1988). Mathematics learning in Japanese, Chinese and American classrooms. In G. Saxe & M. Gearhart (Eds.), *Children's mathematics* (pp. 27–54). San Francisco: Jossey-Bass.

Stigler, J., Fernandez, C., & Yoshida, M. (1996). Traditions of mathematics in Japanese and American elementary classrooms. In L. Steffe, P. Nesher, P. Cobb, G. Goldin, & B. Greer (Eds.), *Theories of mathematical learning* (pp. 149–175). Mahwah, NJ: Lawrence Erlbaum Associates, Inc.

Straker, A. (1996). The National Numeracy Project. *Equals*, *2*, 14–15.

Strauss, M. & Curtis, L. (1981). Infant perception of numerosity. *Child Development*, *52*, 1146–1152.

Suinn, R.M., Taylor, S., & Edwards, R.W. (1988). Suinn Mathematics Anxiety Rating Scale for elementary school students (MARS-E): Psychometric and normative data. *Educational and Psychological Measurement*, *48*, 979–986.

Svenson, O.L. & Broquist, S. (1975). Strategies for solving simple addition problems: A comparison of normal and subnormal children. *Scandinavian Journal of Psychology*, *16*, 143–148.

Svenson, O.L., Hedenborg, M.L., & Lingman, L. (1976). On children's heuristics for solving simple additions. *Scandinavian Journal of Educational Research*, *20*, 161–173.

Swanson, H. (1994). Short-term memory and working memory: Do both contribute to our understanding of academic achievement in children and adults with learning disabilities? *Journal of Learning Disabilities*, *27*, 34–50.

Swanson, H. & Sachse-Lee, C. (2001). Mathematical problem solving and working memory in children with learning disabilities: Both executive and phonological processes are involved. *Journal of Experimental Child Psychology*, *79*, 294–321.

Sylva, K. & Hurry, J. (1995). *Early intervention in children with reading difficulties*, London: School Curriculum and Assessment Authority Discussion Papers, No. 2.

Szanto, G. (1998). Arithmetic disability of adults. *Dissertation Abstracts International*, *59A*, 1911.

Ta'ir, J., Brezner, A., & Ariel, R. (1997). Profound developmental dyscalculia: Evidence for a cardinal/ordinal skills acquisition device. *Brain and Cognition*, *35*, 184–206.

Takayama, Y., Sugishita, M., Akiguchi, I., & Kimura, J. (1994). Isolated acalculia due to left parietal lesion. *Archives of Neurology*, *51*, 286–291.

Tan, L. (1997). *Understanding number in infancy*. Unpublished DPhil thesis, University of Oxford.

Tan, L.S.C. & Bryant, P.E. (2000). The cues that infants use to distinguish discontinuous quantities. *Child Development*, *71*, 1162–1178.

Tasaka, Y. & Shimada, S. (2000). Solving arithmetic word problems: Children born with very low birthweight. *Japanese Journal of Special Education*, *38*, 21–31.

Temple, C.M. (1991). Procedural dyscalculia and number fact dyscalculia: Double dissociation in developmental dyscalculia. *Cognitive Neuropsychology*, *8*, 155–176.

Temple, C.M. (1994). The cognitive neuropsychology of the developmental dyscalculias. *Cahiers de Psychologie Cognitive/Current Psychology of Cognition*, *13*, 351–370.

Temple, C.M. (1997). *Developmental Cognitive Neuropsychology*. Hove, UK: Psychology Press.

Temple, C.M. & Marriott, A.J. (1998). Arithmetical ability and disability in Turner syndrome: A cognitive neuropsychological analysis. *Developmental Neuropsychology, 14*, 47–67.

Temple, E., Deutsch, G.K., Poldrack, R.A., Miller, S.L., Tallal, P., Merzenich, M.M., & Gabrieli, J.D. (2003). *Neural deficits in children with dyslexia ameliorated by behavioural remediation*. Proceedings of the National Academy of Sciences of the United States of America, *100*, 2860–2865.

Thevenot, C., Barouillet, P., & Fayol, M. (2001). Algorithmic solutions of arithmetic problems and operands: Answer associations in long-term memory. *Quarterly Journal of Experimental Psychology, 54A*, 599–611.

Thipkong, S. & Davis, E.J. (1991). Preservice elementary teachers: Misconceptions in interpreting and applying decimals. *School Science and Mathematics, 91*, 93–99.

Thomas, G. & Dowker, A. (2000, September). *Mathematics anxiety and related factors in young children*. Paper presented at British Psychological Society Developmental Section Conference, Bristol.

Thompson, I. (1994). Young children's idiosyncratic written algorithms for addition. *Educational Studies in Mathematics, 26*, 323–345.

Thompson, I. (1997a). The role of counting in derived fact strategies. In I. Thompson (Ed.), *Teaching and learning early number* (pp. 52–61). Buckingham: Open University Press.

Thompson, I. (1997b). Mental and written algorithms: Can the gap be breached? In I. Thompson (Ed.), *Teaching and learning early number*. Buckingham: Open University Press.

Thompson, I. (2000). Issues for classroom practices in England. In J. Anghileri (Ed.), *Principles and practices in arithmetic teaching* (pp. 68–78). Buckingham: Open University Press.

Thompson, I. (2003). Place value: The English disease? In I. Thompson (Ed.), *Enhancing primary mathematics teaching* (pp. 181–190). Maidenhead: Open University Press.

Thorndike, E.L. (1921). The constitution of arithmetical abilities. *Journal of Educational Psychology, 12*, 14–24.

Thornton, C.A. (1978). Emphasizing thinking strategies in basic fact instruction. *Journal for Research in Mathematics Education, 9*, 214–227.

Thurstone, L.L. (1938). Primary mental abilities. *Psychometric Monographs, No. 1*.

Thurstone, L.L. (1941). *Factorial studies of intelligence*. Chicago: University of Chicago Press.

Thurstone, L.L. & Thurstone, T.G. (1941). Factorial studies of intelligence. *Psychometric Monographs, 2*.

Tilton, J.W. (1947). Individualized and meaningful instruction in arithmetic. *Journal of Educational Psychology, 38*, 83–88.

TIMSS (1996). *Highlight of reports from TIMSS: Third international mathematics and science study*. Chestnut Hill, MA: TIMSS International Study Centre.

Tizard, B., Blatchford, P., Burke, J., Farquhar, C., & Plewis, I.F. (1988). *Young children at school in the inner city*. London: Lawrence Erlbaum Associates, Ltd.

Tobias, S. (1993). *Overcoming math anxiety* (2nd ed.). London: Norton.

Tocci, C.M. & Engelhard, G. (1991). Achievement, parental support, and gender differences in attitudes toward mathematics. *Journal of Educational Research, 84,* 5, 280–286.

Topping, K.J. & Bamford, J. (1998). *Parental involvement and peer tutoring in mathematics and science.* London: Fulton.

Towse, J. & Saxton, M. (1998). Mathematics across national boundaries. In C. Donlan (Ed.), *The development of mathematical skills* (pp. 129–150). Hove, UK: Psychology Press.

Trabasso, T. (1977). The role of memory as a system in making transitive inferences. In R.W. Kail & J.W. Hagen (Eds.), *Perspectives on the development of memory and cognition* (pp. 333–366). Hillsdale, NJ: Lawrence Erlbaum Associates, Inc.

Tsuge, M. (2001). Learning disabilities in Japan. In D. Callaghan & B. Keogh (Eds.), *Research and global perspectives on learning disabilities: Essays in honour of William M. Cruickshank* (pp. 255–272). Mahwah, NJ: Lawrence Erlbaum Associates, Inc.

Underhill, R. (1983). *Diagnosing mathematics difficulties.* Columbus, OH: Merrill.

Underhill, R.G., Uprichard, A.E., & Heddens. J.W. (1981). *Diagnosing mathematical difficulties.* London: Merrill.

Uprichard, A.E. & Phillips, E.R. (1977). Intraconcept analysis of rational number addition: a validation study. *Journal for Research in Mathematics Education, 8,* 7–16.

Van Harskamp, N.J. & Cipolotti, L. (2001). Selective impairments for addition, subtraction and multiplication: Implications for the organization of arithmetical facts. *Cortex, 37,* 363–388.

Van Hout, A. (1995). Troubles du calcul et functions de l'hemisphere droit chez l'enfant. *Approche Neuropsychologique des Apprentissages chez l'Enfant, Hors serie 2,* 30–33.

Vandenberg, S.G. (1966). The contributions of twin research to psychology. *Psychological Bulletin, 66,* 327–352.

Van de Rijt, B. & Van Luit, J. (1998). Effectiveness of the Additional Early Mathematics program for teaching children early mathematics. *Instructional Science, 26,* 337–358.

Van Kraayenoord, C.E. & Elkins, J. (2004). Learning disabilities in numeracy in Australia. *Journal of Learning Disabilities, 37,* 32–41.

Van Luit, J. & Schopman. E. (2000). Improving early numeracy of young children with special educational needs. *Remedial and Special Education, 21,* 27–40.

VanLehn, K. (1990). *Mind bugs: The origins of procedural misconceptions.* Cambridge, MA: MIT Press.

Verschaffel, L. & DeCorte, E. (1997). Word problems: A vehicle for promoting authentic mathematical understanding and problem solving in the primary school? In T. Nunes & P. Bryant (Eds.), *Learning and teaching mathematics: An international perspective* (pp. 69–98). Hove, UK: Psychology Press.

Verschaffel, L., DeCorte, E., Lasure, S., Van-Vaerenburgh, G., Bogaerts, H., & Ratinckxx, E. (1999). Learning to solve mathematical application problems: A design experiment with fifth graders. *Mathematical Thinking and Learning, 1,* 195–229.

Very, P.S. (1967). Differential factor structures in mathematical ability. *Genetic Psychology Monographs, 75,* 169–207.

Von Aster, M. (2000). Developmental cognitive neuropsychology of number processing and calculation: Varieties of developmental dyscalculia. *European Child and Adolescent Psychiatry, 9*, 41–57.

Vosse, A.J.M. (1999). Effects and implementation of a peer tutoring program for children at risk. *Pedagogische Studien, 76*, 201–210.

Voyer, D., Voyer, S., & Bryden, M.P. (1995). Magnitude of gender differences in spatial ability: A meta-analysis and consideration of critical variables. *Psychological Bulletin, 117*, 250–270.

Vygotsky, L.S. (1962). *Thought and language*. Cambridge, MA: MIT Press.

Vygotsky, L.S. & Luria, A.S. (1993). *Studies on the history of behaviour*. Hillsdale, NJ: Lawrence Erlbaum Associates, Inc.

Wakeley, A., Rivera, S., & Langer, J. (2000). Can young infants add and subtract? *Child Development, 71*, 1525–1534.

Warrington, E.K. (1982). The fractionation of arithmetical skills: A single case study. *Quarterly Journal of Experimental Psychology, 34A*, 31–51.

Watkins, K.D. (1998). Differential characteristics of memory aptitude as a function of cognitive ability and mathematics achievement in children diagnosed with learning disabilities. *Dissertation Abstracts International, Section B: The Sciences and Engineering, 59*, 3086.

Weaver, J. (1954). Differentiated instruction in arithmetic: An overview and a promising trend. *Education*, Vol. 74, 300–305.

Webb, S. (1995). *Children's use of derived fact strategies in addition and subtraction*. Undergraduate project, University of Oxford.

Wedell, R.A. & Davidoff, J.B. (1991). A dyscalculic patient with selectively impaired processing of the numbers 7, 9 and 0. *Brain and Cognition, 17*, 240–271.

Weinland, S. (1948). Memoir of S. Finkelstein. *Journal of General Psychology, 39*, 243–257.

Werdelin, I. (1961). *The geometric ability and space factor analysis in girls and boys*. University of Lund Press: Lund, Sweden.

Widaman, K.F., Little, T.D., Geary, D.C., & Cormier, P. (1987). Individual differences in the development of skill in mental addition: Internal and external validation of chronometric models. *Learning and Individual Differences, 4*, 167–213.

Wigfield, A. & Meece, J.L. (1988). Math anxiety in elementary and secondary school students. *Journal of Educational Psychology, 80*, 210–216.

Williams, C. & Whitaker, R.L. (1937). Diagnosis of arithmetical difficulties. *Elementary School Journal, 37*, 592–600.

Williamson, K. (Ed.) (1980). *The poetical works of Christopher Smart, Vol. 1: Jubilate Agno* (pp. 92–94). Oxford: Clarendon Press.

Wilson, K.M. & Swanson, H.L. (2001). Are mathematics disabilities due to a domain-general or a domain-specific working memory deficit? *Journal of Learning Disabilities, 34*, 237–248.

Wing, H.D. (1968). *Test of musical ability and appreciation: An investigation into the measurement, distribution and development of musical capacity* (2nd ed.). Cambridge: Cambridge University Press.

Wistedt, I. & Martinsson, M. (1996). Orchestrating a mathematical theme: Eleven-year-olds discuss the problem of infinity. *Learning and Instruction, 6*, 173–185.

Wright, R. (1994). A study of the numerical development of 5-year-olds and 6-year-olds. *Educational Studies in Mathematics, 26*, 25–44.

Wright, R., Martland, J., & Stafford, A. (2000). *Early numeracy: Asssessment for teaching and intervention*. London: Chapman.

Wright, R., Martland, J., Stafford, A., & Stanger, G. (2002). *Teaching number: Advancing children's skills and strategies*. London: Chapman.

Wynn, K. (1990). Children's understanding of counting. *Cognition, 36,* 155–193.

Wynn, K. (1992). Addition and subtraction by human infants. *Nature, 358,* 749–750.

Wynn, K. (1995). Origins of numerical knowledge. *Mathematical Cognition, 1,* 35–60.

Yeo, D. (2001). *Dyslexia and mathematics*. Paper presented at the 5th British Dyslexia Association Conference, London.

Yeo, R.A. (1989). Individual differences. In E.D. Bigler, R.A. Yeo, & E. Turkheimer (Eds.), *Neuropsychological function and brain imaging*. New York: Plenum Press.

Young-Loveridge, J. (1987). Learning mathematics. *British Journal of Developmental Psychology, 5,* 155–167.

Young-Loveridge, J. (1991). *The development of children's number concepts from ages five to nine*. Early mathematics learning project, Education Department, University of Waikoto, New Zealand.

Author index

Subject index

Page numbers for main entries that have subheadings refer to general aspects of that topic. Page numbers for tables are shown in **bold** type.